The Tenant Movement in New York City, 1904–1984

The Tenant Movement in New York City, 1904–1984

Edited by
Ronald Lawson
with the assistance of
Mark Naison

Rutgers University Press

New Brunswick, New Jersey

Manufactured in the United States of America

Library of Congress Cataloging-in-Publication Data

The Tenant movement in New York City, 1904–1984.

Includes bibliographies and index.
1. Rental housing—New York (N.Y.)—History—20th century. 2. Landlord and tenant—New York (N.Y.)—History—20th century. 3. New York (N.Y.)—Social conditions. I. Lawson, Ronald, 1940– II. Naison, Mark, 1946–
HD7288.85.U62N54 1986 333.33′8 86–27894
ISBN 0–8135–1158–5
ISBN 0–8135–1203–4 (pbk.)

For Larry Lipnik

Contents

	Preface		ix
	Acknowledgments		xiii
	Introduction	*Ronald Lawson*	1
	A Pictorial History	*Ronald Lawson*	9
1.	The Landlord as Czar Pre–World War I Tenant Activity	*Jenna Weissman Joselit*	39
2.	New York City Tenant Organizations and the Post–World War I Housing Crisis	*Joseph A. Spencer*	51
3.	From Eviction Resistance to Rent Control Tenant Activism in the Great Depression	*Mark Naison*	94
4.	Tenant Power in the Liberal City, 1943–1971	*Joel Schwartz*	134
5.	Tenant Responses to the Urban Housing Crisis, 1970–1984	*Ronald Lawson with the assistance of Reuben B. Johnson III*	209
	Index of Names		277
	Subject Index		281
	Note on Contributors		289

Preface

IN introducing this book it seems pertinent to discuss its genesis. I arrived in New York City from Australia in September 1971 to pursue postdoctoral work at Columbia University's Bureau of Applied Social Research. While finding my bearings I became involved in a graduate field methods course that focused on Washington Heights, Manhattan, because the bureau was preparing to conduct a major study of that neighborhood. I focused my research on two tenant organizations in different parts of the Heights.

Both organizations proved to be abuzz with activity. Vacancy decontrol had taken effect less than two months earlier, beginning what was seen as a gradual dismantling of New York's twenty-eight-year-old system of rent control. The dire predictions of tenant leaders appeared to be confirmed as their meetings were swamped by tenants telling tales of landlord subterfuge aimed at driving them from their rent-controlled apartments. It seemed to me that the movement at that time showed considerable growth potential: tenants were angry and open to mobilization, tenant organizers were harnessing the anger with innovative strategies, and new young organizers—often veterans of the movements of the sixties—were readily available.

My own interest in collective protest dated from my involvement in the antiwar movement in Australia during the 1960s and from my coverage, in my dissertation, of the early labor movement and of religious movements there. By the early 1970s criticism of the then dominant sociological approach to movements—which interpreted them as aberrant acts of "collective behavior" whose very occurrence needed to be explained—was beginning to emerge. Such criticism was initiated by persons whose experience in movements during the 1960s had led them to view the movements as normal, rational parts of the political process. This perspective, in my view, required a historical approach to the study of a movement: an approach that encompassed the life cycle of a movement and saw it in historical context.

Since I held such a view of movements, and had been trained as a historical sociologist, my new interest in contemporary tenant activism in New York led me to inquire into its precursors. Questions to tenant leaders found that they knew little of any early activity. However, my own preliminary exploration suggested that there had been several periods of considerable mobilization by New York tenants, and I guessed that the tenant movement had considerable continuity. I reported these findings to a seminar at Columbia University, where I expressed interest in following up on what I had discovered.

When Amitai Etzioni, professor and head of the Center for Policy Research (the arch rival of Columbia's Bureau of Applied Social Science), heard about my seminar presentation, he suggested that I write a proposal to the Center for Metropolitan Studies at the National Institute of Mental Health in an endeavor to fund my research idea. I realized that funding would provide me with the opportunity to trace the development of the tenant movement in a key location across time, and in so doing gather an unparalleled body of data that would bear directly on the questions that sociologists were asking about movements. My proposal envisioned two research thrusts: one tracing the emergence and evolution of the tenant movement over time, the other studying the dynamics of tenant mobilization, strategies, and impact during the period of the grant. NIMH responded with a grant of $200,000; however, the award specifically excluded the historical section of the proposed study—I was told to concentrate on the 1970s. Expressing great reluctance to carry out such a restricted project, I argued that much sociological research was of limited value because it was ahistorical and that such a danger was particularly pertinent to the study of a movement. Consequently, NIHM agreed to allow me to divert some of the grant to a study of the history of the tenant movement as I had proposed originally.

The research was carried out by two teams. One researched the period from the mid-nineteenth century until 1970; the other gathered and processed participant observation, in-depth interview, and survey data from the tenant organizations active in the 1970s. Two very different books were planned, each drawing upon the research of both teams. In the first, this history of tenant activism in New York, I would edit the work of the historians and write the post–1970 chapters myself. In the second, I would use the wealth of data collected to test and clarify the competing sociological theories that attempt to generalize about social movements.

We did not rush to complete the book manuscripts after the NIMH grant expired in 1976. In part this was because of funding problems experienced near the end of the grant, which left the research incomplete. Also, my inexperience, at that time, in leading a large research project had no doubt allowed the jubilant pursuit of data to get somewhat out of control. However, the researchers engaged in the historical study committed themselves to complete their research and writing in their own time.

Another important reason for the postponement of publication was that by this time it was obvious that the tenant movement had entered a period of rapid change. Housing abandonment had been recognized as a serious problem, and tenant activists had been responding with new strategies: spending monies withheld in rent strikes on services and repairs, exploiting ordinances that could allow tenants to gain control of their buildings if they were poorly maintained, rehabilitating abandoned buildings through "sweat equity," and setting up low-income cooperatives. By 1976 government housing agencies, desperate to slow abandonment, were beginning to fund strategies where tenants managed or rehabilitated buildings. These initiatives developed rapidly into large programs following a 1977 visit by President Jimmy Carter to a building being rehabilitated by tenants in the Bronx and after the election of Mayor Edward Koch in 1978 allowed the diversion of Community Development funds to housing programs. It was obvious to me that these developments were significant and exciting, and I was unwilling to publish research on the tenant movement that did not include analysis of the evolution and impact of the new strategies. Consequently, I proposed a study of "the impact of tenant strategies on the social process of housing abandonment" to allow me to follow these developments closely and obtained funding to pursue this research. I also carried out studies of the political face of the real estate industry in order to have a better grasp of the context in which the tenant movement was working, and of the track records of the low-income cooperatives formed in the early and mid-1970s. Meanwhile, I had to find and fund two new historians to complete the historical research and remain on top of developments in the traditional wing of the movement myself. I also took the opportunity to return after eight years to the 153 buildings studied originally in 1975, when all had been in the midst of some type of tenant action, to discover the outcomes of both tenant grievances and organization. The extended time, then, allowed for a broadening of the study's data in important ways.

Finally, it is important to describe the division of responsibilities between Mark Naison and myself. I conceived of the project, found the funding, supervised the research, wrote several sections and somehow kept the whole thing together. However, when the book contract came through from Rutgers University Press—together with some excellent suggestions from reviewers—I was about to leave New York for most of two years to work on a research fellowship on another topic. Mark Naison agreed to take responsibility for working with the contributors, including me, in their revisions. That is, he filled the role of manuscript editor.

The analysis upon which the second, theoretical, book is to be based is far advanced. However, it is dependent on the data summarized in this history of the tenant movement. The completion of this history prepares the way for its writing to be finished.

Ronald Lawson

Acknowledgments

It would not have been possible to complete a research project as ambitious as this without the funding made available to it, in whole or part, from many sources. I wish to thank them all for their vision and patience: the Center for Metropolitan Studies (Metrocenter) at the National Institute of Mental Health; the Professional Staff Congress/Board of Higher Education research grants for faculty of the City University of New York (four awards); the New York Community Trust; the Taconic Foundation; the federal Department of Housing and Urban Development; the New York City Department of Housing Preservation and Development; the Graduate and Research Dean, Queens College, City University of New York.

Professor Herbert Gans deserves special thanks for his willingness to trust me to the extent that he cosigned the original research proposal to NIMH, and thus made funding possible (for at that time I was an unknown newcomer to the United States), and then continued to encourage me as I learned to cope with the problems of administering a large research team.

Special thanks also go to Mark Naison, who supervised the completion of the final drafts of all segments, and encouraged and made suggestions to each author, while I was on leave away from New York City. His suggestions concerning my own segments were very valuable.

Many research assistants have helped with this study. Jody Dworetzki and John McLoughlan worked with historical data, while those engaged in contemporary (post-1972) data gathering included Reuben Johnson III, Stephen Barton, Kathleen Schneider, Anita Nager, Stephen Burghardt, Karolynn Siegel, Judy Sandwell, Danny Guenzberger, Steven Kennedy, Mark Bierman, Susan Gibson, Karen Leiner, Shelly Zabrowski, Kim Edel, and Patty Celentano, together with a great many interviewers, mostly selected from among the students at Hunter College and Queens College, the City University of New York.

It is important that we recognize the contributions made by many who have given generously of their time and information: past and present activists and officials whom we have interviewed, librarians and archivists who have made suggestions and helped us find what we needed, colleagues who have given us feedback. The reviewers for Rutgers University Press also contributed very helpful suggestions.

Most of all, I would like to thank the other historians who have contributed to this volume. All proved to be faithful workers who were excellent at the historian's craft. As historians, they had all been socialized to be academic rugged individualists who were used to working alone, and who therefore found my team approach, derived from my sociological apprenticeship, foreign. But they caught my vision of the potential of this study, and their own enthusiasm burgeoned as their research proceeded. I know each one doubted whether we would ever pull the whole historical project together into a completed volume. But as individualists, each took pride in his or her own work, while my definition of the subject matter and the themes resulted in a high degree of teamwork and unity in the final product. It is extremely gratifying to realize the original vision, to find the historical fabric that we have unfolded to be as interesting as it is.

Ronald Lawson

Introduction

Ronald Lawson

THIS account of tenant activism in New York is the first history of an urban social movement studied through the entire length of the twentieth century in a particular setting. As such it allows us to examine the dynamics of a movement over time: the relationship between changing threats and opportunities for the movement constituency and levels of mobilization; continuities and discontinuities in leadership and organization; the evolution of strategies and their short- and long-term impact. It offers new insights into the continuities and dividing points in the history of American radicalism and between working-class and student protest and into the emergence of different ethnic constituencies for radical activity and the role of women in protest.

At the heart of this study lies the tenant-landlord relationship, where the distribution of power is normally sharply unequal. An individual tenant is much more dependent upon his landlord than the latter is upon him: on the one hand, shelter is a basic necessity of life and source of personal identity and moving is costly, both economically and socially; on the other hand, the rent received from a single tenant is likely to amount to only a small portion of a landlord's income. Moreover, the interests of the two parties frequently conflict: a tenant desires security of tenure in well-maintained housing with reliable services and inexpensive rents, while his landlord, wishing to maximize his profits, wants the highest possible rents while often economizing on maintenance and services and retaining freedom to shuffle tenants to his greatest advantage. The low-income housing market, in particular, has tended to attract hustlers and speculators, often recent immigrants who, not much wealthier than their tenants, are willing to engage in a high-risk, high-tension enterprise. Under conditions where the market economy is unregulated (such as prevailed in the United States during the second half of the nineteenth century and continued to do so in most rental markets throughout the twentieth century), and especially when rental housing is in short supply (an all too common situation in most American cities), the asymmetry of the tenant-landlord relationship becomes very pronounced: rents may be raised at the whim of the landlord, and complaints concerning maintenance or services in his building, no matter how justified, render the tenant liable to summary eviction. The result has been frequent reason for confrontation and conflict.

Thus, the key players in this study are tenants and landlords and the tenant and real estate organizations formed to represent their interests. Other prominent participants include legislators who can enact laws that alter the tenant-landlord relationship, government administrators who enforce such laws, and judges and other court officials who settle tenant-landlord disputes. All of the latter groups have tended to be instinctually prolandlord because of their respect for property. Tenant interests have usually been expressed defensively—against the threats of sharp rent increases, the removal of services such as heat in winter, the decay of housing, and various forms of displacement. Unless such threats are chronic, they tend to be intermittent, and therefore to spawn transitory organizations. However, with the passage of time and the gaining of experience, the tenant movement espoused goals that approached these issues assertively, such as the limitation of rent increases through the enactment of rent regulations or the gaining control of housing. Organizations pursuing such goals have tended to be longer lived: the Metropolitan Council on Housing (Met Council) has now existed for twenty-five years and the New York State Tenant and Neighborhood Coalition (NYSTNC) for eleven years.

This book reveals a breadth of protest that scholars have vastly underestimated and that enlarges our understanding of neighborhood life in the periods covered. The protest includes rent strikes that have amounted to major communal revolts, tenant lobbying campaigns that have shaped legislative agendas for rental housing, and impressive experiments in tenant management and ownership in a period of market collapse. Although the record here is replete with failures as well as successes, it indicates that tenant activism has been a major force in shaping the New York City housing market. Tenant organizations have so far been much less stable than labor unions, which also represent people in a sharply asymmetrical relationship that is essential to another of life's fundamental necessities and sources of personal identity, and which many tenant leaders have spoken of emulating. Nevertheless, tenants have demonstrated a remarkable capacity to mobilize during recurring crises and to force concessions from landlords and responses from the political system.

Although the largest, most militant and effective rent strikes took place after World War I and during the Great Depression, the tenant movement has, in general, grown in power and sophistication over the past forty years. Whereas much early tenant protest was exclusively reactive and defensive, ever since the late 1930s the city has seen tenant organizations that have sought to shape housing policy as a whole—offering legislative programs, new court practices, even engaging in construction, tenant ownership, and the fostering of public housing. These organizations have become highly sophisticated at manipulating and using government to protect tenant interests and to enter the housing market as a builder and manager as well as a regulator. To do so they have had to build organizations focusing on multiple levels (building, neighborhood, city, state, and finally national). In sophistication, if not in wealth, the tenant movement came to match, and sometimes surpass, the real estate lobby.

Meanwhile, the rent strike, the strategy with which the tenant movement has been most closely identified, has been transformed. Whereas the initial strikes early in the century were large (with hundreds of buildings involved concurrently), short (culminating in court in a few days), and infrequent (concerted waves of activity years apart), recent strikes have become localized (normally limited to conflict over a single building), much longer (typically lasting several months), and frequent (many actions overlapping one another, but not in a concerted manner). These changes paralleled the growing legitimacy of the strike. Although during the early decades large strikes did, on occasion, achieve some legitimacy in the courtroom, it was not until the late 1960s and early 1970s that the strategy achieved full legitimacy and safety within the law. This was an important watershed, for it made the strategy "risk free" from a legal standpoint if proper procedures were followed—that is, it virtually eliminated the risk of eviction. Consequently, what was once invoked only when there was safety in numbers is now used by tenants in individual buildings to gain bargaining chips with their landlord.

Because housing markets, like labor markets, are often anarchic and unstable, the trend throughout the century, learned through bitter experience, has been to subject them to government regulation and intervention in order to try to assure some degree of public peace and justice. The private housing market has, at several points, produced disastrous conditions for tenants (such as the rent hikes before and after World War I, the massive evictions during the depression, and the abandonment cycle beginning in the late 1960s). Sometimes government policy has itself been disruptive (such as post–World War II urban renewal and the introduction of vacancy decontrol in 1971.) At such moments the tenant movement could generate overwhelming demand for government intervention to ease the crisis. Tenant leaders knew that tenant organizations lacked the stability to regulate the market through their own force and that, although the legal system from time to time demonstrated some flexibility to place tenant needs above property rights, such judicial intervention proved unstable and unpredictable without laws providing a structure of rights for tenants. Hence, government intervention became the goal, and in New York, as time passed, this was, with increasing frequency, achieved.

The history of the tenant movement is also very much a story of the interaction of radicals and mainstream political leaders. In normal times, real estate interest groups are often far more powerful than tenant organizations in shaping public policy. Through campaign contributions and direct political involvement they acquire direct access to political leaders. Moreover, left political organizations have usually conceived of the tenant movement as secondary to labor union concerns or, later, "civil rights work," and have frequently joined in tenant activity only when they have realized that emergencies have created unusual opportunities for popular mobilization based on tenant issues. Much of the organizing activity at such times has been carried on by persons tied to left political groups: initially the Socialist party in the first two decades of the century, then the Communist and American Labor parties from the 1930s to the 1950s and beyond. Civil rights organizations conducted rent strikes in ghetto neighborhoods during the 1960s. And in the early 1970s New Left activists, who had been disappointed when participants in such mass actions as the March on Washington disappeared into the woodwork on returning home, began to organize tenants as a means of creating a movement where the participants could not get lost by going home after the action. These New Left activists worked along side of, or often competed with, the long-term activists with "Old Left" ties. Frequently—after World War I, from the late 1930s through the late 1940s, and from the early 1970s until the present—radical organizations mobilized tenants with such effect that they forced mainstream and machine politicians to become aggressive tenant activists. Although tenant mobilization has never produced mass radicalization (it has, at best, marginally expanded the Left's constituency), it has demonstrated considerable political impact. To compete with the Left, mainstream political clubs suddenly became impassioned advocates of tenant interests, and elected officials began to intervene to assure some stability for housing markets.

Although radicals were the most important facilitators of grass roots activism, they were by no means the only ones who successfully organized tenants or represented their interests. Religious groups (especially once the civil rights movement had raised their consciousness and shown them what was possible) and apolitical community leaders were also important in some instances. The volatility and size of the tenant vote has also been a force operating on political leaders. The whole picture suggests that grass roots activism has been a far more important part of policy-making than commentators have realized.

This is not to overlook the limits and constraints placed on tenant action. The poor have very limited resources and are difficult to organize because of their multiple problems and low expectations resulting from previous experience with the political system. Both the political and the legal systems are biased toward property owners, to the point where red scares have been invoked to intimidate movement leaders. Moreover, the impact of movement strategies can easily be undercut by coopting the movement by, for example, funding certain activities at the expense of others or offering salaries to its leaders.

The data on the tenant movement both support and challenge the conclusions of Frances F. Piven and Richard A. Cloward who, in *Poor People's Movements*, argue that mass defiance rather than formal organizational structures make movements successful and that the structures actually blunt militancy and therefore lessen movement impact.[1] On the one hand, there are examples of the use of disruption by tenants to change policy, such as when the widespread rent strikes following World War I resulted in the introduction of rent regulations. On the other hand, however, stable organizations, such as NYSTNC (1973–), which use research and lobbying, were able to have considerable input into legislation and to effect the "daily life" of landlord-tenant relations to a significant degree. Indeed, the more sophisticated and well organized tenant organizations were, the more they were able to influence policy. An optimum situation is one that combines stable organization with mass protest, usually, in this instance because of the structure of the tenant movement that evolved, with different organizations using different strategies.

The basic organizational levels of the tenant movement are building and neighborhood organizations; the first federation was added in the mid-1930s. Because there were multiple levels to the movement's structure, each was able to specialize functionally and thus marshall the appropriate expertise: while building organizations were the basic organizing unit and neighborhood organizations provided them with organizing skills and focused on local issues, federations represented the interests of tenants to outside authorities. The existence of building organizations and neighborhood organizations, matching local concerns and identities, facilitated both the mobilization of the tenant constituency and the emergence and promotion of leaders. Many of those in leadership positions at the neighborhood and federation levels, especially women who became increasingly prominent as time passed, began their activity in the tenant movement by helping to organize their own buildings.[2] Moreover, specialization at each level allowed the adoption of positions and strategies suiting particular situations. Thus, federations could afford to work within the system in their political strategies, while, concurrently, affiliated neighborhood organizations utilized unorthodox or extralegal strategies, such as organizing rent strikes or seizing control of buildings, in their combat with uncooperative landlords or encroaching abandonment. Similarly, strategic experimentation was eased by the existence of multiple levels and organizations. For example, some building organizations around 1970 were able to test the effectiveness of spending accumulated rent monies on services such as heating or on repairs, without committing the whole movement to the strategy until it had been shown both safe and successful. Once multiple federations emerged in the 1970s, they too could adopt different stances toward authorities, so, for example, the radical demands of tenants who sat in the offices of legislative leaders during the annual mass mobilizations of Met Council in Albany increased the credibility of the more reasoned demands of NYSTNC lobbyists who maintained an ongoing presence there during legislative sessions.

As rental housing has become increasingly important throughout the nation, and as rapid rent increases, condominium conversions and other forms of gentrification, and abandonment crises have hit other cities, the threat of anarchy in private housing markets has become a growing concern. The only weapon that tenants have had against these problems has been organization, and the structure that has been adopted has usually followed the New York pattern of multiple levels. The spreading movement has recently spawned a new level of organization, a superfederation aptly named the National Tenants Union. That is, tenant organizations are becoming increasingly significant, and tenant interests are likely to be expressed with a new sophistication, stability, and coherence.

Another theme that emerges from this recounting of the history of the tenant movement in New York concerns links to particular ethnic traditions of political protest and self-assertion. The lion's share of rent strikes in New York City up until the mid-1930s took place in the neighborhoods of Eastern European Jews, where the strike as a mode of economic bargaining had wide currency and a romantic flavor that it did not command in other neighborhoods. For example, Jews and Italians at the turn of the century lived in adjoining neighborhoods on the Lower East Side where both faced severe housing conditions and spiraling rents. However, while the Jews conducted the first rent strikes, the Italians suffered in silence. In the mid-1930s the tenant movement acquired some new ethnic arenas, notably in black ghettoes. But at the same time it also spread to a "cosmopolitan" professional class, which applied labor tactics to middle-class housing issues (in addition to working-class ones). This group, gradually disseminating techniques of tenant mobilization through a wide spectrum of liberal and left organizations, made tenants as a lobby more consistently influential than they had been previously. However, while the class base of the movement broadened, ethnically the leadership remained primarily Jewish and black as late as the early 1970s, after which time Puerto Ricans also became prominent.

The tenant movement has been, to a large degree, dominated by women activists. Women organized the first rent strikes, much of the daily activity of the movement has been undertaken by women, and they became increasingly prominent among higher-level leadership as time passed. The dominance of women in the movement partially accounts for its previous "invisibility." This book therefore helps uncover an unwritten history of female self-assertion within the intersections of the "domestic" and "civic" spheres. The dominance of women was true at all periods of the movement's history, and was especially notable during the first rent strikes, the strikes of the early 1930s, the World War II consumers' movement, the post–World War II campaign to preserve rent controls, and the Save Our Homes struggles against Robert Moses and urban renewal during the 1950s, which led to the founding of Met Council, which was, and is, also strongly dominated by women. Indeed, one of the most remarkable tales of grass roots activism in this work is that of working-class Jewish women associated with the Communist party who kept landlords on the defensive for three generations. The line runs from the Crotona Park rent revolts in the early 1930s, via the consumers leagues, the American Labor party, and the Save Our Homes organizations, to Met Council, where some of them are still involved. These women, leaders and followers alike, helped establish a tradition of protest and activism, of organization and policy-making, which is unlikely to leave tenants unorganized again. They are the pioneers of modern tenant organization, much like the John L. Lewises, Mike Quills, and Sidney Hillmans of the labor movement.

This history of the tenant movement affirms popular insurgency even under difficult conditions. It confirms that elites do *not* always have their way, that ordinary people—working class and poor, women, immigrants, minorities—do help shape political agendas when they are organized and mobilized. It is not a story of revolutionary victory or the coming of a socialist republic. Its victories are usually defensive and often narrow, and they are sometimes swept away by larger change. But the record does show that ordinary people can fight to defend their interests against the most powerful forces.

NOTES

1. Frances Fox Piven and Richard A. Cloward, *Poor People's Movements* (New York, 1979).
2. See Ronald Lawson and Stephen E. Barton, "Sex Roles and Social Movements: A Case Study of the Tenant Movement in New York City," *Signs*, Winter 1980.

A Pictorial History *Ronald Lawson*

1. New York City's first mass rent strike broke out in 1904 among Jews on Manhattan's Lower East Side; the issue was rapidly escalating rents. Part of the source of tenant bitterness was their sense that they were being exploited by poor but ambitious fellow Jews who, as "listers" or "cockroach landlords," leased whole buildings from landlords and then profited from the rents they charged for individual apartments. The socialist *Jewish Daily Forward* depicted this bitterness in a cartoon published during the strike. Its lengthy caption read: "The man is not a capitalist. He's showing off as a capitalist. The house is not his—he's just a 'lister.' He rented the house on a lease. He wants to get rich in a hurry. The woman is the wife of an oppressed tenant. He is asking for another $4 per month. She is asking for pity, but he says he is a landlord and doesn't have any" (March 20, 1904).

2. The leaders and organizers of the rent strikes in both 1904 and 1907 were young women. Indeed, most of the grass roots leaders throughout the history of the tenant movement in New York, and most of the participants, have been women. Illustration 2 shows one of these women, with her fist raised, addressing a group of tenants outside a Lower East Side building in December 1907. From *The Independent*, January 1908. Lewis W. Hine Collection, U.S. History, Local History and Genealogy Division. Courtesy the New York Public Library, Astor, Lenox, and Tilden Foundations.

3. The rebellions by tenants took the Socialist party by surprise, for their doctrines focused attention on the workplace. However, once the 1907–1908 strike demonstrated the potential of tenant discontent, the Socialists set up a committee, dominated by young men, to try to expand the strike and give it overall direction. This established a pattern of male leadership of the coordinating organizations within the tenant movement—a pattern that only began to change in the 1960s. Illustration 3 shows a meeting of this committee. Note the portrait of Karl Marx on the far wall. From *Harper's Weekly*, January 25, 1908.

4. Tenement children, too, were moved by the spirit of the strikes. Illustration 4 shows a group on the Lower East Side hanging a landlord in effigy in December 1907. From *The Independent,* January 1908. Lewis W. Hine Collection, U.S. History, Local History and Genealogy Division. Courtesy the New York Public Library, Astor, Lenox, and Tilden Foundations.

5. The strikes of 1917–1920 encompassed many of the neighborhoods of the city. Illustration 5 shows tenants outside a Harlem building where every tenant went on strike in September 1919. As strike momentum built, the fears of landlords, politicians, and the conservative media led to accusations of striker disloyalty. When Abraham Levew, the landlord of this building, charged that the committee of three leading the tenants was really a soviet, one of them, Anne Breitman, retorted that she would slap anyone's face who said she was not 100 percent American. Courtesy *UPI/Bettman Newsphotos*.

6. As the strikes spread, evictions multiplied. Illustration 6 shows rent strikers in Brownsville, having been evicted by their landlord for refusing "to pay exorbitant rents imposed on them," with their furnishings piled up on the sidewalk. Courtesy *UPI/Bettmann Newsphotos.*

7. In the early 1930s rent strikes broke out yet again in many parts of New York City. But unlike the earlier strikes, which protested rent increases, these instead demanded rent reductions, for the depression had left tenants unable to pay the prevailing rent levels. Illustration 7 shows a strike: "But it is not higher wages but lower rents that these strikes are demanding. Housewives and their children (93 lease holders are affected) [are shown] doing picket duty in front of their homes in Williams Ave., Brownsville, Brooklyn. All have received notices of eviction." Courtesy *UPI/Bettmann Newsphotos.*

8. Sometimes crowds of the unemployed were attracted to evictions and responded by attempting to move the furniture of the evicted tenants back into their apartments. On January 27, 1933, "police reserves were called out to battle 500 jobless men and women who rioted when seven writers and artists were evicted from 'Paradise Alley,' a colony of artists and poets at Ave A and 11th St" on the Lower East Side. Courtesy *UPI/Bettmann Newsphotos*.

9. Nowhere was the resistance to evictions greater than in the Bronx, where the Communist party was best organized. One of their strongholds was the workers' cooperative colony on Allerton Avenue. On February 1, 1932, "Mounted cops, 50 patrolmen and a like number of detectives help[ed] to evict four Bronx families who refused to pay rent at 665 Allerton Avenue. Thousands of communists rallied to help these families resist the city marshal who sought to evict them. Many bruised bodies and battered heads resulted from this rent strike, the second in a week. Notice how one man has been knocked down practically under the very hoofs of a police horse." Courtesy *UPI/Bettman Newsphotos.*

10. The middle-class tenants at Knickerbocker Village, Manhattan, organized when they found their new apartments were not completed on the day they moved in. Later, in March 1936, when they received publicity for joining the picket lines of their striking service workers, the tenants were contacted by other neighborhood tenant organizations. The result was the formation of New York City's first tenant federation, the City-Wide Tenants Council, in which Knickerbocker Village tenants played central roles. Courtesy *UPI/Bettmann Newsphotos.*

11. In October 1936 the City-Wide Tenants Council supported a demonstration organized by the Consolidated Tenants League of Harlem, which protested rent increases in buildings that were changing from white to black tenantry. UPI reported that "4,000 white and colored persons" took part in the parade. The Consolidated Tenants League was the first substantial, long-lived black tenant organization. Courtesy *UPI/Bettmann Newsphotos*.

12. Meanwhile, America's first public housing, First Houses, on Manhattan's Lower East Side, had been completed. Illustration 12 shows a view of the opening ceremony, at which Eleanor Roosevelt presided. Public housing, having first been demanded by the Socialist-led tenant leagues during the unrest following World War I, had long been advocated by tenant leaders. Courtesy *UPI/Bettmann Newsphotos.*

13. When, after World War II, the federal administration began to dismantle wartime rent controls, tenants in New York State mounted a relentless campaign to pass legislation that would continue them. On February 9, 1947, 1,800 "marchers" who had been bussed to Albany from New York City demonstrated around the state capitol. Courtesy *UPI/Bettmann Newsphotos.*

14. Under state rent control, once it was imposed, the chief mechanism for rent increases was tenant turnover. The tenant movement therefore concentrated on countering the real estate interests' efforts to weaken the system or have the legislature impose across-the-board rent increases. One such campaign took place in 1953. Illustration 14 shows an interracial delegation from the Bronx Council on Rents and Housing about to board a train to Albany (March 3, 1953). The racial base of the tenants involved in the rent control struggle, which had previously been almost exclusively white, was broadening. However, tenant efforts that year could not prevent a general 15 percent increase in units where rents had not already increased by at least that amount as a result of tenant turnover since the imposition of state controls. Courtesy *UPI/Bettmann Newsphotos.*

15. In the winter of 1963–1964 a rent strike erupted in Harlem. It was led by Jesse Gray, a tenant organizer there since 1953 and now head of the Community Council on Housing. The focus of the strike was not rent levels but a new issue: poor maintenance and services. In illustration 15 Gray (*left*), Major Williams, an organizer, and Alexander Joseph, a tenant, display rats caught in two Harlem tenements to reporters, December 30, 1963. Courtesy *UPI/Bettmann Newsphotos.*

16. As the Harlem rent strike gained momentum and publicity, it spread to other neighborhoods, including the Lower East Side, where for the first time New York Hispanics were drawn into the movement in large numbers. Illustration 16 shows Gray speaking there at a rally on January 31, 1964. Courtesy *UPI/Bettmann Newsphotos*.

17. Urban renewal ravaged poor and working-class neighborhoods in New York City throughout the 1950s and 1960s. However, residents of the neighborhood surrounding Manhattan's Cooper Square, working with planner Walter Thabit, developed an alternative plan whereby the buildings of the renewal area would be razed and replaced in stages rather than simultaneously so that the residents of the community would not be displaced. Although their plan received wide publicity and ultimately official endorsement, it faced thirty years of roadblocks. On November 19, 1964, "members of the Cooper Square Community Development Committee brought out everything from babies to dogs while keeping an all night vigil outside [the Mayor's official residence at] Gracie Mansion in protest over the delay in erecting low rent housing at Houston and Chrystie Streets" (*New York Post* caption). The first part of a truncated plan was realized only in 1985. *New York Post* photograph by Engel.

18. The introduction of the rolling rent strike, a new form of the old strategy, lengthened tenant-landlord struggles. When landlords of decaying buildings were slow to respond, the tenants often invented innovative ways to increase pressure. In the winter of 1971–1972, striking tenants at 565 Crown Street, Brooklyn, picketing the home of Councilmember Howard Golden, demanded that he fire his aide, Milton Kessler, who was their slumlord. Illustration 18 shows the president of the building's tenant organization (*left*) and Michael McKee, then an organizer and vice-president for the Metropolitan Council on Housing. A year later McKee became one of the founders of the New York State Tenant and Neighborhood Coalition, a rival federation. Photo by Gary W. Foster.

19. When the tenants returned home from the action pictured in illustration 18, they found that Kessler was in their building, a rare happening, and waited at the entrance to confront him. Kessler, however, used his political ties to secure a police escort from the building. He adopted a pose commonly employed by criminals when face to face with a camera. Photo by Gary W. Foster.

20. The decay of buildings and their abandonment by landlords led young minority tenants to experiment by taking control of such buildings and turning them into low-income cooperatives. Initially the way was pointed by equally young middle-class innovators who knew how to manipulate bureaucratic structures. Illustration 20 shows a 1973 title transfer, in the mayor's office, of an in rem building at 334–336 East Eighth Street on the Lower East Side to a not-for-profit tenant cooperative corporation. Several of the key low-income tenant ownership pioneers, together with two city officials and a tenant from the building, are pictured: (*left to right*) Milton Musicus, administrator, Municipal Services Agency; Louis Morales, coordinator of Adopt-a-Building; Juan DeLeone, tenant; Roberto Nazario, coordinator of Adopt-a-Building; Philip St. Georges, intern, Sweat Equity Program, Housing and Development Administration; Ira Duchan, commissioner, Department of Real Estate; and William Eddy, director, Adopt-a-Building. Eddy was later one of the founders of the Urban Homesteading Assistance Board (UHAB), and then an Episcopal priest; St. Georges became, successively, a staff member and then the director of UHAB, assistant commissioner of the Department of Housing Preservation and Development and head of the Division of Alternative Management Programs, the regional director of the National Co-operative Bank in New York and then vice-president at its national headquarters in Washington; Nazario became president of both Adopt-a-Building and the board of the Association of Neighborhood Housing Developers, and then, after time studying at Harvard, an officer of the Development Training Institute in Baltimore headed by Father Joe McNeely, who had been assistant secretary of HUD during the Carter administration.

21. The small landlords, who typically owned the buildings housing poor tenants, were now pressured by sharp increases in fuel costs and the specter of encroaching abandonment. Their organization, the American Property Rights Association, fixed the blame for their shrinking profit margins on rent regulations and the politicians who supported them. Lacking the funds of the real estate organizations representing larger operators, they utilized such grass roots strategies as demonstrations. Illustration 21 pictures a demonstration during fall 1976, which was part of a campaign, coordinated by several diverse real estate groups, aimed at persuading the legislature to allow the Emergency Tenant Protection Act to lapse in 1977. Photo by Laureanne Pare.

22. NYSTNC and its organizing and training arm, the People's Housing Network, sponsored twelve "schools for organizers" during the period 1973—1980. In spring 1977 it found that classes demonstrating sweat equity were attracting increasing interest. Illustration 22 shows one such class in progress at Fordham University. Robert Schur (*left*), director of the Association of Neighborhood Housing Developers and the genius behind all strategies establishing low-income cooperatives, was the tutor. Photo by Michael McKee.

23. In October 1977 President Jimmy Carter, accompanied by Patricia Roberts Harris, head of the federal Department of Housing and Urban Development, and Mayor Abraham Beame, visited the South Bronx. Their first stop was on Charlotte Street, where they saw the devastation caused by the abandonment process. The second stop in the South Bronx was at 1186 Washington Avenue, where the People's Development Corporation was engaged in sweat equity rehabilitation. The visit provided Carter with hope and inspiration, and sweat equity in general and PDC in particular with valuable publicity. One result was a vast increase in the flow of funds to groups utilizing sweat equity. Courtesy *UPI/Bettmann Newsphotos.*

24. Sweat equity rehabilitation allowed for the rearrangement of interiors, with attractive designs such as sunken living rooms. Illustration 24 shows the president of the People's Development Corporation, Ramon Rueda (*standing*), addressing members in 1186 Washington Avenue, the South Bronx, as the rehabilitation neared completion in 1978. Photo by Ron Diamond.

25. Establishing a pattern of tense, rowdy meetings, both tenant and real estate organizations began to pressure the Rent Guidelines Board, which annually set maximum rent increases in rent-stabilized apartments. Illustration 25 shows a demonstration organized by the Metropolitan Council on Housing preceding a RGB meeting during the summer of 1979. Photo by Chuck Rubenstein.

26. In 1978 the city became the largest landlord in New York City as a result of changes in regulations governing the seizure of buildings for nonpayment of taxes. All these buildings were in various stages of decay and likely to be at least partly vacant, while the incomes of their tenants generally fell far below the city's median level. Consequently, the city found the management of its new real estate portfolio a considerable financial drain. The Koch administration, noting that transfer to city ownership removed housing from prevailing rent regulations, subsequently announced rent increases, which drew both scorn and anger from tenants (March 5, 1982). Photo by Bernard Moore.

27. In the ten years after 1973, NYSTNC became a significant force in Albany housing politics. Illustration 27 shows Bill Rowen, NYSTNC chairperson, telling Richard Runes, counsel to Republican senator John Daly, chair of the Senate Housing Committee, that the tenants refused to leave his office until they had seen the senator (May 1983). Photo by Tom Robins for "City Limits."

28. NYSTNC's successful campaign in 1983 to move responsibility for the enforcement of rent regulations from the landlord-operated Rent Stabilization Association to the state Division of Housing was seen as a victory. However, the endeavor of the senate Republican leadership to placate the real estate industry by giving the RSA responsibility for designing the new code was a threat. Consequently, the tenant movement protested against adoption of the code when hearings were held by the city administration in February 1984. Their efforts were successful: the code was rejected.

Among those who spoke against the RSA code at a tenant-organized press conference were Bonny Brower, director of the Association of Neighborhood Housing Developers, and Jane Benedict, chairperson of the Metropolitan Council on Housing—two of the three major tenant federations. Women leaders had at last achieved prominence in the upper levels of the tenant movement in New York. Illustration 28 shows politicians lining up to speak behind the two tenant leaders: Assemblyman Eliot Engel, city councilman Robert Dryfoos, and state senators Leon Bogues and Franz Leichter were anxious to show their support for the tenant position. Photo by Tom Robins for "City Limits."

29. The tide turned on the Lower East Side in the early 1980s: tenants had helped stabilize the neighborhood through their management and rehabilitation of buildings abandoned by their owners, and now, as real estate prices in Manhattan revived, owners and speculators realized the potential value of a neighborhood abutting the now fashionable East Village and close to the financial district. The process of abandonment ceased almost entirely, but tenants were suddenly faced with a new threat from speculators anxious to remove low-income tenants in order to prepare their buildings for higher-paying tenants. But the community leaders who had saved their homes and neighborhood from the ravages of abandonment were not about to surrender it to gentrification without a struggle. Illustration 29 shows a banner on East Ninth Street in 1984. Photo by Mel Rosenthal.

30. As rent levels escalated as a result of speculation, gentrification, and cooperative conversions, the number of homeless climbed. The latter included both families and single persons who simply could not find homes they could afford and were forced to live in shelters and on the streets. The tenant movement was slow to realize the seriousness of this issue and how relevant it was to its own causes. However, on May 4, 1985, housing activists organized a protest march in conjunction with the Coalition on the Homeless. Their route led them through midtown Manhattan to Trump Tower, a symbol of the probusiness, antipoor policies of Mayor Koch's administration because of the tax breaks its developer had been given—subsidies that tenant leaders argued could have been used instead for sorely needed housing (May 4, 1985). Photo by George Cohen.

1. The Landlord as Czar *Jenna Weissman Joselit*

Pre–World War I Tenant Activity

Rent day is like the Day of Judgement . . . we never know what our fate will be.
—*Jewish Daily Forward*
March 5, 1908

IN the spring of 1904, several hundred residents of the Lower East Side, New York's immigrant Jewish quarter, took to the streets in protest against their landlords and refused to pay their monthly rent. Property owners in the area, taking advantage of a decided shortage in rental housing, had recently increased tenement house rents by an additional 20 to 30 percent. But area residents, largely seasonal garment trade workers and small businessmen, could hardly afford the existing rent, which swallowed anywhere from one-quarter to one-third of their income, let alone an increment. "What is to become of the family whose sole breadwinner earns 60¢ a day and whose rent has been increased from $8.50 to $13 a month," wondered one resident.[1] Still another related that many Lower East Siders felt they "lived and worked for the landlord."[2]

At first, individual tenants and then, as protest spread "like an angry wave" over the entire neighborhood, groups of tenants asked their landlords not to raise the rent lest wholesale evictions ensue.[3] When the property owners refused, tenement house dwellers held protest meetings, picketed the homes of their landlords, and conducted rent strikes. "We are all pledged not to pay you the increase in rent," tenants informed their landlords. "If you wish to turn us out you can do so, but notice will be sent all over the East Side and no new tenants will move in."[4] Striking residents also printed up cards, in both Yiddish and English, warning their neighbors "to keep away from the house at ——— Street. In the name of your children we are asking you not to hire rooms in that house, as the house is on strike because the rent is raised every month and we want to put a stop to it once and for all. Keep away."[5]

On the surface, Lower East Side residents were demonstrating against rent increases they could little afford. On a deeper level, however, they were protesting against the tenuousness of their status as tenants. The most recent rent hike was, to them, not only a financial affront but also a psychological one, indicating that when it came to housing, the "landlord was czar."[6] Without a lease (or any other curb regulating the housing market), the tenants felt his power—and often, his capriciousness—at every turn. Some landlords had a *minhag* (custom) of determining the rent according to family size, charging 50¢ additional per child above the base rent.[7] Still others routinely raised the rent after making alleged improvements in the building. "One poor woman desirous of celebrating the Passover in a becoming manner asked her landlord to whitewash her ceilings, which grievously needed it," reported a local Jewish magazine. "In January, three months before the Passover, he raised the rent fifty cents a month . . . on account of the superior accommodations she would have when Passover really came and her ceilings were really whitewashed."[8]

For the most part, tenants were passive in their dealings with the landlord or his designated representative, the lessee. "That there was anything wrong with living as we lived, we never suspected," one resident explained. "To live, a family of eight in three rooms seemed to us quite normal, as was being without a bathroom and sharing the toilet with three neighbors."[9] Others, less innocent perhaps, knew that they lived in substandard conditions and that they had considerable cause for complaint but felt themselves too raw, too inexperienced in American ways to challenge the landlord's way of doing business. Then there were those Lower East Siders who, deliberately choosing inactivity over collective protest, preferred to keep their dissatisfactions to themselves. Tenement dwellers, Irving Howe writes, "knew that by American standards, they were victims of an outrage. . . . But they also remembered that in the old country many of them had lived in hovels . . . so they responded to both the American immediacy and the European memory, submitting as best they could to their daily burdens, determined to escape as quickly as possible."[10] In fact, "escaping as quickly as possible" was, for most Lower East Siders, the preferred route: unable to pay the mandated rent or dissatisfied with their unlit hallways and limited bathing facilities, tenants moved elsewhere: up north to Harlem, across the river to Brooklyn. By exercising what sociologists have called the "exit option," tenants defused the potential for protest.

But in 1904, New York's housing market permitted no such option. Housing, especially for New York's tenement population, was in short supply. "There are hardly any 'To Let' signs," reported the *New York Herald* at the time, "and every place that is in the least desirable seems to have been taken."[11] And on the Lower East Side, as its population continued to grow, available housing supply dwindled to the point where, one observer noted, "there is a famine in the supply of available tenements."[12] For one thing, many sections of the Lower East Side had been torn down to make way for local municipal improvements—parks, schools—and the building of the Williamsburg Bridge; construction of the bridge in 1900 forced the razing of what had once been home to over seventeen thousand local residents.[13] For another thing, even as the Lower East Side's housing supply decreased, the neighborhood, magnet to thousands upon thousands of newly arriving Eastern European Jews, continued to grow. Within five years, since the turn of the century, its population had expanded by over 14 percent.[14]

With the "famine" in available Lower East Side housing on the one hand and the landlord's determination to take advantage of that situation by continuous rent raising on the other, it was no wonder, then, that tenants manifested their discontent in a "spontaneous outburst" of rent withholding and protest.[15] "Those in close touch with the district," reported David Blaustein, director of the area's largest social settlement house, the Educational Alliance, "had seen the storm far off for a long time."[16] An example of the "new combativeness" of Lower East Side residents—the "rental agitation" of 1904—reflected that community's increasing politicization.[17] Referring rather self-consciously to themselves as "strikers," to their non-cooperatings neighbors as "scabs," to building-level tenant groups as "tenant unions," and to the withholding of their rent as a "rent strike," Lower East Side tenement dwellers drew on familiar political rhetoric—on the language of the labor union—in conducting their protest. They also borrowed many of its techniques of protest as well—the use of pickets, outside demonstrations, marches, canvasing the neighborhood for support; each strategy calculated to force the collective hand of local real estate interests was drawn from the neighborhood's embryonic, but powerful, trade union movement. "The trade union movement in the Jewish quarter has been growing apace," reported Abe Cahan. "It has had its ups and downs, its spurts and its periods of weakness, but upon the whole, trade unionism has taken root. The spirit which impels one to struggle for his rights, to combat robbery, has imbedded itself," he concluded, "in the hearts of our workingmen. . . . This is the case with the present rent strikes. They are the outcome of the same spirit, the offspring of that same struggle against Capital, which has grown up in our quarter owing to the work of Socialists and trade unionists."[18]

Even more to the point, perhaps, was that the "rent wars" of 1904 were of a piece with an earlier, more delimited incident in which local Lower East Side residents, angered by conditions in the marketplace, took matters into their own hands. Two years earlier, in the spring of 1902, Lower East Side housewives had organized a communitywide boycott of local kosher butchers. The price of kosher meat at the time had jumped from a barely affordable 12¢ a pound to an unaffordable 18¢ a pound. When small retail butchers were unable to persuade the "meat trust" to lower the wholesale price of beef, area residents assumed responsibility for making kosher meat available and organized themselves into the Ladies Anti-Beef Trust Association. Relying on informal neighborhood ties and on local institutions as well—the synagogue, the labor union, the mutual aid and benefit society—members of this association, exerting pressure on their relatives and friends, urged them not to enter butcher shops or to purchase meat until the meat trust, and with it the small meat retailer, lowered the price of meat. Once the boycott was well underway—even the city's kosher restaurants had stopped serving meat—male communal leaders, including David Blaustein himself, organized the Allied Conference for Cheap Kosher Meat, claiming that they would now "bring order to the great struggle for cheap meat." Under its aegis, boycott activity continued until the meat wholesalers agreed, under considerable pressure, to reduce the price of wholesale meat to prestrike levels. "With this issue," writes Paula Hyman, "immigrant housewives found a vehicle for political organization . . . they temporarily turned their status as housewives to good advantage and used the neighborhood network to stage a successful three week boycott."[19]

Much the same can be said of the 1904 tenant protest. Here, too, women were its central actors. Drawing, once again, on their experiences as consumers and managers of the household budget, East Side women used the neighborhood as a staging ground for their antilandlord protests. They held meetings to discuss strategy, picketed buildings where tenants were forcibly evicted for nonpayment of rent, organized building-level "tenant unions," and went from tenement to tenement drumming up support for their activities. "Local Jewish women," explained the *Jewish Daily Forward*, "began the rent strike and through their efforts and enthusiasm, they spread it. Through their strength, even the blackest strike was won and without their remarkable activities, the strike would not have been possible."[20]

Participants in the 1904 "rental agitation" were fully aware of the similarities between this episode and the preceding one and exploited those similarities. Repeatedly, such prominent Yiddish newspapers as the *Jewish Daily Forward*, drawing parallels between the two events, invoked the earlier protest to fuel the current one. Urging Jewish residents to hold firm in the face of evictions, that paper trumpeted that "this strike can be as great as the meat strikes" and advised Jewish housewives "to take the rent question into their hands as they did the meat question."[21] Linking the two events together served to legitimate them and made one seem a natural consequence of the other. And both, as the *Forward* liked to remind its readers, had common origins as "great folk struggles." "The meat strike," the socialist paper went on to say, "was a child of the trade strikes . . . and the rent strike, in turn, comes from the same source."[22]

The similarities between the two events were structural as well. Like the 1902 meat strike, male communal leadership, two years later, stepped in to direct the rent protest, once grass roots protest was well underway. Within weeks of its initial outburst, tenant protest had grown so large and the Lower East Side was "seething with activity and protest" that male delegates from the United Hebrew Trades, the Workmen's Circle, and various locals joined together to form the New York Rent Protective Association (NYRPA).[23] Modeling itself after one of the Lower East Side's most popular social institutions—the *landsmanshaft* or Jewish fraternal and mutual aid society—the NYRPA provided small sums of money to recently evicted tenants. Like the *landsmanshaft*, which provided money to its unemployed, disabled, or needy members, the NYRPA was designed to be "an immense mutual benefit society for Jewish tenants of the Lower East Side."[24] "Every tenant," one of its founders explained, "will pay dues and the funds so raised will be available to pay the rent of any member of the association who cannot raise the money (for rent)."[25] In addition to providing financial benefits, the NYRPA provided advice and legal counsel as well. Hoping to become "the address" for tenant-landlord problems, NYRPA staff would help disgruntled tenants in court, organize tenant groups in individual buildings, and plan rent strikes.

Ultimately, the NYRPA foundered on the issue of politics. Some of its one thousand members maintained that without an avowedly political base—that of the Socialist party—tenant protest was not likely to get off the ground. Others held that in withholding their rent, they were acting as tenants; "we are not here as Socialists nor as labor unionists but as tenants," this group explained. Unable to resolve their differences, the Socialist faction of the NYRPA went its own way and seceded from the parent organization; the NYRPA, itself, dissolved soon thereafter.[26]

Though Lower East Side residents failed, in 1904, to establish a sustained, ongoing, institutional base from which to conduct future rent strikes and other forms of tenant activity, the rent wars of 1904 appeared to them as a successful venture. The threatened evictions failed to materialize, and, if newspaper accounts are to be believed, the overwhelming majority of Lower East Side landlords rolled back rents to prestrike levels, some even going so far as to sign leases with their tenants promising to hold the rent steady for at least one year. Even more important, perhaps, than the material gains won by striking tenants were the psychological implications the 1904 rent protest held out for area residents. As tenants, residents saw the value of collective protest. The 1904 rent strike, noted the *Forward* in its aftermath, "puts tenants on a new level,"[27] while another contemporary observed that "the tenants of the East Side have learned their lesson. They see that a long pull and a strong pull and a pull altogether will save. . . . It must be borne in mind as a most important feature of this whole affair, that the tenants fought their own battle."[28]

Beginning in late December 1907 and crescendoing a month later, the "greatest rent wars" the Empire City had ever seen took place as thousands of residents throughout Manhattan and Brooklyn collectively withheld their rents in protest against yet another round of impending rent hikes.[29] The 1904 protest, it seemed, had succeeded only temporarily in holding down rents; within a year of its passing, local real estate interests began incrementally once again to raise the rent. Early in December, landlords announced that as of the new year, rent would be increased by an additional dollar or two. Coming on the heels of successive waves of rent hikes in which, for example, two-and-one-half "dark rooms" now rented for $16 or $17 instead of the 1904 price of $11 or $12, tenants were caught off guard by the latest rent hike.[30] What is more, 1907 was a depression year in which anywhere from seventy-five to one hundred thousand men on the Lower East Side were unemployed. If in ordinary times when employment was more or less steady tenement dwellers were hard put to come up with an additional 50 cents or $1 for the rent, what could they possibly do when opportunities for work were negligible. "A difference of $1 in the rent," related one disgruntled resident, "means all the difference in the world."[31]

"Born in the shabby rooms of the tenements where mothers saw things going from bad to worse," tenant protest, once again, spread throughout the Lower East Side "like a fire."[32] As in 1904, local housewives initially led the protest, their concern with and ultimate participation in rent strikes stemming from their role as homemaker and manager of the household budget. Described alternately as "missionaries" or as the "great army of protestants," they canvased the neighborhood for support, wrote circulars denouncing "rent robbery," and urged residents not to pay the additional rent.[33] "We, the tenants of 3M," read the text of tenant resolutions, "having realized our present misery come to the following conclusions. Whereas the present industrial depression has affected us most severely; and whereas the rent for the last two years has risen skywards . . . therefore we resolve to demand of you to decrease the rent immediately."[34] For many area residents, withholding their rent pending a more reasonable settlement with the landlord was their only option. "I simply did what any sensible girl would do," one of the rent protestors explained. "I am not a labor leader or a regular striker and I am also not a troublemaker. I simply joined the strike because I saw it was impossible to exist on a small salary these days and then pay exorbitant rents to the landlords."[35] The rent strikes, added social reformer Rose Pastor Stokes, herself a former resident of the area, come out of "pure necessity."[36]

Almost immediately, the 1908 "tenant uprising" was brought under the "systematic and organized control" of the Eighth Assembly District or local branch of the Socialist party, a party heavily represented and favored by Jewish garment workers and others.[37] As January rent day drew closer, one eyewitness recalled, tenants became increasingly agitated over their inability to pay the new rent; "this agitation in turn formulated itself into a question which at last found expression at a meeting of the 8th Socialist party."[38] Under its aegis, the rent strike spread to Brooklyn and Harlem and ultimately engaged several thousand tenants. What is more, Newark, New Jersey, residents sent a delegation across the river to the Lower East Side to discuss planning a similar protest in their city, while members of the International Federation of Italians conferred with the members of the Socialist party directing the strike on how best to conduct a rent strike in the city's Italian neighborhoods. Staff located at the Socialist party's downtown headquarters provided tenants with advice on how to approach their landlords for a rent reduction and, when that failed, on how to organize a rent strike. When property owners appeared ready to negotiate a possible settlement, Socialist party members spelled out the proper negotiating techniques to the tenants and, in some instances, negotiated directly with the landlords on the tenants' behalf, even appearing for them in court. Several socialist unions, meanwhile, joining in the fray, pledged financial assistance to dispossessed or needy tenants. More dramatically still, the members of the "Hebrew local" of the Teamsters Union refused, in their capacity as marshals, to dispossess striking tenants.[39]

Thanks to the direction and leadership of the Socialist party, the 1908 tenant rebellion was perhaps better and more tightly organized than in the past. Lending its name, organizational base, and personnel to the cause, the Socialist party not only indelibly marked tenant protest as a left wing activity (an association that persisted for quite some time) but also adumbrated its involvement, several years later, in the major garment industry strikes of the prewar era. During the shirtwaist makers' strike of 1909–1910, the Socialist party assisted the ILGWU, the fledgling garment union, by providing it with financial support and pickets. Yet there were several drawbacks in being associated with the Socialists for, in the minds of many New Yorkers, rent striking was seen increasingly as a Socialist venture. New York City's police, for example, frightened by what they took to be the revolutionary fervor of the 1908 protestors, not only refused to grant them the right to parade through downtown streets but also forcibly disbanded such gatherings. For another thing, tenant-landlord confrontations this time around were considerably more violent than they had been previously. Egged on by the Socialists, tenants hung their landlords in effigy and hung red flags (actually petticoats dyed red) from their windows.[40]

The media, for its part, was far less supportive of the 1908 rent strike than it had been of the one four years before. What the press described, somewhat kindly, in 1904 as a "tenant-landlord conflict," a "rental agitation," or a "folk struggle," they now depicted as a "rent war," a "tenant uprising," or a "tenant rebellion"; groups of tenants were seen as an "army" and tenant-landlord confrontations as "skirmishes."[41] Undoubtedly, the Socialist nature of the agitation alarmed many. The *American Hebrew*, New York Jewry's middle-class newspaper, sharply criticized its downtown coreligionists for "not acting wisely." The rent strike, commented the weekly, "is a typical example of how not to do things."[12] *Charities and Commons*, in turn, noted that "the use of red flags and the violent opposition to their removal has already to some extent alienated public sympathy from their cause."[43] Protesting tenants, then, were seen in 1908 as dangerous and unruly, as a group to be controlled and quieted. Alarmed by what seemed to them to be a clear misreading of the situation, Lillian D. Wald and James Hamilton, two of New York's leading social workers, wrote to the editor of the *New York Times* to explain what was occurring on the Lower East Side and elsewhere throughout the city. "We deem it only just to say," the social workers related, "that the agitation through public meetings and the like has been conducted in a calm and orderly manner. The people of the Lower East Side are hardworking, self respecting and lawabiding . . . and it is our observation that the movement has been conducted in such a manner as to deserve respect."[44]

The social workers' appreciation for the dilemma faced by Lower East Side and other tenants did nothing to alleviate a growing sentiment against them, particularly on the part of the municipal court judges who dispensed eviction proceedings. Insisting that "there must be no lawlessness nor red flags" and that a "rent strike cannot be entertained as an excuse for not paying rent," the magistrates issued several thousand dispossess notices.[45] Ultimately, this action broke the back of the 1908 protest, to say nothing of the esprit de corps of the protestors. Although several hundred tenants successfully secured rent reductions of a dollar or two, most were not so fortunate: they were either evicted from their homes or, alternatively, "yielded at the last moment" and paid the new rent.[46]

Writing in the strike's aftermath, Rose Pastor Stokes applauded the tenants for organizing. Regardless of whether they won reductions, she noted, tenants should feel that the "fight itself must result in great good. It makes [the tenants] conscious of the common interests of their class, this fighting together."[47] However conscious tenants might have been of their "common interests" as tenants, they failed to develop an institutional base from which to protect those interests. The 1908 rent protest, like its predecessor, lasted only a short time; it disappeared as quickly as it had first appeared. The organizations that emerged to defend the tenants against the "rent robbery"—the building-level tenant unions or the Socialist party's involvement—similarly disappeared, leaving no enduring structure. Tenant activity, it seemed, was ad hoc and temporary: once tenants secured what they regarded as gains or were simply unable to proceed any further with their protests, the "rental agitation" subsided. Several thousand strong at the height of the 1908 protest, New York's tenants had the possibility to effect some measure of change in the nature of the tenant-landlord relationship—to make a case for tenants' rights and to press for the accountability of the property owner. Ultimately, though, as one contemporary observed at the time, "no marked change in the condition of the East Side has been brought about" by the 1908 rent strikes.[48]

What is more, there was "no marked change" in the condition of the New York City tenement house dweller in the years following the great rent strike of 1908. In the period preceding the outbreak of World War I, tenant activity was sporadic and, for the most part, limited to the city's Jewish neighborhoods. Small-scale protests, in which tenants threatened to withhold their rent in protest against an impending rent hike, erupted from time to time on the Lower East Side, Harlem, and the Bronx; a few protests centered on the issue of inadequate heat and poor building management.[49] Nothing comparable to the 1908 protest took place until several years after the Great War. And while one can find scattered hints of some tenant activity among other New York City residents at the time, it assumed completely different forms than it had earlier.[50] Black residents of Harlem, for example, occasionally formed block associations, wrote petitions, and held rallies in protest against excessively high, and discriminatory, rents.[51] They did not, however, commonly resort to rent strikes until years later. Only after their policicitization on other fronts did black New Yorkers use forms of collective protest within the context of housing-related grievances; the latter technique remained a hallmark of Jewish tenant activity.

NOTES

1. *New York Herald* (hereafter cited as *NYH*), Apr. 10, 1904.
2. Archibald Hill, "Rental Agitation on the Lower East Side," *Charities*, Apr. 16, 1904. See too Louis Freedman, "Rise in Rentals on the Lower East Side," *Jewish Charity*, Feb. 1904. The following account is drawn largely from the *Jewish Daily Forward* (hereafter cited as *JDF*), Mar. 17–May 21, 1904; *New York Times* (hereafter cited as *NYT*), Apr. 4–May 5, 1904; *New York Sun* (hereafter cited as *NYS*), Apr. 6–May 4, 1904; *NYH*, Apr. 4–May 5, 1904.
3. *NYT*, Apr. 8, 1904.

4. David Blaustein, "Cockroach Landlords," *New Era* 4, no. 6 (May 1904): 2.
5. Ibid., p. 5.
6. *JDF*, June 1, 1906, Mar. 5, 1909, Sept. 12, 1916.
7. Ibid., Mar. 6, 1905.
8. Quoted in Blaustein, "Cockroach Landlords," p. 5.
9. Zalmen Yoffeh, "The Passing of the East Side," *Menorah Journal*, Dec. 1929, p. 274.
10. Irving Howe, *World of Our Fathers* (New York, 1976), p. 154.
11. *NYH*, Apr. 6, 1904.
12. Ibid.; *Real Estate Record and Builder's Guide*, Jan. 4, 1908.
13. *Real Estate Record and Builder's Guide*, July 27, 1901.
14. Cited in Thomas Kessner, *The Golden Door: Italian and Jewish Immigrant Mobility in New York City, 1880–1915* (New York, 1977), p. 33.
15. *JDF*, Apr. 7, 13, 1904.
16. Blaustein, "Cockroach Landlords," p. 1.
17. Howe, *World of Our Fathers*, p. 124.
18. Abe Cahan, "What Sense Is There In These Rent Strikes," *Worker*, Apr. 17, 1904.
19. Paula E. Hyman, "Immigrant Women and Consumer Protest: The New York City Kosher Meat Boycott of 1902," *American Jewish History* 70, no. 1 (Sept. 1980): 91–105, especially p. 92. See too Paula E. Hyman, "Culture and Gender: Women in the Immigrant Jewish Community," in *The Legacy of Jewish Migration: 1881 and Its Impact*, ed. David Berger (New York, 1983), pp. 157–168. See too Mari Jo Buhle, *Women and American Socialism, 1870–1920* (Urbana, 1981).
20. Editorial, "The Role of Women in the Rent and Other Strikes," *JDF*, May 21, 1904. Also, *NYT*, Apr. 8, 1904; *NYH*, Apr. 8, 10, 1904; *NYS*, Apr. 12, 1904.
21. *JDF*, Mar. 18, 1904.
22. Cahan, "What Sense in Rent Strikes," p. 4.
23. *NYS*, Apr. 8, 1904; *NYT*, Apr. 10, 1904; *NYS*, Apr. 11, 1904; *NYT*, Apr. 8, 11, 1904.
24. *NYS*, Apr. 11, 1904; *NYT*, Apr. 11, 1904.
25. *NYT*, Apr. 18, 1904; *NYS*, Apr. 12, 1904.
26. *NYT*, Apr. 12, 1904; *NYH*, Apr. 12, 1904; *NYT*, May 3, 1904.
27. Blaustein, "Cockroach Landlords," p. 6.
28. Ibid. In the years that followed, tenants continued to hold rent strikes. Faced with a rent hike or an unwarranted eviction, tenants protested by withholding their rent. In the spring of 1905, for example, tenants on a Lower East Side Pike Street tenement collectively withheld their rent in protest against what they believed to be an unfair rent hike. Similarly, late in 1907, tenants forced to move from their homes in order to make way for an entrance onto the newly erected Manhattan Bridge held protest demonstrations. For all that though, tenant activity was rather limited in scope; a brief flurry involving one or two buildings, it was a far cry from the communitywide protest of 1904. If, at the first sign of a rent problem, the *Jewish Daily Forward* trumpeted, "Another rent war is here," its excitement more accurately reflected journalistic license than it did the actual social reality. See *JDF*, Apr. 21, 1904, Apr. 3, 1905; "East Side Rents," *American Hebrew*, Sept. 15, 1905.
29. *NYT*, Dec. 28, 1907. Because of the size of the protest, New York's metropolitan newspapers paid it a good deal of mind. General accounts of the 1907–8 rent strike can be found in the *JDF*, Dec. 24, 1907–Jan. 22, 1908; *Wahrheit*, Dec. 26, 1907–Jan. 10, 1908; *Judisches Tageblatt*, Dec. 26–31, 1907; *NYT*, Dec. 26, 1907–Jan. 24, 1908; *New York World* (hereafter cited as *NYW*), Dec. 27, 1907–Jan. 15, 1908; *New York Evening Journal* (hereafter cited as *NYEJ*), Dec. 26, 1907–Jan. 24, 1908. *Daily People* and *Worker*, two Socialist publications, were also consulted.

30. *Daily People*, Jan. 3, 1908; *Wahrheit*, Dec. 27, 1907; *American Hebrew*, Jan. 10, 1908.
31. Quoted in *Daily People*, Jan. 3, 1908; Charles Bernheimer, "High Rents on New York's East Side," *Charities and Commons*, Jan. 18, 1908.
32. *New York Globe and Commercial Advertiser*, Dec. 26, 1907; *NYEJ*, Dec. 26, 31, 1907.
33. *NYEJ*, Jan. 26, 28, 1908.
34. *NYW*, Dec. 30, 1907; *Worker*, Jan. 4, 1908. See too, Charles Bernheimer, "Rent Strikes and Crowded Neighborhoods," *Outlook*, Jan. 1908.
35. *New York American*, Dec. 30, 1907; *NYEJ*, Dec. 31, 1907. On the women participants in particular, see *New York American*, Dec. 26, 27, 28, 30, 1907; *NYT*, Dec. 26, 27, 1908; *NYEJ*, Dec. 27, 28, 31, 1907; Victor Rousseau, "Low Rent or No Rent: The Tenement Dweller's Rebellion in New York," *Harper's Weekly*, Jan. 25, 1908, pp. 148–152.
36. *NYW*, Jan. 9, 1908.
37. *New York Globe and Commercial Advertiser*, Dec. 26, 1907; *NYT*, Dec. 30, 1907; William Mailly, "The New York Rent Strike," *Independent*, no. 64, Jan. 1908. The New York Socialist party was heavily Jewish, for the Lower East Side garment worker, the party's backbone, "made up the single largest fraction of the enrolled Socialists," accounting for at least one-third of its membership. Charles Leinenweber, "The Class and Ethnic Bases of New York Socialism, 1904–1915," *Labor History* 22, no. 1 (Winter 1981): 31–56, especially pp. 39, 43.
38. Mailly, "New York Rent Strike," p. 150; author's interview with Pauline Newman, June 12, 1975.
39. *JDF*, Jan. 3, 1908; *NYEJ*, Jan. 2, 1908; *NYW*, Jan. 15, 1908; *Worker*, Jan. 18, 1908. See too, Jeffrey Gurock, *When Harlem Was Jewish*, 1870–1930 (New York, 1979), pp. 72–73.
40. *NYS*, Jan. 6, 1908; Mailly, "New York Rent Strike"; *Wahrheit*, Dec. 28, 29, 1907.
41. See, for example, Rousseau, "Low Rent"; *NYW*, Dec. 27, 29, 1907, Jan. 3, 1908; *NYEJ*, Jan. 4, 1908.
42. *American Hebrew*, Jan. 3, 10, 1908.
43. *Charities and Commons*, Jan. 11, 1908.
44. *NYT*, Jan. 11, 1908.
45. *JDF*, Jan. 2, 1908; *NYEJ*, Dec. 31, 1907; *New York Globe and Commercial Advertiser*, Jan. 6, 1908; *NYEJ*, Jan. 7, 1908.
46. *NYEJ*, Jan. 3, 1908; "Outcome of Rent Agitation," *Charities and Commons*, Feb. 8, 1908.
47. *NYEJ*, Jan. 3, 1908.
48. "Outcome of Rent Agitation."
49. In the years that followed, tenants continued, on occasion, to engage in protest behavior. During the years 1909–1916, for example, small-scale examples of tenant activity erupted on the Lower East Side, Harlem, and the Bronx. In 1909, tenants in an East 100th Street tenement, angered by what they regarded as the dishonest management of their building, threatened to withhold rent until the landlord conducted his affairs more honorably. Shortly thereafter, Lower East Side residents in one tenement house went out on a rent strike in protest against a rent hike. Moreover, on the eve of World War I, the failure of one landlord to provide his tenants with what they saw as a sufficient amount of steam and hot water provoked them into threatening a rent strike. See, *JDF*, Apr. 2, 1908, Apr. 5, 1909, Dec. 30, 31, 1916.
50. The Society to Lower Rents and Reduce Taxes on Homes must be mentioned in this context as well. Strictly speaking, it was not a tenant association for it neither serviced the immediate needs of the city's apartment house dwellers nor counseled them on how to handle landlord-related problems. Formed by civic reformer Benjamin Clarke Marsh in 1913, the society was essentially a land and tax reform organization, concerned primarily with reducing urban congestion and only incidentally with the plight of tenants. Marsh and his followers believed that a reduction of the

building tax on building improvements would have salutary effect on living conditions, most particularly on the high cost of rent. Armed with the slogan, "One-half tax equals lower rents," Marsh crusaded among New York tenement and apartment house dwellers for their support. To that end, he published a magazine, *Tenant's Weekly* (later it came out monthly), as a forum through which the society's ideas could be publicized. Though Marsh's organization ultimately failed to lift itself off the ground, its short-lived history suggests that, increasingly, tenants were being seen as a political constituency. On Marsh, see Benjamin Clarke Marsh, *Lobbyist for the People* (Washington, 1953); *Tenant's Weekly*, June 1, 1914; *Municipal Facts*, Sept. 17, 1911; "Lower Rents as a City Slogan," *Survey*, Mar. 15, 1913.

51. See, for example, *New York Age*, Sept. 28, Oct. 5, Nov. 23, Dec. 28, 1916; "Housing Conditions among Negroes in Harlem, New York City," *Publication of the National Urban League*, vol. 4, no. 2, Jan. 1915.

2. New York City Tenant Organizations and the Post–World War I Housing Crisis

Joseph A. Spencer

THE decade following World War I is one of the most significant periods in the history of New York City tenant activity due to the extent that renters organized against landlords as well as the gains achieved through such mobilization.

Lack of construction, increased demand for apartments, and rampant speculation in New York's tenement neighborhoods led to increasing landlord-tenant bitterness during the last years of the war. In the face of repeated rent increases, many families organized to resist. Relying on help from the Socialist party and its allied labor unions, tenants built effective building- and neighborhood-level organizations in several working-class communities of the Bronx, Brooklyn, and Manhattan and forced hundreds of landlords to rescind rent increases or improve building conditions. Tenant leaders were much less successful, however, in achieving broader goals such as legislative limits on rent increases and stronger code enforcement provisions. Furthermore, they failed in efforts to build a larger citywide organization and translate renter support into Socialist victories at the polls.

Nevertheless, government officials could not treat the situation lightly. By early 1919, eviction cases clogged the municipal courts, and thousands of families suffered eviction each month. Approximately twenty-five thousand apartment dwellers had affiliated with a tenant league, and the crisis was spreading into more and more of the city's neighborhoods. Many felt that unless something were done, the Socialists would eventually reap major political benefits from their advocacy of the tenants' cause.

In the spring of 1919, elected representatives responded by appointing committees to deal with the housing shortage. The most important was the Mayor's Committee on Rent Profiteering, which competed with the leagues by arbitrating landlord-tenant disputes and providing legal aid to renters through local Democratic clubhouses. Although the committee helped thousands of families, the cycle of rent increases, strikes, and evictions grew worse. By the end of 1919, tenant leagues existed in a dozen neighborhoods, and the Socialists had won several key victories in the November elections.

At this time, however, several factors combined to change significantly the context in which the postwar housing struggle was fought. The first was the rise of the Red Scare—the wave of rampant antiradicalism and nativism that swept the country in late 1919 and early 1920. The tenant movement became the target of widespread red-baiting, with league organizers and members harassed in the courts and on the picket line. The five Socialist members of the state assembly were suspended and eventually expelled from the legislature, a development that symbolized the general exclusion of the tenant leagues from the negotiation process over legislative remedies to deal with the crisis.

Meanwhile, several new tenant organizations emerged in certain sections of the Bronx and Manhattan. Generally led by persons with ties to local Democratic and Republican organizations, these groups opposed rent striking. Not surprisingly, they were quickly recognized by government officials as the "legitimate" representatives of tenant interests. With the support of such groups and labor unions associated with the established parties, the legislature in April 1920 passed a series of laws that gave tenants limited rights to challenge large rent increases and protected the tenure of some apartment dwellers.

While these "April Laws" led to a noticeable decrease in the number of rent strikes, it soon became clear that they were not really a solution. Tenants still had no real legal defense against most rent increases, and loopholes in the law actually sparked a tremendous increase in eviction proceedings. In response to pleas from the municipal court judges and the conservative tenant associations, the legislature met in special session in September 1920 and passed the Emergency Rent Laws, a series of statutes that granted tenants much more substantial protections against arbitrary rent increases and unjust eviction.

Following passage of the Emergency Rent Laws, the tenant movement experienced major changes. The Socialist tenant leagues faded from the scene, victims of both the court-based remedies passed in September and the ideological warfare that split the party during 1920. Several of the conservative associations in the Bronx and Manhattan, on the other hand, matured into stable organizations with memberships in the thousands. Throughout the early and middle 1920s they provided a range of legal and social services to desperate families. They also served as allies of state and local housing officials; it was their cooperative "pressure" and vacancy-rent surveys that justified the periodic extension of the laws throughout much of the decade.

Yet the orientation and tactics of tenant leaders after 1920 failed to serve the broader and longer-term interests of tenants. Concerned with legitimacy and their own relationships with government officials, they limited their goals almost exclusively to the administration and maintenance of the rent laws and failed to press for more basic advances such as public housing or tougher code enforcement.

Eventually this reactive strategy produced failure. During the decade, New York's residential housing supply expanded rapidly, fueled by large tax incentives for new construction. The resulting high vacancy rate made it increasingly difficult to justify the continuation of "emergency" limits on rents. Thus, starting in 1926, the legislature began to exempt increasing numbers of apartments—based on rent per room—from renewals of the Emergency Rent Laws. For the tenant associations, this spelled the start of a cycle of decline: each reduction in the number of tenants covered by the rent laws decreased the constituency available to resist further cuts. By 1928 the movement was so weak that it could put up only token resistance, and the rent laws were phased out over the next two years.

American involvement in World War I produced chaos in New York City's housing market. Defense industries received top priority in the allocation of manpower and materials, thus inflating the cost of construction at a time when war-oriented investment opportunities drew off needed capital. As a result, tenement construction, already on the decline since 1911, came to a standstill. Only 1,481 apartments were completed in 1919—a 94 percent decrease from 1915.[1]

The decline in residential construction came at a time when wartime prosperity, fueled by defense jobs, was attracting thousands of families to New York City. Under such pressure the vacancy rate fell precipitously, from 5.6 percent in 1916 to just 0.36 percent in April 1920.[2] Many families, faced with rising rents and the decreasing availability of suitable apartments, were forced to move into smaller or more deteriorated quarters. This reversed a trend in which thousands of substandard units had been abandoned during the previous decade. Thirty-six thousand "old law" (i.e., pre-1901) apartments, vacant in 1916, had been reoccupied by 1920.[3]

This downward movement occured at a time when the city government lacked a commitment to protect the well-being of tenement dwellers. Under the cost-conscious Mayor John Hylan, the Tenement House Department budget was continuously slashed. While the number of inspectors was set by law at 206 for 103,000 buildings, Commissioner Frank Mann economized by not replacing other departmental personnel who resigned or entered the armed forces. He ordered his staff not to report any "trivial or unnecessary violations" and even deferred action on structural shortcomings. Consequently, buildings that had been grossly inadequate for decades suffered further decay. By the summer of 1919 Mann was forced to admit that even the city's low vacancy rate was misleading since most of the empty apartments were uninhabitable.[4]

Although factors of increased demand and limited building were in themselves capable of producing a housing shortage of crisis proportions, the situation was further exacerbated by intense speculation in tenement housing. A speculator would purchase a building, immediately raise rents, and then resell at a profit, based on its increased rental income. Thousands of properties changed hands in this fashion, with some houses in the Bronx and Brooklyn sold several times in one month.[5]

Another major grievance was the lessee system, through which landlords with more buildings than they could personally manage would lease certain properties to individuals for a fixed yearly fee. The lessee, usually a local small businessman without sufficient capital to purchase a building of his own, made his profit by increasing rents and curtailing services. In areas where the system was prevalent, especially the Jewish communities of the Lower East Side, Williamsburg, and Brownsville, the lessee was hated—perceived as a traitor seeking profit from the exploitation of his fellow countrymen.[6]

The origins of the postwar tenant movement are somewhat obscure. The first major precursor, however, was a January 1917 rent strike in the Crotona Park section of the Bronx. This was a predominantly lower-class neighborhood with a heavy concentration of Russian Jewish families that had emigrated from the Lower East Side in search of improved living conditions. In the best of times these families had trouble paying their rent.[7] They became even more burdened, and restive, in the face of repeated rent increases and the failure of their landlords to provide heat and hot water. In late December 1916, five hundred to one thousand tenants in twenty-five buildings owned by two major real estate firms were organized by the Socialist Women's Consumers League of the Bronx. At the urging of Theresa Malkiel, a Socialist Party State Committee member, the tenants rejected a rent increase demanded for January 1, 1917, and refused to pay any rent until heat and hot water were restored. They formed the Bronx Tenants League, collected a small strike fund, and organized a picket force of the "huskiest women." Leon Malakiel, a Socialist lawyer, agreed to represent the strikers and immediately filed complaints of code violations with the Health Department and the Tenement House Department.[8]

Within a week the landlords responded with a flood of eviction notices. The back of the strike was broken when the first cases came to court. Municipal court judge Michael Scanlon ruled that 296 tenants had no recourse at law because they had no written leases; they had to pay their rent or vacate.[9] Most had no choice but to give in. As one local paper commented, "It is to be presumed that if the five hundred tenants are ejected from their present quarters, that they will not be able to obtain flats elsewhere in the Bronx."[10]

The leaders of the Bronx Tenants League vowed to continue their efforts on behalf of tenants, despite the disintegration of the strike. On January 17 they held a meeting and, formally establishing their organization, enrolled 150 charter members. They also announced plans to form affiliates in all of the city's boroughs to fight for lower rents, better building maintenance, code enforcement, and legal aid for indigent tenants.[11] Despite their excellent intentions, however, a widespread following failed to develop, and there is no evidence of organized tenant activity for the rest of 1917.

Landlord-tenant bitterness resurfaced one year later, however. The early months of 1918 were unusually harsh, with temperatures hovering around the zero mark for over a month. To make matters worse, the city faced a wartime coal shortage and many landlords failed to supply heat and hot water. By the end of January the Bronx alone had 450 heatless buildings.[12] Residents of the other boroughs endured similar hardship. A social worker serving the East Harlem and Yorkville areas noted: "Conditions are beyond description. Gas is frozen, homes are dark, no water in the toilets, sanitary conditions unspeakable, faces blue and pinched from the bitter cold and ever so many kiddies down with pneumonia."[13]

In response to these conditions, thousands of families throughout the city refused to pay their full rent. Many had purchased their own heaters or fuel and demanded reimbursement in the form of rent reductions. Landlords reacted not only by denying their immediate responsibility, but also by asserting that the payment of rent did not entitle one to heat and hot water.[14] When they sought to evict nonpaying families, however, some municipal court judges disagreed and allowed 10 percent reductions to offset tenant fuel expenditures. Yet for several reasons, appeal to the courts was not an adequate tenant remedy. Justices with sympathy for strikers usually granted reductions only to those with written leases—a small minority in that period. Furthermore, since the laws governing such cases were vague, decisions varied from one judge to another. Thus building owners could bring a family into court month after month until the case came up before a prolandlord judge.[15]

Sensing their vulnerability, tenants sought strength in numbers. The Bronx Tenants League emerged from a year of dormancy to capitalize on tenant discontent. Again in cooperation with the Women's Consumers League, it mounted a No Heat, No Rent campaign and organized several large rent strikes in the East Tremont, Morrisania, and Mott Haven sections. A key to the group's success was the legal assistance it offered distressed tenants. Attorneys Morris Gisnet and Alexander Kahn won temporary reductions for hundreds of families in January, February, and March 1918.[16] Socialist assemblyman Samuel Orr, who had been elected from the Fourth Assembly District the previous November, also took an active part in the league's work; at the height of the crisis he introduced several bills in the legislature which would have required landlords to maintain a minimum temperature of 68 degrees at all times and allowed rent reductions if this were not done.[17] Although these bills were throttled in the assembly, they attracted attention to the league and enhanced its reputation among tenants.

Although sporadic rent striking occurred throughout upper Manhattan, the only successful attempt to organize tenants beyond the building level took place in Washington Heights. In late February 1918, representatives of twenty-seven buildings, led by William Herman, an executive with the State Industrial Commission, met and formed the Washington Heights Tenants League. Within several weeks they claimed a membership of over three hundred and had achieved half a dozen victories, both in court and through negotiation with landlords. Their success was largely attributable to the fact that most members, many of whom were professionals, had written leases that were recognized in court and gave them leverage in bargaining with building owners.[18]

Brooklyn landlords and tenants were also involved in a series of struggles. In the Williamsburg section a young Socialist lawyer, Joseph Klein, won a succession of rent cases in the municipal courts and then, in early March, began to organize buildings and negotiate directly with the owners. By April he had established the Williamsburg Tenants League and was threatening to lead a widespread rent strike against all profiteering landlords.[19]

Tenants were also coalescing in Brownsville. The local consumers league had backed several large strikes in the early months of 1918, but the major confrontation did not occur until late April. Landlord demands for a May 1 increase of from three to five dollars per month found tenants in a mood to resist—the neighborhood already being in the throes of labor strikes by bakers, shoemakers, and barbers. On the eve of May Day the Socialist party daily, the *New York Call*, reported that "entire blocks are being organized" and that one thousand families were withholding rent. The ensuing struggle was bitter and long lasting. The courts were filled with eviction cases; in some instances landlords emptied entire buildings. Although many families were forced to retreat back to the cheaper, more deteriorated apartments of the Lower East Side, many more remained and fought. Evicted families moved in with neighbors and picketed struck buildings, often threatening prospective tenants. Groups of strikers and guards hired by landlords battled outside of buildings.[20]

The tenant activity of early 1918 led to an escalation of the landlord-tenant struggle and contributed to a hardening of attitudes on both sides. This was certainly true of building owners, who argued that they had suffered several lean years prior to the war when overbuilding in the Bronx and Brooklyn had depressed rents. Now when wages and prices were rising steadily, they felt entitled to share in the general prosperity.[21] The refusal of their tenants to pay rent, and especially the actions of judges and politicians in support of strikers, shocked and angered many realtors. One Bronx owner with a flair for hyperbole captured the mood of his colleagues: "Tenants control our property, move in and out of it as they please, pay rent or withhold it as they please and treat with the landlords or ignore them as they please. Politicians seeking votes are now organizing disgruntled tenants to oppose the rights of landlords."[22]

To counteract the effect of the "professional agitators" they blamed for tenant unrest, many landlords formed local organizations to augment the older, established real estate lobbying groups. The Bronx Federation of Real Estate Owners, the Bronx Landlords Protective Association, and the Brownsville Taxpayers and Real Estate Owners Association battled tenants by appealing court decisions that granted rent reductions, evicting tenant "ringleaders," developing a standard lease that waived a tenant's right to heat, and coordinating requests for rent increases.[23]

Tenants had also achieved a new level of solidarity and strength. Unlike other previous rent strike episodes, the winter 1918 agitation did not disintegrate with the arrival of warmer weather. Rather, during the rest of the year the better-organized groups—the Bronx Tenants League, the Williamsburg Tenants League, and the Brownsville Consumers League—continued to add members, and new leagues were formed in East Harlem and the Borough Park section of Brooklyn.[24]

All of these successful organizations were marked by a supportive relationship with the Socialist party. That is not to say that membership in the leagues was restricted to party members. But the link between the two was close. The leagues flourished in areas of Socialist electoral strength and held meetings in Socialist halls. Socialist lawyers and officials played key leadership roles, while women of the consumers leagues allied with the party did much of the organizing. In addition, the *New York Call* gave the leagues their best press coverage. This relationship gave the tenant organizations access to a wide variety of resources that they would otherwise have had to develop on their own.

Thus when landlords in a number of neighborhoods sought yet another round of increases for October 1, 1918, thousands of households were prepared to resist. Many had no choice: there were no other apartments available, and they were being asked to pay twenty-five to thirty dollars per month for quarters that had cost twelve to fifteen dollars a year before.

When used properly by tenant organizers, the rent strike became a most effective tactic. The building owner could usually obtain dispossess orders from the municipal court, but in order to carry out the evictions he had to hire movers, at a cost of ten to twelve dollars per family. In a well-organized building of fifteen to twenty units, this expense might well exceed the income from the proposed increases. If the landlord decided to evict regardless of the cost, however, his troubles were not over. The ousted tenants would move in with neighbors and picket his building, often threatening prospective tenants. Thus many owners, faced with the possibility of such spirited resistance, chose to negotiate a settlement with the tenants league. Generally a contract was drawn up that granted half of the requested increase in return for a one-year lease and the promise of repairs. The league would then hold all rent until the specified repairs were completed.[25]

While such tactics brought many local victories, movement leaders experienced considerable difficulty in achieving goals that went beyond the building level. In late May 1918, leaders from various leagues met and formed the Greater New York Tenants League (GNYTL). Working with the Socialist party, GNYTL representatives drafted a call for state legislation to limit rent increases, regulate lessees, raise the court fees for landlords instituting eviction proceedings, and provide legal aid for indigent tenants. Yet there was little response. Governor Charles Whitman spent a few minutes with a tenant delegation, but refused to call a special session of the legislature. Local officials, led by Mayor John Hylan, condemned rent profiteering but pleaded a lack of authority to deal with the problem.[26]

Even more disturbing was the failure of the Socialists to capitalize on the housing crisis in the November elections. The previous fall's campaign had been extremely successful for the Socialists. As the only party opposing the war, they had received nearly 22 percent of the vote for mayor in a four-way contest and had elected ten assemblymen and seven aldermen. Now, party leaders hoped to do even better, with the tenant leagues serving as a source of new supporters. Several candidates, such as Samuel Orr, A. I. Shiplacoff, and Joe Klein, had served as tenant leaders themselves. The leagues, polling the contestants of all parties concerning their rent policies and eventually endorsing the Socialists at campaign rallies, asserted that only they could be trusted to pass protenant legislation. The election produced major setbacks, however. The Socialist share of the vote declined slightly in most districts, and a fusion movement by Democrats and Republicans succeeded in unseating eight of the party's assemblymen. Only Charles Solomon of Brownsville and August Claessens of East Harlem survived.[27]

Other factors may have been largely responsible for these disappointing results, however. First, a large percentage of those who participated in rent strikes were already supporters of the Socialist party. Second, the armistice followed the election by less than a week, and with peace so near, the party undoubtedly lost many of the antiwar votes that had swelled its tally the previous November. Therefore, while many distressed tenants may have turned to the Socialists, the addition of their ballots may only have served to offset the loss of peace votes.

Nevertheless, the developments of late 1918 did reveal a deeper weakness in the growing movement. Tenants were willing to participate in rent strikes when they or their neighbors were threatened, yet they proved reticent to maintain long-term league participation or support programs that went beyond the local level. Thus, although its component groups had led scores of strikes in various areas, GNYTL could report only 1,321 dues-paying members by the end of 1918.[28]

Nevertheless, the defeat of most Socialist incumbents in November 1918 did not allow Democratic and Republican officeholders to ignore the housing crisis. The declining vacancy rate—2.18 percent in March 1919[29]—and continually rising rents were producing potential tenant leaguers at a rapid pace. In the early months of 1919, therefore, many politicians began to take a more active interest in housing. In the forefront were those who had won fusionist victories in areas of Socialist strength. They feared that increasing numbers of tenants would soon come to echo the sentiments of one man who complained that "My family and myself have always been staunch Democrats but if we get no relief we will have to look to the Socialist party even though we despise their doctrines. They may give us a chance to live."[30]

Sensing similar discontent among many families in their districts, several Bronx and Brooklyn assemblymen warned that their constituents were being "driven toward socialism" by rent profiteering.[31] Similarly, the announcement of yet another round of rent increases for May 1 inspired a flood of protest letters to Mayor Hylan. One implored him to "Keep these Rent Profiteers on the run." A Brooklyn woman wrote of a situation so bad that her husband had attempted suicide by swallowing iodine. A third correspondent returned to a familiar antilandlord theme; "If Bolshevism ever comes to this country, there is no one to blame but such types of persons as this organized band of thieves."[32] These letters reflected the seriousness of the housing crisis. Working-class families throughout the city were faced with rapidly escalating rents. Landlords were demanding as much as fifty and sixty dollars per month for four- and five-room apartments, far more than many families were able to pay. On one day in early April, a Bronx municipal court judge ordered the eviction of three hundred families and later remarked that he had never before seen the courts burdened with so many rent cases.[33]

Forced to respond in some fashion, leaders on both the city and state level opted to appoint committees. On April 14, 1919, Mayor Hylan created the Mayor's Committee on Rent Profiteering, composed of safe Democratic supporters. The committee was chaired by Nathan Hirsch, a property lawyer, and included the Reverend A. Roy Petty of Judson Memorial Church, Edward Hannah, president of the Central Federated Union, Peter Brady, president of the Allied Printing Trades Council, and Harry Bloch, an attorney. Less than a month later, the legislature appointed its own Joint Legislative Committee on Housing under the leadership of Senator Charles Lockwood, a Republican from Brooklyn who had defeated Socialist incumbent A. I. Shiplacoff on a fusion ticket the previous November. The Lockwood committee immediately launched into a search for scapegoats: over the next nine months it conducted an exhaustive investigation of the building trades unions and building materials suppliers, both alleged to be engaged in restrictive practices that inflated the cost of construction.[34]

The Mayor's Committee, meanwhile, had mounted a more substantive program to aid desperate tenants. Churches and armories were turned into temporary shelters for evicted families and their possessions. With the cooperation of the Democratic party organizations in the boroughs, the committee recruited 150 volunteer lawyers to represent indigent tenants in the municipal courts. Its major accomplishment, however, was the establishment of a panel to arbitrate landlord-tenant disputes.[35] While these efforts provided more direct relief than the Lockwood committee's witch-hunt, neither body was willing to mount a politically costly attack on the source of rent profiteering.

This conservatism was demonstrated at the special session of the legislature held in June 1919. While Governor Alfred E. Smith had originally called the session to consider the women's suffrage amendment to the federal constitution, he granted the Mayor's Committee's request that the housing situation be added to the agenda and invited the chairman Nathan Hirsch to submit recommendations. In doing so, the committee ignored a strong call from the municipal court judges for a temporary rent freeze, mandatory one-year leases, and restrictions on an owner's right to evict. Instead it submitted a far weaker package of bills, which were quickly endorsed by the Lockwood committee and passed by the legislature. The resulting laws increased from ten to twenty days the period of notice required before an owner could dispossess a tenant without a written lease as well as the maximum stay of eviction that a judge could give to such a tenant. More fundamental questions of rent levels, unjustified eviction, and building deterioration were ignored.[36]

Yet it was such questions that were creating turmoil in the city's working-class neighborhoods. The case of Sophie Epstein serves as a good example. In the summer of 1919 Sophie Epstein lived with her husband, who was a dressmaker, and three children in a tenement on East 138th Street in the South Bronx. When the landlord sought to nearly double the rent in the Epsteins' building and four adjoining houses, Mr. Epstein and several other tenants decided that they could not pay the increase. Forty of the sixty threatened families joined together, selected a strike committee, raised a fund of ten dollars per family, and sought aid from the Bronx Tenants League.

When the landlord took them to court and sought evictions, a lawyer from the tenants league represented the strikers and scheduled a hearing for the following week. Meanwhile, with the men at work, the leadership of the strikers fell largely to Sophie Epstein. Although unaccustomed to such a leadership role, she did not shrink from it. Under her direction, the tenants picketed the local synagogue, of which the landlord was president, and placed Rent Strike signs in their windows. Then, when the tenants' lawyer was unable to appear at the eviction hearing, Sophie Epstein presented their case. "It really fell upon my shoulders," she recalled nearly sixty years later, "and I went through it heroically, so green, not knowing that I went through it." Her pleas were to no avail, however, and Judge Harry Robitzek ordered twelve evictions.

Several days later a city marshall carried out the evictions of three families, including the Epsteins. That night the men guarded the furniture on the street while the women and children slept with neighbors. The next day the tenants committee went to city hall to see Captain Charles Goldsmith, head of the Mayor's Committee arbitration panel, who obtained an injunction delaying the remaining evictions. Sophie Epstein returned to 138th Street, triumphantly stopped the marshall from evicting the other families, and gave a rousing speech to the strikers.

Several days later Goldsmith brought the tenants and the landlord together and reached a settlement. The strikers received a one-year lease containing a promise of repairs in return for an increase of just one dollar per apartment per month. Tenants in two adjacent buildings who did not organize and strike were eventually forced to pay a larger increase.[37]

The case of the Epstein family and their neighbors indicates the intensity of building-level struggles throughout 1919. Tenants used every resource at their command—the Socialist tenant leagues and the Mayor's Committee, social pressure within the neighborhood and religious congregations, and their combined economic power to withhold rent. More important, tenants like Sophie Epstein drew upon talents and reserves of courage that they had not previously exercised.

As noted above, the Mayor's Committee sought to provide desperate families like the Epsteins with an alternative to the Socialist-led leagues. Its hearing officers tried to negotiate settlements similar to those obtained by league organizers: compromises on rent increases, one-year leases, and repairs. In the early fall Hirsch attempted to expand the committee's role. The volunteer lawyers who served in the municipal courts interceded with the judges to delay many eviction proceedings until arbitration could be given a chance. The arbitration hearings, which had been held in Manhattan, were extended to central locations in the Bronx, Brooklyn, and Queens. These hearings were often highly charged mixtures of farce and tragedy. A group of East Bronx tenants arrived at one in a motorcade headed by a jazz band playing "Homesick Blues." But at another meeting three thousand angry tenants stormed the building and jeered the landlords, while one frustrated man assaulted the chairman. Such physical attacks upon participants were commonplace. Chief arbiter Charles Goldsmith became a near folk hero and was regularly featured in newspaper accounts of the committee's work.[38]

By the end of 1919 Hirsch's staff had settled an impressive number of cases; the chairman claimed success in 95 percent of the thirty thousand disputes heard since April. Despite charges from the Socialists that it was a "landlord's forum," the committee's negotiation sessions appear to have been conducted fairly; arbitrators generally attempted to elicit evidence of building conditions, expenses, and profit levels upon which to base their recommendations.[39] The real problem stemmed from a lack of authority to enforce agreements and protect those tenants who sought the committee's aid. Chairman Hirsch admitted that many landlords reneged and that some sought revenge against strike leaders and participants.[40] Such faults notwithstanding, the Mayor's Committee was successful in one of its primary tasks. It gave thousands of tenants the opportunity to reach agreement with their landlords without further clogging the courts or turning to the Socialists.

Tenant leaders were quick to ridicule the relief efforts of the Mayor's Committee and to point out the weaknesses of its arbitration machinery. For example, A. I. Shiplacoff told one league meeting, "What the suffering tenants of this city are asking for is not army cots in churches, fly filled tents and army barracks. They're asking for the right to live in their own homes."[41] And indeed, the success of the committee did not seem to slow the growth of the tenant movement. In late April a number of Brooklyn progressive organizations, led by the Socialists and the consumers league, established the Brownsville Tenants League. Pledging to resist further rent increases, the leadership originally planned a general rent strike. While this failed to develop, the organization did lead dozens of strikes during the following summer and fall.[42]

Meanwhile, Socialist assemblyman Charles Solomon and his supporters formed the Brooklyn Tenants Union (BTU) in the same area and quickly demanded 10 percent rent reductions. The building owners balked, however, with one owner's lawyer telling the BTU leaders, "We've got the money and it's money that counts." The BTU retaliated with a rent strike against the eight buildings owned by the president of the landlords association. Over the next ten weeks, tenant leaders were beaten, houses were picketed, prospective tenants threatened, and one building completely emptied. The tenants ultimately achieved victory, but not before 72 of 192 striking families were evicted.[43]

A large strike in the Williamsburg section that same summer showed that tenants could draw upon varying types of support to achieve victory. Four hundred and fifty families in seventeen jointly owned buildings struck on August 1, 1919, under the auspices of the Williamsburg Tenants League. In a rare example of cooperation with the Mayor's Committee, the tenants took the case to arbitration, but the landlord refused to accept an adverse ruling. On September 4 the owner obtained eviction notices for the strikers. Soon a city marshall, fifty policemen, and thirty union movers arrived to dispossess the tenants, but the moving men refused to do so when the striking women displayed their tenant league membership cards and insisted that they too were "union members." Despite the willingness of the landlord to expend the six thousand dollars required to evict the families, three additional attempts to recruit a work force were unsuccessful. In desperation, the owner offered to settle; he received one-third of the increase originally demanded in return for a nine-month lease and improvements in the buildings.[44]

In the late summer the Lower East Side was successfully organized. The absence of this strongly Socialist area from the ranks of the tenant movement during nearly three years of agitation is perhaps accounted for by the fact that its rents had remained relatively low. It had served as a "safety valve," with thousands of families from newer neighborhoods in upper Manhattan, the Bronx, and Brooklyn retreating back to its cold-water flats. In time, however, it again became crowded, rents began to rise, and residents became restive. In response, Socialist alderman Abe Beckerman established the East Side Tenants League at the party's headquarters on Avenue C and within several weeks was leading fifteen rent strikes and claiming at least one thousand members.[45]

Thus by late 1919 the tenant movement had achieved considerable stability, with effective local organizations in a dozen working-class neighborhoods in the Bronx, Manhattan, and Brooklyn. While some Socialist claims of one hundred thousand members were clearly exaggerated, the more-often-stated figure of thirty-five thousand members among the various organizations is probably accurate, if the criterion used is participation in, or active support for, a rent strike rather than long-term dues-paying membership.[46]

While certainly disturbed by the continued growth of the tenant movement, municipal officials were equally alarmed by the large number of cases for which neither the leagues nor the Mayor's Committee could find a settlement. As landlords attempted to squeeze more rent from their tenants or to evict them to bring in a new family at a higher figure, the courts became clogged. A total of 96,623 families faced eviction proceedings in 1919, with the majority of these cases coming before the bench in the fall months. Many judges were hearing several hundred cases per day, and evening sessions had to be introduced. Under these circumstances, some freely admitted their inability to deal with each tenant fairly. Usually a tenant would be allowed to pay his old rent for another month and then vacate.[47] As a result, the October 1, 1919, "moving day" was described as the most congested in the city's history; over seventy-five thousand families in just the Bronx and Manhattan changed apartments. One city paper noted that "Usually on New York's moving day a trend in a definite direction may be noticed, but this is an unusual year. At one time most of the population was flocking to the Bronx, at others they chose new homes on Washington or Morningside Heights or in the suburbs. This year they count themselves among the elect if they have any place to which to go."[48] The market for apartments was so brisk that the real estate section of the *Tribune* headlined, "Goldmines No More Profitable Than Realty These Days."[49] One Bronx judge charged that the wholesale use of dispossess proceedings by many landlords was causing serious distress, which made tenants "easy prey for agitators who are Bolsheviks and other forms of radicals."[50]

The recurring fear of a radicalized tenantry is explicable by the degree to which the period of rent striking coincided with the postwar Red Scare. The nativist antiradicalism that the Wilson administration had fostered during the war remained virulent throughout 1919. Early in the year large mobs, often led by veterans in uniform, attacked meetings and parades organized by immigrant and left-wing political groups. In July a major antiblack riot occurred in St. Louis. Labor unrest, at a high level throughout the year, peaked in the fall with major conflicts in the steel, coal, and railroad industries. The federal Justice Department, under A. Mitchell Palmer, attributed the increase in labor strife to radicals and responded with a series of raids in November 1919 and January 1920 in which thousands of alleged subversives were arrested. The hysteria engendered by the Red Scare did not subside for several months, after Palmer's prediction of a nationwide revolt for May 1 proved groundless.[51]

In New York City the tenant movement had experienced red-baiting well before the Red Scare. Landlords had long sought to label organizers as "Bolsheviks" or to claim that their buildings were being seized by tenant "Soviets."[52] But the fall of 1919 saw the start of a concerted campaign against the tenant leagues because of their radical potential. In the municipal courts, some judges began to single out league members and treat them more harshly. One East Side justice bragged that he had "stamped out the Tenant's League." Another judge, in Harlem, found three women strikers guilty of assault, then offered to release them if they revealed information concerning the organizers of their group.[53]

In early October, at the request of Nathan Hirsch, Mayor Hylan instructed Manhattan district attorney Anthony Swann to begin grand jury investigation of "certain east side organizations" that had led a "score or more" rent strikes. Hirsch claimed, "We have records of cases where in effect the tenants undertook to set up Soviet government, and we know of others where the actions of these leaders have been little less than anarchistic. Many of those who join these societies are foreign born, and they have no idea that their actions have been in direct violation of the law."[54]

Throughout October, Hirsch, Swann, and their allies issued a series of statements to the city's newspapers, which nourished fears of the tenant movement. They thoroughly detailed the links between the leagues and the Socialist party and claimed that tenant leaders encouraged the willful destruction of apartments. One judge warned, "I know that if this poisonous virus is not removed these people [league organizers] will lead this great mob of people into anarchy, riot and revolution."[55] Taking the estimates of the most unrealistic tenant leaders at face value, they charged that the Socialists would soon convince 250,000 families to withhold rent—a force that even the police and the National Guard could not evict.[56] Furthermore, the Socialists were accused of using supposed antirent rallies to promote the party's candidates and of diverting strike funds into its campaign coffers.[57]

The Socialists denied that they had misled tenants, yet freely admitted that they hoped to gain votes as a result of their protenant activities. Abe Beckerman observed, "If we can handle the rent situation it is only natural that the people we helped would vote for us. We don't only take Socialists into our tenant leagues. We take anybody and we don't expect all the Democrats and Republicans to vote for us because we bring their rents down, but gratitude ought to give us enough of their votes to win the election."[58]

Indeed, the Socialists realized that they had a potent issue and put it to good use. In the 1919 campaign the party's candidates attacked Republican and Democratic incumbents for their failure to resolve the housing crisis and for their lack of sympathy for tenants. They promised, if elected, to seek a standard one-year lease and restrictions on rent increases and the right of eviction.[59] As an off-year election, the contest was not well covered by the press, but it appears that housing was a key issue. Several years later, an aide to Assemblyman George Jesse, a Republican from Washington Heights, recalled that "The rent question had become more acute and I heard Mr. Jesse make many speeches and I do not think that he ever made a speech during the campaign of [1919] in which he did not state that he was in favor of some law to protect tenants of the City of New York."[60]

The election resulted in a limited victory for the Socialists. Faced with fusion in many races, the party increased its share of the vote by several percentage points in most districts and succeeded in electing five assemblymen (two from the Bronx and one each from East Harlem, the Lower East Side, and Brownsville) and four aldermen. The head of the ticket, candidate for president of the Board of Aldermen James O'Neal, received 121,000 votes—just 20,000 short of Morris Hillquit's mayoral tally in 1917. These results are even more significant since many tenants who might have voted Socialist—those evicted in October and early November—were disenfranchised due to their change of residence.[61]

Socialist satisfaction was short-lived, however. When the assembly convened on January 7, 1920, one of the most noteworthy Red Scare episodes began. After being duly sworn in with their colleagues, the five Socialists were summoned to the front of the chamber by Speaker Thaddeus Sweet and denounced for having been elected on a platform "inimical" to the best interests of the United States and the state of New York. By a vote of 140 to 6 they were suspended until their fitness to serve could be considered.[62] A bitter three-month battle ensued, with the right of the Socialists to serve debated in the press as well as in the assembly chamber. But ultimately Sweet's control of a solid bloc of upstate Republicans proved decisive, and the five were expelled on March 31, 1920.[63]

Meanwhile, as the Red Scare was focusing attention on the Socialists and their allies in the tenants movement, new and more conservative forces were becoming involved in the housing crisis. First were the Community Councils of National Defense. Over sixty of these neighborhood-oriented bodies had been formed during the final months of the war to aid in civil defense, the reemployment of veterans, and the reporting of all types of profiteering. By late 1919 about a dozen councils remained active in a number of programs—Americanization, the improvement of neighborhood health and transportation facilities, and campaigns against rising food prices. As the housing crisis continued to grow in severity, several councils in upper Manhattan and the Bronx established committees to aid tenants.[64] In early 1920 they were joined by two new tenant groups. The Washington Heights Tenants Association, led by Harry Allen Ely, was an outgrowth of the Audubon Community Council. By far the most influential, however, was the Fair Play Rent Association of the north-central Bronx. Initially founded at the end of January, the organization grew rapidly and had over thirty-five hundred members in more than two hundred buildings by mid-March.[65]

Although good data concerning the makeup of most of the community councils and conservative tenant associations is lacking, it can be established that they differed from the Socialist-led tenant leagues in several very important respects. The latter represented a predominantly Jewish, and to a lesser extent Italian, working-class constituency, had a Jewish leadership, and maintained alliances with the Socialist party, the consumers leagues, and the labor unions of the United Hebrew Trades. The community councils and conservative tenant associations present a different picture. Their membership, which was open to landlords as well as tenants, appears to have been considerably more middle class and was concentrated in areas of better housing. The leadership was largely Irish-American, with some Germans and old-stock Americans.[66] They had close political ties to local Democratic and Republican organizations. For example, Fair Play's president, George Donnelly, had once been secretary to the Bronx borough president.[67] Their allies were the municipal unions (police, firemen, teachers) and various patriotic groups such as the American Legion and the Sons of the Revolution.[68]

As the respective political allegiances of the two forces would suggest, the greatest differences between the Socialist groups and the conservative tenant organizations concerned ideology and tactics. Leaders of the community councils and newer tenant associations were both strongly anti-Socialist and unalterably opposed to rent striking. This attitude is best illustrated by the founding of the Fair Play Rent Association (FPRA). Faced with a rent increase they did not wish to pay, the residents at 2789 Valentine Avenue felt legally bound to do so. Their frustration led to the formation of the association—dedicated to the election of protenant legislators and the use of "moral force" to effect legal remedies. From its inception, the FPRA was careful to note that it did not interfere in individual cases and that it bore no ill feelings toward most landlords. Under the motto "Fair play to the landlord and tenant, and jail to the profiteer," the organization invited the cooperation of building owners.[69]

While the leadership of the tenant associations and community councils certainly possessed sympathy for families pressed by rising rents, evaluation of their broader motives is difficult. Their close ties to local Democratic and Republican leaders suggest that their efforts may have represented a covert attempt to blunt the political impact of the Socialist tenant movement, but this cannot be demonstrated. It does seem certain, however, that one of their key goals was to direct tenant discontent into legitimate channels, namely the legislative process and the courts. In this sense the conservative groups functioned much as the Mayor's Committee.

At the same time that the conservative tenant associations were being founded, the organized labor establishment was also growing restive. The various unions of the 350,000-member Central Federated Union (CFU) had negotiated contracts in 1919 on the basis of assurances from President Woodrow Wilson that postwar inflation was at an end. Such had not been the case, however, and CFU president Edward Hannah, who was also a member of the Mayor's Committee, came under increasing pressure from rank and file. Union labor, he reported, felt that it was receiving fair dollar wages but that the increased cost of living, with rents a major factor, was lowering real income.[70]

In early February 1920 a delegation from the CFU, headed by Hannah and Ernest Bohm, met with Mayor Hylan to demand legislative curbs on rent increases. Bohm reportedly told the mayor: "We mean business. We do not intend to permit action to be put off indefinitely. Our membership has been hard hit by rent profiteering and they are in no mood to be put off by kind words."[71]

One month later CFU delegates met to consider further action. In an incident typical of early 1920, the *Times* and the *World* erroneously reported that the delegates had endorsed a general strike and had instructed membership not to pay exorbitant rents. Although the *Times* corrected itself the next day and admitted that the idea of a general strike had been rejected by the CFU, the impact remained.[72]

Indeed, the very hint of such action by its labor supporters spurred the Hylan administration to cooperate. The mayor threatened to increase the property assessments of landlords who raised rents. He called a conference of real estate men and building trade union leaders to explore possible means of stimulating building, after which the CFU and the Mayor's Committee jointly proposed a $20 million city bond issue for public housing. Most important, however, was the city administration's endorsement of a CFU proposal that municipal judges be given the discretionary power to determine the reasonableness of rent increases.[73]

For Socialist tenant leaders, the early months of 1920 represented a period of great uncertainty. New participants were entering the housing struggle, while league members faced discrimination in the municipal courts, and the Socialist party's elected representatives, expected to advance protenant legislation, had been suspended. The maintenance of the movement appeared in jeopardy unless the proper tactics could be utilized. Most of the leagues responded by adhering to the fundamental, building-level activities that had contributed to their early growth. While avoiding the courts as much as possible, tenant leaders continued to lead rent strikes and negotiate settlements with landlords. The Harlem Tenants League alone signed over four hundred leases in the period from October 1919 to March 1920.[74]

Some individuals within the movement demanded the use of more extreme tactics, however. In early March the Brownsville Tenants League, under the leadership of Leo Gitlin, began to organize a general rent strike for May 1. Members of the Brownsville group had advocated such a step in 1918 and 1919, but had met with opposition from the other leagues. Now Gitlin began to mobilize and predict success. His bulletins reported a steadily increasing following: 2,000 on March 5; 10,000 two weeks later; by March 22, 500 organized buildings with 29,000 tenants ready to withhold rent.[75]

In retrospect, it is clear that Gitlin represented only a small minority in the tenant movement and that he greatly exaggerated the extent of his following.[76] But the significance of the general-rent-strike threat rested not in its actual strength but rather in the fact that it was widely accepted as bona fide. There were several reasons for that acceptance. First was the widespread realization that thousands of tenants were indeed angry and desperate. Another round of increases on May 1, the city's heaviest moving day, might have been the last straw.[77] Second, until Gitlin was denounced by other Socialist tenant leaders in mid-April, the *Call* accepted his statements as accurate and added to their impact by incorrectly linking all rent strikes to the "general strike movement in Brownsville and other sections of the city."[78] Last, and most important, was the fact that Gitlin's campaign was a prophesy fulfilled. Caught up in the Red Scare hysteria, Hirsch, District Attorney Swann, and others had warned of Socialist attempts to organize hundreds of thousands of tenants. Thus they were predisposed to accept the general-rent-strike threat as genuine, regardless of its substance.

Conservative tenant leaders and city officials responded to the threat of a tenant uprising by increasing pressure on the legislature. Edward Murphy of the Inwood Community Council told an assembly committee: "We are playing with fire. If you had the sentiments expressed by sober-minded, law abiding citizens in my district, you would know that action must be taken now. They have been driven into a condition that is no good for any country."[79] State senator Loring Black, Jr., of Brooklyn warned of a "social revolution beyond description on May 1." Fiorello La Guardia, recently elected president of the Board of Aldermen, predicting that tenants would refuse to pay rent if not aided, noted, "You can't dispossess every tenant in the city." Municipal court judge Joseph Callahan insisted that landlords would have to trust the courts—"Somebody must stand between them [landlords] and the Bolsheviki of this state."[80] Lastly, Judge Harry Robitzek told a legislative committee, "if you do not give us legislation I have no hesitancy in telling you that you cannot prevent the socialist voting population in the Bronx from increasing from 30,000 in the last election to one hundred and fifty thousand."[81]

In a 1962 article Stanley Coben argued that the Red Scare represented an attempt to deal with "a number of severe social and economic dislocations," such as inflation, disillusionment over the war, labor strife, and scattered acts of terrorism, "which threatened the national equilibrium." Many Americans responded by reaffirming their own national values—through the 100 percent Americanism movement—and by attributing responsibility for the nation's problems to foreign influences.[82] Statements made by public officials and representatives of the conservative tenant groups indicate that a similar process shaped attitudes about the housing crisis—indeed that such attitudes epitomized the Red Scare mentality.

Thus the profiteering landlord became stereotyped as a "Bolsheviki Russian Jew landlord." A letter to Governor Smith from an "American Jew" demonstrates the virulence of such views: "I hope that you will pass those rent bills to kill those Bolsheviki profiteering Russia Jew landlords. . . . The Russian Jews pass a remark that they will make the American people kiss their hands and feet. If you will let me carry a gun and look out for me, I will kill these Russian dogs in a few hours."[83]

Such unrestrained bigots were not alone in promoting this stereotype, however. At a meeting of the Board of Aldermen in March, Republican Fred Smith of Brooklyn asserted that "Most of the rent profiteers are Hebrews." While testifying at a hearing in Albany, La Guardia responded to a heckling landlord by shouting, "Yes, hiss, my friends. You people who emigrated from the pales of Russia but a short time ago." Not surprisingly, the legislature also received numerous requests to restrict the rights of aliens or those who did not speak English to lease or own property.[84]

The rent-striking tenant was often portrayed in an identical fashion—as an alien ignorant of American law and norms of behavior. Unable to pay the high rents demanded by profiteers, he turned in desperation to the organizers of the Socialist tenant leagues who sought political advantage in his plight by organizing illegal rent strikes and antilandlord vandalism and cheated him through fraudulent demands for strike funds.

The solution to the crisis, conservative spokespersons argued, was to be found in compromise legislation. They repeatedly expressed the belief that most tenants and landlords (implicitly American tenants and landlords) could cooperate with a well-informed legislature to develop the proper remedies. As a representative of the Fair Play Rent Association told the Lockwood committee:

> Now, I am through but I have got just this to say. I am an American woman. The American form of government has never failed us since it was established and it will not fail us now, and you men will help us now that you realize and understand the situation down there. You are going to pass laws. You are going to protect landlords. They have got

> rights under the constitution. And you are going to help the rest of us, because I tell you, gentlemen, that between the Bolshevism of the poor, helpless, ignorant, illiterate alien, that came here believing that this was the golden land and finds out it is not the land of plenty and between the Bolshevism of the people that will squeeze every last dollar out of their fellow men and women and then in the name of patriotism put it in Liberty Bonds, I am going to tell you that between the Bolshevism below and the Bolshevism up above, it is a case of God help the rest of us in the middle.[85]

By late March, Socialist tenant leaders were also looking toward the legislature for assistance. Although rebuffed in the past, they agreed to join a coalition to pressure Albany. The driving force behind this effort was the United Hebrew Trades (UHT), which called a mass meeting for March 29. Six hundred and forty-eight delegates from several hundred organizations, such as Jewish labor unions, consumer societies, synagogues, fraternal orders, Socialist party locals, and ten tenant leagues, gathered at Beethoven Hall on Fifth Street and formed the United Tenants Organization (UTO). Although some representatives advocated the use of a general rent strike as the ultimate tactic, the UTO's sixty-member executive committee adopted a milder approach. The new organization decided to seek favorable court decisions, work for the designation of housing as a public utility, and petition the legislature for legislation similar to that sought by the CFU, namely laws giving judges discretion to set fair rents.[86]

The United Hebrew Trades (UHT) had entered the tenant struggle for several reasons. Of great importance was leadership's desire to aid union members who were directly affected by rising rents and deplorable housing conditions. Many also wished to support their allies in the Socialist-led tenant leagues. But the major impetus was the fear of growing anti-Semitism. As noted above, the central position of Jews on both sides of the controversy, combined with the irrational passions of the Red Scare, were contributing to an increasing number of anti-Semitic attacks. In seeking compromise solutions to the housing crisis, the leaders of the UHT and other Jewish organizations hoped to defuse the situation.[87]

Ironically, this last ditch attempt by the UHT, the Socialist tenant leagues, and their supporters to seek compromise was totally misunderstood. The *New York Times*, prolandlord and alarmist from the outset, headlined its page-one story "Organize Revolt against Rents" and reported that "The delegates were exhorted to combine, not as they had been doing, in houses, but in entire blocks and in sections of the city, and to withhold all rents they deem oppressive."[88] The next day, Arthur Hilly, who had succeeded Nathan Hirsch as chairman of the Mayor's Committee, charged the

United Tenants Organization with fomenting a general rent strike and condemned such action as a "planned display of Red flagged disorder."[89]

By this time, however, the shape of the legislature's response had been largely determined. In mid-March state senate and assembly leaders had conferred with Charles Lockwood and members of the Bill Drafting Department. They produced a package of bills that reflected the key aspects of the proposals offered by conservative tenant leaders and by the CFU and UHT.[90] After a series of hearings in late March, the bills were slightly modified, with concessions made to all parties. This compromise slate was passed overwhelmingly on March 31 and signed by the governor on the following day. Ironically, the assembly had voted to expel its Socialist members just hours before passing the housing bills.

The April Rent Laws, as these statutes came to be known, included several major provisions:[91]

> *Chapter 137* granted to municipal court judges power to grant stays of eviction lasting up to one year when convinced that the tenant was unable to find similar quarters at a rate equal to that which he had been paying.
>
> *Chapter 136* allowed a tenant to defend against eviction for nonpayment on the grounds that the rent demanded was "unjust, unreasonable and oppressive." On increases of 25 percent or less the burden of proof was on the tenant. Larger increases had to be justified by the landlord.
>
> *Chapter 130* extended until October 1 following occupancy all written leases that did not specify the duration of tenancy.
>
> *Chapter 133* required landlords to establish "to the satisfaction of the court" that a tenant was "objectionable" when such charges were made as the grounds for a summary eviction. Previously, a landlord had only to swear that he was acting in "good faith."

The housing situation remained tense for several weeks following passage of the rent laws. Arthur Hilly continued to predict a large-scale tenant uprising for May Day, with a thousand buildings "organized into a kind of a soviet" and widespread sabotage,[92] but Socialist tenant leaders dismissed such charges. On April 21 representatives of the United Tenants Organization and its component groups condemned Leo Gitlin, the leader of the alleged general rent strike, as irresponsible. Harry Rich of the Brooklyn Tenants Union told the *Call*, "If there is any rent strike being planned in Brooklyn or Brownsville by any such large bodies of tenants, I have never heard of it." He insisted that since April 1 his members had been "satisfied in nearly all cases with the decisions of the Brownsville justices under the laws."[93] When May Day arrived, Hilly's fears were, in fact, proved groundless as only 392 tenants were reported on strike.[94]

Despite their initial positive reception, however, it soon became apparent that the April Rent Laws were inadequate and, in the long run, capable of producing an even greater crisis than that which had prompted their passage. In effect, the laws had created three categories of tenant: Those with written leases were safe until their agreements expired. They were the only lucky ones. The second category included month-to-month tenants—those without any written lease. Thousands received demands for 25 percent increases during the spring and summer. According to chapter 136 they could fight such demands in court as "unjust, unreasonable and oppressive," but this proved virtually impossible. Judge Robitzek noted that "I do not know of a single tenant who has been able to establish that the 25 percent was unreasonable. You see, the figures are all in the possession of the landlord and it is impossible."[95] Tenants who lost such cases were invariably given stays of from one month to a year. Robitzek alone claimed to have granted ten thousand between April 1 and the end of July. But eventually these stays would expire and thousands of families would be on the street.[96]

The third category of tenancy represented the greatest danger. Chapter 130 provided that written leases of unspecified duration would expire on October 1. Landlords were under no obligation to renew these leases, and therefore began notifying such tenants months in advance to move on September 30—since new tenants were not covered by the rent laws and could be charged much higher rents. The city faced the prospect of sixty thousand evictions from this provision alone.[97]

During the summer of 1920, as the implications of the April Laws became apparent, pressure for new legislation grew. But the roles of the major groups were markedly different from what they had been earlier in the year. For the Socialist tenant leagues, the spring and summer months represented a period of relative inactivity. The *Call*, generally eager to publicize any example of organized tenant protest, mentioned only one mass meeting and a handful of strikes during the entire period.[98] There were several reasons for this quiescence. As was noted previously, the level of rent striking was directly related to the extent of tenant discontent. During the spring, there was general satisfaction with the operation of the laws, based primarily on the wholesale granting of long-term stays by the courts. Most families remained calm so long as they did not face immediate ouster.[99]

Ironically, the limited activity of the tenant leagues was probably also the result of their close relationship with the Socialist party. Ordinarily this bond benefited tenants by providing trained leaders, meeting halls, a newspaper, and other resources that the leagues would otherwise have had to develop independently. After March 31, however, the Socialist party devoted itself almost entirely to the reelection of its expelled assemblymen in the fall campaign. In the case of those who held key positions in both the party and a tenant league, this may have led to neglect of housing problems.[100]

The conservative tenant associations, on the other hand, were quite active during the summer months. In late July a new organization, the University Heights Tenants Association, was formed in the Bronx. Early in the following month the Fair Play Rent Association established a second branch in the Mott Haven–Morrisania section. Most important, however, was Fair Play and the Washington Heights Tenants Association pressure for a special session of the legislature to pass additional rent laws. On August 10 a delegation estimated at two thousand tenants met with Governor Smith in Albany and presented him with a petition containing six thousand signatures; the delegates predicted riots unless the April Laws were strengthened. Three days later Smith issued a call for the special session.[101]

Despite the timing of these events, tenant associations were not the dominant influence on Smith or the legislature. For with the end of the Red Scare and a reduction in the level of rent striking, political leaders no longer viewed the housing crisis as the cutting edge of a social revolution, but rather as a specific, though grave, political-administrative problem. In fact, the most significant pressure came from the municipal court judges. They had been at the center of the storm from the outset. Several members of the bench had argued for greater discretionary powers as early as the spring of 1919, but government officials had opted for appointment of the Mayor's Committee and the Lockwood committee. The April 1920 laws had also represented a partial yet poorly conceived concession to judicial requests.

By the summer of 1920, each day was offering further demonstration that the April Laws were inadequate. Now the judges spoke out even more forcefully. At legislative hearings held in July and August, judges testified to the gravity of the situation—thousands of stays of eviction which would soon come due, thousands of tenants denied lease renewals, and ever-increasing court calendars. It was their pressure, more than that of any other group, that spurred the legislature to action.[102]

When the special session convened on September 20, there was little doubt that it would have to act quickly. Architect and housing reformer Clarence Stein captured the mood of the situation perfectly when he wrote in the September issue of the *Survey*, "In New York City this summer the housing situation is calm. It is the calmness that comes before the storm."[103]

The president of the Board of Municipal Court Judges was more specific when he warned:

> the dispossess proceedings against tenants *during the month of October* will exceed in number the record for the whole year of 1919. If the hard-hit public is to be relieved, action must be taken within a period of ten days after the Legislature convenes, otherwise our new May Day, October first, will find us in a terrible condition. Our courts will be packed with frantic men and women. You will have to act quickly.[104]

Further encouraged by a strong message from the governor, the legislature on September 27 passed the Emergency Rent Laws, a series of statutes incorporating the recommendations of the judges.[105]

> *Chapter 944* reenacted all provisions of chapter 136 but eliminated the 25 percent clause, thus allowing the municipal court judges to determine the reasonableness of all increases and placing upon the landlord the burden of proof. To assist the judges in making their determinations, landlords seeking increases were required to submit a bill of particulars setting forth figures as to gross income and expenses.
> *Chapter 942* was directed at the threat of evictions for those whose leases expired on October 1. It severely restricted the rights of landlords to deny lease renewals to such tenants.

Enactment of the Emergency Rent Laws of 1920 marked a historic occasion—save for a federal statute governing the District of Columbia passed several months before, it was the first rent control program passed in the nation.

Although the impact of the Emergency Rent Laws remained a subject of debate throughout the 1920s, several effects of the legislation were clear from the outset. Most notable were the designation of the municipal courts as legal arbiters with authority over disputed rents and a reduction in radical tenant activity.

As noted earlier, the level of rent striking during the summer of 1920 had been relatively low. The decrease in rent striking was even more dramatic following passage of the September laws. The only major strike noted in the news media was that of forty-five hundred tenants led by the Bronx Tenants League in the East Fordham section—and that was for a 7 percent rent reduction demanded by garment workers who had received a 20 percent wage cut. On the whole, it would appear that the Socialist-led groups were satisfied with the Emergency Rent Laws. In early October several thousand members of the Workmens Consumer League of Brownsville held a victory parade in which they carried signs reading No More Moving and Victory Is Ours.[106]

As tenants rejoiced, the thousands of lease termination cases slated for October 1 worked their way into the municipal courts, where the crowding of court calendars surpassed even spring 1920 levels; indeed, the number of cases continued to increase during late 1920 and early 1921. Judge Robitzek of the Bronx municipal court reported that the backlog of cases would take several years to hear and complained that the Board of Estimate had "turned a deaf ear" to judicial requests for additional clerks and courtroom facilities.[107] Robitzek's prediction proved accurate: the courts remained clogged with rent cases as late as 1925. This is understandable since neither landlords nor tenants had much to lose by going to court. In contesting a rent increase, a tenant was assured of his apartment at the old rent pending hearing of the case, often after a delay of several years. If the tenant eventually lost the case, he was required to pay the increase retroactively, but many families moved quietly before their cases came to trial. Landlords were encouraged to sue because they were assured the old rent, collected arrears if victorious and if the tenant had not moved, and could even include legal costs in bills of particulars filed with the court.

Faced with a steadily mounting caseload, the municipal court justices sought to develop practical guidelines for the administration of the rent laws. After much confusion and several higher court reversals, a common approach evolved. Landlords were allowed to bring suit only in the court district in which the building was located, or that in which they lived. This prevented landlords from forcing tenants to appear in distant court districts in Staten Island or Queens. More important, the justices agreed that a "reasonable rent" would be that which gave the landlord an 8 percent profit on the market value of his property. While this system encouraged many "paper exchanges" of buildings to enhance their market value figure, it was used throughout the 1920s.[108]

Against this background, both major components of the tenant movement experienced a significant transformation. The Socialist-led wing of the movement went into decline shortly after passage of the September laws. It is most likely that the serious schism that split the Socialist party itself also weakened its dependent tenant organizations. The party's split over the Communist issue started in February 1919 with the organization of the Left Wing Section and was completed during the Chicago Emergency Convention in August of the same year. National dues-paying membership, which had peaked at 108,504 in 1919, declined to only 13,484 by 1921. Although the New York local remained the strongest of the remnants, it was obviously much weaker after the traumatic summer of 1919.[109] Another major factor inhibiting the activities of Socialist tenant leaders was the repression associated with the Red Scare. Whatever the exact reasons, there is no evidence of Socialist-led tenant activity after early 1921.

The conservative tenant associations and community councils experienced a far different fate—continued growth, an expanding role in landlord-tenant matters, and increased unity. The relative complexity of the Emergency Rent Laws accounted for this in large part, since most tenants needed assistance in using them properly. The tenant associations were well suited for this role. Their leaders had good ties with both city and state officials and had consistently advocated legal, legitimate alternatives to the rent strike. Above all, association leaders wished to retain the status and prestige gained during the 1920 crisis. Thus, while the Socialist tenant leagues ceased activity, the conservative tenant associations readily increased their efforts.

In doing so, they continued to concentrate their activities in the Bronx and the northwest section of Manhattan. Although there may have been some slight, independent activity in Brownsville, East New York, and Yorkville during the early part of the decade, the areas of previous Socialist tenant league strength were not really represented in the movement after 1920.

Of the conservative groups, several deserve special attention. The Washington Heights Tenants Association (WHTA) grew out of the Audobon Community Council in late 1919. Headquartered on Saint Nicholas Avenue, WHTA maintained a large membership—consistently above seven thousand—and was one of the most effective and vocal tenant organizations of the decade. This was due, in large part, to the organization's leader, Harry Allen Ely. A vigorous, seventy-one-year-old self-proclaimed "soldier of fortune," Ely led most of the movement's lobbying efforts and published a short-lived periodical *The Tenant*. He was an acerbic critic of landlords and city officials; indeed, he was found guilty of criminal libel for maligning a municipal court judge in 1925. He obviously had the allegiance of his members; following his conviction, a meeting of the WHTA raised $600 in bail money in only ten minutes.[110]

Another strong group from Manhattan was the Academy Tenants Association. Led by attorney Lucille Zeumer, Academy represented several thousand tenants on the West Side from 96th to 125th streets. Zeumer, who also represented other Manhattan tenant groups, kept Academy functioning from its founding in 1924 through the end of the decade and remained a major movement spokesperson after many other tenant leaders had passed from the scene.[111]

The best organized borough was the Bronx, with each of several territories served by a specific group. The South Bronx Tenant and Civic League recruited in the entire area south of 149th Street. The Melrose Tenant and

Civil League was responsible for the section from 149th to 167th streets. The Tremont League handled tenants living north of 167th Street and east of the Grand Concourse. Its jurisdiction coincided slightly with that of the Fair Play Rent Association, which gave its boundaries as north of Tremont Avenue and west of the Grand Concourse and Third Avenue. In addition, several other organizations served smaller subsections of the borough. The University Heights League was active in the area bounded by Fordham Road, 180th Street, the Grand Concourse, and Sedgewick Avenue. The Bronx Protective Tenants Association organized the largely Italian East Fordham Road section.

Although each group was autonomous within its own territory, there was a good deal of cooperation among the various organizations. The Melrose, South Bronx, Tremont, and University leagues were united in an umbrella organization called the Bronx Council of Tenant Leagues. The council's chief attorney, Agnes Craig, handled most lobbying activities and was the borough's most prominent tenant representative during the decade. Many of the city's neighborhood tenant groups were also affiliated with the Federation of Tenant Associations (FTA). Founded in February 1921 by several Bronx organizations, including the Fair Play Rent Association and the Tremont League, the FTA was described as "made up for the most part of tenants of the so-called middle class" and "perhaps the strongest organization of its kind ever attempted." The federation's first president was Thomas Moore of the Tremont League, but Harry Allen Ely soon assumed leadership. The FTA's center of power seemed to shift also, with the Washington Heights and other Manhattan groups becoming its most active affiliates. Under Ely's aggressive leadership, the federation served as a key lobbying force into the late 1920s.[112]

For obvious reasons, it is difficult to make accurate estimates of tenant organization strength during the 1920s. In 1923 the Bronx groups claimed a membership of 25,000 to 30,000, with all members of dues-paying families included. Two years later the Bronx Council alone listed a constituency of over 11,000 families paying dues of one dollar per year. Adding an equal number for the Manhattan membership gives a broad estimate of over 20,000 member families throughout the city, representing perhaps 80,000 to 100,000 persons. Such figures are plausible when one considers the number of rent cases in the courts and the fact that the tenant organizations provided the cheapest and most accessible legal assistance available to poor tenants.[113]

Although each individual organization active during the 1920s had unique qualities, they all focused their efforts on providing basic tenant services, especially legal assistance. As noted earlier, the September statutes were extremely complicated from the outset, and were further amended almost every year from 1921 to 1929. Without proper legal advice, a tenant could easily forfeit valuable rights.[114] Soon after passage of the September 1920 laws, the major tenant associations moved to provide attorneys who might advise tenants and, for a modest fee, represent them in court. At well-attended weekly meetings, members and nonmembers alike asked an endless assortment of questions—How can I get repairs and not pay an increase? What is this paper and what does it mean? As late as 1925 tenant leaders spoke of meetings with three hundred to four hundred attendees and an ever-increasing level of complaints. The leaders, usually reelected year after year, became experts in landlord-tenant law and served as assistants to association attorneys.[115]

As the crowded dockets of the municipal courts indicated, large numbers of landlord-tenant disputes found their way into the courts. Tenant lawyers often succeeded in having cases dismissed due to technicalities such as the landlord's failure to give written notice of an increase. When such procedural defenses failed, tenants usually requested jury trials; this delayed their cases considerably and ultimately increased the chances of victory. With time, tenant lawyers gained proficiency in criticizing landlords' bills of particulars and convincing judges and juries that rent increases were unwarranted. Veteran attorneys handled tremendous numbers of cases. As early as October 1923 Agnes Craig claimed to have represented eight thousand tenants, with another three thousand cases pending. Charles Marks, an attorney for the Manhattan organizations, handled so many cases that he was accused by landlords of reaping a fortune from the housing crisis.[116]

Most tenant organizations, especially those in the Bronx, also provided some assistance to needy families. Each group followed a different procedure: some dispensed aid on an ad hoc confidential basis; others reviewed requests for aid at membership meetings. The South Bronx Tenant and Civic League, which had a separate Social Service Committee, serves as a good example. Originally it granted funds with little supervision, but eventually all allocations had to be reviewed by membership. Occasionally money was donated to churches, the Veterans of Foreign Wars, or other groups, but the vast majority of funds went to families who needed rent money to avoid eviction. The league paid $401 in rents for poor families in 1924, approximately 12 percent of its expenditures that year. By 1926, however, most of the Bronx tenant groups were experiencing a decline in income and began to shift more of the burden to charitable and philanthropic agencies; more and more cases were referred to the Salvation Army, Jewish Charities, and Catholic Charities.[117]

Another activity closely associated with social work was tenant education. Some tenant leaders accepted, in part at least, landlord assertions that tenants themselves were primarily responsible for unsanitary housing conditions. Tenant associations frequently featured guest speakers from the Health, Street Cleaning, and Tenement departments who urged tenants to keep dumbwaiters, air shafts, hallways, and fire escapes clean and clear.[118]

The movement's major goal, however, was continuation of the Emergency Rent Laws. Thus lobbying was the key focus of the groups during the 1920s. The laws were renewed in 1922 with little opposition since it was clear to everyone that an emergency still existed. In 1923 the protection afforded by the statutes was extended to cover tenancies entered into after 1920.[119]

The first apparent struggle over renewal of the laws occurred in late 1923, with tenant organizations playing a major role. Actually, the outcome was never in doubt, but to understand the situation one must look at developments from 1920 to 1923. The Emergency Rent Laws had been passed originally under the state's implied police power. That is, the legislature argued that the acute postwar housing shortage created a grave situation that justified limitations on the traditional rights of property holders. In 1923 the courts remained clogged, the vacancy rate remained below 1 percent, and rents for new tenancies continued to rise. For both political and practical reasons, Governor Smith and the legislature were determined to extend the laws beyond their February 1924 termination date. Furthermore, leading realtors accepted the situation and made no serious attempts to prevent extension.[120]

The governor and tenant advocates feared, however, that the courts might deny the constitutionality of extension by claiming that the level of crisis existing in 1920 was no longer apparent. On the advice of public interest lawyer Samuel Untermyer, Smith ordered the state's Commission on Housing and Regional Planning, chaired by architect Clarence Stein, to hold hearings that would document the continued presence of a serious housing shortage.[121]

Stein set the hearings for October 1923 and asked tenant leaders to collect relevant data. Each organization, conducting a survey of its neighborhood or territory, compiled detailed information on vacancies, rents, conditions, and special landlord-tenant problems. At several hearings held at city hall, Agnes Craig, Harry Allen Ely, and other tenant representatives documented the case for extension. Each witness told a similar tale: no vacancies in low- or moderate-rent apartments, with many families harassed and forced out by landlords because the laws did not cover new tenants. Many speakers noted a tremendous increase in "doubling up," that is, two families living in one apartment. Asked what would happen if the Emergency Rent Laws were not extended, Martin McCarthy of the Melrose

League responded, "I tell you, I think there would be an uprising, because if you come to those meetings, you would see the feelings of these women when they come in."[122]

The testimony of tenant leaders provided the Stein commission with the evidence required; its report to the legislature, based largely on a tenant organization survey covering eighty-five hundred families, cited a 14 percent increase in rents since 1921, over eighty-five thousand eviction cases pending in the municipal courts, and few vacancies in moderate-rent apartments.[123] With such justification, the legislature extended the Emergency Rent Laws through February 15, 1926.

By late 1925, however, the need for renewal was not as generally accepted. Landlords argued that the crisis was over; a survey of five thousand landlords, property owners, and managers conducted by a leading trade periodical found that 86 percent were opposed to extension although 32 percent admitted that poorer tenants still required some protection. The Real Estate Board of New York was only willing to accept a brief extension while the housing crisis was studied by a new legislative committee.[124]

Tenant leaders were unwilling to compromise, however. In a repeat of their 1923 efforts, they cooperated with the Stein commission in compiling data on rents and housing conditions. Replies from several thousand tenants demonstrated the continued shortage of affordable apartments, even more "doubling up," and a large number of new rent cases in the courts. In some regards, the situation was growing worse. Landlords were seeking increases of 80 to 100 percent, and those who were thwarted by the courts were decreasing maintenance expenditures to compensate. Lastly, tenant representatives charged that some owners were switching their tactics in court; experiencing little success in obtaining rent increases, they were now seeking to evict tenants on false pretenses. Furthermore, judges and district attorneys were doing little to stop such obvious attempts at evasion of the law.[125]

Once again, the threat of social upheaval was used to underscore tenant demands. Agnes Craig warned that failure to extend the Emergency Rent Laws would produce "wholesale evictions right straight through the Bronx. I think we will go back to the same conditions as existed in 1920." Stanley Cromwell of the Tremont League was more vivid in predicting that "Riots and bloodsheds [*sic*] will prevail if they are prematurely dropped."[126]

In addition, tenant leaders sought to mobilize political pressure against the legislature. Prior to 1925, tenant organizations had been almost deferential in tone; now they were more demanding. From October 1925 to February 1926, various tenant associations and community councils held at least a dozen mass rallies to demand satisfaction from elected officials. The

Home News described a meeting of the Hamilton Community Council as "one of the best attended tenant's meetings ever held in upper Manhattan" and reported that the aisles were full and many persons were turned away.[127]

Such demonstrations of tenant organization strength, timed in part to coincide with the November elections, had a marked effect. Politicians of both major parties competed with one another in expressing support of tenants; this was especially true of legislators in districts with strong tenant organizations. A prime example was Assemblyman Abe Grenthal, a Republican from central Harlem's Nineteenth District, who announced on September 25, 1925, that he was basing his reelection campaign on the rent issue. Three weeks later he promised if reelected to introduce legislation extending the Emergency Rent Laws.[128]

While cloaking themselves in the robes of tenant advocacy, many politicians also found it beneficial to attribute opposing sympathies to their adversaries. Thus Grenthal charged, "the landlords want me beaten, as I have the tenant forces too well organized." Using a similar approach Republican candidate for Manhattan borough president John R. Davies charged in a speech before the Washington Heights Tenants Association that landlords had contributed $30,000 to the campaign of Julius Miller, his Tammany opponent. Miller responded three days later by claiming that he was one of the "fathers" of the Rent Laws and that he too favored extension.[129]

Such statements were indicative of broader political support for tenants. On October 13, 1925, several incumbent Manhattan assemblymen, including the Democratic leader of the assembly, endorsed extension. One week later they were followed by twenty-three Republican candidates from New York County. The next day all eight GOP assembly candidates from the Bronx fell into line. Not to be outdone, on October 21, sixty-two Democratic candidates, representing all five boroughs, gave the Rent Laws their support. By election day each party was demanding extension and claiming credit for passage of the original statutes.[130]

Such promises were honored. In February 1926 the legislature extended the Emergency Rent Laws until June 1, 1927. The victory was not total, however, as all apartments renting at more than twenty dollars per room per month were exempted. Tenant leaders, particularly Ely, arguing that coverage of only certain rent levels marked the law as class legislation and made it more vulnerable to rejection by the courts, vigorously opposed this provision. But legislators and other protenant reformers, such as Lawson Purdy of the Charity Organization Society, insisted that an emergency could be demonstrated only for the less expensive apartments and that the exclusion of costly flats thereby enhanced the constitutionality of the statute.[131]

The extension of the laws in early 1926 marked a turning point. It was

Table 2.1
Apartment Construction in New York City, 1917–1930

Year	*No. of New Buildings*	*Net Gain in Apartments*
1917	760	14,241
1918	130	2,706
1919	95	1,624
1920	237	4,882
1921	309	6,835
1922	1,173	25,804
1923	1,794	32,000
1924	3,919	55,450
1925	2,857	42,573
1926	3,869	63,186
1927	4,617	79,253
1928	3,538	72,724
1929	1,855	53,812
1930	739	24,544

the last time during the 1920s that a strong tenant movement would exercise its power. To understand the reasons for this, one must examine certain developments in the city's housing situation during the decade.

In 1921 the legislature had passed an enabling act for local municipalities wishing to grant property tax exemption on new residential construction. Under New York City's ordinance, all construction started between 1920 and 1926 was exempt from local taxation until 1932; this allowed a builder to recoup up to one-third of construction costs through tax relief.[132] The program sparked a tremendous surge in residential building. As shown in table 2.1,[133] the years 1918 and 1919 represented low points in the war-induced construction decline. By 1922, however, construction had climbed to record levels. During the entire decade, New York experienced a net increase of over one hundred thousand apartment units.

Such a tremendous addition to the city's housing stock had a major impact on apartment availability. As indicated by table 2.2,[134] the city had experienced less than a 1 percent vacancy rate during the early 1920s. But by 1925 the rate began to climb toward its prewar level, and by 1927 it exceeded 5 percent, the rate usually considered necessary for a fluid, healthy rental market.

The real impact of the housing boom was a major topic of debate between realtors and housing reformers. Tenant advocates insisted that little

Table 2.2
Rate of Vacancies in Rental Apartment Units, New York City, 1919–1928

Year	*Rate (%)*
1919	2.18
1920	0.36
1921	0.15
1922	Not available
1923	0.37
1924	0.80
1925	2.23
1926	3.46
1927	6.63
1928	7.76

of the new construction benefited lower- and lower-middle-income tenants, since the new apartments were too expensive for such families. Figures support this contention. For example, only 17 percent of the apartments completed in 1924 rented for less than fifteen dollars per room per month.[135]

Real estate representatives viewed the situation from a "trickle down" perspective. They argued that the movement of more affluent families into new, tax exempt buildings created vacancies for poorer tenants in older, decent buildings. This seems to have been partially true, insofar as vacancies in "old law" tenements—the city's worst type of housing—did rise during the period. But it must also be noted that by 1928 there was a balance between vacancies in old and new structures (51,291 in "new law" buildings to 50,867 in "old law" tenements). This indicates that the trickle-down effect was limited: many families were still too poor to move up the housing ladder despite a surplus of newer apartments in the middle and upper segments of the market.[136]

These major changes in the housing market had significant effects on both the tenant movement and the Emergency Rent Laws. It is in this context that the battle for extension that took place in late 1925 and early 1926 marked a significant turning point. First, in the face of a rising vacancy rate and continued construction of moderately expensive apartments, tenant leaders chose to base their arguments on the shortage of low-rent apartments alone. This opened the door to gradual erosion of the Rent Laws, which began with the decontrol of apartments renting for more than twenty dollars per room. Second, such erosion served to reduce the appeal of the tenant organizations by reducing the number of families who could use the laws or be called upon to fight for their retention.

In fact, the loosening of the housing market and the limitations on rent law protection seem to have had an immediate impact on the movement. While it is extremely difficult to chronicle the decline of grass roots organizations, scattered evidence indicates that within a year—by early 1927—most tenant associations had lost much of their strength. Several organizations were giving out door prizes to encourage attendance; others held weekly socials to "keep the interests of the members at the proper pitch."[137] When a new series of hearings commenced in early 1927, tenant leaders were pessimistic about the chances of renewing the Rent Laws; certainly their lobbying efforts were less impressive. The *Times* noted that "the delegations to the hearing were not as large as in former years and were easily seated in the Assembly, where they had once filled the Chamber."[138]

Despite the weakening of the movement, however, politicians still respected the voting power of rent payers and chose compromise. In March 1927 the legislature extended the Emergency Rent Laws to June 1, 1928; but coverage was limited to existing tenancies in apartments renting at less than fifteen dollars per room per month. Once again, the field of beneficiaries, and thus the movement's constituency, had been narrowed.[139]

In the ensuing year, the city's tenant organizations declined even further. By late 1927 the Fair Play Rent Association had ceased to meet regularly. The Tremont League met on alternate Tuesdays rather than weekly. Although the South Bronx and Melrose groups still drew between 150 and 200 people to their meetings, this represented only about one-third of the average attendance during the peak years of activity. More important as an indicator of organizational decay was the trend in memberships: a hard core of old-timers remained, but dues from new members were declining.[140]

This loss of strength was all too evident in March 1928 when the State Board of Housing, which had replaced the Stein commission, considered further extension of rent control. Gone were the days when special hearings, held in New York City, focused a prestigious spotlight on tenant representatives. Rather, small tenant delegations traveled to Albany to testify before legislative committees. Much worse than the loss of prestige, however, was the fact that tenant appeals were ignored. After a series of pro forma hearings, the board recommended that the Emergency Rent Laws be allowed to lapse, noting that while many poor families still faced a housing problem, "the condition which confronts them is not temporary, . . . it does not arise out of the economic adjustments following the war, . . . [and it] is not an emergency in the meaning of the law."[141]

Once again, however, practical politics intervened at the eleventh hour when the Republican-controlled legislature seized the opportunity to pose as tenant protectors while also embarrassing Governor Smith. It passed a revised rent law that continued controls on apartments renting for fifteen dollars per room until December 1, 1928, and controls on apartments renting at ten dollars or less until June 15, 1929. Governor Smith had two options—veto the rent bills in a year in which he was running for president or repudiate his own Board of Housing. He chose the latter and the Emergency Rent Laws were extended once more.[142]

One year later the scene shifted to city hall. Since there was no hope that the legislature would again cooperate, tenant leaders looked to the Board of Alderman for protection. Several of the Bronx groups roused themselves and held rallies and demonstrations. In addition, a Negro organization, the Harlem Tenants League, mobilized some support in the black community. Yet most observers acknowledged, even if indirectly, that the postwar crisis was over. Agnes Craig told tenants to fight increases by "calling the landlord's bluff. If your landlord insists on having a huge increase in rent and takes your case to court, move out and get an apartment elsewhere. There are plenty of vacant apartments in the Bronx."[143] Nevertheless, the Board of Aldermen chose expediency and passed a city rent control ordinance for apartments renting at ten dollars or less per room. This was a political decision with no real impact for, as everyone expected, the new law was immediately declared unconstitutional. By the fall of 1929, for the first time in nearly a decade, New York City tenants were without rent control.[144]

The events and processes that both led to and followed enactment of the Emergency Rent Laws warrant study, for they provide excellent insights into the development of tenant organization tactics and strategies, the dynamics of movement building, the ways in which change is effected, and the problems associated with maintaining and adding to tenant protections once achieved.

The Socialist tenant leagues were clearly the organizational catalysts of the postwar movement. Despite limited resources, they greatly improved upon the building- and neighborhood-level rent strike. Picketing, demonstrating at the place of business if the owner was a local merchant, threatening prospective replacement tenants, and exerting pressure within local religious congregations made it extremely difficult for landlords to achieve large rent increases or evict families who resisted. While rent striking has gained legal legitimacy and hence greater efficacy in the past twenty years, the actual organization and implementation of a building-level rent strike has probably not changed significantly since its maturation in 1919 and 1920.

Successful organizing and rent striking resulted in major accomplishments on two fronts. The most basic, and most often overlooked, were the individual victories won against local landlords. Direct action, coupled with effective use of the courts and even the competing Mayor's Committee, enabled thousands of families to resist exorbitant rent increases, avoid eviction, and win improved building conditions.

The leagues' most important achievement, albeit indirectly, was the legislation passed to deal with the housing crisis. The Emergency Rent Laws were revolutionary in that the right of a property owner to charge what the market would bear was subordinated to the larger public good. Of course, the precedent was somewhat limited by their administration since an established profit level was the key criterion for determining whether a requested increase was reasonable; thus the right to a profit was not entirely secondary to the needs of poor families. One can also argue that the tax exemption program of the 1920s was also a major milestone, given the amount of construction that was subsidized.

It must also be recognized, however, that the laws passed in 1920 only represented a limited victory. Indeed, it is significant that the Socialist leagues failed to develop support for more far-reaching goals such as public housing, among non-Socialists ensnared in the crisis. This partly reflects how difficult it is to maintain a family's participation in a local tenant organization once its immediate problem has been successfully dealt with. More important, however, the failure of the Socialists to build a larger agenda resulted from the particular chain of events during the postwar period.

The achievement of a major policy or programmatic change requires four major steps. The issue must be raised and recognized; it must be introduced into the decision-making arena; it must pass through the decision-making process; and, lastly, it must be fully implemented.

In this case, such change took place only in response to an extremely widespread crisis and only through the complementary efforts of a variety of groups—the tenant leagues and the more conservative associations, as well as third parties—some of whom did not view each other as allies.

The issue initially gained legitimacy because of two interrelated factors. First, the impact of the post–World War I housing crisis, unlike the situations in 1904 and 1908, was so widespread and serious that it could not be ignored. Second, the Socialists proved capable of mobilizing desperate tenants and capitalizing politically on the inability of the city and state to respond effectively. Had the crisis not developed such broad and multifaceted implications, significant change would not have resulted.

While the Socialists advocated controls on rents and public housing, they only achieved mass support for direct, local activities such as rent strikes. Government officials responded by ignoring the calls for far-reaching (and politically costly) solutions and by undercutting the appeal of the tenant leagues. Creation of the Mayor's Committee was a clear attempt to blunt the appeal of the Socialists while directing discontent into legitimate channels.

Given the situation by late 1919—rents rising throughout the city, widespread striking, thousands of evictions, and Socialist victories in November—it is not surprising that the Red Scare hysteria had a great effect on the movement. Officials and established party leaders, whether genuinely or calculatedly, linked the real anger and desperation of tenants to paranoid images of a larger left wing threat. Meanwhile, the conservative tenant associations emerged—or perhaps were created—to replace the Socialists as the designated "proper" representatives of tenants just at the time when the crisis was most threatening and it was obvious that substantive legislative action was needed.

Thus with the Socialist assemblymen, two of whom were actually tenant leaders, excluded from their seats, a coalition of the conservative tenant associations, the Central Federated Union, the municipal court judges, and Democratic and Republican leaders combined to treat the needs of the city's apartment dwellers. After cursory consideration of public housing, they pushed through the April Laws and then, five months later, the Emergency Rent Laws. In effect, they had coopted the momentum and pressure built by the Socialists and yielded as little as possible during a skillful retreat.

With the fading of the Socialist leagues after September 1920, conservative tenant leaders had a freer hand. Ironically, it is their failure to expand the tenant agenda and gain additional benefits that is most tragic. They had a good relationship with state and local officials, legitimacy in the broader sense, and a sizeable and still quite desperate constituency, yet they made no attempt to use these advantages proactively. This was partly due to ideology; most felt a larger government role in housing was inappropriate. Others may not have wanted to risk their influence by seeming militant. Whatever the motives, from the outset they demonstrated a willingness to work within the existing legal and economic framework. As a result, the organizations that survived into the 1920s adopted a "service agency" perspective, with tenants often viewed as clients, and avoided confrontation with realtors or government leaders.

Initially this posture exerted a positive influence: the leaders of such organizations received the cooperation and support of government officials and eventually assumed a quasi-governmental role as fact finders and facilitators of rent law administration. Yet they also made themselves "prisoners" of the laws by stressing their continued belief in legitimacy and the justification of rent control as an "emergency" measure.

Seen from this perspective, subsequent developments during the decade are understandable. During the early 1920s, at the height of the housing shortage, there was little difficulty in maintaining rent control; in fact, the laws were slightly broadened in 1922 and 1923. But during this period, tenant leaders mounted no pressure for major new advantages—a broader, permanent rent control program, effective code enforcement, public housing. In viewing themselves as partners in the state's housing program, they allowed government officials to define the parameters of organized tenant activity.

The very seeds of the movement's destruction were sown when the leaders accepted the premise that tenant rights would expand and contract in direct proportion to the scope of the housing shortage. Once started in 1926, the process of gradual decontrol was irreversible. By 1928, when the State Board of Housing recommended that the Emergency Rent Laws be allowed to lapse, only 193,000 families—about 10 to 12 percent of the city's population—were covered by rent control. Tenant leaders had allowed their following to be stripped away step by step, until those that remained were not strong enough to resist the final defeat. Over a ten-year period they had let rent control and the potential for even larger gains slip through their fingers.

NOTES

1. Works Progress Administration Historical Records Survey, Box 3647, New York City Municipal Archives, (hereafter cited as WPA Survey); Katherine J. Meyer, "A Study of Tenant Associations in New York City with Particular Reference to the Bronx," Master's thesis, Columbia University, Department of Sociology, 1928, p. 8.
2. *Report of the State Board of Housing Relative to the Housing Emergency Arising out of the Recent World War*, New York State Legislative Document (1928) No. 85, p. 21.
3. Tenement House Department figures cited in Clarence Stein, "The Housing Crisis in New York," *Survey* 44 (Sept. 1920): 659–661.
4. Frank Mann to Mayor John Hylan, Mar. 5 and Oct. 11, 1918, Hylan Papers, Box 276, New York City Municipal Archives (hereafter cited as Hylan Papers); *New York Times*, Aug. 10, 1919, secs. 2 and 4.
5. The widespread nature of this speculation is detailed in *Report of the Mayor's Committee on Taxation and Investigation of Mortgage Loans and the Mayor's Committee on Rent Profiteering* (New York, 1919), pp. 39–40 (hereafter cited as *Report of the Mayor's Committee*); *New York Times*, Dec. 3, 1919; *New York Call*, Apr. 18, 1919.
6. *Report of the Mayor's Committee*, pp. 39–41; *New York Times*, Feb. 24, 1918, sec. 7.
7. Ada H. Muller, "A Study of a Bronx Community," Master's thesis, Columbia University, Department of Political Science, 1915, pp. 15–26. Muller noted that the vast majority of families had an income of less than fifteen dollars per week and that in 1915 (even before the onset of the housing crisis) Hebrew Charities had a heavy caseload in the area.
8. *New York Call*, Dec. 31, 1916, Jan. 1, 2, 4, 1917; *New York Times*, Jan. 1, 1917; *Daily North Side News* (Bronx), Jan. 2, 4, 1917.
9. *New York Call*, Jan. 6, 1917; *Daily North Side News*, Jan. 6, 1917.
10. *Daily North Side News*, Jan. 3, 10, 1917.
11. Ibid., Jan. 19, 1917; *New York Call*, Jan. 18, 1917.
12. *New York Tribune*, Feb. 6, 1918; *New York Times*, Feb. 10, 1918, sec. 4; *Daily North Side News*, Jan. 29, 1918.
13. *Home News* (East Harlem and Yorkville

ed.) Jan. 6, 1918. (Unless otherwise specified, *Home News* citations are for the Bronx edition.) At this time the city's health code had no provision requiring a landlord to provide heat.

14. *Daily North Side News*, Feb. 24, 1918; *New York Times*, Feb. 10, 1918, sect. 4; *New York Tribune*, Jan. 30, 1918. The Bronx alone had twenty-five hundred eviction cases between Dec. 1917 and the end of Feb. 1918; *Daily Forward*, Jan. 12, 20, 1918.

15. *New York Call*, Feb. 8, 10, 16, 1918; *Home News* (West Harlem and Washington Heights ed.), Jan. 13, 1918; *Daily North Side News*, Feb. 24, 1918; *Home News* (East Harlem and Yorkville ed.), Feb. 10, 1918.

16. *New York Call*, Feb. 8, 10, 16, 1918; *New York Tribune*, Jan. 30, 1918; *Daily Forward*, Jan. 12, 20, 26, Feb. 9, 1918.

17. *New York Times*, Feb. 5, 1918; *Home News* (Harlem ed.), Feb. 10, 1918.

18. *Home News* (Harlem ed.), Feb. 27, Mar. 3, 10, 1918; *New York Tribune*, Mar. 12, 1918.

19. *New York Call*, Feb. 16, Mar. 13, 31, Apr. 9, 1918.

20. Ibid., Apr. 30, May 19, 21, 28, June 2, 1918; *Brooklyn Standard Union*, May 3, 1918; *Daily Forward*, Jan. 28, 31, Feb. 1, 3, 4, 23, 1918.

21. *New York Tribune*, May 16, 1918.

22. *Daily North Side News*, Jan. 28, 1918.

23. Ibid., Feb. 24, Apr. 14, 1918; *New York Times*, Feb. 10, 1918, sec. 4; Apr. 7, 1918, sec. 3; *Daily Forward*, Jan. 29, Feb. 23, 1918.

24. *New York Call*, Aug. 13, 16, 20, 26, 29, Sept. 1, 4, 9, 17, Oct. 5, Dec. 31, 1918; *Home News*, Aug. 8, 20, 25, Sept. 10, 19, 1918; *Daily Forward*, Sept. 2, 1918.

25. *New York Call*, Dec. 31, 1918; *New York Tribune*, Nov. 1, 1919.

26. *New York Call*, June 8, 21, July 4, 5, Aug. 24, Sept. 9, 1918; on one day, for example, Judge Robitzek of the Bronx Municipal Court heard twelve hundred dispossess motions. *Daily North Side News*, July 5, 1918; *Daily Forward*, Aug. 22, 24, Sept. 11, 14, 1918; *Home News*, Aug. 23, 1918.

27. *New York Call*, Oct. 22, 25, 29, 1918; *New York Times*, Nov. 7, 8, 1918; *Daily Forward*, Sept. 26, Nov. 7, 1918; James Weinstein, *The Decline of the Socialist Party in America: 1912–1925* (New York, 1967), p. 154. Both the Socialist party and the tenant movement suffered a tragic loss even before the election with the premature death of Joseph Klein.

28. *New York Call*, Dec. 14, 1918.

29. *Report of the State Board of Housing*, L.D. (1928) No. 85, p. 21.

30. Letter to the New York State Reconstruction Commission quoted in *New York Times*, Apr. 17, 1919.

31. *New York Times*, Feb. 23, 1919, IX.

32. A selection of these letters is contained in Hylan Papers, Box 348, "Hylan Housing, 1918–1919."

33. *Daily Forward*, Apr. 9, 11, 1919.

34. *Home News*, Feb. 19, 1919; *New York Call*, Jan. 11, 31, Apr. 10, 1919; *New York Times*, Mar. 11, May 8, 1919; *Daily Forward*, Apr. 16, 1919; *Joint Legislative Committee on Housing, Hearings, 1919–1920*, 7 vols., unpublished.

35. *Report of the Mayor's Committee*, pp. 38–39; *New York Times*, Apr. 30, May 3, Sept. 2, Oct. 22, 1919; *Home News*, Nov. 2, 1919.

36. Nathan Hirsch to Governor Alfred E. Smith, June 12, 1919, and Charles Lockwood et al. to Smith, Smith Papers, Box 260-46; *New York Times*, May 8, 1919.

37. Author's interview with Sophie Epstein, Oct. 29, 1975.

38. *Report of the Mayor's Committee*, pp. 41, 43, 51; press release of the Mayor's Committee, dated Nov. 9, 1919, Smith Papers, Box 260-46; *Home News*, Sept. 11, 24, 1919; *New York Times*, Sept. 24, 1919, Sept. 14, 1919, sec. 7.

39. *Report of the Mayor's Committee*, p. 48; *Bronx Home News*, Sept. 4, 21, Dec. 9, 1919; *New York Call*, Apr. 25, 1919.

40. *Report of the Mayor's Committee*, p. 42.

41. *New York Call*, May 4, 1919.

42. Ibid., Apr. 22, 25, May 6, 1919; *New York Times*, May 7, 1919; *Daily Forward*, Apr. 25–30, 1919.
43. *New York Call*, Apr. 26, May 3, 5, July 17, 20, 25, 1919; *Daily Forward*, Apr. 3, 1919.
44. *Brooklyn Eagle*, Sept. 5, 6, 7, 1919; *New York Call*, Sept. 5, 1919; *New York Times*, Sept. 5, 6, 1919.
45. *New York Call*, Sept. 10, 1919; *New York Times*, Oct. 18, 1919.
46. *New York Tribune*, Oct. 31, 1919; *New York Sun*, Oct. 21, 1919; *New York Call*, July 17, 1919.
47. *Report of the Joint Legislative Committee on Housing, September 20, 1920*, L.D. (Special Session, 1920) No. 11, p. 5; *Home News*, Sept. 20, Oct. 2, 12, 1919.
48. *New York Tribune*, Oct. 1, 1919.
49. Ibid., Oct. 12, 1919.
50. *Home News*, Nov. 30, 1919.
51. Ibid., Sept. 20, Oct. 2, Nov. 30, 1919.
52. *New York Times*, Sept. 4, 1919; *New York Call*, Sept. 11, 1919.
53. *New York World*, Oct. 7, 1919; *Joint Hearing of the Senate and Assembly Committees on Cities*, Mar. 23, 1920, mimeographed transcript in Smith Papers, Box 260-46 II. (Hereafter cited as Hearing Transcript, Mar. 23, 1920.)
54. *New York World*, Oct. 4, 1919; *New York Call*, Nov. 22, 1919.
55. *New York Tribune*, Nov. 23, 1919.
56. Ibid.
57. Ibid., Oct. 18, 31, 1919.
58. *New York Tribune*, Oct. 8, 31, 1919; *Home News*, Oct. 21, 1919.
59. *Home News*, Nov. 2, 1919; *New York Call*, Oct. 2, 1919; *New York Times*, Oct. 6, 1919.
60. Ward V. Tolbert to Governor Alfred E. Smith, Nov. 3, 1923, in Smith Papers, Box 200-51-1.
61. *New York Times*, Nov. 6, 1919; *Home News*, Oct. 7, Nov. 6, 1919.
62. Thomas E. Vadney, "The Politics of Repression: A Case Study of the Red Scare in New York," *New York History* 49 (1968): 58–74.
63. Melvin I. Urofsky, "A Note on the Expulsion of the Five Socialists," *New York History* 47 (1966): 41–51.
64. *Home News*, Oct. 5, Nov. 9, 13, 16, 18, 20, 1919; Fleetwood Community Council to Smith, Feb. 25, 1920, Smith Papers, Box 260-46.
65. *Brooklyn Eagle*, Mar. 4, 5, 12, 1920; *Home News*, Feb. 1, 5, 8, Mar. 7, 9, 1920; Hearing Transcript, Mar. 23, 1920, pp. 75–77; *Commission of Housing and Regional Planning Hearings*, 1923, p. 318, (hereafter cited as Stein Commission, Hearings, 1923).
66. The following is a list of last names of all community council and conservative tenant association leaders listed in the press in 1920: Boyle, Sullivan, McGlynn, Crowley, Donnelly, Craig, Ely, Arthur, Goldfarb, McPherson, Ryan, Cooney, Anson, Murphy, Cahil, and Gray. In addition, two of the community councils met in parish houses of Catholic churches. *Home News*, Nov. 13, 16, 1919.
67. *Home News*, Feb. 5, Mar. 16, 25, 1920.
68. Ibid., Feb. 29, 1920; *Evening World*, Mar. 9, 1920. A *Home News* account of a Fair Play Rent Association meeting on Feb. 23, 1920, demonstrates the patriotic fervor of the organization. The meeting began with a "patriotic program": three men presented a dramatization of the Spirit of '76, a man dressed as George Washington gave a speech, and the daughter of FPRA founder Patrick McGlynn recited a poem entitled "The True American."
69. *Home News*, Feb. 1, 5, 8, 12, 29, 1920.
70. *New York Times*, Feb. 9, Mar. 7, 1920; *New York Call*, Mar. 8, 1920; *Daily Forward*, Mar. 3, 1920.
71. *New York Times*, Feb. 9, 1920.
72. Ibid., Mar. 7, 8, 1920; *World*, Mar. 7, 1920.
73. *New York World*, Mar. 19, 1920; *New York Journal*, Mar. 13, 1920; *New York Times*, Mar. 12, 7, 1920.
74. *New York Call*, Mar. 25, 1920.
75. Ibid., Mar. 5, 18, 22, 1920.
76. It was not until mid-April that other

tenant leaders disavowed any connection with Gitlin and branded him a sham.
77. *New York Times*, Mar. 7, 1920; *Brooklyn Eagle*, Mar. 7, 1920.
78. *New York Call*, Mar. 19, 1920.
79. *New York Tribune*, Mar. 4, 1920.
80. *New York Call*, Mar. 4, 10, 24, 1920; Hearing Transcript, Mar. 23, 1920, pp. 18, 64, 65; *New York Tribune*, Mar. 4, 1920.
81. Hearing Transcript, Mar. 23, 1920, p. 120.
82. Stanley Coben, "A Study in Nativism: The American Red Scare of 1919–1920," *Political Science Quarterly* 79 (Mar. 1964): 52–75.
83. "American Jew" to Smith, Mar. 25, 1920, in Smith Papers, Box 260-46, pt. 1.
84. *Brooklyn Eagle*, Mar. 17, 1920; Hearing Transcript, Mar. 23, 1920, p. 66; Report of the Mayor's Committee, Appendix; *Home News*, Mar. 9, 1920.
85. Hearing Transcript, Mar. 23, 1920, pp. 77, 122.
86. *New York Call*, Mar. 30, Apr. 21, 1920; *New York Tribune*, Mar. 31, 1920; *New York Times*, Mar. 30, 1920.
87. *Daily Forward*, Mar. 16–19, 21, 28–31, 1920.
88. *New York Times*, Mar. 30, 1920.
89. Ibid., Mar. 31, 1920.
90. *New York Tribune*, Mar. 4, 1920; *Home News*, Mar. 2, 1920; *Brooklyn Eagle*, Mar. 9, 17, 1920; *New York Call*, Mar. 10, 1920.
91. For the full text of the laws see Edgar Lauer and Victor House, *The Tenant and His Landlord* (New York, 1921), Appendix A. Besides the major provisions mentioned in the text, the April Rent Laws gave tenants several other advantages. Chapter 135 allowed tenants to make an oral answer before the clerk, thus eliminating the expense of hiring an attorney; chapter 132 allowed the court to give affirmative relief without the defendants having to file a separate action; chapter 131 made it a misdemeanor for a landlord to harass tenants by curtailing services.
92. *New York Call*, Apr. 21, 1920.
93. Ibid., Apr. 1, 18, 24, 1920.
94. Ibid., May 2, 1920.
95. *Joint Legislative Committee on Housing Hearings*, July 29, 1920, p. 2947.
96. Ibid., pp. 2936, 2937, 2966.
97. *Joint Legislative Committee on Housing Hearings*, July 19, 1920, pp. 2853–2854; *Report of the Joint Legislative Committee on Housing*, L.D. (Special Session, 1920) No. 11, p. 5.
98. *New York Call*, June 9, 22, 23, July 1, 8, 10, 31, 1920.
99. *Joint Legislative Committee on Housing Hearings*, July 22, 1920, p. 2912; *New York Call*, July 31, Aug. 4, 1920; Stein, "Housing Crisis in New York," p. 659.
100. Examination of the *Call* for the summer of 1920 demonstrates the extent to which the reelection effort dominated party activities. The campaign was successful, as all five were reelected at a special election prior to the special session.
101. *New York Call*, Aug. 3, 11, 1920; *Home News*, Aug. 1, 12, 1920.
102. *Joint Legislative Committee on Housing Hearings*, July 1920, *passim.*
103. Stein, "Housing Crisis in New York," p. 659.
104. *Report of the Joint Legislative Committee on Housing*, L.D. (Special Session, 1920) No. 11, p. 5. Emphasis in original.
105. Text of the laws can be found in Lauer and House, *Tenant and Landlord*, Appendixes A, B.
106. *New York Times*, Dec. 3, 1920, Oct. 3, 1920.
107. Ibid., Jan. 21, 1921.
108. Ibid., Nov. 3, 1921.
109. For a detailed account of the Socialist party schism, see David Shannon, *The Socialist Party of America* (New York, 1955), chap. 6.
110. *New York Times*, Jan. 24, Feb. 4, 11, 1925.
111. *New York State Commission on Housing and Regional Planning Hearings*, 1925, p. 61. (Mimeograph, hereafter cited as Stein Commission Hearings, 1925.)
112. Stein Commission Hearings, 1923 and 1925, *passim;* Mayer, "Study of Tenant Associations," *passim;* Smith Papers, 200:51; *New York Times*, Feb. 8, 1921.
113. Stein Commission Hearings, 1923,

pp. 81, 172–179; Stein Commission Hearings, 1925, p. 52.
114. For example, if a tenant paid a rent increase for three months, he forfeited his right to charge subsequently that it was unreasonable.
115. Stein Commission Hearings, 1925, pp. 70–140 *passim.*
116. Stein Commission Hearings, 1923, p. 285.
117. Mayer, "Study of Tenant Associations," pp. 21–23.
118. Ibid., pp. 24–26.
119. Stein Commission Hearings, 1923, p. 101.
120. Stewart Browne to Alfred E. Smith, Jan. 2, 1924, Smith Papers, Box 200: 51-1.
121. Samuel Untermeyer to Alfred E. Smith, Mar. 5, 1923, Smith Papers, Box 200:102.
122. Stein Commission Hearings, 1923, pp. 7–333 *passim;* quote from p. 237.
123. New York State Legislative Document (1924) No. 43, pp. 11–14, 22, 27.
124. *New York Times*, Dec. 8, 1925, Jan. 5, 1926.
125. Stein Commission Hearings, 1925, pp. 4–144 *passim.*
126. Ibid., pp. 12, 58.
127. For details of such tenant meetings, see the *Home News*, Oct. 24, 1925–Feb. 15, 1926.
128. *Home News*, Sept. 25, 1925; *New York Times*, Oct. 17, 1925.
129. *Home News*, Sept. 25, 1925; *New York Times*, Oct. 13, 16, 19, 1925.
130. *Home News*, Oct. 14, 22, 1925; *New York Times*, Oct. 21, 22, 23, 1925.
131. *New York Times*, Jan. 16, Feb. 6, 1926.
132. WPA Survey, Box 3603, "Housing Guidebook for NYC," pp. 35–36.
133. Data from Real Estate Board of New York, *Apartment Building Construction in Manhattan, 1902–53* (New York, n.d.), pp. 9, 18, 119.
134. *Tenth Report of the Tenement House Department (for the Years 1918–1929)* (New York, 1930), pp. 162–163.
135. WPA Survey, Box 3634, "Housing in New York, First Draft," *passim.*
136. *Tenth Report of the Tenement House Department*, pp. 162–163.
137. *Home News*, Feb. 5, 1927.
138. *New York Times*, Feb. 9, 1927.
139. Ibid., Mar. 22, 24, 1927; Apr. 24, 1927, sec. 10.
140. *Home News*, Mar. 12, 15, 1928.
141. *New York Times*, Mar. 10, 1928.
142. Ibid., Mar. 14, 22, 1928; *Home News*, Apr. 7, 1928.
143. *Home News*, May 18, 1929.
144. The legislature had, however, reenacted protections against unjust eviction and provisions for stays of eviction in certain hardship cases.

3. From Eviction Resistance to Rent Control

Tenant Activism in the Great Depression

Mark Naison

THE period between 1929 and 1943 was a time of extraordinary ferment among tenants and of innovation and experimentation within the sphere of housing policy. The era began with organized tenant activism at a low ebb; with the exception of a small Harlem-centered movement, there was little protest against the expiration of the last of the Emergency Rent Laws passed after World War I. But the coming of the Great Depression created crises in the housing market, which stimulated mass tenant protest and a powerful liberal-philanthropic coalition for housing reform. First came an antieviction movement, led by Communists, that sought to reduce the impact of mass unemployment on beleaguered tenants; then came a campaign for tenement house upgrading led by social work and philanthropic organizations; then came a campaign for public housing supported by liberals and tenant activists; and then a campaign for wartime rent control led by a broad spectrum of the city's Left. The political forces unleashed here were extremely diverse, but they were united by one significant trend: the failure of a depression-weakened housing market and private construction industry to provide safe, affordable housing to the third of the city's population who were unemployed or underemployed.

Under the press of depression conditions, the terms of debate in housing policy shifted dramatically. For the first time in American history, a broad-based housing coalition developed that emphasized aggressive government intervention in the private housing market. "Private capital," WPA head Harry Hopkins told a crowd at the opening of First Houses, New York's first public housing project, "has never spent a dime to build a house for the poor person." Settlement houses joined with Left-led tenant organizations to lobby for code enforcement, rent control, and the construction of public housing, while liberal public officials endorsed tenant protests as needed catalysts for reform. "You will never get anything unless you demand it," Tenement House Commissioner Langdon Post told a group from the City-Wide Tenants Council in 1937. "Nothing was ever gotten in this country except when the people forced it." Important differences existed within this coalition as to the role of public subsidies and market incentives in slum clearance and the construction of public housing; but the fact remains that two major, lasting innovations in the city's housing market came out of the reform effort—a program of low-income public housing and the imposition of a centrally administered system of rent control.[1]

Tenants organizations also displayed some new aspects that were to become permanent features of the city's political landscape. First, black tenant organizations became influential actors in the city's tenant movement and housing reform coalition. From the 1929 Harlem Tenants League which protested expiration of the Emergency Rent Laws, to the mid-depression Consolidated Tenants League which pioneered new forms of legal defense for tenants, to the Harlem-wide coalition fighting for wartime rent controls, black tenant leaders played a leading role in developing tactics to improve conditions for individual tenants and in shaping the agenda of housing reformers. Alongside the Jewish community, blacks emerged as a solid ethnic base for tenant activism.

Second, the radicalization of depression-era professionals inspired a new form of citywide tenant federation that employed a uniquely effective "mix" of tactics: expert legal representation of individual buildings and tenants, reinforced by rent withholding and picketing; careful research on housing issues, which led to legislation projecting a "tenant perspective"; and aggressive lobbying for tenant interests in cooperation with liberal and left wing organizations. Forming coalitions with grass roots tenant organizations in the city's ethnic neighborhoods, middle-class tenant advocates—lawyers, public relations experts, architects, and the like—created a set of strategies and a style of organizing that has survived, with some modification, to the present day. The City-Wide Tenants Council, founded in 1936, displayed professionalism and expertise comparable to philanthropic housing organizations, yet projected a commitment to mass mobilization and an identification with the downtrodden characteristic of the Left. Although City-Wide declined in the mid-1940s, its methods of organizing were adopted by tenant groups associated with trade unions, consumer groups, and left wing political clubs.

However, these innovations in organization came only after years of mass tenant protest that were far more violent and less precise in their targets. During 1932 and 1933, a Communist-led rent strike movement erupted in the Bronx, Brooklyn, and the Lower East Side, which almost reached the proportions of the post–World War I tenant revolt, but which produced no major innovations in legal strategy, no legislative accomplishments, and no permanent forms of tenant organization on a local or citywide level. Concentrated in Jewish neighborhoods, these rent strikes evoked violent opposition from landlords and police and a concerted effort by judges and city officials to neutralize the movement's effects. Failures in the sphere of housing policy, they helped create a climate in the city conducive to liberalized relief policies and the creation of a "safety net" of income maintenance programs that helped keep the poor in their homes.

There are structural explanations for this discontinuity between the two major waves of tenant activism. In the early 1930s, a massive loss of income by all city residents threw housing markets into disarray; tenants could not pay their rents, landlords could not meet their mortgages, and courts received a flood of eviction and foreclosure cases they lacked the capacity to process or enforce. The atmosphere of desperation on both sides created a climate conducive to violence, especially in neighborhoods where there was a tradition of collective action in response to economic setbacks. By the mid-1930s, however, the development of a broad-based home relief system, along with the establishment of federal work relief programs, had removed the atmosphere of mass desperation—most knew they could at least get funds for food and some kind of shelter. Serious issues still remained for tenants—building safety, affordable rents, protection from arbitrary evictions, racial discrimination—but these were issues that could be dealt with more calmly because of a greater sense of security regarding the basic necessities of life (as well as a subjective sense of government responsiveness to the needs of low-income people).

But economic determinism alone cannot explain the pattern of tenant activism of the period; one must also look at the history of the organized Left, particularly the Communist party, to understand why tenant protest shifted from mass communal uprisings to the actions of professional advocacy organizations. Communists did not "control" the City-Wide Tenants Council or its affiliates the way they did the Unemployed Councils of the early 1930s, but they were a definite presence in its ranks, influencing its policies and its network of alliances. The politics of antifascism dictated this more subtle approach: not only did the Party shift its emphasis from revolution to reform, but it actively courted middle-class professionals and enrolled a sizable group in its ranks. The City-Wide Tenants Council embodied the ethos of the Popular Front Left: simultaneously seeking respectability and projecting identification with the downtrodden; mingling mass protest techniques with sophisticated political bargaining; incorporating struggles against racial discrimination into movements for social reform. This style of organizing lasted well beyond the depression. Tenant organizations resembling City-Wide thrived during the 1950s, 1960s, and 1970s, long after the Communist party ceased to be the dominant force on the American Left.[2]

The Great Depression, therefore, represented a watershed in the history of tenant activism. Tenant organizations were inactive when the decade began, but by World War II they had become a powerful force in the political life of the city and state. Seeking government action to control rents, they fought for the constructions of public housing, worked to improve conditions in slum tenements, and strove to limit the disruptive impact of urban renewal. More than any other time, the 1930s was the period when the tenant movement "came of age."

The Harlem Tenants League

The first harbinger of the new tenant activism came nearly a year before the Great Depression struck. In February of 1928, a black Communist named Richard Moore, recognized for his knowledge of black history and his oratorical gifts, turned a quiet meeting of the Washington Heights Tenants League at the Harlem Public Library into an impassioned protest against the expiration of the city's Emergency Rent Laws. Pointing out that blacks were penned in their neighborhoods by rigid segregation and lacked bargaining power with their landlords, he warned that the expiration of controls on apartments renting for fifteen dollars per month (in December of 1928), and on those renting for ten dollars per month (in June of 1929) would provoke a wave of rent increases in Harlem. Upon his suggestion, tenants present formed a Harlem Tenants League, elected him president, and began holding protest meetings in the community and sending delegations to meetings of the Board of Aldermen, where the rent law was being discussed.[3]

In April of 1929, two months before the expiration of the ten-dollar-a-room controls, the league captured Harlem's attention with a campaign to resist impending rent increases and an attack on Harlem's politicians, editors, ministers, and landlords. Spurred by a series in the *Daily Worker* documenting the hardship of Harlem tenants, the league claimed that Harlem churches and real estate concerns that owned or managed Harlem property profited from segregation's toll on the black working class. "The capitalist caste system," Richard Moore wrote, "which segregates Negro workers into Jim Crow districts makes these doubly exploited black workers the special prey of rent gougers. Black and white landlords and real estate agents take advantage of this segregation to squeeze the last nickel out of the Negro working class who are penned in the black ghetto. Rents in Negro Harlem are already often double and sometimes triple those in other sections of the city." The league held meetings at the Harlem public library, sponsored marches through the streets of Harlem, and organized individual buildings to resist rent increases. Many of the buildings the league organized were owned by black churches and landlords.[4]

The league's attack on the black middle class, it soon became clear, owed more to the Communist party's sectarian enthusiasm (partly inspired by a recent Comintern edict), than to an accurate assessment of the behavior of local leadership. On June 6, 1929, the Republican and Democratic district leaders of Harlem sponsored a meeting at Abyssinian Baptist Church to demonstrate community support for the preservation of rent control and to urge tenants to bring their housing problems to their local political clubs. Every important Harlem politician, and both Harlem newspapers, lobbying for the preservation of rent controls, pointing out that blacks of *all classes* faced unfair rents because of segregation in housing. When the city's Board of Aldermen, in June of 1929, passed an ordinance preserving rent controls for apartments renting under fifteen dollars per room, it was partially in response to the pressure of black elected officials (the Socialist party and remnants of the 1920s tenant leagues also made their voices heard). Nevertheless, a certain cynicism characterized this gesture, as the ordinance was soon declared unconstitutional on the grounds that the city had intruded on matters of state concern.[5]

The Harlem Tenants League and Harlem's political leadership both took action once the city's rent control ordinance was struck down. For the Tenants League, the preferred tactic was a "Harlem wide rent strike." During the summer and fall of 1929, the league solicited complaints from individual tenants, held meetings in buildings scheduled to receive rent increases, and tried to persuade tenants to strike when negotiations failed. Such tactics proved of limited effectiveness; the league claimed that strikes took place on an intermittent basis and that non-Communist sources displayed no evidence to support even those limited claims. At this stage in Harlem's history, Communists lacked the cadre (they had less than twenty black members in the neighborhood), the reputation, and perhaps the right issue to arouse militant, risk-taking action on the part of Harlem tenants. Some Harlemites would attend Party protest meetings, march in Communist parades, and bring their complaints to Party tenant organizers, but the tactic of the strike was still unfamiliar and was frought with risk because of the tight housing market blacks faced in a segregated city (blacks evicted could take little comfort from the city's 7.5 percent vacancy rate because they were barred from most apartments). Nevertheless, the Tenants League agitation represented an important step in implanting a culture of collective protest among Harlem tenants, an effort that would bear greater fruit once the depression struck.[6]

Simultaneously, Harlem political leaders used their influence in Albany to propose legislative remedies for the special problems of black tenants. In 1930, Assemblymen Francis Rivers and Lamar Perkins proposed, and won, passage of legislation that expanded the bargaining power of tenants living in deteriorated buildings, or those who lacked alternative sources of housing than the premises on which they resided (which in 1930 meant largely blacks). Rivers's bill, which became section 1446(a) of the Civil Practice Act, provided that if a tenant could offer proof of a serious enough violation of the Multiple Dwellings Law or Health Department Code such as to "constructively evict" that tenant from the premises, the court might stay summary proceedings for nonpayment of rent, provided the tenant deposited all rent owed with the clerk of the court. The Perkins bill, which became section 1436(a) of the Civil Practice Act, provided that if tenants were served with an increase of rent, they might apply to a judge for a stay of eviction of up to six months if the tenant could not find equivalent shelter at comparable rentals. Subject to interpretation by the municipal courts, which were vulnerable to community pressure and political influence, these bills gave some additional leverage to black tenants fighting "rent gouging" in a segregated market and a potential weapon to all tenants living in "old law" tenaments (which included over two million people). Their passage demonstrated the growing importance of black political leaders in the struggle for housing reform and the recognition by the political leadership of the state that black tenants faced special problems in their quest for safe, affordable housing.[7]

Communists in the Lead: Early Depression Eviction Protests and Rent Strikes

The protest meetings of the Harlem Tenants League and the legislative efforts of Harlem's elected officials represented efforts to remedy the special problems of blacks within a steadily loosening housing market. But the depression, which hit the city and the nation with shocking rapidity, changed the context in which all discussion of housing issues took place and the basic texture of landlord-tenant relations. First, the rapid spread of unemployment undermined the capacity of most tenants to pay predepression rents, and some tenants to pay any rent at all. Second, the loss of rental income made it difficult for many landlords, especially marginal operators, to meet their mortgage bills, insurance payments, and utility costs and caused some to relinquish their properties and others to reduce routine maintenance. Third, the private construction industry, which had boomed during the 1920s, became instantly unprofitable, even for luxury buildings.[8]

Landlord-tenant relations became suffused with desperation. Facing tenants who could not pay, landlords improvised. Some, hoping that better times would bring them repayment, allowed tenants to stay on rent free. Others accepted labor exchanges in return for rent. Others lowered rents to more acceptable levels. But a good many responded to the crisis in "rational" economic terms and tried to force nonpaying tenants to leave. During 1932, the municipal courts of the city issued dispossess notices at two and three times predepression levels.[9]

Tenants scrambled desperately to retain or find apartments. Some made arrangements with landlords along the lines mentioned above. Others went to their local political club (or church or synagogue) to get help in "softening" their landlord's stance or to get a donation of a month's rent. Some did not pay rent, saved their money, moved out, and gave a downpayment to another desperate landlord, and moved once again when the dispossess arrived. But a good many simply left when the landlord asked, moved in with friends and relatives, or waited until the marshal put their furniture on the street. Although actual evictions—complete with marshals and police—were relatively few (less than 5 percent of dispossesses resulted in evictions), hundreds of thousands of people left their apartments for smaller ones, fell into the status of lodgers, or became part of the army of homeless that slept on streets, lived in Hoovervilles, or rode the rails. During the first three years of the depression, the city's vacancy rate rose precipitously, to over 9 percent in the Bronx and sections of Brooklyn and to over 15 percent in some low-income neighborhoods.[10]

City officials, though sympathetic to the problems of impoverished tenants, were overwhelmed by the misery facing them. The mayor's office, the police, and the municipal courts all tried to avoid massive displacement of tenants. The Mayor's Committee on Unemployment, set up by Mayor Jimmy Walker (and funded by private donations), asked to investigate cases of impending eviction to see if aid could be provided to avoid that contingency. Municipal court judges tried to encourage negotiations between landlords and tenants to achieve settlements short of eviction. And city police and marshals demonstrated a visible reluctance to evict destitute tenants; indeed, landlords in the Bronx actually sued one marshal to force him to carry out eviction orders that were issued by the courts. But such individual humane gestures could not fully blunt the force of the law or the inexorable logic of a private housing system that required the payment of rents to function. In the absence of government programs that put rent money in the hands of the unemployed, the dispossession and relocation of tenants proceeded on a massive scale and at considerable human cost.[11]

None of the tenant organizations that had been active in the 1920s, whether of Socialist or "conservative" origin, developed a strategy to organize tenants in this crisis. It fell upon the Communist party, an organization that had been marginal to the housing campaigns of the 1920s, to spearhead tenant activism, and it did so in a manner that provoked a great deal of hysteria and more than a little disorder.

At the time the depression struck, the Communist party in New York City was hardly a household word. Composed largely of Eastern European Jewish immigrants living in self-contained neighborhoods, it possessed a messianic air of certainty about its revolutionary ideals, which derived more from faith in the Soviet Union than knowledge of American conditions. But despite its sectarianism and insularity, the Party had two great advantages in dealing with the depression—a cadre that was experienced in collective struggle (both in American trade unions and European revolutionary movements) and a willingness to act outside the law and the established rules of political discourse to make its demands heard. While other groups on the Left tried to understand the crisis before organizing mass protest, Communists literally leaped onto the barricades as soon as the depression struck and demanded that federal, state, and city governments provide direct aid to the unemployed; Communists organized marches, rallies, and disruptions of government agencies to reinforce its demands.[12]

By the fall of 1930, Communist-led Unemployed Councils had begun to experiment with two tactics that had a direct impact on the housing market—eviction resistance and rent strikes. The first of these, eviction resistance, proved to be one of the most effective weapons in the Party's arsenal. Coming upon instances where tenants had been forcibly evicted, Communist organizers would move the furniture back from the street to the apartment, while appealing to neighbors and passersby to resist marshals and police if the eviction were repeated. Since many marshals and police were reluctant to evict (and since landlords had to pay marshals for evictions), such actions often bought time for beleaguered tenants and gave Communists a new-found respect. Through the fall of 1930 and the spring and summer of 1931, Communists employed this tactic in almost every city neighborhood where they were active, although the bulk seem to have occurred in poor communities where the depression hit early and hard—Harlem, the Lower East Side, Hell's Kitchen, the South Bronx, Brownsville, and Coney Island. In some of these neighborhoods the Party was relatively weak (the Lower East Side and Brownsville were the only ones where the Party had a mass membership), but eviction resistance did not require active support from the population or even the political sympathy of the victim. Given the overextended schedules of marshals and police, a handful of Party cadre could move the furniture back, provided the rest of the neighborhood was sympathetic or indifferent. Hundreds, possibly thousands, of such incidents occurred during the early depression years; some of them led to confrontations with police in which hundreds of people participated, but most of them led to some peaceful resolution, be it retention of the apartment by the tenants or a delay in their departure. "The practice of moving evicted families back into their homes has become frequent of late on the Lower East Side," declared the *New York Times* in describing the arrest of a group of eviction protesters, "but this was the first time that the police had arrived in time to seize any of the participants in such demonstrations."[13]

Rent strikes proved to be more difficult to organize. In the winter of 1931, Unemployed Councils tried to organize tenant leagues in buildings in their neighborhoods to force reductions in rent commensurate with tenant losses in income. Apparently, the tactic did not spread very rapidly; between March of 1931 and January of 1932, only seven rent strikes are mentioned in the *Daily Worker* (none in the *New York Times*), and four of those took place in the Lower East Side, a Party stronghold. Unlike eviction resistance, rent strikes required organizational experience and a willingness to take risks on the part of tenants as well as Unemployed Council organizers; tenants had to form committees, develop demands, negotiate with landlords, and keep their ranks firm with a subtle combination of persuasion and intimidation. Such a prospect was not appealing to people who lacked experience in collective protest or a strong belief in the "moral legitimacy" of the strike as an economic weapon. But Communist-led rent strikes posed a deadly threat to depression-era landlords. By demanding that building owners sharply reduce rents in response to mass unemployment, Communists were insisting that landlords "carry" their tenants, irrespective of its effect on their profit margins or their ability to hold onto their investment. A tactic forged in mass desperation, devoid of any respect for the landlord's economic problems, it posed an implicit threat to private ownership of housing. Predictably, landlords responded to such strikes with the vehemence of hungry people about to have the bread snatched out of their mouths.[14]

The Battle of the Bronx

The Great Rent Strike War of 1932 began in a quiet section of the Bronx just east of Bronx Park and west of the White Plains Road elevated line. A neighborhood of modern elevator buildings with spacious rooms, adjacent to a park, the zoo, and the botanical gardens, it seemed an unlikely place for a communal uprising. But by an accident of geography and sociology, this neighborhood contained one of the largest concentrations of Communists in New York City. On the corner of Bronx Park East and Allerton Avenue stood the "Coops"—two buildings populated entirely by Communists who had moved to the neighborhood as part of a cooperative housing experiment and had remained when the buildings reverted to private ownership. Filled with people for whom "activism was a way of life," it was a formidable presence in the community. The Coops were "a little corner of socialism right in New York," one activist recalled, "it had its own educational events, clubs for men and women, lectures, motion pictures." But the rest of the neighborhood's population, while not so militantly radical, came from comparable backgrounds to the Coops people. The majority were Eastern European Jews, skilled workers and small businessmen who had accumulated enough income to move out of the East Side and the South Bronx, but were hardly secure in their middle-class status. More important, many of them grew up in environments in which socialism and trade unionism provided models of heroism and moral conduct, and more than a few had extensive activist backgrounds, whether in bitter garment strikes in New York City or clandestine revolutionary struggle in Europe. Although relatively "privileged" compared to many New York workers ("Certain comrades . . . wanted to ridicule the movement," one rent strike organizer wrote apologetically, "not realizing that these 'better paid workers' are members of the American Federation of Labor, many of them working in basic industries"), they suffered serious losses of income and employment and were not about to sink quietly into poverty and despair in response to the "invisible hand" of the market. When Unemployed Council activists began to organize them into tenant committees, they responded in a manner that perplexed and enraged landlords and city officials.[15]

In early January of 1932, the Upper Bronx Unemployed Council unveiled rent strikes at three large apartment buildings in Bronx Park East—1890 Unionport Road, 2302 Olinville Avenue, and 665 Allerton Avenue. In each of these buildings, the majority of the tenants agreed to withhold their rent and began picketing their buildings to demand 15 percent reductions in rent, an end to evictions, repairs in apartments, and recognition of the tenants committee as an official bargaining agent. In all three instances, landlords, moving quickly to dispossess leaders of the strike, argued that the demands were extortionate; judges readily granted them notices of eviction.[16]

But the first set of attempted evictions, at 2302 Olinville Avenue, set off a "rent riot" in which over four thousand people participated. As the city marshals and the police moved into position to evict seventeen tenants, a huge crowd, composed largely of residents of the Coops, gathered in a vacant lot next to the building to support the strikers, who were poised to resist from windows and the roof. When the marshals moved into the building and the first stick of furniture appeared on the street, the crowd charged the police and began pummeling them with fists, stones, and sticks, while the "non-combatants urged the belligerents to greater fury with anathemas for capitalism, the police and landlords." The outnumbered police barely held their lines until reinforcements arrived. As the police once again moved to disperse the crowd, the strikers agreed to a compromise offer that called for two- to three-dollar reductions for each apartment and the return of evicted families to their apartments. "When news of the settlement reached the crowd," the *Bronx Home News* reported, "they promptly began chanting the Internationale and waving copies of the *Daily Worker* as though they were banners of triumph."[17]

At 665 Allerton Avenue, the attempted eviction of three tenants evoked disorders of nearly equal magnitude. The same elements all appeared: tenants barricading apartments and hurling objects at marshals and police; sympathetic crowds gathering and engaging police in hand-to-hand combat; the shouting of Communist slogans and ethnic-political epithets ("Down with Mulrooney's Cossacks"—an insult reserved for police—being the favorite). "The women were the most militant," noted the *New York Times;* they constituted the majority of the crowds, the arrestees, and those engaged in physical conflict with the police. This time, the evictions did occur, but only with the help of over fifty foot and mounted police and a large and expensive crew of marshals and moving men.[18]

Bronx property owners moved quickly to try to contain the movement. At first, they tried arbitration. Following the evictions at 665 Allerton, landlords in Bronx Park East asked a blue ribbon committee of Bronx Jewish leaders to arbitrate the dispute, convinced that an impartial examination of the building's books would show that the landlord could not meet the strikers' demands without operating at a loss. But the strike leaders at 665 Allerton contemptuously rejected arbitration and indeed the whole notion that a "reasonable return" on one's investment represented a basis for negotiation. "When times were good," strike leader Max Kaimowitz declared, "the landlords didn't offer to share their profits with us. The landlords made enough money off us when we had it. Now that we haven't got it, the landlords must be satisfied with less." Faced with this kind of bargaining position, landlords felt they had no choice but to pull out the stops to suppress the movement. By the second week of February 1932, two major organizations of Bronx landlords had formed rent strike committees that offered unlimited funding and legal support for any landlord facing a Communist-led rent strike. Using the considerable political influence and legal expertise at their disposal, they developed a strategy that included "wholesale issuance of dispossess notices against striking tenants," efforts to win injunctions against picketing in strikes, agreements by judges to waive normal delay periods in evictions, and efforts to ban rent strikes by legislative enactment. "The situation has become much graver than most persons suppose," one landlord spokesman declared. "The strikes are spreading rapidly and scores of landlords are facing financial ruin or loss of their properties as a result of them." Former state senator Benjamin Antin told landlords: "This is a peculiar neighborhood. It is the hot bed of Communism and radicalism. The people in this neighborhood are mostly Communists and Soviet sympathizers. They do not believe in our form of government."[19]

The landlord mobilization broke the back of some of the strikes—mass evictions took place at 665 Allerton Avenue and 1890 Unionport Road—but it did not discourage Communists from continuing rent strikes in Bronx Park East or spreading the movement to other neighborhoods. During January and February of 1932, Communist-led strikes for rent reductions began breaking out in Brownsville, Williamsburg, and Boro Park (in Brooklyn), and in Crotona Park East, Morrisania, and Melrose in the Bronx. Like Bronx Park East, these were neighborhoods primarily inhabited by Eastern European Jews, possessed of a dense network of radical cultural and political organizations, but they were poorer, more troubled, and harder hit by the depression. Irving Howe's description of Crotona Park East, the neighborhood where the second wave of Communist rent strikes attracted the greatest following, gives a sense of the grim atmosphere in which the Party's message was received:[20]

> The East Bronx . . . formed a thick tangle of streets crammed with Jewish immigrants from Eastern Europe, almost all of them poor. We lived in narrow, five story tenements, wall flush against wall, and with slate covered stoops rising sharply in front. There was never enough space. The buildings, clenched into rows, looked down upon us like sentinels, and the apartments in the buildings were packed with relatives and children, many of them fugitives from unpaid rent. Those tenements had first gone up during the early years of the century, and if not so grimy as those of the Lower East Side in Manhattan or the Brownsville section of Brooklyn, they were bad enough. . . . Hardly a day passed but someone was moving in or out. Often you could see a family's entire belongings furniture, pots, bedding, a tricycle, piled upon the sidewalks because they had been dispossessed.

In neighborhoods like these, Communists' appeals to strike invoked both indigenous traditions of militancy and a certain desperate practicality—since people were getting evicted anyway, why not put up a fight? Using the networks they possessed in fraternal organizations, women's clubs, and left wing trade unions, aided by younger comrades from the high schools and colleges, Communists were able to mobilize formidable support for buildings that were on strike and to force police to empty out the station houses to carry out evictions. Nowhere was this more apparent than in the strike of five buildings on Longfellow Avenue between 174th and 175th streets, which the Greater New York Taxpayers Association made a test case of its efforts to suppress the movement. Three separate waves of eviction provoked confrontations between police and neighborhood residents, the largest of which involved three thousand people "hurling stones, bottles and other missiles." On another occasion, a mob of fifteen hundred fought the police for an hour and then took off after the landlord when they saw him moving through the crowd. The strike finally was broken, but only after more than forty evictions, an injunction against picketing, and numerous arrests and injuries. The police needed full-scale mobilization to suppress such strikes. "The police have set up a temporary police station outside one of the buildings," read the *Daily Worker* description of a Brownsville rent strike. "Cops patrol the street all day. The entire territory is under semi-martial law. People are driven around the streets, off the corners, and away from the houses."[21]

For rent strike organizers and sympathizers, and for landlords and city officials, the issues the strike evoked transcended housing and were not readily conducive to "rational" negotiation. For Communists, rent strikes represented a way of arousing popular militance and of recruiting people into the unemployed movement and the Communist party. The Party had no systematic analysis of housing issues and no legislative solution to the housing crisis; in the one theoretical article in the Party press dealing with the rent strike movement, the emphasis was on "Building or organizations, on getting rent strikers . . . to join our unions, to form shop committees . . . to recruit them for the Party." Although some strikes resulted in rent reductions for the tenants, many, if not most, resulted in eviction of some of the strikers. Communists almost seemed to relish the confrontations resulting from evictions, regarding them as experiences that would radicalize the masses. Witness the rhetoric following the eviction of a rent striker on Seabury Place, in Crotona Park East: "A crowd of between 1,500 and 2,000 people witnessed the eviction of Zuckerman and his family. . . . Orators delivered blistering speeches from the fire escapes in denunciation of the policemen, the landlords, the marshall . . . the capitalist system, the vested interests, and the imperialist designs of Japan in the Far East." The Unemployed Councils had no coherent legal strategy to prevent evictions, or to argue the legitimacy of the rent strike before municipal judges—their major courtroom strategy appeared to consist of "intimidation by numbers."[22]

Given the Party's disdain for legal niceties, its rejection of arbitration, and its open appeal for conflict between citizens and police, it is not surprising that municipal judges, city officials, and police, normally quite sympathetic to tenants in distress, regarded the Communist rent strike movement as a pestilence to be stamped out. During the Longfellow Avenue protests, a municipal court judge warned striking tenants that "There are 18,000 policemen ready to keep order" and immediately issued dispossesses for all tenants who had withheld rent. Two weeks later, another judge granted an injunction restraining the picketing of Longfellow Avenue buildings. In the same strike, "the Mayor's Committee, police, and city marshalls . . . suspended their ordinary routine in evictions and [would] not withhold service of writs of eviction to investigate the neediness of the families."[23]

This fierce counterattack, for a time, appeared to put a damper on Communist-led rent strikes. In May of 1932, the *Real Estate News* described the injunction against picketing as a "body blow" that "broke the Bronx rent strikes," and events of the next six months appeared to bear out that claim. From May of 1932 to December of 1932, all articles on rent strikes in the *Bronx Home News* and the *Daily Worker* described disorders provoked by evictions rather than newly launched rent strikes—the landlords, not the strikers, appeared to have taken the offensive.[24]

However, in December of 1932 and January of 1933, the Unemployed Councils began a new wave of strikes that rapidly assumed far greater proportions than the last one. Beginning in Crotona Park East, the strikes spread into Brownsville, Williamsburg, Boro Park, the Lower East Side, and much of the East Bronx. In February of 1933, a panicked *Real Estate News* writer warned that "there are more than 200 buildings in the Borough of the Bronx in which rent strikes are in progress, and a considerably greater number in which such disturbances are brewing or in contemplation."[25] The reappearance of massive rent strikes appeared to owe less to deteriorating housing conditions than to a strategic decision by Communists to use the tactic as a component of a new campaign to mobilize the city's unemployed. During the winter of 1932–1933, Communist organizing among the unemployed expanded in breadth and effectiveness. Party leaders not only organized hunger marches on Washington, Albany, and city hall, but initiated demonstrations and sit-ins at neighborhood relief bureaus that had been set up by the state to dispense direct relief to the unemployed. The simultaneous deterioration of employment prospects in the private sector, and a growing receptivity of public officials to providing aid to the unemployed, gave Communists both a ready constituency and a target amenable to pressure. Party leaders responded by doing everything in their power to dramatize the hardship of the population and to stimulate mass action by the unemployed. Rent strikes had a proven capacity to inspire popular militancy, and the Party urged its organizations of the unemployed and neighborhood cultural groups to make rent and eviction issues primary concerns.[26]

The campaign took hold first, and most strongly, in densely packed blocks of tenements at the southeast corner of Crotona Park (a neighborhood whose huge stretches of abandoned buildings made it a national symbol of urban decay in the 1970s). During December of 1932, rent strikes broke out on Franklin Avenue, Charlotte Street, Bryant Avenue, and Boston Road, all within five blocks of each other. Attempts by landlords to break the strikes with evictions produced street battles of epic proportions. "News of the impending eviction of the Lerner and Pzelsky families spread like wildfire," wrote the *Bronx Home News* about a Franklin Avenue disorder:

> Jeers and epithets were hurled at the police as they were jostled, shoved and manhandled. . . . A woman tenant appeared on a fire escape and screamed to the crowd to do something. This time, the efforts of Sergeant Maloney and his small force were unavailing. They were overrun, kicked, clawed and scratched. For more than an hour, the battle raged. Policemen were scratched, bitten, kicked and their uniforms torn. Many of the strike sympathizers received rough handling and displayed the scars of battle when order was again restored.

Evictions on Charlotte Street, occurring two weeks later, inspired a street battle with two thousand participants. The size of these protests reflected the movement's unique ability to tap the energies and organizational skills of neighborhood women, who used networks developed in child rearing to mobilize the community and exploited the "myth of female fragility" to neutralize police attacks. "The women played a very big part in the rent strikes," one Franklin Avenue tenant wrote. "When the police went for the men, the women rushed to protect them. . . . While the men were busy looking for work, the women were on the job." "On the day of the evictions we would tell all the men to leave the building," another activist recalled. "We knew that the police were rough and would beat them up. It was the women who remained in the apartments, in order to resist. We went out onto the fire escapes and spoke through bullhorns to the crowd gathered below."[27]

By early January, strikes for rent reductions had broken out in an artists colony on the Lower East Side, in several tenements in Brownsville and Williamsburg, and in elevator apartment houses in Bronx Park East. Communist party leaders now felt they had the nucleus of a citywide movement. "With demonstrations of 3,000 to 5,000 people," wrote the *Daily Worker:*[28]

> with tenants of one house after another organizing, with block committees, unemployed council branches, workers clubs . . . uniting around tenant grievances, a hot fight against high rents and evictions is spreading through the working class sections of New York.
>
> Today is a high point in the struggle in the three main centers of conflict; the Bronx, the Avenue A section of Manhattan, and Williamsburgh.

> The battle is on! Go this morning to the nearest picket line and put up a united front, mass struggle against the greedy landlords of New York.

The Party's strategy of mobilizing its full network of organizations to picket rent-striking buildings and of organizing street rallies and protest marches through striking neighborhoods made the movement far more intimidating and effective than it had been the year before. "Yesterday, 1,500 people massed in front of 1433 Charlotte Street," one account read, "preventing the eviction of eight tenants. . . . Speaking and picketing went on all day. There were 35 speakers from the Prospect Workers Club, Bronx Workers Club, the International Labor Defense, the International Workers Order, the Women's Council, and the 170 Street Block Committee." Although evictions did occasionally take place, many tenants won substantial reductions by striking and some won reductions merely by threatening to strike. In late January of 1933, the secretary of the Bronx Landlords Protective Association warned of "scores of landlords capitulating to demands of tenants threatening to strike" and claimed that landlords' capacity to collect rent was being seriously impaired. "Rent strikes can be compared to epidemics," he asserted, "for when a strike breaks out in one apartment house, strikes start in nearby houses or landlords are forced to capitulate to threats of tenants. Some landlords have been forced to reduce their rent a number of times."[29]

Although several hundred buildings throughout the city may have been organized, the rent strike "epidemic" spread only to neighborhoods that had strong Communist party organization. The majority of participants (using names of evicted tenants or arrested protesters as a guide) were Jewish, with some representation of Italians, Slavs, and blacks. Irish-Americans, though composing a large percentage of the city's working class, were almost entirely absent from the striking group (they tended to deal with tenant grievances through their local political clubs rather than through the Left). Launched by Communists as part of a comprehensive unemployment strategy, the strike had the aura of a communal revolt by Eastern European immigrants. In neighborhoods like Crotona Park East, evicted tenants were taken in by their neighbors until they could find new housing, and tenants opposed to the strike faced intimidation and harassment. The expressive elements of the strike—the picketing, the marching, the songs sung and the slogans shouted—embodied the anxieties and hopes of people who had recently escaped an oppressive past and now faced the prospect of descent back into poverty. But despite the foreign accents and sectarian slogans, the movement had considerable force ("The entire East Bronx is full of fire," one landlord lamented). Making a worse case analysis, landlords feared that the communal pressures at the strikers' disposal would make it impossible to collect rent in large sections of the Bronx and thereby undermine the political and legal climate necessary to profitably operate rental property.[30]

By the last week of January 1933, the two major associations of Bronx landlords had developed a "concerted drive against rent strikes" which included "every legal device at their command." It included some tested tactics—a central fund to pay the mortgages and legal expenses of landlords engaged in strikes; eviction of striking tenants; requests for injunctions against rent strike picketing. But it also included some new approaches—requests for "criminal conspiracy" indictments against rent strike leaders; circulation of a "red list" of tenants who had participated in rent strikes; and demands that the mayor's office develop a coordinated program to suppress the strike. In approaching city officials, landlords emphasized the importance of "taking the streets away from the strikers," since they believed that "picketing has always been the most important weapon of Communists in conducting rent strikes."[31]

City officials and judges appeared to share this sense of urgency about the Communist "rent revolt." In late January, Mayor John O'Brien called a conference on the rent strike situation, which included the police commissioner and chief magistrate, representatives of the district attorney's office, the office of corporation counsel, and savings banks and mortgage companies. Within the next two months, several actions followed that significantly increased the risks of participation in strikes. In mid-February, Magistrate William Klapp of the Bronx Supreme Court, holding two rent strikers on charges of "criminal conspiracy," argued that they had "intimidated and threatened" tenants who were not ready to join in the strike. Two weeks later, Magistrate John McGoldrick of the Bronx Supreme Court granted an injunction restraining nontenants from picketing a house that was on strike. Finally, in the last week of March, City Corporation Counsel Edward Hilly issued a ruling that the "picketing of apartment houses in rent strike demonstrations is unlawful" and conveyed to city police "authority for the arrest of such pickets." This last action, based on the dubious ground that "there is no such thing known to law as a rent strike," represented the most serious effort by the city's law enforcement establishment to suppress the rent strike movement. Several days after it was issued, the counsel for the Bronx Landlords Protective Association claimed that the ruling "had such a sweeping effect that not a single rent strike is now in progress in the Bronx, although the borough seethed with such demonstrations before the circular was sent out."[32]

Without question, the Hilly ruling put a damper on the rent strike movement. Sporadic strikes continued to occur—in the East Bronx, in Brownsville, in the Lower East Side—but the "epidemic" quality of the movement disappeared; arrests of pickets made the strikes more difficult and dangerous to carry out. However, the Unemployed Councils did not relinquish their drive to prevent evictions of tenants or to assure that rent levels were commensurate with incomes. Instead, they changed their target from the landlord to the home relief system. During the spring and summer of 1933, Unemployed Councils throughout the city began taking large numbers of tenants to the home relief bureaus and having them sit in until they were given funds to pay rent. "In Williamsburgh," the May 19, 1933, *Daily Worker* claimed:

> half a dozen workers who refused to leave the Bureau . . . forced the Home Relief Bureau to pay the rent in spite of previous repeated refusals. In Coney Island, over 30 families secured their rent by similar actions. In Manhattan and the Bronx, the Home Relief Bureaus were forced to revoke the "no rent" order in cases of workers participating in these militant actions. . . . In Harlem, struggles against the marshall and the restoring of workers furniture to their homes hastened . . . the payment of rent to Negro families.

Three weeks later, the *Worker* claimed, "Rent checks [were] . . . being issued to nearly 500 unemployed families in the Bronx by the Home Relief Bureau . . . as a direct result of picketing, demonstrations, and anti-eviction fights led by the Unemployed Councils."[33]

The Unemployed Councils' campaign to shift the onus of preventing evictions from individual landlords to the government proved a shrewd tactic. Stymied in their effort to sustain a massive rent revolt (partly by effective repression, partly because landlords could not profitably make concessions), Party organizers found the city government amenable to collective pressure because of new funds made available by the Roosevelt administration and because of a political climate increasingly receptive to government aid to the unemployed. In June of 1933, Mayor O'Brien issued an order to city marshals instructing them to inform "the rent consultant of the home relief bureau" upon issuance of a dispossess and to give the bureau time to provide aid prior to the implementation of any eviction. In addition, if evictions did occur, marshals were ordered to guard tenants' furniture until a representative of the home relief system arrived. The thrust of this action was to make the home relief bureaus serve as a cushion for tenants who were behind in their rent, either by helping them remain in their apartments or by securing new quarters.[34]

O'Brien's program, coupled with a gradual expansion of home relief funds and the implementation of New Deal work relief programs, rapidly eased the early depression eviction crisis. Communist organizations of the unemployed still served as watchdogs for tenants with rent problems, but their actions increasingly took the form of advocacy at the relief system. Through the mid-depression years, Communist organizations of the unemployed still participated in eviction resistance, but rarely organized rent strikes. If tenants had difficulty paying their rent, Unemployed Councils (and later the Workers Alliance) took them to the relief bureaus, where they acquired semiofficial recognition as bargaining agents for the city's poor, and persuaded relief officials to release sufficient funds to keep them in their apartments.[35]

The Communist rent strike movement of the early 1930s must therefore be judged a qualified success, but in the sphere of income maintenance, not housing policy. Communist organizers did not succeed in establishing the legitimacy of the rent strike, did not leave a viable legacy of courtroom strategy, and did not develop an effective campaign for legislation aiding low-income tenants. Their analysis of the economics of housing ranged from the primitive to the nonexistent. But they did give some unemployed tenants an opportunity to resist eviction from their homes and others a chance to dramatize a level of personal suffering that the mechanisms of the private housing market could not alleviate. Unable to offer "responsible solutions" to tenant problems, they helped force government into an income strategy that gave unemployed tenants a much-needed sense of security.

Housing Reform and the Roots of the City-Wide Tenants Council

The decline of Communist-led rent strikes left something of a vacuum in grass roots tenant activism. Rent strikes and militant tenant associations did not reappear on a significant scale until the summer and fall of 1934, and they were launched under different auspices and among very different constituencies.

Nevertheless, the years 1933 and 1934 saw the emergence of a powerful housing reform coalition in New York City, rooted in settlement houses and philanthropic organizations, but with a significant base in the administration of a newly elected mayor, Fiorello La Guardia. Concerned with deteriorating conditions among the city's two million inhabitants of old law tenements, reformers lobbied for the construction of low-rent public housing and the improvement of health and living conditions in the city's slums. By the time a grass roots tenant movement did reemerge, the reformers represented a formidable ally, offering tenant leaders office space, funds, and help with lobbying on issues of common concern.

One important component of the reform coalition was the Lower East Side Public Housing Conference. Organized in a neighborhood with the largest concentration of old law tenements in the city (and the highest rates of foreclosure and tax delinquency), the conference brought together settlement houses, mothers clubs, and religious organizations to lobby for housing reforms that could not be won on a neighborhood level. Led by professional social workers, it organized delegations of slum dwellers to Washington and Albany, published a journal, took legislators on tours of the slums, and sponsored a Better Housing Week to raise public awareness of the need for government-funded low-income housing. A brilliant advocate for slum dwellers, it avoided organizing individual buildings or engaging in confrontations with landlords; its forte was legitimizing once-controversial legislative proposals.[36]

The Emergency Committee on Tenement Safety represented a group of comparable origins and purposes, organized by the city's settlement houses to "obtain passage of housing legislation to provide minimum standards of safety, health, and decency for tenement dwellers." Spurred by a rash of fire deaths in old law tenements, the committee lobbied for four bills reforming the state Multiple Dwellings Law: one requiring the fire retarding of halls and stairs within two years, another requiring a toilet for every family within two years, the third prohibiting the use of rooms without windows after January 1, 1939, and the fourth conferring on the Tenement House Department broader powers to order the demolition of abandoned buildings that constituted a nuisance. The bills, passed during the 1934 session of the legislature, gave the Tenement House Department significant weapons to press for the upgrading, or eventual demolition, of tenements that did not meet minimum standards of health and safety.[37]

Another important asset of the housing reform movement was the support it received from Mayor Fiorello La Guardia and his tenement housing commissioner, Langdon Post. Post and La Guardia used their offices to lobby for the construction of public housing, and Post proved singularly effective in using his authority to force the abandonment and demolition of hazardous slum properties. A forceful advocate of political mobilization by slum tenants, Post, during his first three years in office, forced the abandonment of over fifteen hundred tenements and pressed the owners of thousands more to upgrade their properties. Beginning his efforts at a time when there was a high vacancy rate in slum neighborhoods (due to evictions and doubling up of families), Post's policies, combined with massive slum clearance by New Deal agencies and an improvement in the economic climate, contributed to a significant tightening of the housing market by the end of 1936. Convinced that government-sponsored housing was the only permanent solution to the housing needs of the poor, Post announced he was "going to create a housing shortage because that is the only way we will get decent housing." The actual *pace* of public housing construction fell short of Post's hopes (as of the fall of 1936, only one low-income project, First Houses, had been erected in New York City, with two more under construction), but his definition of reform priorities coincided with that of liberal housing advocates and a new wave of tenant organizers that emerged in the mid-depression.[38]

The Rebirth of Activism

During the summer and fall of 1934, two rent strike movements erupted that were to have a lasting impact on organized tenant activity in New York. The first of these, launched among middle-class blacks in Harlem's Sugar Hill, led to the formation of the Consolidated Tenants League; the second, among tenants of Knickerbocker Village, a large limited-dividend housing development on the Lower East Side, produced the Knickerbocker Village Tenants Association. Both strikes achieved success employing sophisticated legal and public relations strategies disdained by early-depression Communists and openly welcomed the help of housing reformers inside and outside of government. Each movement generated tenant organizations of great permanence and strength, the leadership of which played key roles in the rebirth of a citywide tenant movement.

The Harlem rent strike of 1934 erupted in a neighborhood undergoing rapid ethnic change and among a population that had become highly politicized during the depression. The first building to go on strike, 281 Edgecombe Avenue, was a large, modern elevator building that was changing from white to black tenancy; many of its first black residents were lawyers, doctors, and entertainers. But the black residents of the building soon discovered that the status of moving to a Sugar Hill address came at the price of rents nearly double that charged former white residents, of elevators that seldom worked, and of poor building maintenance. This kind of profiteering at the expense of black tenants had occurred throughout Harlem's emergence as a black community, and in another time, the tenants might have gritted their teeth and accepted the situation. But in 1934, Harlemites increasingly turned to the boycott and the picket line to solve their problems. The community was the scene of a boycott of store owners on 125th Street to force them to hire black clerks; of sit-ins and protests to force nondiscriminatory relief policies; and of marches and rallies to free the Scottsboro Boys. The tenants of 281 Edgecombe, having seen the effectiveness of such tactics (the 125th Street boycott and the relief campaigns achieved major victories), decided to apply them to their own situation; they called a rent strike and began picketing the building to demand lower rents and better building conditions. At the same time, they retained two skilled attorneys,

Julius Archibald and Vernal Williams, to represent their interests in municipal court.[39]

The Edgecome strike, the *Amsterdam News* asserted, "fired the minds . . . of Harlemites who have long suffered under the burden of exorbitant rents." Tenants in several other buildings launched strikes for lower rents, and the buildings involved formed a United Tenants League to coordinate their demands. By mid-September of 1934, the movement, helped by near-unanimous tenant support and intimidating mass picketing (which the La Guardia–appointed corporation counsel did not try to stop), won victories in all the buildings it had organized; owners agreed to reductions of three to ten dollars a month plus repairs.[40]

News of the strike's success brought dozens of requests for aid from tenants throughout Harlem and inspired strike leaders to form a permanent organization. In October of 1934, they joined with leaders of a group that had organized rent strikes on 150th Street—the New York Tenants League—into a Consolidated Tenants League and began offering negotiation services and legal representation to Harlem tenants willing to pay the organization's dues (two dollars initiation, two dollars per year). From the time of Consolidated's founding, its major leaders, chairman Donellan Phillips and attorney Vernal Williams, perceived it as a professional service organization capable of supporting a full-time staff. Committed participants in Harlem's struggle for racial justice (Consolidated took part in numerous campaigns against racial discrimination in housing and employment), they also observed that Harlem's unique housing conditions enabled people with legal and organizational skills to pursue tenant advocacy as a career. Harlem's landlords, their rents inflated by discrimination, could afford to make substantial concessions without sacrificing "reasonable" profit; organizers with the talents to extract such concessions could find a large market for their services, especially among middle-class blacks. Harlem Communists, who had worked within Consolidated from the beginning, did not know what to make of this approach; in 1934, they attacked Consolidated leaders for their "opportunism"; two years later, they courted their support. But the strategy worked. By 1938 Consolidated claimed over five thousand dues-paying members and supported a full-time staff of organizers and lawyers.[41]

Consolidated's great contribution, Heinz Norden of the City-Wide Tenants Council claimed, was its development of an effective "legal defense of tenants brought to court by landlord's actions." Consolidated's lead attorney, Vernal Williams (who had earlier won notoriety for his defense of Marcus Garvey), proved to be expert in using every available statute, along with judicial delays and appeals to common sense, to persuade judges to postpone evictions and serve as mediators between landlords and tenants. Sometimes using section 1436(a) of the Civil Practice Act to win six-month postponements of rent increases (giving landlords a strong incentive to make a deal), sometimes claiming that landlords had violated "proper consideration" in failing to provide promised services, sometimes claiming that multiple violations provided grounds for six-month stays of eviction, Williams developed an extraordinary track record in winning reversals of rent increases and agreements to improve building service. "It is not too much to say that an entire new body of tenant law was created in Harlem," Heinz Norden asserted. "For the first time, tenants began to get a break in the courts." Williams's success, in striking contrast to that of Communist lawyers in the early 1930s, derived from his deference to the judges and the reasonableness of his claims as well as his legal expertise. Consolidated's lawyers always proclaimed their willingness to negotiate and their respect for the profit margins of landlords, and judges in Harlem's municipal court (who saw Williams and other Consolidated attorneys literally hundreds of times) learned to regard a Consolidated case, almost by definition, as well prepared and reasonable. Some of this experience did not easily translate to the rest of the city (the magnitude of the rent discrimination faced by Harlemites, including black public officials, contributed to a protenant atmosphere in the Harlem municipal court). But Consolidated's courtroom success provided encouragement to tenant activists elsewhere seeking a balance between mass action and legal representation.[42]

The Knickerbocker Village rent strike, employing appeals to public officials and the media more than courtroom advocacy, provided an equally innovative model of tenant organization. The setting of this conflict was a sixteen-hundred-unit complex located in a deteriorated neighborhood just north of the Brooklyn Bridge (Manhattan side), which had been financed with a loan from the Reconstruction Finance Corporation that limited its developers to a 6 percent profit and rents of no more than $12.50 per room. Designed as a model project for middle-class New Yorkers, Knickerbocker Village attracted a tenant population of young, college-educated professionals—professors, architects, social workers, teachers, lawyers, civil servants, and businessmen. Arriving on moving day with high expectations, they found the buildings unfinished and the management poorly prepared for their arrival. Elevators did not work; apartments lacked finished floors, bathroom and kitchen fixtures, and painted walls; "model" features of the development—laundry rooms, radio hookups, children's playrooms—proved inoperable or poorly equipped. Worse yet, management representatives, failing to take tenant complaints seriously, offered insolent responses or avoided contact altogether.[43]

Knickerbocker Village residents, who had developed an instant camaraderie during the move-in fiasco (and who were not accustomed to this treatment in their professional lives), swiftly mobilized to ease their predicament. Less than three weeks after moving day (October 1, 1934), over six hundred Villagers came to a meeting at a local public school and voted to withhold their next month's rent unless management agreed to a long list of demands, including repairs of apartments, elevators, and public areas, and reimbursement of tenants for moving expenses. The strategy tenants pursued demonstrated a shrewd understanding of politics, public relations, and the weight conferred by their own professional status (the strike committee had forty-four lawyers and seventeen journalists among its supporters). Within one week, the strike committee had set up meetings with the mayor, the State Housing Board, and the Village management (the Fred M. French Company), and had managed to secure four full-length articles in the *New York Times*. In addition, the strikers formed a legal defense committee, a newsletter, and a social activities committee to help firm up their support with the rest of the tenants. By mid-November the Knickerbocker Village management, reeling under the force of this organizational blitzkrieg, agreed to negotiate; a compromise was reached that resulted in repairs of unfinished apartments and nearly $25,000 in reimbursements to aggrieved tenants.[44]

The successful strike generated tremendous esprit de corps among politically active tenants. One week after the French Company settled tenant claims, strike leaders announced that they were forming a permanent Knickerbocker Village Tenants Association to undertake a program of cultural and educational activities within the housing complex. The tenant leaders, ranging politically from New Dealers to Communists, approached the association as an opportunity to create a social and cultural environment that reflected the "activist" currents of the time, but they ran up against the grim opposition of the French Company, which saw the association as a threat to its control of the project. The company refused to grant meeting space to the association, set up a rival tenant group, funded an antiassociation newsletter, and finally, in the summer of 1935, informed seventeen association leaders that their leases would not be renewed because of their "evident unhappiness" with conditions in the project.[45]

The effort to evict association leaders, even more than the strike, radicalized many residents of the project. Although the association lost an eleven-month court battle to force renewal of the leases, it used the issue of arbitrary management tactics to expand its following among the tenants and create strong ties with public officials, journalists, and civic organizations concerned with housing reform. To the French Company's dismay, a whole new group of association leaders emerged who expanded its cultural and political activities, kept its newsletter alive, and expanded association membership to over a thousand tenants, thus swamping its management-sponsored rival. "Knickerbocker Village became a beehive of activity," one tenants leader recalled, "one of the most interesting places in New York to live in." For the new tenant leadership, the recalcitrance of the French Company became a metaphor for the problems all tenants faced in winning recognition of their rights to free association and collective bargaining, and they became evangelists for tenant activism in their Lower East Side neighborhood and the city as a whole.[46]

The Knickerbocker Village leaders possessed some unique assets in their efforts to serve as the catalysts for a citywide tenant movement. First, they possessed professional skills, and they projected a cosmopolitan style that no militant tenant activists had previously commanded. College educated and "Americanized" (no foreign accents here, even among the "ethnics"), they combined a romantic faith in mass action with a hardheaded knowledge of the law, public relations, and the legislative process. Second, their radicalism, although sincere, lacked the rough edges displayed by immigrant Socialists and Communists. Recent converts to the Left, they affected a nonpartisan aura that never compromised their professional expertise or jeopardized smooth social relations with liberals. Third, they had the backing of a strong, stable tenant association that provided both a model and a source of financial and political support for their activities. At a time when housing reform had become a major issue in city politics, Knickerbocker Village activities were uniquely situated to bring together a grass roots tenant movement that sought links with liberal reformers in the settlement houses and the city government.

The Citywide Tenants Council

Very early in their association's history, Knickerbocker Village tenant leaders displayed interest in broadening their base of operations. In 1935, with the cosponsorship of the Lower East Side Public Housing Conference, they formed a City-Wide Housing Conference, only to see it disintegrate. "Letterheads were printed, and about a dozen affiliates obtained," one activitist recalled, "but the movement . . . failed to catch on." In March of 1936, Knickerbocker Village leaders made another attempt at citywide organization, this time with a more activist orientation. Inspired by the support displayed by tenants for striking building service workers (which at Knickerbocker Village and other middle-income developments took the form of picket lines, fund-raising, and harassment of strikebreakers), KV leaders decided that "the time had come to set up a permanent tenant group in defense of tenant rights." Gaining the support of the Consolidated Tenants League, the only other tenant organization in the city with a secure popular base, KV leaders invited representatives of eighteen other tenant associations (most from individual buildings) to a meeting at the Mecca

Temple to rally support for the building service strikers and create a new tenant organization. Featuring speeches by Congressman Vito Marcantonio, Building Service Union leader James Bambrick, and Newspaper Guild leader Heywood Broun (all of whom advised tenants to employ labor union tactics), the meeting attracted two thousand participants, five hundred of whom signed cards displaying interest in a citywide organization. Several weeks later, the organizing committee, dominated by Knickerbocker Village representatives, held its first meeting at an office donated by a sympathetic businessman. The group constituted itself as a direct membership organization—the City-Wide Tenants League, and elected Heinz Norden, an editor and translator from Knickerbocker Village, as its first chairman.[47]

Norden, who served as City-Wide's major leader for the first four years of its existence, represented the quintessential "Popular Front personality." A skilled writer, administrator, and speaker, Norden viewed the Communist party as the major inspirational force on the Left and was willing to defer to its judgment on matters of national and international policy so long as it did not compromise his sense of professionalism or interfere with his day-to-day activities. He sought the help of Party organizations in building City-Wide, while carefully avoiding direct Party control. But at the same time, he never encouraged any policy or relationship that might offend Party activists, whose skills and labor the movement needed. Norden felt most comfortable in a coalition of liberals and radicals, and he helped endow City-Wide with an "ecumenical" air that allowed it to thrive at a time when Communists had discarded much of their revolutionary bravado and some of their sectarian arrogance in the interests of fighting fascism.

For the first five months of its existence, the new organization had rough sledding. First, the predominantly middle-class tenants who helped found the organization drifted away once the building trades strike ended. With the exception of the Knickerbocker Village Tenants Association, none of the building organizations activated during the strike displayed any long-term stability. Second, Consolidated Tenants League leaders, who represented the largest tenant association in the city, resented the direct membership structure of City-Wide. Dependent on membership dues for their employment, they did not want City-Wide to compete with them for individual members. These problems might have been insurmountable had not City-Wide's hard-pressed leadership discovered two new constituencies: working-class tenants seeking help with individual housing complaints and left wing unions and civic groups seeking advice on housing policy. As Norden described it:[48]

> Word about the Tenants League had got into the newspapers and a procession of tenants from the slums began to appear at its . . . office with immediate, concrete problems—rent rises, dispossess proceed-

> ings, landlord-tenant disputes. Somehow, the League always managed to have a volunteer lawyer in court, an organizer in the house, and slowly but surely it began to chalk up its first victories in the form of settlements and court decisions. It also embarked on the activity which proved to advance its fortunes more than any other. It sent speakers to address union, civic, fraternal and political groups—anyone who would listen.

During the fall of 1936, City-Wide leaders began to develop a new organizing strategy. First, they decided to change City-Wide's structure from a membership organization to a federation of self-governing neighborhood tenant associations. The function of the central office would be to develop legal and legislative strategy, coordinate fund-raising and public relations, and conduct an educational program on housing issues for organized tenants and the entire "progressive" community. Second, they decided to promote the formation of tenant associations in slum neighborhoods. The first experiment with this policy took place on the Lower East Side. City-Wide organizers enlisted the support of settlement house leaders and social workers (themselves deluged with housing complaints) in the creation of a Joint Committee for Tenants Organizing. After several months of canvasing houses, holding public meetings, and handling individual complaints, the committee felt it had sufficient support to create a permanent organization, which it called the East Side Tenants Union. In November of 1936, the new group, along with City-Wide itself, moved into donated headquarters in the Church of All Nations and began soliciting membership and organizing tenants. Within a month, the group had several hundred members and three dynamic leaders—Wilma Saunders, Sophie Black, and Marcia Moore.[49]

In December of 1936, two crises erupted in low-income neighborhoods which dramatized the salience of City-Wide's new strategy and helped put the organization on the map. The first took place among six hundred families living in tenements that had been condemned by the city to make way for the South Bronx approach to the Triborough Bridge. To hasten their departure, officials responsible for the bridge construction (headed by Robert Moses) stopped providing services in the tenements and announced the start of demolition just two weeks before Christmas. When tenants and local businessmen protested these policies, City-Wide leaders offered help in publicizing their grievances. Under their direction, neighborhood residents began picketing city hall, sending delegations to relief officials and sympathetic legislators, and holding mass meetings in the community to which the press was invited. The campaign embarrassed city officials and won major concessions, including a stay of demolition, the restoration of building services, the granting of emergency food, clothing, and medical care, and the payment of moving expenses by the Emergency Relief Bureau. City-Wide emerged from the campaign with considerable credibility in the neighborhood (a South Bronx Tenants League later formed nearby) and with a strategy to insure fair treatment of tenants displaced by government construction projects.[50]

Less than a week after this crisis broke, a group of savings banks owning property on the Lower East Side decided to board up tenements under their control rather than comply with the fire retarding and sanitary requirements of the Multiple Dwellings Law, whose deadline for compliance was January 1, 1937. Over seven hundred families on the Lower East Side (and an unknown number of others in other poor neighborhoods) received eviction notices that gave them less than a month to find new quarters in the dead of winter. Worse yet, this action came when, according to the *New York Times*, New York was "on the verge of a shortage of low rent housing that many observers fear may be as grave as that of 1921." More than forty thousand apartments had been removed from the low-rent market since 1933 (through demolition, abandonment, and transfer to nonresidential use), and evictees faced grave difficulty finding quarters at comparable rents. The East Side Tenants Union, less than a month old, leaping into the fray, threw up picket lines around the banks in question and sent delegations to the tenement house commissioner and the mayor demanding that the evictions be postponed and that tenants be assured of full services until they could find other quarters at comparable rents. In response to these complaints, and the equally vociferous protests of settlement house leaders, the mayor directed the New York City Housing Authority to hold hearings to help find a solution to the problem.[51]

The hearings, held during the last two weeks of December 1936, provided an excellent opportunity for City-Wide to publicize its work and recruit new affiliates. City-Wide leaders used the occasion to present a Tenants Housing Program that offered solutions to the immediate crisis and suggested long-term remedies for low-income tenants. For the bank evictions, City-Wide offered a solution based on the Triborough Bridge settlement: stays of eviction, intervention by the city to assure proper services to tenants, and payment by the Emergency Relief Bureau of the moving expenses of tenants forced to leave. It categorically rejected postponing enforcement of the Multiple Dwelling Law, preferring to see tenements closed or repairs charged to landlords rather than the persistence of dangerous conditions. As long-term solutions, City-Wide proposed a moratorium on evictions, the passage of laws prohibiting rent increases in buildings containing violations, the passage of a "prior lien" law allowing the city to make repairs in tenements and charge them to landlords, the large-scale construction of low-rent public housing, and the passage of laws prohibiting racial discrimination in the renting of apartments or the fixing of rent levels. This program, presented in a low-key, professional manner, affirmed City-Wide's ties with liberal housing advocates, but it also helped City-Wide recruit a grass roots tenant advocacy group, based in the Brownsville section of Brooklyn, called Brooklyn Rentpayers. Rentpayers representatives at the hearings (who had the same "progressive" political views as City-Wide leaders) immediately endorsed the Tenants Housing Program and expressed interest in affiliating. Their recruitment gave City-Wide the critical mass of local affiliates it needed to complete the transition to a tenants federation. In late December of 1936, at a meeting in Harlem, the organization changed its name to the City-Wide Tenants Council and elected Donelan Phillips of Consolidated as its chairman and Heinz Norden as its executive secretary. The council's charter members included three neighborhood tenants associations—the Consolidated Tenants League, the Brooklyn Rentpayers, and the East Side Tenants Union—along with the Knickerbocker Village Tenants Association and the Lower East Side Public Housing Conference. With this composition, the council could legitimately claim to represent the interest of slum tenants, even though much of the leadership at its central office was middle class.[52]

During 1937 the council experienced substantial growth; it added more than ten new affiliates and emerged as the recognized voice of tenants' interests in the municipal courts, the city housing bureaucracy, and the city council and state legislature. Drawing upon ties with settlement houses, left wing trade unions, and unemployed organizations, council organizers helped form local tenant leagues in the South and East Bronx, Williamsburg, Flushing, midtown Manhattan, Greenwich Village, Chelsea, Yorkville, Coney Island, and downtown Brooklyn. At the same time, the council recruited a volunteer "staff" of more than one hundred lawyers (through the left wing National Lawyers Guild); developed a housing research component (with the help of the left wing Federation of Architects, Engineers, Chemists, and Technicians); and developed a lobbying operation in concert with three key organizations involved in housing reform—the Charity Organization Society, the Housing Committee of the United Neighborhood Houses, and the Housing Section of the Welfare Council.[53]

The City-Wide Tenants Council's growth, accomplished entirely with volunteer labor (it had eight to ten unpaid organizers on staff), reflected the genuine need for tenant advocacy in the city's poor neighborhoods, where housing conditions had become unsettled. Rapidly declining vacancy rates, the impact of slum clearance projects and public works, and the abandonment and upgrading of tenements as a result of code enforcement left many poor tenants vulnerable to arbitrary evictions and rent increases. As City-Wide gained publicity for defending low-income tenants, its organizers found themselves deluged with individual requests for help. Recognizing that they lacked the resources to help all complainants on a one-to-one basis, they tried to encourage tenants to create self-sufficient building organizations that enlisted the support of activist organizations in their neighborhood for picketing and publicity. In neighborhoods where a critical mass of buildings organized themselves, City-Wide organizers fostered the creation of neighborhood tenant leagues that had the capacity to handle complaints themselves.[54]

The style of organizing City-Wide employed, both from its central office and its neighborhood leagues, represented a shrewd combination of mass protest tactics and legal representation. Unlike tenant organizers in the early 1930s, City-Wide organizers employed mass picketing and rent withholding only after other strategies failed and only when they had strong assurances that tenants would not be penalized for their use. Convinced that the tenant movement would be built by practical victories, City-Wide organizers encouraged tenants to meticulously build their case by recording violations, getting inspectors to buildings, and initiating negotiations with landlords. "*If* the landlord refuses to negotiate," Heinz Norden wrote, "*if* there are violations of the law or patent unfairness on the part of the landlord; and *if* there is sufficient support and sentiment on the part of the tenants, picketing may be resorted to and as a last resort, a rent strike declared. The Council, however, realizes that the rent strike is to be invoked *only* if all other methods fail, and then only if there is a good chance of success." When conducting a strike, council organizers insisted that strict financial controls be employed (with money deposited in a trustees account and possibly with the court) and that picketing be conducted with precision and care. "The Council . . . stays strictly within the law," Norden boasted. "In only one instance was a City-Wide organizer ever arrested and none was convicted of any offense."[55]

Despite Norden's strictures, City-Wide affiliates, if pressed, could play rough. In October of 1937, two leaders of Brooklyn Rentpayers chained themselves to the door of a Brownsville building to prevent the eviction of two families on rent strike. Rentpayer pickets at the building engaged in a shoving match with the police when they tried to unlock the protesters. But unlike their early 1930s counterparts, Rentpayer organizers did not define the police as the enemy. Indeed, they accepted the offer of a local precinct captain to mediate the dispute and agreed to the setlement he worked out. The incident dramatized two key features of City-Wide strategy: a willingness to submit disputes to third-party mediation (or arbitration) and the use of the strike as a precise instrument to win concessions, rather than a generalized instrument of neighborhood rebellion.[56]

With this mixture of militancy and caution, City-Wide affiliates seem to have accumulated a good track record in winning gains for tenants they represented (in November of 1937, City-Wide claimed it had won settlements for tenants in twenty-six buildings around the city). Their success ratio—much higher than that of early 1930s groups—stemmed from a number of sources. First, City-Wide organizers simply did not defend tenants unless they had solid grievances and did a great deal of the work in organizing their building and negotiating with the landlord. Second, City-Wide had energetic and talented young lawyers at its disposal who shared information about how to handle tenant grievances (for example, City-Wide lawyers discovered that most "notices of rent increases were not in the form required by law" and could be easily challenged on a technicality). Third, the legal climate facing organized tenants had changed for the better from the early 1930s. By 1939, as a result of a series of landmark cases (and a political climate more conducive to collective protest), most municipal judges recognized the right of tenants to picket in rent disputes. Rent strikes proved to be a more questionable proposition, but judges generally declined to evict if tenants paid their back rent on demand. Finally, City-Wide affiliates could draw upon the Communist party network to staff picket lines should rent disputes enter the "militant" stage. Almost every City-Wide neighborhood affiliate had a working relationship with a local unit of the Workers Alliance—the Communist-led organization of the unemployed—and many had close ties with American Labor party clubs. These two organizations could be counted on to supply pickets, speakers for street rallies, and members for delegations to landlords or the municipal courts, which gave tenant leagues added political muscle in local disputes.[57]

The effectiveness of City-Wide's tactics in handling individual building disputes, despite the hopes of its organizers, did not result in the development of stable membership organizations "on the trade union model." Most tenants, City-Wide leaders recall, lost interest in the organization once their individual grievances were settled, and individual building organizations, except in large developments, generally disintegrated quickly. Even the neighborhood tenant leagues, some of which lasted for years, generally depended upon the enthusiasm of a handful of volunteer lawyers and organizers rather than a stable dues-paying membership (Consolidated was the one exception). Depression-idled professionals, rather than slum tenants, proved to be the glue that held City-Wide together. Solving the problems of slum tenants simultaneously appealed to their idealism and enabled them to hone skills and make connections that might be useful to their careers. Lawyers, architects, writers, and public relations experts gravitated to City-Wide in sufficient numbers to keep the organization going despite the absence of sufficient funds to hire a full-time staff. By 1940 City-Wide claimed more than twenty affiliates in city neighborhoods and government-sponsored housing developments and had helped publicize effective methods of tenant advocacy to scores of left wing trade unions and neighborhood organizations. Not a mass movement by any stretch of the imagination, it had helped bring important legal, technical, and organizational resources into the lives of slum tenants and had helped some stave off rent increases and improve conditions in their buildings.[58]

City-Wide also played an important role in the political arena: it contributed a "tenant perspective" to public deliberations on issues like the construction of low-income housing, code enforcement, rent control, and strategies of urban redevelopment. It mobilized tenant delegations to meetings of the city council, state legislature, and U.S. Congress; issued annual Tenants Housing Programs with specific legislative recommendations; and represented tenant interests through its seats on the board of the Citizens Housing Council, a high-powered housing reform organization founded in 1937. Skilled in mobilizing slum tenants for demonstrations and lobbying, City-Wide organizers also helped bring left wing unions and American Labor party clubs into the housing reform coalition, which added to its political influence on a statewide level. Sympathetic to the Communist party, City-Wide organizers, Heinz Norden observed, "influenced . . . the Socialists and the Communists far more than vice versa. . . . before the tenants movement got under way, the radicals seem to have paid very little attention to housing."[59]

The legislative activities of City-Wide resulted in some accomplishments and some disappointments. On the question of code enforcement, City-Wide found itself at odds with a new policy of the La Guardia administration to use market mechanisms to encourage repairs, rather than administrative action to force them. During the winter of 1937, the mayor, despite City-Wide's vociferous protests, supported a six-month moratorium on the fire retarding and upgrading of old law tenements. When City-Wide and its allies won the passage of a prior lien bill in the state legislature (allowing the city to repair violations in old law tenements and charge the repairs to landlords), the city council passed regulations crippling enforcement of the bill and appropriated limited funds to implement it. With a growing shortage of low-income housing (and in response to pressure from landlords and banks), La Guardia decided to give code enforcement lower priority. In 1938 he replaced Langdon Post with Alfred Rhenstein, "a builder with close ties to banking and realty groups," and instituted a policy aimed at offering positive incentives (tax incentives and rehabilitation loans) to tenement owners seeking to upgrade their properties. As a result, the boarding up of tenements slowed considerably in the late 1930s, and what rehabilitation did occur often resulted in increased rents.[60]

On the issue of government construction of public housing, City-Wide registered slightly greater success. Along with other public housing advocates, it lobbied successfully for the passage of the federal Housing Act of 1937, which made subsidies and loans available to states that wished to construct low-income housing. One year later, City-Wide lobbied for the passage of a public housing amendment to the New York State Constitution and supported the La Guardia administration's efforts to construct low-income projects with available funds. But the size of the public housing program in the city fell short of City-Wide's expectations. The federal government appropriated less than a billion dollars for public housing (much of it in loans, not direct subsidies) rather than the 10 billion City-Wide recommended. The state legislature failed to appropriate the $300 million for public housing that the constitutional amendment had authorized. Although the city government did accelerate its construction of low-income housing, all the projects together accommodated slightly more than ten thousand families at the beginning of World War II. This represented an important gain for low-income tenants, but not the systematic effort to rebuild the slums that City-Wide had hoped for.[61]

City-Wide's agitation for rent control did not, in the late 1930s, result in a centrally administered system limiting rent increases and prohibiting evictions, but it did help pass the Minkoff Act of 1939, which prohibited rent increases in old law tenements that did not comply fully with the provisions of the Multiple Dwellings Act. Since over 90 percent of old law tenements contained major violations, this bill represented a form of rent control for low-income tenants. Introduced by an American Labor party assemblyman from the Bronx, supported by major housing reform groups and the city administration, the Minkoff Act reflected an alliance of liberals and the Left that would have been impossible five years before, a coalition that City-Wide did much to bring together.[62]

City-Wide's lobbying with city bureaucracies, in some respects, exceeded its legislative work in importance and effectiveness. During 1937, City-Wide and the Workers Alliance conducted a successful campaign to force the Emergency Relief Bureau to scale rents to the type of housing clients occupied as well as to the size of their families, thereby protecting clients from displacement during the upgrading of tenement properties. City-Wide also placed steady pressure on the New York City Housing Authority to influence the location, eligibility requirements, and patterns of tenant recruitment in New York City housing projects. City-Wide instructed its neighborhood affiliates to lobby for housing projects in their communities and supply Housing Authority officials with names of eligible tenants. Once projects were constructed, City-Wide organized tenant associations in them. By 1941 tenant associations had become strong in several of the larger projects—Red Hook, Vladek, Williamsburg, and Queensbridge—

and had won priority access to public facilities and informal recognition of their right to negotiate for individual tenants (especially on the sensitive issue of "income ceilings" for project residents).[63]

The breadth of City-Wide's concerns, and the range of its organizational linkages, certainly surpassed those of any previous tenant organization in the city's history. City-Wide's shifting group of volunteer lawyers, organizers, and researchers accumulated expert knowledge of the legal representation of tenants, the economics and politics of housing, and the operation of city housing and relief bureaucracies. The sophistication of City-Wide's legislative proposals and public relations work equaled that of the real estate lobby and traditional housing reform organizations. But the organizational structure that sustained this effort proved fragile. Never did City-Wide's fund-raising produce over one thousand dollars per year. Only in 1939 did it acquire the funds to hire a full-time staff member, and it paid him the munificent sum of fifteen dollars per week. The slum tenants who benefited most from City-Wide's work lacked the resources to subsidize it, or the political skills and inclinations to build the kind of stable organizations that could give City-Wide real permanence. City-Wide survived on the politically motivated idealism and skills of underemployed professionals, both of which were vulnerable to shifts in the political climate and improvements in the economy.[64]

The Wartime Tenants Movement and the Struggle for Rent Control: Organizational Diffusion and Political Success

The coming of World War II had an unsettling effect on the organized tenant movement in New York City, particularly on the City-Wide Tenants Council. The core group of volunteer activists who kept the organization going, most of them sympathetic to the Communist party, followed Party priorities in allocating their energies and defining City-Wide's political stance. From the signing of the Nazi-Soviet Pact to Hitler's invasion of the Soviet Union, they imparted a strong antiwar tone to City-Wide's work by accusing the president and Congress of taking needed funds away from the federal low-rent housing program to subsidize war preparations. Once the Soviet Union and the United States entered the war, this group made a complete about-face and urged City-Wide affiliates to "Assist the Work of Civil Defense" and participate in "Help Win the War Activities." Key male leaders of the organization, such as Heinz Norden and Donald Schoolman, along with scores of lawyers and local organizers, caught up in the Left-approved spirit of patriotism, volunteered for the armed forces. Talented women leaders replaced them, notably Grace Aviles and Catherine Masters, but their advocacy of tenant issues, given their political perspective, inevitably became fused with the task of mobilizing the civilian population to provide support for the armed forces (blood and clothing drives) and to serve as monitors against "profiteering" in the consumer economy. As a result, the more organizationally fragile locals of City-Wide gradually disintegrated or fused with the left wing consumers movement. By 1943 City-Wide, renamed the United Tenants League in deference to the "Win the War" spirit, had become a much smaller organization, with its primary base in city housing projects and limited-dividend developments such as Knickerbocker Village rather than in neighborhood tenant leagues.[65]

However, the gradual decline of the City-Wide Tenants Council did not mean that tenant activism ceased or that the interests of low-income tenants lost all weight in the political arena. Rather, techniques of tenant protest and advocacy, in the courtroom, the city bureaucracy, and the legislative arena, spread to a wide range of progressive organizations—American Labor party clubs, civil rights organizations, neighborhood consumer councils, and CIO unions. Possessing far greater resources than City-Wide, these organizations, employing methods City-Wide activists pioneered, facilitated their own organizational growth. Concentrating on two main issues, rent levels and evictions, they helped engineer one of the most far-reaching victories in the history of the New York tenant movement: the imposition by the Office of Price Administration of a system of wartime rent controls covering all of New York City.[66]

The federal government's experiment in the setting of rent levels came as a result of a nationwide decline in housing construction, exacerbated by a migration to cities of workers seeking employment in defense industries. In many urban areas, a rapid tightening of the housing market occurred, marked by overcrowding and rapid rent increases. The federal government responded to the housing shortage (and the shortage of other consumer commodities) by passing the Emergency Price Control Act of 1942 and establishing an Office of Price Administration with the power to freeze rents and prices in designated localities. Shortly after the act was passed, the United Tenants League, the Citizens Housing Council, and consumer organizations began to press Mayor La Guardia to have the OPA immediately freeze rents in New York City. La Guardia made such a request, but the OPA, claiming the city's vacancy rate (7.5 percent in 1940) was too high for mandatory controls, initially refused to take action. It did declare the city a "defense rental area," but instead called for a voluntary limit on rent increases, monitored by the mayor's office.[67]

The failure of the OPA to impose rent controls became the rallying point for a coalition of civil rights organizations and left wing political groups. In Harlem, where the housing market was particularly tight, city councilman Adam Clayton Powell, Jr., mobilized the People's Committee that had engineered his election to collect one hundred thousand signatures on a petition to have Harlem declared a "war emergency area" subject to immediate controls. The Consolidated Tenants League, handling scores of cases of buildings facing rent increases, supported the campaign; the league claimed that Harlem landlords consistently violated voluntary restraints. And Communist party clubs, left wing unions, and the National Negro Congress joined the drive by collecting petitions among their followers and even organizing rent strikes in individual buildings.[68]

In other parts of the city, the "progressive" wing of the American Labor party (which had split into pro-Communist and anti-Communist factions after the Nazi-Soviet Pact) made the struggle for rent control a major political priority. Congressman Vito Marcantonio, an advocate of rent control and public housing who employed "tenant clinics" as part of his service operation, pressed the issue on a federal level, but ALP candidates throughout the city also made rent control an issue in their campaigns for the assembly and the city council. Michael Quill, head of the Transport Workers Union and a power in the CIO industrial union council, campaigned on the rent control issue in seeking (successfully) a council seat from the Bronx, as did CP-ALP candidates Benjamin Davis, Jr. (from Harlem), and Peter Cacchione (from Brooklyn). At a time when the Communist Left generally eschewed confrontation tactics, consumer issues emerged as a "respectable" form of militancy, with the struggle for price stability assuming the character of a patriotic crusade. All over the city, ALP clubs (following the Marcantonio model) began setting up in their offices tenant clinics that served as advocates in landlord-tenant disputes, and occasionally they employed rent strikes. Staffed largely by women, some of whom had worked with City-Wide in its heyday, these organizations became heirs of a tradition of neighborhood tenant activism at a time when City-Wide lost the power to sustain it.[69]

The struggle for rent control, supported by the mayor, the city's Left, liberal housing groups, and a neighborhood consumer movement, assumed added urgency as a result of the riot that broke out in Harlem on August 1, 1943. The looting, window smashing, and battles with police that erupted that night provoked a nervous OPA to open a branch office on 135th Street and begin monitoring Harlem rents and prices. The Consolidated Tenants League, Powell's People's Committee, and left wing unions and neighborhood groups began flooding the office with complaints. At the same time, the city's CIO unions, especially Mike Quill's Transport Workers Union and the Left-led National Maritime Union, began warning the mayor and the OPA that when lease renewals came up on October 1, 1943, landlords would violate voluntary restraints and institute massive rent increases. The mayor, hardly insensitive to the combined political influence of the ALP, the Harlem community and the CIO unions, escalated his pressure on the OPA as well. On November 1, 1943, the OPA finally relented and declared New York City a War Rental Area with mandatory ceilings retroactive to the levels of March 1, 1943. From this point on, tenant associations, ALP clubs, and unions focused their attention on the OPA as the major point of reference for tenant complaints and began serving as de facto vigilance committees to insure enforcement of the edict.[70]

The imposition of controls, and the manner in which they were imposed, proved to be a watershed in housing policy in New York City. Long a part of the agenda of the organized tenant movement, rent control came not because that movement had accumulated new organization strength, but because tenant work and tenant issues had been adopted by civil rights groups, trade unions, consumer organizations, and left wing political clubs. Having fought for controls so long and so hard (OPA controls came with much less of a struggle in other cities), and having defined the issue as central to their identity (and sometimes their political power), these organizations developed a powerful stake in rent control's survival. After the war, even in very different economic settings, controls would prove difficult to reverse. Tenant activism, expressing itself through numerous forms, had emerged as a permanent force in the political life of the city.

NOTES

1. *New York Times*, July 3, 1936, Mar. 8, 1937.
2. The most useful works dealing with the Popular Front phase of American Communism are Joseph Starobin, *American Communism in Crisis, 1943–1957* (Cambridge, Mass., 1972), and Al Richmond, *A Long View from the Left* (Boston, 1973).
3. Interview with Richard B. Moore, Nov. 14, 1973, conducted by Mark Naison; *New York Amsterdam News*, Jan. 9, 1930, Sept. 17, 1928.
4. *Daily Worker*, Apr. 8, 10, 13, 15, 16, 19, 25, 1929.
5. *New York Amsterdam News*, June 5, 1929; *Daily Worker*, June 8, 1929; William B. Rudell, "Concerted Rent Withholding on the New York City Housing Front: Who Gets What, Why, and How?" paper, Yale Law School, Spring 1965, pp. 36–37.
6. *Daily Worker*, June 12, 25, July 1, 2, 4, 1929; *Revolutionary Age*, Nov. 1, 1929.
7. *New York Times*, Apr. 16, 1930; Rudell, "Concerted Rent Withholding," pp. 37–38.
8. *Bronx Home News*, Jan. 31, 1932; *Real Estate News*, Jan. 1931, p. 12.
9. *Real Estate News*, Jan. 1931, pp. 12–13; *Bronx Home News*, Apr. 27, 1932.
10. New York City Housing Authority, *The Failure of Housing Regulation* (New York, 1936), pp. 12–17; Roy Peel, *The Political Clubs of New York* (New York, 1935), pp. 210–212; *New York Times*, Feb. 26, 1932, Jan. 15, 1933; "No Rent Where There Is No Work," *New Leader*, Dec. 17, 1932, p. 5.
11. *Real Estate News*, Jan. 1931, pp. 12–13; Apr. 1931, p. 126; *New York Times*, Feb. 14, 1932; *Bronx Home News*, Jan. 10, 13, 1932.

12. *Daily Worker*, Dec. 9, 30, 1929; Mark Naison, *Communists in Harlem during the Depression* (Urbana, Ill., 1983), pp. 24–26.
13. *New York Amsterdam News*, Oct. 8, 1930; *Real Estate News*, Apr. 1931, pp. 126, 131; *New York Times*, June 3, 1931; *Daily Worker*, Oct. 6, Dec. 13, 1930, Jan. 5, Mar. 13, May 20, June 22, Aug. 19, 22, Sept. 17, 1931; Interview with Theodore Bassett, Dec. 14, 1973, conducted by Mark Naison.
14. *Daily Worker*, Mar. 18, 28, May 12, June 13, Aug. 6, 1931; *Working Woman*, Oct. 1931, p. 12.
15. Kim Chernin, *In My Mother's House: A Daughter's Story* (New York, 1983), pp. 100–101; Interview with Sophie Saroff, Oral History of the American Left Collection, Tamiment Library; "The Utopia We Knew: The Coops," *Cultural Correspondence*, Spring 1978, pp. 95–97; "The Political Significance of Rent Strikes," *Party Organizer*, Feb. 1932, pp. 23–24.
16. *Bronx Home News*, Jan. 10, 22, 1932; *Daily Worker*, Jan. 5, 8, 1932.
17. *Bronx Home News*, Jan. 23, 1932; *New York Times*, Jan. 23, 1932; *Daily Worker*, Jan. 23, 1932; Interview with Sara Plotkin, Jan. 23, 1976.
18. *Bronx Home News*, Jan. 28, 29, Feb. 2, 1932; *New York Times*, Jan. 30, Feb. 2, 4, 1932; *Daily Worker*, Jan. 26, Feb. 2, 1932.
19. *Bronx Home News*, Jan. 31, Feb. 3, 5, 7, 8, 1932; *New York Times*, Feb. 10, 1932.
20. *Daily Worker*, Jan. 9, 18, 23, 28, 1932; *Real Estate News*, Feb. 1932, pp. 54–55; Kenneth Alan Waltzer, "The American Labor Party: Third Party Politics in New Deal–Cold War New York, 1936–1954," Ph.D. diss., Harvard University, 1977, pp. 149, 153–154, 162; Irving Howe, *A Margin of Hope: An Intellectual Autobiography* (New York, 1983), pp. 1–2.
21. *New York Times*, Feb. 27, Mar. 13, 16, 1932; *Real Estate News*, Mar. 1932, p. 90; *Bronx Home News*, Feb. 12, Mar. 16, 1932; *Daily Worker*, Feb. 25, Mar. 1, 8, 1932.
22. "Political Significance of Rent Strikes," p. 23; *Bronx Home News*, June 8, 1932.
23. *Bronx Home News*, Mar. 10, 1932; *New York Times*, Mar. 25, 1932; *Real Estate News*, Apr. 1932, pp. 134–135.
24. *Real Estate News*, May 1932, p. 152; *Bronx Home News*, May 27, June 8, Sept. 4, 10, 1932; *Daily Worker*, May 21, 30, June 1, Sept. 10, 1932.
25. *Real Estate News*, Feb. 1933, p. 50.
26. Naison, *Communists in Harlem during the Depression*, pp. 76–78; *Bronx Home News*, Nov. 27, 1932; *Hunger Fighter*, Sept. 1932, pp. 1–4; Mar. 1933, pp. 1–4.
27. *Daily Worker*, Dec. 7, 22, 1932, Jan. 4, 6, 1933; *Bronx Home News*, Dec. 7, 1932, Jan. 5, 15, 1933; *New York Times*, Dec. 7, 21, 1932, Jan. 6, 17, 1933; *Working Woman*, Mar. 1933, p. 15; Chernin, *In My Mother's House*, pp. 96–97.
28. *Working Woman*, May 1933, p. 18; *New York Times*, Jan. 12, 17, 28, 31, 1933; *Daily Worker*, Jan. 9, 11, 12, 14, 19, 1933.
29. *Daily Worker*, Jan. 9, 11, 20, 24, 28, 1933; *Bronx Home News*, Jan. 25, 1933.
30. On Irish-Jewish tension in New York, see Ronald H. Bayor, *Neighbors in Conflict: The Irish, Germans, Jews, and Italians of New York City, 1929–1941* (Baltimore, 1978), esp. pp. 87–108; *Daily Worker*, Jan. 31, Feb. 1, 4, 9, 11, 14, 15, 23, 1933; *Bronx Home News*, Feb. 1, 1933.
31. *Bronx Home News*, Jan. 15, 18, 25, Feb. 15, Mar. 26, 1933; *Real Estate News*, Jan. 1933, pp. 12–13; Feb. 1933, pp. 50–51, 59; *New York Times*, Jan. 15, Feb. 1, Mar. 12, 1933.
32. *Bronx Home News*, Jan. 25, Feb. 21, 24, Mar. 9, 26, 1933; *New York Times*, Mar. 31, 1933; *Real Estate News*, Mar. 1933, p. 83; *Brooklyn Eagle*, Mar. 27, 1933.
33. *Bronx Home News*, Mar. 28, Apr. 11, June 1, 1933; *New York Times*, Mar. 28, June 1, 1933; *Daily Worker*, May 1, 11, 13, 18, 19, 31, June 3, 1933.
34. *New York Times*, June 8, 1933; *Real Estate News*, June 1933, pp. 164–165; *Bronx Home News*, June 8, 1933.

35. Interview with Sophie Saroff; Frances Fox Piven and Richard A Cloward, *Poor People's Movements: Why They Succeed, How They Fail* (New York, 1977), pp. 76–82; Naison, *Communists in Harlem during the Depression*, pp. 257–259.
36. *Woman Today*, Aug. 1936, pp. 6–7; "The Citywide Tenants Council, A History," typescript in Heinz Norden Collection, Tamiment Library, pp. 7–8.
37. *New York Times*, Mar. 28, 30, Apr. 5, 1934.
38. New York City Housing Authority, *Failure of Housing Regulation*, pp. 2–17; Welfare Council of New York, *Rent Control: Four Options* (New York, 1937), pp. 2–4; *New York Times*, Sept. 23, 1936, Jan. 3, 1937.
39. *New York Amsterdam News*, Aug. 11, 18, Sept. 1, 1934; *Negro Liberator*, Aug. 18, 1934; on the atmosphere of protest in Harlem during the spring and summer of 1934, see Naison, *Communists in Harlem during the Depression*, pp. 115–124.
40. *New York Amsterdam News*, Sept. 1, 8, 1934; *New York Age*, Sept. 29, 1934; *Negro Liberator*, Sept. 1, 1934.
41. *New York Amsterdam News*, Oct. 6, 1934; *New York Times* Mar. 21, Apr. 6, 1935; *Negro Liberator*, Sept. 8, 29, Oct. 13, 1934; Interview with Donnelan Phillips and Thomas Murray, Apr. 10, 1976; Norden, "Citywide Tenants Council," pp. 3–4.
42. Norden, "Citywide Tenants Council," pp. 3–4; Rudell, "Concerted Rent Withholding," p. 63; interview with Hope R. Stevens, Aug. 3, 1981, conducted by Joel Schwartz.
43. Norden, "Citywide Tenants Council," pp. 5–6; Heinz Norden, "Knickerbocker Village: Background Story," p. 1, and Aubrey Mallach, "Landlord Tenant Relationships in Government Sponsored Housing Projects," pp. 32–34, typescripts in Heinz Norden Collection.
44. Norden, "Citywide Tenants Council," p. 6; Mallach, "Landlord Tenant Relationships," p. 40; *New York Times*, Oct. 23, 24, 25, 31, Nov. 12, Dec. 1, 1934.
45. *New York Times*, Dec. 10, 1934; Norden, "Citywide Tenants Council," pp. 6–7; Mallach, "Landlord Tenant Relationships," pp. 41–60.
46. Norden, "Knickerbocker Village," p. 1; Mallach, "Landlord Tenant Relationships," pp. 52–60.
47. Norden, "Citywide Tenants Council," pp. 8–9; *Daily Worker*, Mar. 9, 10, 12, 13, 17, 1936.
48. Norden, "Citywide Tenants Council," pp. 9–11.
49. Ibid., pp. 11–12; *Woman Today*, Aug. 1936, pp. 7–8.
50. Norden, "Citywide Tenants Council," p. 60; *Daily Worker*, Dec. 2, 3, 4, 1936.
51. *New York Times*, Dec. 9, 16, 1936, Jan. 3, 1937; *Daily Worker*, Dec. 15, 16, 23, 1936.
52. Norden, "Citywide Tenants Council," pp. 12–13; *New York Times* Dec. 18, 19, 24, 1936; *Daily Worker*, Dec. 16, 19, 24, 29, 30, 31, 1936, Jan. 1, 1937.
53. City-Wide Tenants Council Minutes, Dec. 1, 1937, Norden Papers; *The Tenant*, vol. 1, nos. 1–3; vol. 2, no. 1; Norden "Citywide Tenants Council," pp. 21–22, 29–30, 41; *New York Times*, Feb. 2, July 22, 1937.
54. Norden, "Citywide Tenants Council," pp. 18–19; Interview with Donald Schoolman, Feb. 1, 1976, conducted by Joseph Spencer.
55. Norden, "Citywide Tenants Council," pp. 20–21.
56. *New York Times*, Oct. 26, 27, 1937; for City-Wide's position on arbitration, see Heinz Norden, "The Relationship between Landlords and Tenants in Low Rent Housing," report submitted to Citizens Housing Council, Feb. 17, 1938, Norden Papers.
57. "How Tenants Organization Keeps Down Rents and Improves Housing Conditions," Nov. 1937, typescript; City-Wide Tenants Council Minutes, Dec. 1, 1937, Norden Papers; *The Tenant*, vol. 2, no. 4; Norden, "Citywide Tenants Council," pp. 20–21, 45, 56; *New York Times*, May 7, 1937.
58. Interview with Donald Schoolman, Feb.

1, 1976; *Daily Worker*, Feb. 14, 1939; *The Tenant*, vol. 2, no. 4; Mallach, "Landlord-Tenant Relationships," p. 36.
59. Norden, "Citywide Tenants Council," pp. 25–29, 50–52, 60; "The Tenants Housing Program, 1937," "Legislative Program, 1940: Citywide Tenants Council," in Norden Papers; *New York Times*, Jan. 25, Feb. 17, 27, 1937.
60. *New York Times*, Jan. 19, Apr. 8, 23, 4, June 22, Sept. 25, 1938; Norden, "Citywide Tenants Council," pp. 30–31; *Housing Newsletter*, Mar. 4 and Apr. 16, 1940, in Norden Papers.
61. *New York Times*, July 17, 1937; Norden, "Citywide Tenants Council," pp. 25–27; City-Wide Tenants Council, "Suggested Program of Work for Summer," June 4, 1940, "Legislative Program, 1940," in Norden Papers; *Daily Worker*, Feb. 14, 1939.
62. Norden, "Citywide Tenants Council," pp. 27–29.
63. Ibid., p. 45; "Suggested Program of Work for Summer," June 4, 1940; *The Tenant*, vol. 2, no. 4; Heinz Norden to the editor, *New York Times*, July 19, 1938; Grace Aviles, Memorandum to New York City Housing Authority (1941); "Calling All Tenants," (published by Hillside Tenants Association), "Queensbridge News," (published by Queensbridge Tenants Association), in Norden Papers.
64. Interview with Donald Schoolman, Feb. 1, 1976; also see *Housing Newsletter*, issue running from Jan. 5 to May 6, 1940, Norden Papers.
65. City-Wide Tenants Council, "Resolution on Housing and Peace," June 20, 1940; and "Plan for Tenant League Activities to Augment and Assist the Work of Civilian Defense and 'Help Win the War' Activities," in Norden Papers; Interview with Donelan Phillips, July 11, 1972; City-Wide Tenants Council, "Resolution: Priorities—Housing and National Defense," Oct. 20, 1941, in Fiorello H. La Guardia Papers, Municipal Archives and Records Center; *Daily Worker*, Feb. 22, Apr. 23, Aug. 31, 1942.
66. Interview with Mamie Jackson, Jan. 1975; *New York Age*, Apr. 26, 1941; Norden, "Citywide Tenants Council," pp. 56–57.
67. Davis R. B. Ross, *Preparing for Ulysses: Politics and Veterans during World War II* (New York, 1969), p. 238; Daniel D. Gage, "Wartime Experiment in Federal Rent Control," *Journal of Land and Public Utility Economics* 23 (1947): 52; Memorandum, Federal Price Administrator to Fiorello H. La Guardia, July 26, 1943, Grace Aviles to Mayor La Guardia, Aug. 27, 1942, Aviles to Leon Henderson, August 27, 1942, in La Guardia Papers, Box 153.
68. *New York Age*, July 4, 1942, Aug. 1, 15, Sept. 19, 1942; *New York Amsterdam News*, Sept. 19, Oct. 17, 1942; *Peoples Voice*, Aug. 1, Sept. 21, Oct. 17, 31, 1942; *Daily Worker*, July 21, Sept. 20, 30, Oct. 1, 1942; Telegram, Ferdinand Smith to Mayor La Guardia, Oct. 7, 1942, La Guardia Papers, Box 2772.
69. *Daily Worker*, Sept. 24, Oct. 6, 14, 22, 23, 27, Dec. 22, 1942; Joseph Curran and Saul Mills to Mayor Fiorello H. La Guardia, July 16, 1942, La Guardia Papers, Box 153; Lawrence Lader, *Power on the Left: American Radical Movements since 1946* (New York, 1979), p. 13.
70. *New York Times*, Aug. 3, 7, 20, 1943; Interview with Donelan Phillips and Thomas Murray, Oct. 1, 1975; Dominic J. Capeci, Jr., *The Harlem Race Riot of 1943* (Philadelphia, 1980), pp. 86, 159; Max Goldfrank to Mayor Fiorello H. La Guardia, Aug. 6, 1942, Memorandum, Joseph Platzker to Hn. F. H. La Guardia, Sept. 21, 1942, Telegram, Michael J. Quill to Mayor Fiorello H. La Guardia, Oct. 6, 1943, La Guardia Papers, Box 153; *Daily Worker*, Aug. 20, Sept. 10, 29, 30, Oct. 1, 3, 10, 14, Nov. 1, Dec. 27, 1943.

4. Tenant Power in the Liberal City, 1943–1971

Joel Schwartz

At the height of World War II, tenant organizations confronted the greatest challenge to their hard-won influence in New York City. In 1943 liberal government intervened on the housing front with federal rent controls and a state urban redevelopment law. Tenant leaders, of course, had long hoped to bring public policy to their side of the housing struggle. But few could have anticipated that wartime expedients would become abiding measures with the most profound impact on the city's housing environment and the role of tenant power within it. From modest beginnings, government would soon arrogate vast authority to reshape the housing landscape and become the great rent arbiter, giant landlord, and mass evictor. How influential would the tenant movement remain among the new housing programs that it had campaigned so hard to bring about? Could it continue to shape the legal process of rent bargaining that had been the central function of local councils? Could it continue to bring tenant views to bear on the development of public housing and city planning? For that matter, could the movement survive at all, as New York moved into an era of liberal housing policies? First mobilized amid the anger of the Great Depression against landlord police, landlord judges, and landlord politicians, could tenant consciousness exist in a city whose political leaders vowed to move heaven and earth to solve the housing crisis?

The following essay will explore the salient issues presented by the tenant movement's confrontation with the liberal city. Foremost is the tenant version of the dilemma that faced all radicals in post–New Deal America. Could tenant unions maintain effective rent bargaining, their economic bread and butter, during the expansion of government rent regulation? Would tenants continue to rely on the collective strength of local councils after rent protection became a public benefit? These were vital considerations for the American Labor party clubs, which provided the cadre of tenant action in the 1940s and aspired to translate rent protests into comprehensive radical attacks on Truman liberalism. To the consternation of ALP organizers, their neighborhood followers appeared less driven by a collective sense of proletarian dispossession than by a determination to hold on to their virtual proprietary rights as "statutory tenants" under the rent laws.

As the rent strikes by blacks and Hispanics in the early 1960s bear out, this radical dilemma lost none of its poignancy. Leaders like Jesse Gray stirred a potent collective fury, only to have it dissipated by the anxiety of tenants to get on the waiting list for an apartment in the New York City Housing Authority.

A related question remains as overshadowing as the Housing Authority itself. To what extent was radical action undermined by the smooth efficiency of such large-scale organizations? The susceptibility of tenants may not have been much different from that of other rank-and-file movements that have been absorbed by giant, welfare-capitalist organizations. But to point an accusing finger at the Housing Authority is to overlook the acquiescence, if not the complicity, of tenants themselves, and to forget that in the 1930s, an important component of the tenant movement sprung up in the quasi-public, "limited-dividend" projects (which the state subvened in exchange for a limit on the interest earned by mortgage investors), where leaders sought collective bargaining with their institutional landlords. This approach partly stemmed from the City-Wide Tenants Council's attempts to forge a united front with liberal Democrats and partly from the understandable inclination of tenant organizers to avoid the drudge work in scattered, dingy walk-ups. More than its partisans cared to admit, the movement often fed off these corporate housing promotions, whether Stuyvesant Town and other urban redevelopment projects in the 1940s or Model Cities projects in the 1960s. Tenant radicals inspired much of the War on Poverty's Community Action Program, but tenant organizations rarely avoided becoming a recruiting arm of the Housing Authority.

Another question concerns the ability of tenants to move beyond their status as passive consumers of shelter to that of active developers, an idea that was perfectly absurd to commercial realtors and no less presumptuous to the liberal reformers who regarded themselves as patrons of public housing. Nevertheless, in the 1930s, local tenant unions and the City-Wide Tenants Council had intruded into this sacrosanct area, first demanding collective bargaining on management issues in the limited dividends, then taking advantage of government requirements that citizen advisory bodies accompany the development of city planning and public housing. Later in the decade, the City-Wide, claiming to speak for responsible rank-and-file interests, had participated in that advisory mechanism, wrung tacit recognition from the Housing Authority, and conferred with the housing liberals over blueprints that shaped the city's postwar future. Could the tenants maintain this presence? Perhaps in the long run that was precluded by urban "modernization," the trend in metropolitan development that would lodge decision making in the hands of centralized, professional staffs, as much the case in the pre-1945 Housing Authority as in the more elusive

Slum Clearance Committee under Robert Moses. But as the evidence suggests, it was one thing for downtown corporate elites to try to centralize housing decisions and quite another for tenant leaders to relinquish their involvement. As we will see, organized tenants in the pursuit of strategic, united-front goals may have withdrawn from a critical review of urban redevelopment during World War II. Afterward, cold war suspicions wrecked the credibility of tenant opposition to Title I redevelopment, when that program was in its most vulnerable stage. Tenant involvement was throttled less by evolutionary forces than by circumstances, by calculated decisions, and by politics. These might-have-beens in city planning may not sit well with readers convinced that Moses alone was responsible for Title I and its relocation havoc.

The sense of lost opportunities becomes sharper in the alternative-planning phase of the Metropolitan Council on Housing and the War on Poverty's stimulus of advocacy planning in the early 1960s. For a brief moment, Met Council, an unlikely coalition of Old Left stalwarts and Christian seekers, of community workers and gadfly architects, set an ambitious agenda for neighborhood planning. Determined to make the city listen to community aspirations, Met Council would leave an indelible, New Left sensibility on how the city should plan for people. But whether Met Council's advocacy planners were faithful instruments of community intent or initiators and doers in their own right remained questionable. Much the same ambiguity tainted the citizen planning machinery of Model Cities in the late 1960s. Tenant participation in housing development remained a chimerical goal, whose realization usually taught sorry lessons about an urban reform tradition convinced that housing was a complex, technical subject and that housing projects must be made to pay their own way. On those rare occasions when tenants became managers, they found themselves behaving like landlords who had bills to meet, rents to collect, and occupants to evict.

The ability of the tenant movement to deliver on its promises, of course, was closely related to its ability to recruit followers and to incite a mass involvement, or at least to convey to landlords and city officials the impression of the same. Distinguishing between matter-of-fact assessments and adversarial boasts remains a continuing headache. We will encounter numerous details of street-level mobilization, of the number of tenements organized, of rent strikers, of court cases, of union members, of crowds in meeting halls, of leaflets passed out. We will have to sort through the romantic, self-serving claims, some of them grown to movement myths, from the hard facts. Many remain too elusive to pin down. Some come from first-person reminiscences, a fascinating oral history. But the accounts are often thirty, even forty years old; some inevitably blend hazy recollections of

1937 with those of 1947. They demand corroboration with the written record. Admittedly, this reliance on literary evidence means reliance on those middle-class liberals who left a solid accounting and who usually staffed the government and reform agencies that tenants often confronted. There seems to be no way around this obstacle except to reckon with its biases and make the best of its legacy, to balance written reports with movement claims to recruitment and influence. We will be on safe ground if we judge the tenant movement by the same hard standards that its leaders would have applied to its operations—whom did it influence, what policies did it bring about, what results did it accomplish? We could dwell on the interesting questions of mobilization strategies and tactical repertories, but we cannot afford to abstract these apart from the landscape of the city. And it is this larger perspective that requires an answer to these more important questions. Did tenant organizations make a difference in the city's housing environment? Had organized tenants not existed, would the city's housing policies and accomplishments have been any different?

Rent Wars, 1943–1955

For five years, New York City's tenant unions had been at the center of the struggle for rent control, but by 1943 they had slipped to the edge of the great civic crusade that suddenly made controls a reality. The U.S. Office of Price Administration (OPA) imposed controls on the city largely because of general anxieties well orchestrated by the Fiorello H. La Guardia administration. When the mayor led a broad coalition of liberal and civic groups clamoring for restraints on rising rents, organized tenants found themselves just one among many interests appealing for an emergency measure whose time had come. But the realities of total war that had taken the primacy of rent control away from tenant lobbyists had also changed the structure and priorities of their movement. The struggle to maintain wartime morale brought new membership and new influence to the leagues in the public projects. The new Soviet-American friendship in the aftermath of the Teheran Conference encouraged radicals to bury old tenant grievances and forge genial relations with liberal Democrats, even if they were landlords. At the same time, the OPA rent system quickly overshadowed the rent bargaining that had been the central function of tenant unions for a generation.[1]

The war on the home front had forced organized tenants to set aside many of the housing issues that had matured during the depression. A few weeks after Pearl Harbor, the City-Wide Tenants Council virtually ended its five-year role as the advocate for renters in private apartment houses. In

February 1942 an emergency convention adopted the name United Tenants League of Greater New York (UTL), but the hurried new committee assignments made clear that UTL energies would go to the struggle to bolster community morale for the "People's War." By December the UTL even dropped its half-hearted agitation for OPA controls. The issue had never been relevant to tenants in the limited dividends and public projects, who enjoyed subsidized low rents. The project leagues now had more immediate worries, as the federal government curtailed new housing construction except around defense plants, gave occupancy preference to defense workers and military personnel, and pressed the New York City Housing Authority to evict families whose incomes exceeded a maximum ceiling. As war wages increased during 1942, the Queensbridge Tenants League (QTL), the largest of the public project councils, became the most insistent voice behind the UTL's call for a moratorium on public housing evictions and an increase in the income ceiling to three thousand dollars.[2]

During 1943 the UTL, spearheaded by the Queensbridge contingent, skillfully reached beyond the Housing Authority to sympathetic liberals in Washington. It managed to arrange a joint meeting at New York's Town Hall with the prestigious National Public Housing Conference, which called attention to the plight of excess-income tenants. In the wake of a war production crisis in Long Island City aircraft plants, the UTL warned the U.S. War Manpower Commission that Housing Authority income ceilings were keeping two thousand skilled Queensbridge women off the labor market and provoked nervous Washington inquiries about whether the Housing Authority was "impeding" the war effort. The UTL's persistence, backed by a barrage of telegrams from Queensbridge, Fort Greene, and Williamsburg, forced the Housing Authority to raise the maximum in June 1943 to three thousand dollars with an added rent surcharge. At Queensbridge this qualification touched off stormy protests, which the QTL barely contained. When hotheads threatened to withhold rent, the Queensbridge manager marveled at how the QTL leader "sat on them saying this is no time for rent strikes." This "popular feeling," the manager reported, "was only checked and controlled by the experienced members of the QTL who proposed that we first work out an organized system of collective bargaining for the adjustment." Having wrung a satisfactory modus vivendi from the Housing Authority, the project leagues maintained a genial advisory posture for the duration.[3]

The concentration of the tenant movement in the public projects, along with the Communist Left's emphasis on wartime unity, shaped the UTL's complacence toward the 1943 issue of urban redevelopment. Within weeks after the state legislature passed the Mitchell-Hampton Redevelopment Companies Law in spring 1943, the La Guardia administration and the Metropolitan Life Insurance Company unveiled plans for Stuyvesant Town, a middle-income project that would sprawl across the Lower East Side—and displace some thirty-eight hundred site families. Liberals who questioned the project's massive, bull-dozer character were outraged when Metropolitan Life divulged its intent to limit occupancy to whites. At Board of Estimate hearings, liberals from the City-Wide Citizens Committee on Harlem, the United Neighborhood Houses, and the Citizens Housing Council bitterly attacked this "walled," "Jim Crow" city. Radical response, however, was generally muted. Only the United Tenants League and Queensbridge Tenants League sent denunciations. Communist councilman Peter V. Cacchione voiced perfunctory skepticism, while the American Labor party speaker simply urged "some provision" for site tenants.[4]

Shocked site tenants already had a voice—a UTL affiliate, the Stuyvesant Tenants League, which rallied the protests of local civic groups and churches. But Stuyvesant Tenants remained good neighborhood liberals, who, more than anything else, resented the insurance giant and expected fair play from the powers-that-be. They were quickly mollified by the Community Service Society's sympathetic study of their rehousing needs and, more decisively, by Metropolitan Life's "efficient" field services that were handled by the Tenant Relocating Bureau, Inc., organized by liberal realtor James Felt. The Community Service Society had to admire Tenant Relocating's professional solicitude, but applauded the special consideration that the Housing Authority gave evictees, including referrals to the Fort Greene Houses. Any lingering opposition was further undercut by cool heads on the UTL, who urged cooperation with Metropolitan Life for a painless relocation. Above all, Stuyvesant Tenants was advised not to break with the La Guardia administration. Without vehement opponents on the site, liberals' arguments against irresponsible corporate redevelopment faded.[5]

In 1943 redevelopers, also setting their eyes on Harlem, conjured up plans that proved an effective solvent of tenant league resistance. In the weeks following the August 1 Harlem riot, James Felt hurriedly completed his idea for a nonprofit corporation to operate Harlem tenements with a paternalism modeled after England's Octavia Hill Association. Economies in the management of adjoining buildings, he argued, would cut maintenance costs without sacrificing operating standards. An interracial board of trustees would oversee an all-black staff of rent collectors and social workers. Felt solicited the interest of Donelan J. Phillips and Vernal J. Williams of Harlem's Consolidated Tenants League, who believed they were being offered a part in the management. But Felt had no such plans; he conceived it all along as an Urban League operation recruited from Harlem's social work establishment. But a far more serious intrusion on Harlem's tenant consciousness was Metropolitan Life's Riverton at 135th Street and Fifth Avenue, an "interracial" development that the insurance giant hoped would make amends for Stuyvesant Town. Affronted by the company's arrogance, Donelan Phillips nevertheless had to disagree with white liberals and welcome Riverton's much-needed 1,232 middle-income units. Trying to save face, he boasted that his Consolidated Tenants League could steer the Metropolitan's housing direction. "Negroes have their own insurance policies," he said, "and can make demands" on the company. He was sadly mistaken. The league's strength had been its traditional services—its opening of Jim Crow apartments, its rent bargaining, and its pressure against arbitrary landlords. All this would be rendered obsolete by Riverton's fixed rent schedule, its institutionalized waiting list, and its glib interracialism.[6]

These corporate blueprints, filled with portents for the city's future, got only an uncritical glance from the United Tenants League, more concerned with progress of the People's War. UTL president Grace Aviles refused to join the liberals in their rebuke of Metropolitan Life's cynical gesture at Riverton. More important, amid the Stuyvesant Town debate, the UTL quietly dropped its traditional objections to private-sector redevelopment. The May 1944 UTL convention called federally aided redevelopment "essential to meet our postwar needs" and added that "we cannot justifiably oppose federal aid to urban redevelopment just because that aid is going to private industry." Within days after eviction rumors raced through East 14th Street, the UTL convention resolved that the New York City Housing Authority should finish its Jacob Riis and Lillian Wald projects to absorb refugees from the Stuyvesant Town site. With explicit praise for the Mitchell-Hampton Law, the United Tenants League statement reiterated, "As part of the overall housing program, encouragement should be given to private capital to invest in the field." "If private real estate owners and builders ignore this market, or fail to meet its demands, public housing can and must do the job." But, as the *Daily Worker* added in its coverage of the 1944 tenant convention, the UTL "is of the mind that private capital will be prepared for the challenge."[7]

In the meantime, OPA rent regulation severely weakened many UTL affiliates that had made rent bargaining in the courts the heart of their community appeal. At first, the OPA's operations in Harlem proved a boon for the Consolidated Tenants League, which tried to acquaint Harlem with the new argot of "prevailing" rents, "comparable" services, and landlords' "hardship" increases. Becoming the OPA's self-appointed mediator and propagandist, the league never handled so many cases or enrolled so many new "units"—twelve in December 1943, and twenty-one in January 1944, each with eight to ten tenants. But Harlemites quickly swamped the OPA's 135th Street office with desperate pleas about rents, hot water, painting, and repairs. The OPA soon became a one-stop housing office, whose volume business undercut most other voluntary efforts. The narrow grounds for

OPA certificates of eviction reduced fears of landlords' thirty-day notices and much of the work of the magistrate's courts. Harlem was deluged with OPA leaflets: "WHEN IN DOUBT ASK THE RENT DIRECTOR," was the message that the Consolidated, along with other groups, feverishly distributed.[8]

In white, lower-middle-class neighborhoods, the UTL's dwindling affiliates had little choice but to throw in their lot with the growing consumer movement. The OPA, declaring war on price gougers, had enrolled middle-class volunteers from the League of Women Voters, the League of Women Shoppers, and other groups mobilized by the civilian defense effort. As rents steadied compared to the jump in market-basket prices, tenant leaders quickly shifted allegiance to these neighborhood vigilantes. The Mid-Queens Consumer Council, in fact, was behind the most important rent protest of 1943, a mobilization of 250 tenants in Rego Park–Forest Hills against rent increases and evictions, climaxed by a housewives' invasion of the OPA's Long Island City office. The trend in consumer advocacy was furthered by the vogue in "nonpartisan" wartime conferences during the winter of 1943–1944. In Brooklyn, the Non-Partisan Conference on Legislation in Wartime, the Brownsville Neighborhood Council, and the Conference of Brooklyn Consumers Councils brought civic groups, consumer councils, and women's clubs into the united front against war profiteers. Meeting at local hotels or neighborhood YMHAs, conferees generally agreed on liberal civic goals, mentioned fair housing and improved health services in the same breath as the Atlantic Charter, and resolved to struggle for community betterment while winning the People's War.[9]

In this atmosphere, the independent tenant voice of the 1930s withered away. Many tenant veterans had been drafted or volunteered for war service, their places taken by women activists who readily joined the consumers' home front. At Knickerbocker Village, Queensbridge, Williamsburg, and Fort Greene, the preoccupation was the output of nearby war plants, insofar as it could be inspired by civic festivals staged by the projects. Left with a few satisfied, inactive tenant councils in the public projects and some old letterhead affiliations, the United Tenants League disappeared sometime during 1945.[10]

Postwar housing controversies soon stirred the consumers-and-tenants out of their wartime complacence. Within a year after V-E Day, tenant councils became one of the most raucous elements of the city's Left. Their often brazen tactics drew attention from the fact that, at the behest of their neighbors, they pursued an eminently conservative goal—the retention of OPA controls and what that meant for community stability. But given the country's revulsion against wartime restrictions, and against the OPA in particular, this course proved a long, dogged retreat. Tenant groups sided with President Harry S. Truman in his 1946 showdown with congressional Republicans over OPA extension, demanded Governor Thomas E. Dewey provide standby state controls if federal authority lapsed (which it did, for twenty-five days after June 30, 1946, when Truman vetoed an unacceptable OPA bill), lobbied in 1947 against attempts by the Republican-controlled Eightieth Congress to water down OPA, and later tried to influence the new federal Office of the Housing Expeditor (OHE), OHE rent control offices, and OHE citizens boards that advised on the pace of local decontrol. At best, they were able to delay, or occasionally confuse, but never halt the inexorable postwar pressures to restore free market rents and incentives for housing.[11]

These were the stakes for tenants when President Truman drew the political battle lines during summer 1946, and the city's consumer and tenant councils staged vivid media events to dramatize fears for OPA. The Bronx Consumer Coordinating Council organized a June Buyer's Strike against clothing, appliance, and furniture stores that became the focal points for neighborhood Save OPA rallies. On July 26 the New York Consumers Council and its Brooklyn and Queens affiliates held a Buy Nothing Day aimed at the large chain stores, the "milk trust," and the black market in meat. Prominent stores, such as Macy's Parkchester, Hearn's, and Sachs, announced their scrupulous adherence to voluntary price limits, while local consumer and tenant councils had even greater success intimidating smaller shopkeepers in radical strongholds, like the Allerton Avenue section of the Bronx. The Brooklyn Borough Hall section of the American Labor party mobilized housewives for baby carriage parades, while the Brownsville Consumer and Tenant Council, formed that June, won neighborhood favor with a two-week strike and noisy pickets at butcher shops and clothing stores on Pitkin Avenue. Local consumer and tenant groups seemed the only protection for community standards against the cynical maneuvers in Washington.[12]

These were just the opening skirmishes, however, of the bitter campaign during spring 1947 to influence the housing policies of the Eightieth Congress, whose new Republican leaders were intent on scrapping rent and price controls. Amid post-election fears, American Labor party radicals and consumer and tenant leaders organized the Emergency Committee on Rent and Housing (ECRH) to mobilize scores of local unions, consumer and tenant leagues, and ALP storefronts. The ECRH sent a powerful lobby to Capitol Hill, but could not prevent passage of the Housing and Rent Act of 1947. While the law extended OPA defense-rental ceilings (to be administered by regional rent offices within the newly created Office of the Housing Expeditor), it also allowed 15 percent increases on apartment "turnovers" and on varied categories of "improvements"; removed rent ceilings on new multiple dwellings as well as on apartment hotels; and on July 1 ended the required OPA certificates of eviction. Back in New York, these provisions touched off citywide fears of evictions and "pandemonium" in Manhattan's residential hotels. A stunned Mayor William O'Dwyer embraced the city council's rent laws, which froze residential hotel rents and set up a City Rent Commission to adjust "hardship" inequities and ration sharply the number of approved evictions. But the ultimate mobilizer of tenant fury were the loopholes of the 1947 federal law, which permitted landlords to negotiate 15 percent "voluntary" rent increases with tenants and to petition the OHE rent control office for rent increases based upon "hardship." Landlords took advantage of these loopholes en masse: from July to December 1947 the New York rent office approved over 250,000 leases containing "voluntary" 15 percent increases.[13]

Throughout the city, tenants flocked to local consumer and tenant councils for help against the "hardship" scourge. Brooklyn saw the overnight growth of eighteen tenant and consumer councils (one each in Coney Island, Brighton Beach, Sheepshead Bay, several in Flatbush, and others scattered throughout the borough). Most had been quickly improvised by nearby ALP and Communist clubhouses. Probably, the center of this activity lay in predominantly Jewish Brownsville, along Powell Street and Blake and Pitkin avenues, neighborhoods also in the shadow of new public housing projects. Here the Brownsville Tenants Council mushroomed to more than four hundred members, met every Wednesday at local ALP headquarters, and conducted an ongoing rent clinic and complaint night against building violations. Not far away, the Stuyvesant Tenants Council claimed a membership of five hundred families, a potent force in stopping evictions and "keeping the rent control front firm." Amid all the confusion about the new federal rent law, the ALP's rent clinics were a comforting presence in many localities.[14]

Information about these Brooklyn groups, including the banner units proudly described in the *Daily Worker*, reveals an inadvertent conservatism that prevailed, whatever may have been the aims of their leaders. One of the most active, the Ocean Front Tenants League, founded in 1945, was described by a *Worker* reporter in 1948 as "an established part of community life in Brighton Beach." It claimed some seventeen hundred members (out of fifty thousand area residents), with a summer intake of twenty-five tenant cases on each of three nights per week at its Neptune Avenue office. While the Ocean Front League placed a premium on grass roots organization, it really depended upon walk-in clients, predominantly elderly Jews who feared landlord demands for "hardship" increases. During mid-1948, however, tenant counciling gave way to the all-out effort for Henry Wallace, the Progressive party's presidential candidate, and for Lee Pressman, running on the Progressive ticket for Congress. The Boro Park Tenants and Consumers Council was another spring 1946 upstart in the OPA struggle. By 1948, leaders boasted six hundred members in the Orthodox Jewish and ALP heartland of the Sixteenth Assembly District, an area of two-, four-, and six-family houses on quiet residential side streets. "The Council is known in the neighborhood," summed up a laudatory *Daily Worker* article, "for aiding evicted families, for sending delegates to Washington on price and rent lobbies, and for collecting thousands of signatures for worthy causes." But its weekly sessions at the local YMHA were dominated by routine housing complaints as well as responses to landlord demands for 15 percent increases. Despite its radical claims, the Boro Park Council was an expeditor of tenant complaints to the rent control office, a fairly effective goad of landlords to provide heat, to paint, to make repairs, and to provide other services. While leaders saw the need for grass roots mobilization, and even proposed setting up "block groups which will work on the problems on each given block," the idea was never carried out. In any case, like the Ocean Front, the Boro Park Council soon turned its attention to canvasing the larger apartment dwellings for Henry Wallace.[15]

Manhattan's consumer and tenant councils also rode the "hardship" tide and were equally dependent on ALP activists who mastered the rent control game. On the Upper East Side, the Yorkville Tenants League, operating out of the local ALP clubhouse, cultivated a legal service that claimed to have handled hundreds of eviction cases in the magistrate's courts and rent reduction applications with the housing expeditor. Further north, Congressman Vito Marcantonio's East Harlem club illustrated the full-service ALP at the height of its power. His office staff took on the whole array of neighborhood housing problems—not only "hardship" increases, but evictions and complaints about heat or hot water, garbage, and repairs. When tenants approached his ALP headquarters, the staff sought the individual tenants' names, sent out a form letter, and arranged a meeting at the ALP clubhouse. Marcantonio's eager, young aides gave a pep talk, handed out pamphlets, such as "Tenant Rights Concerning Painting, Repairs, Rent and Hot Water, and Rent Increases" (written by an assistant), and the indispensable temperature charts. When necessary, the staff arranged for power of attorney to deal with the housing expeditor. Always, the meticulous follow-up included personal letters from "Marc" and a friendly huddle at ALP headquarters. Understandably, landlords charged that the congressman had "trumped up petty complaints" for his radical cause, but the painstaking tenant work seemed more like the traditional Tammany ministry to the poor. Hispanics on East 100th Street pledged to him in early 1949, "You have votes in the building where we live, we fite for you when Election comes. You can ask to your peoples if they come here to take sign for anything you need in the political."[16] But Marcantonio's success at moving grievances from tenement stairwells to the ALP clubhouse and then to the housing expeditor also inhibited the formation of independent tenant groups in East Harlem, except as they existed as names on his mailing lists.

By all accounts, however, the Bronx was the tenant movement's spearhead. No other borough combined so many key ingredients: a tradition of neighborhood Jewish radicalism, local working-class institutions (ALP clubs along with the lodges of Michael Quill's Transport Workers Union), plus a special rancor in landlord-tenant relations going back to the early 1930s. The Bronx also began with a strong consumer-and-tenant cadre, thanks to Helen Harris, a junior high school teacher who had guided a wartime consumer group into the Bronx Emergency Council to Save Rent Control. During the 1947 struggle against the "hardship" challenge, the Bronx Emergency Council boasted forty-five thousand members in thirty-three "autonomous" neighborhood branches and a storefront headquarters with eight full-time organizers and an attorney. Local councils charged a dollar initiation fee and three dollars annual dues, which went for legal expenses and mass distribution of leaflets, such as the "Tenants Bill of Rights." Among the most active were the Archer Avenue Consumer Committee and the Morrisania Consumer Coordinating Committee, which organized housewives in Fleetwood, the Grand Concourse, and Yankee Stadium areas, the Highbridge Consumers Council, and the tenant councils on Burnside Avenue, Gunhill Road, and Claremont, all areas of solid six-story, lower-middle-class buildings.[17]

Behind many of these neighborhood leagues lay spontaneous outbreaks among tenants who had worried for months about their rights under the new federal rent law, then panicked with a sudden notice of eviction or blew up at a landlord's pompous message that his 15 percent increase would provide more security of tenure. The *Bronx Home News* reported numerous "spontaneous meetings" where "tenants banded together in many large apartment houses and defied threats by landlords to 'pay up or get out.'" It did not take long for some tenant, either on his own or at the prompting of an outsider, to suggest that they take their landlord's "coercive" letter to the local rent office or the Bronx Emergency Council. A typical uprising saw one hundred tenants, mostly housewives, from 2100–2120 Wallace Avenue, jam the local OPA office to protest an abrupt notice of hardship increases. Actually, as one husband noted, "This thing's been smouldering for several years now." At 2100 Wallace the landlord had gradually cut concessions and skimped on heat, while next door he had the nerve to tell the mothers to keep their noisy kids out of the courtyards. "It was one grievance after another. But when we got those sudden notices from the OPA, we boiled over." Rent officials rushed to the trouble spot, making sure that local newspapers reported their rapid response. Bronx rent director Albert J. Haas, a political fixer one step ahead of the firestorm, quickly notified tenants that he would reopen the case and weigh their arguments. But just as rapidly on the scene were representatives of the Pelham Parkway Consumers Council. A few days later the ALP announced that negotiations with the landlord on Wallace Avenue were just one of several being handled by ALP volunteer attorneys.[18]

Fears of evictions and hardship increases made the Bronx a political battleground, where Democrats, the ALP, and upstart Liberals contended for the allegiance of Jewish tenants, that crucial swing vote in the borough's multiple dwellings. At the outset, the ALP stole a march on the rent issue. In late 1946, the Parkchester ALP haunted subway exits with leaflets charging the Republicans with betraying tenants and put the incumbent GOP assemblyman on the defensive. Then, with a battery of volunteer attorneys, the Bronx County ALP inaugurated free legal services. The party kept up the pressure during the fall 1947 municipal elections, when ALP workers, canvasing apartment houses, distributed over one hundred thousand informational folders on tenant rights. But Bronx Democrats were not to be outdone. As part of its decisive break with the ALP and bitter campaign to defeat proportional representation, the county party threw open fourteen clubhouses to acquaint tenants with their rights. Bronx boss Ed Flynn personally marshaled the volunteer attorneys for clubhouse service. Competing Liberals responded with open-air, rent control rallies. By October they had also turned their clubhouses into legal centers, one at their Bronx headquarters at 2707 Wallace Avenue, another on Southern Boulevard, and the third astride the contested ground on East Tremont Avenue.[19]

All these activities were a prelude to the all-out war in 1948 for the hearts and minds of Bronx tenants. On the eve of the Progressive party's presidential campaign for Henry Wallace, the *New York World Telegram* headlined that seven tenant and consumer councils, including those in Hunt's Point, Williamsbridge, the Stadium, Tremont, and the Concourse, were headquartered in local ALP storefronts placarded for Wallace. It reported widespread complaints against the radicals' high-pressure recruiting, which engendered feelings that "when a council representative moves in to organize an apartment house, [residents] have nowhere to turn." Their tactics touched off counterattacks by local Democrats and Liberals, some of them affiliated with the new, avowedly anti-Communist, Americans for Democratic Action. Liberals stepped up their Bronx rent struggle, leafleting, holding thirty outdoor rallies, and assembling a phalanx of volunteer lawyers at county and district headquarters. "We have been flooded with 'phone calls,' with individuals calling in person, and with delegations seeking such assistance," said Liberal party director Ben Davidson. Attacking the notion that the Communists were the only activists in the struggle against landlord claims, the Liberals' Rent Control Committee reported that federal officials granted rent increases "roughly the same as that awarded in the case of tenants 'protected' by the [ALP] councils. Yet, in relation to the legal work they provide, the councils charge exorbitant fees."[20]

Among the Democrats, the Bronx Emergency Council, and their Liberal rivals, tenants could pick and choose their legal response to landlord "hardships"—a thicket of redress that often constrained landlords, particularly small owners, who had trouble with the OPA forms and could not afford attorneys. Federal rent enforcers preferred to pursue cases against large realtors, particularly in projects where articulate tenants supplied compelling affidavits and where the rulings might have greater impact as class actions. But small operators often fell prey to strong tenant councils ready to pounce on "hardship" requests. One landlord blamed delays in his petition for a rent increase on "the tenants' committee, having access to all our books of accounts, through the [federal] Office of Rent Control have questioned every insignificant item of expenditure and income." Small owners in areas like Tremont faced formidable tenant leagues, armed with leaflet campaigns and weekly rent clinics. In February 1948 Bronx rent director Albert Haas admitted that borough tenants had generated some twenty-nine thousand complaints against landlord initiatives, 50 percent more than in Brooklyn, despite the latter's greater population. Bronx tenants had, in fact, held their landlords to one of the lowest percentages of "hardship" increases in the nation. During March 1948 the rate of approved applications ran 32 percent, compared to 45 percent citywide and a national average of 61 percent.[21]

While postwar tenants wielded political clout in the rent offices and in city hall, that power rested on limited and shifting foundations. Despite widespread anxieties about OPA controls, tenant activism had remained a phenomenon of working- and middle-class Jewish neighborhoods. The Bronx bastions were those sections that the tenant and consumer councils had closed down on their Buy Nothing Days in July 1946: Tremont Avenue, 174th Street, Southern Boulevard and Prospect Avenue, the Allerton Avenue area, and 167th and 169th streets east of Grand Concourse. No extensive outbreaks occurred in the growing black ghetto in Morrisania or in the Puerto Rican barrio emerging in Mott Haven and Melrose. In Harlem the level of tenant protest appeared to have declined since the seasons of agitation led by Adam Clayton Powell, Jr., and the National Negro Congress in 1942. Brooklyn told much the same story. Few signs of organized protest appeared in the emerging black ghetto in Brownsville and Bedford-Stuyvesant compared to the anger against arbitrary rent increases and apartments withheld from the rental market in white, lower-middle-class neighborhoods on their periphery.[22]

What passed for a tenant "movement" also depended to a great degree on the organizational finesse and shifting priorities of neighborhood radicals. Just as Communist united-front goals appeared to have dictated the 1942 dissolution of aggressive tenant councils, so evidence points to a reverse strategy behind the blossoming of the tenant and consumer councils during 1946. Certainly, ALP and Communist clubs gave coherence to the sometimes formless anger in the neighborhoods.[23] But the rage of the depression was gone. Baby carriage parades and Buy Nothing Days were the acts of exasperated consumers quite satisfied to hang on to their lower-middle-class standards, if only the politicians would have let them. A half decade of OPA bureaucracy had also taken the bite out of many local tenant groups. They had lost whatever gumption they once had to physically challenge landlords and the police; it seemed pointless in any case. Processing rent forms was more effective and far more respectable among middle-class radicals still cultivating the united-front sensibilities of liberal Democrats. The danger, of course, remained that with this growing efficiency at forwarding rent-reduction forms to borough offices, radical tenant councils would become just another voluntary social welfare agency, like the settlement house, the institutional church, or the political clubhouse—effective at helping individuals in distress but without the power to stir collective action for basic social change.

With the end of the "hardship" crisis and the establishment of complaint routines at the housing expeditor, tenant council strength eroded rapidly. At the City-Wide Tenants Council's old bastions—the limited dividends and public housing projects—tenant consciousness encountered the ironic perils of upward mobility. In Long Island City's Sunnyside Gardens, affluent renters had to decide whether to buck the Gardens Tenant Association and purchase the townhouses being converted by a speculator. Despite great acrimony, the private sales went on. At Knickerbocker Village and Hillside Gardens in the Bronx, rising incomes had forced many occupants beyond the income-eligibility limits that the state established years before for these limited-dividend projects. Management seized the opportunity in 1947 to get rid of affluent—and troublesome—dissenters and put the old tenant councils on the defensive. As in 1934, the Knickerbocker Village Tenants Association tried to enlist the sympathies of city housing reformers, but this time the middle-class leadership at Knickerbocker Village could not convince liberal Democrats that the state should continue to subsidize the patently nonpoor.[24]

At the same time, a greater challenge faced the toughest tenant cadre in the city—the project councils of the New York City Housing Authority. During the winter of 1946–1947, the Housing Authority began what it called an "intensive drive to clear the projects of ineligible tenants" whose incomes had risen over the ceiling set in 1943. The Queensbridge Tenants League abruptly renewed its adversary role as spearhead of a new Inter-Project Tenants Council, comprised of tenant leaders from Queensbridge, Red Hook, Fort Greene, and Williamsburg. With leaflets and placards that warned, "IF YOUR FAMILY INCOME IS $2355 A YEAR OR OVER YOUR TURN IS COMING!" the Inter-Project mobilized tenants and maneuvered to stave off evictions. When the Housing Authority finally claimed that federal dictates had tied its hands and would force the removal of three thousand affected tenants, the Queensbridge Tenants League wondered where these families could go: "These prospective evictees are occupying low-income houses through no fault of their own—but rather due to the critical housing situation. Limited dividend apartments are not only insufficient to meet the demand, but are also out of reach for many people whose incomes are just over the amount permitted in low-income housing. Homes are offered for sale at exorbitant prices—their quality is notoriously inferior. No one likes to make a bad investment." Management replied by emphasizing its first responsibility to the "many thousands" of low-income families on Housing Authority waiting lists, then divulged to the newspapers that 2,953 families in ten projects earned more than the $3,000 ceiling.[25]

The project leagues continued to present plausible alternatives, such as exempting the wages of secondary earners, veterans benefits, and disability pensions; but they were steadily losing moral influence in a city impatient to move ahead with expensive public improvements. At Queensbridge, Red Hook, Fort Greene, and Williamsburg, managers curtailed the leagues' use of community rooms, particularly for Wallace presidential rallies in 1948. Meanwhile, the Housing Authority, documenting its case against excess tenant income, counted 438 such families at Red Hook, 514 at Williamsburg, and 736 at Queensbridge, the centers of white, radical protest. In early 1949 a "program of mass evictions" got underway. Ninety-day vacate notices were sent to excess-income families, with suggestions that they consider rental or purchase of middle-income shelter in new developments, such as Fresh Meadows or Hollis Gardens in Queens. The Inter-Project Council demanded that Mayor William O'Dwyer declare a housing emergency and an immediate halt to evictions. But the council implicitly undermined its working-class rhetoric by pursuit of a transfer policy that would have given these tenants priority on the waiting lists of the Housing Authority's middle-income garden apartments or of Stuyvesant Town, Jim Crow and all. While public housing radicals later blamed their dwindling forces on the Truman administration's witch hunts in the projects, the radicals were clearly losing ground to the affluence that had lifted many tenant supporters out of public housing well before their ranks were purged. In reality, the Queensbridge Tenants League had become a mere letterhead years before its name was added to the attorney general's "list" of "subversive" organizations.[26]

Postwar prosperity and middle-income housing developments undermined the tenant's movement everywhere. As working-class and lower-middle-class Jews experienced upward mobility, tenant agitation switched from the Lower East Side, Chelsea, Morrisania, and Brownsville to the Upper West Side and Yorkville, the Grand Concourse–Tremont neighborhoods in the central Bronx, and Rego Park in middle Queens, where it expired in an alien environment of quasi-suburban garden apartments, whose families withdrew to the preoccupations of child rearing. These were difficult places to stir tenant consciousness, let alone organize a tenant union.[27]

The movement never balanced this lost strength on the Lower East Side, Yorkville, and Chelsea with new recruits from black and Hispanic Harlem or the emerging ghettoes of Brownsville, Bedford-Stuyvesant, and Morrisania. A few organizational forays into the black community were the work of the ALP and Communists, although they left the South Bronx and Bedford-Stuyvesant untouched until the all-out political canvas in 1948. Whenever they tried, however, they ran up against strong countertrends, especially the enormous safety valve on tenant discontent provided by public housing. In East Harlem, for instance, Congressman Marcantonio's office expedited the applications for Housing Authority apartments for some nine hundred constituents in the last half of 1949, and nearly three thousand more during 1950. At the same time, the postwar fair-housing movement deflated the tenant councils' appeal to Harlem's middle class. Thanks to the Brown-Sharkey-Isaacs antidiscrimination law and activists on the New York State Committee on Discrimination, blacks once limited to the segregated Paul Lawrence Dunbar or Riverton Houses could consider "interracial" housing on the edge of Harlem and in the "open" suburbs beyond. Before the war, Walter White and Roy Wilkins of the NAACP helped organize their Colonial Park Apartments, while Communist city councilman Benjamin H. Davis boasted that he had made his residence a unit of the Consolidated Tenants League. In 1950 one of the fifteen blacks admitted to Long Island City's Queensview Co-ops was NAACP leader Henry Lee Moon, whose *The Negro Balance of Power* described the concentration of the black vote in key northern ghettoes. Councilman Davis was unseated in a watershed postwar election by black Democrat Earl Brown, who later moved into Morningside Gardens, another interracial co-op.[28]

Despite the narrow neighborhood base and the loss of rent bargaining to federal bureaus—or perhaps because of these trends—the organized remnant poured its remaining energies into rent control politics. This amounted to a series of adroit publicity events designed to preempt liberal efforts to determine the contours of federal decontrol. Tenant radicals were remarkably successful in derailing plans for gradual decontrol and in placing their own demands for rent protection on the public agenda. But their tactics remained limited, defensive ploys that failed to wrest authority over rent control away from the housing reformers, liberal realtors, and their academic allies, who formed the coalition favoring the gradual, but determined, restoration of market rents.

Radicals hinged their campaign on the Housing and Rent Act of 1947, which authorized governors to suggest nominees for the Rent Control Advisory Boards that would propose the scope and pace of local decontrol to the housing expeditor. When Governor Thomas E. Dewey suggested Democrat Joseph B. McGoldrick to head the New York City board, composed of Republicans prominent in real estate and civic endeavors, the Emergency Committee on Rent and Housing (ECRH), the ALP, Progressive Citizens of America, United Harlem Tenants League, National Lawyers Guild, and Greater New York CIO Council all howled against Dewey's failure to name tenants or workers. Such denunciations forced the McGoldrick board, which favored deliberate, phased decontrol, not to urge the outright dismantling of federal rent protection in the New York area. With the ECRH and some 140 other tenant and building councils on constant watch, the state legislature, prodded by the governor and Mayor O'Dwyer, overwhelmingly validated the city council's eviction controls. Throughout early 1948, the ECRH badgered the McGoldrick board to clear its backlog of tenant complaints and lobbied with the housing expeditor for assurances that local rent boards would seat tenant representatives. Even during the disastrous Wallace presidential campaign, the New York Tenant Councils, the ALP's vehicle to enroll apartment dwellers for Wallace, peppered O'Dwyer and Dewey with demands for two-year, statewide controls, a rollback of all rents to 1947, and a procedural thicket against further "hardship" increases.[29]

Governor Dewey somehow managed to placate these demands, while acceding to the fierce realtors' lobby. In late 1949, with the New York Tenant Councils calling for standby state protection and liberal voices like Charles Abrams, the Regional Plan Association, and the United Neighborhood Houses urging a statewide takeover, Governor Dewey convened a legislative fact-finding commission to investigate the role of controls during the housing emergency. Tenant radicals, poised for downstate hearings and city hall vigils, presented witnesses who vented the popular distrust of the housing expeditor and the preference for staunch local authority. The New York Tenant Councils demanded a city administrative commission with bona fide tenant representation, procedures for tenant rebuttal evidence, and a flat prohibition against rent increases in buildings with Multiple Dwellings Law violations. Political realities and GOP patronage needs, however, made a statewide board inevitable. Governor Dewey's bill established a state rent commission and favored landlords with a generous March 1, 1950, freeze date and rent comparability formulas, but balanced this with a six-month moratorium on rent increases to enable McGoldrick, the new state rent administrator, to conduct a scientific study of the rental market. Having finessed this solution to spiraling rents, Governor Dewey expected an easy reelection.[30]

In a series of maneuvers, tenant radicals still attempted to dominate the rent issue. They initiated lawsuits (cosponsored by the New York Tenant Councils and former congressman Leo Isaacson) to uphold the city's eviction laws. Paul L. Ross, chairman of the New York Tenant Councils and the Committee to End Discrimination in Stuyvesant Town, entered the 1950 mayoral race as the rent payer's champion, running a left wing populist campaign against Mayor O'Dwyer's flagrant machine politics and Robert Moses's alleged deals with real estate cronies. The ALP stalked McGoldrick board hearings around the state, with dire warnings of sellouts to landlords, and managed to turn one Manhattan hearing into a marathon of invective. While McGoldrick denounced attempts "by disruptive elements to inflame the public," he had no choice but to emphasize that any rent increases would affect only a small number of "hardship" cases. Nevertheless, as the city's foremost student of scientific property earnings, McGoldrick sent recommendations to the legislature that pegged rent increases to a fixed return on capital investment. He also favored negotiated, voluntary 15 percent rent increases and wider grounds for eviction, particularly for landlords planning to subdivide apartments. The Dewey-McGoldrick package—the state commission, fixed-return formula, and voluntary 15 percent increases—became the new staple of state controls.[31]

While controversy embroiled different aspects of state rent control, the Dewey-McGoldrick system proved durable over the next decade. During the debates over revision in spring 1953, housing liberals on the influential Citizens Housing and Planning Council were disturbed by McGoldrick's inadequate 4 percent return on assessed values. They favored a 15 percent rent "catch-up" for tenants who had not paid any increase since 1947, while the Metropolitan Fair Rent Committee argued for an across-the-board 20 percent. The legislature's Temporary State Commission to Study Rents favored renewal with an increased net-return formula, vacancy decontrol, and an exemption on luxury apartments. Although tenant radicals railed againt this "open capitulation to landlords," Governor Dewey signed the two-year extension, which granted a 15 percent "equalization" adjustment and increased the net annual return for "hardships" from 4 to 6 percent. Subsequent Democratic leaders ventured no major changes on Dewey's handiwork. Robert F. Wagner, Jr., the Manhattan Democrat who successfully campaigned for mayor in 1953 by attacking Dewey's "rent gouging," was shrewd enough not to take over the rent program when the Democratic legislature offered the city a local-control option. When liberal Democrat W. Averell Harriman succeeded Dewey as governor in 1955, he appointed Charles Abrams as state rent administrator, a move popular with tenant groups from the Village, the Lower East Side, and Yorkville. But it was Abrams who directed the state's series of market-rent studies that eventually provided the rationale for the systematic lifting of selected controls.[32]

During this heyday of liberal Democratic rent control, the old American Labor party neighborhood clubs, where they survived at all, perfected their tenant work amid competition from nearby settlements and Reform Democratic clubs. Tenant radicals had slipped into conservative, safe rent advisement not much different from social casework. Whether in Chelsea or Yorkville, ALP storefronts and their subsidiary councils were practicing rent advisement and the expediting of individual rent claims with federal and state offices, thus becoming veritable extension agents of the rent control system. Rarely did the councils venture outside the system—and withhold rent. As a mild sort of intimidation connected with rent-decrease petitions pending at the state rent office, Esther Rand's East Side Tenants Union occasionally encouraged tenants to hand their rent checks collectively to a tenant council officer. Not a single instance of rent withholding appears in all the extensive tenant work performed by Marcantonio's ALP clubhouse; nor is there evidence that ALP clubs in Chelsea or Yorkville departed in any significant way from this caution. Tenant radicals had ended up as deputies of the liberal status quo. Desperate to distinguish their services, they had little choice but to shuffle rent-reduction forms faster than the Reform Democrats were doing down the block.[33]

Title I: Challenge and Response, 1949–1963

As the American Labor party clubs settled into routine neighborhood service, they soon found that they could not isolate rent counciling from the demolition that was becoming the chief by-product of Title I redevelopment in New York City. The Title I program became synonymous with Robert Moses, his ruthless political-construction complex, the wanton destruction of neighborhoods, and the scattering of their residents. To a generation of critics, notably Robert A. Caro in his blistering biography of Moses, Title I was also synonymous with reckless power that went unchecked until a small band of urban liberals rallied the conscience of the city. Few observers (including Caro), however, fully appreciated the extent of neighborhood opposition or the spearhead for that opposition provided by radical tenant councils and ALP clubs. But they were ever present, with their eviction protests, their city hall vigils, and their legal challenges, thus shaping the climate of neighborhood resistance as well as the disillusionment with large-scale redevelopment, which forced liberals to their agonizing reappraisal. Out of the rubble of countless defeats, tenant radicals would emerge with a critical understanding of the interaction between neighborhoods and the greater city that would become a fundamental aspect of the liberalism of the 1960s. And they would fashion a tenant coalition that would thrust that new consciousness onto the councils of the city.

Tenant radicals failed at first to grasp the full implications of urban redevelopment or the vital necessity of maintaining good relations with housing liberals, the allies they would need in the struggles to follow. The misunderstanding began at Stuyvesant Town in 1943, when the United Tenants League's blanket endorsement of private-sector initiatives undercut what might have been a liberal-Left coalition to humanize the scale of Metropolitan Life's inner-city plans. The divergence widened as cold war suspicions poisoned relations between liberal Democrats and radicals, who seemed determined to politicize the OPA rent crisis for the Wallace presidential campaign. What were otherwise common grounds against redevelopment became further occasions for acrimony. In 1947, when tenant radicals belatedly tried to exploit the Jim Crow issue with their Tenants Committee Against Discrimination in Stuyvesant Town, liberals from the Citizens Housing Council, the American Jewish Committee, and the Ethical Culture Society responded with their own implicitly anti-Communist, open-housing lobby—the New York State Committee on Discrimination in Housing. When liberals held a 1948 Conference on City Planning to challenge Moses's ideas for large-scale redevelopment, the tenant councils were noticeably absent. During the special mayoral election of 1950, ALP candidate Paul L. Ross snubbed Citizens Union queries about city planning, while two Republican property owners' candidates welcomed the notion of urban reconstruction limited by the vetoes of neighborhood planning boards. By then it was already too late to restore the splintered coalition.[34]

This fateful division handed the initiative to Moses's redevelopment machine, a phalanx of experienced realtors and public contractors, many of them alumni of the New York City Housing Authority's largest clearance jobs and long reconciled to shoving thousands aside for housing progress.[35] They found their instrument in the new law that Moses had helped draft, Title I of the Federal Housing Act of 1949. Title I authorized the U.S. Housing and Home Finance Administration to contribute two-thirds of the "write down" costs incurred by local redevelopment authorities to acquire and prepare "blighted" residential acreage for resale to private developers. It also contained formal safeguards for local, democratic decision making, such as public planning commission hearings to define blighted areas and city council votes to condemn property and to authorize the required, local one-third contribution. But it was generally acknowledged that Moses stood the system on its head. His Committee on Slum Clearance (CSC) secretly arranged with favored realtors to pick choice sites and cleared votes on the City Planning Commission and Board of Estimate before site residents could respond. The master of visionary blueprints, Moses drove his CSC staff to churn out a glossy agenda for the city's redevelopment: Corlears Hook, Harlem and North Harlem, Washington Square South, South Village, Williamsburg, Delancey Street, Manhattantown, Morningside-Manhattanville, and others, which would transform New York's cityscape and force at least one hundred thousand people from their homes by 1960.[36]

While the CSC held the initiative in packaging and promoting projects, it was often forced to dicker with local opposition, play a game of divide and conquer, and wield as its trump card the promise (or threat) of public housing projects. In the complex shuffle among government agencies and civic groups, tenant groups usually played a peripheral, yet often influential, role, creating the tension that forced liberals to intervene. When the CSC unveiled its "Corlears Hook" Title I for the Lower East Side in 1950, the ALP and its Manhattan Tenants Council tried to organize the 878 site families, an effort joined by a few Socialists and the local Tammany congressman. But the project suffered no major delays, except for those involved in the removal of a few isolated Puerto Rican families and some small businesses along Grand Street. The CSC enjoyed much the same sway at "Godfrey-Nurse" and "North Harlem," Title I sites on the Harlem periphery. Both were praised in the black press, and none of the community's tenant groups challenged these efforts at redevelopment. CSC proposals for "Washington Square South" and "South Village," however, poked into a locale whose institutions ranged ideologically from St. Anthony's Roman Catholic parish to the Little Red School House. The intrusion on the Square roused a committee of old Moses foes, such as Charles Abrams and planner Robert C. Weinberg, and middle-class residents stirred by the area's brownstone heritage. A large, effective Village protest forced Moses to withdraw, but not before liberals conceded that some plan should be adopted "before local opposition crystallized to a point where no redevelopment in Greenwich Village could be accomplished." Some were ready to appease Moses with the "blight" to the south and east of West Broadway so that he might keep his hands off what they considered the real Village center.[37]

"Manhattantown" (later renamed Park West) comprised six square blocks between 97th and 100th streets, Central Park West to Amsterdam

Avenue, with five thousand families, which the CSC marked for clearance in 1951. ALP workers and their Manhattan Tenants Council, quickly arriving on the scene, helped tenants form an opposition group, gathered over a thousand protest signatures, and held demonstrations at city hall. In December 1951, local Protestant clergy and the editor of *El Diario* convened an emergency conference at the Grace Methodist Church on West 104th Street and denounced the dissolution of "one of the oldest Negro communities in New York outside of Harlem," a transparent strategy to force blacks and Puerto Ricans back across 110th Street. Few prominent liberals cried out against the proposal, while the controversy over relocation was defused when the state housing commissioner offered eighteen hundred public housing units for site families who cooperated. Nevertheless, the Manhattan Tenants Council, with Manhattantown protesters leading the way, rallied resisters in Harlem, North Harlem, and Manhattanville into a United Community to Save Our Homes, which brought suit against the Title I contracts in state supreme court. While fighting a losing cause, ALP radicals achieved two important breakthroughs. They had raised a rallying cry in Save Our Homes and had established the liaison that made possible citywide protests from scattered sites. In the process, their inflammatory, aggressive attacks had also unnerved liberals, who preferred urban redevelopment without incident.[38]

How far liberals would go to suppress the contrary arguments presented by tenant radicals is revealed in the controversy surrounding the Title I project for Morningside Heights. The struggle against urban decay on this edge of Harlem dated back to 1947, when Columbia University and the Riverside Church founded Morningside Heights, Incorporated (MHI), a consortium of local churches, hospitals, and educational institutions to stimulate the upgrading of housing that would "stabilize" the area's "exposed fringes." Soon after enactment of Title I, David Rockefeller, chairman of the Riverside Church board of trustees, solicited Robert Moses's interest, particularly in potential superblocks north of 122d Street. Working closely with the CSC on redevelopment plans, MHI director Lawrence W. Orton organized a cadre of local redevelopment enthusiasts, the Morningside-Manhattanville Community Advisory Committee. With elaborate publicity, the CSC and MHI soon released plans for "Morningside," six high-rise middle-income, cooperative apartment buildings. As an afterthought, the CSC also announced it was trying to commit the Housing Authority to build sixteen hundred low-income units for "Manhattanville," the companion development straddling the Harlem boundary at 125th Street.[39]

The developers, however, had not anticipated the anger of site residents nor the resourcefulness of local ALP radicals. Led by a site tenant, Elizabeth Barker, ALP stalwarts organized a Save Our Homes committee operating out of an Amsterdam Avenue storefront. At preliminary Board of Estimate hearings, seventy residents warned lawmakers that "they would rather have no housing than housing not suited to their incomes." The head of the Community Advisory Committee, Father George F. Ford of Corpus Christi Church, also had to face his parishioners' resentment at being torn from everything familiar. Troubled by the unexpected hostility, particularly by the charge of "Negro removal," MHI considered reshaping the plan to attract the more amenable of the ALP radicals. MHI hoped to get a stronger Housing Authority commitment for the low-income Manhattanville component or perhaps a foundation to finance less expensive co-ops. Some suggested pursuing the inquiry from the Brotherhood of Sleeping Car Porters to sponsor limited-dividend housing (north of 125th Street). Aware that they had to strengthen the promise of low-income housing to site residents, Father Ford, Orton, and Rockefeller conferred with Robert Moses about community "tensions." When Rockefeller suggested that the CSC emphasize its guarantee of adequate public housing, Moses petulantly questioned their own support for the project and warned that he would ask the Board of Estimate to defer consideration of the project at its November 15, 1951, meeting. In the meantime, the Committee to Save Our Homes collected five thousand signatures from site residents and rounded up several hundred persons for the Board of Estimate hearings. While the Housing Authority came through with $23,000,000 for "Manhattanville," with priority to families displaced from the Title I site, 250 protesters remained unmollified and boisterous. At the hearings, they sneered at the "luxury" co-ops that would force blacks back to "walled-in Harlem" and cried victory when the board laid the project over to spring 1952.[40]

This delay provided both sides with time to regroup. MHI and the Community Advisory Committee hired social workers to organize a Manhattanville Civic Association, "a broadly-based cross-sectional organization for community improvement," open to "residents only." Nevertheless, Save Our Homes packed the association's first meeting, booed down a conciliatory resolution, and resolved "to see the high rent cooperative plan defeated." Furthermore, the Save Our Homes appeal to site residents increased over the winter, as tenants brooded over their uncertain future and landlords began to cut services in anticipation of imminent clearance. Save Our Homes well cultivated these concerns. It established a Tenant Information Service to advise on a wide range of rent control and Multiple Dwellings Law violations, while trying to maintain site residents' morale. For its part, MHI spent the winter lining up prestigious endorsements, including testimonials from the Liberal party, Negro Labor Committee, the Brotherhood of Sleeping Car Porters, and the Morningside Cooperative Society. Even so, the opposition proved more effective than ever. For the April 1952

Board of Estimate hearings, Save Our Homes orchestrated pleas from residents, a committee of small-store owners, and another parish priest. Before Elizabeth Barker was thrown out of the hearing, she "shocked," boasted the *Daily Worker*, seasoned professionals with her detailed analysis that showed the feasibility of nine-dollar-per-room public housing for the Morningside site. MHI regarded further Board of Estimate action as inadvisable and agreed to a delay until the fall, in hopes that the opposition would melt away with the first chance to apply for the co-op apartments.[41]

During spring and summer 1952, when much of Truman liberalism seemed under a cloud, anxieties among redevelopment liberals and Washington's impatience with Title I in New York reached a crisis. Both were crystallized to a great degree by the Save Our Homes furor. In March, liberals on the influential Citizens Housing and Planning Council (CHPC) warned Washington that Robert Moses's cavalier practices had risked "an unfavorable public reaction" against Title I, especially when "Communist dominated groups are piling misrepresentations and falsehoods on top of the weak relocation structure." When the Housing and Home Finance Administration dismissed these fears, the CHPC argued for a "go slow" policy that would allow only one major clearance project, as an experiment in the careful relocation of site tenants. After fruitless negotiations with the city, the CHPC, joined by the NAACP, United Neighborhood Houses, and Americans for Democratic Action, publicized its opposition, warning about the mischief of "Communist dominated groups" and the adverse impact on Title I of relocation that was "improperly handled." Liberals' anxieties had some justification. In May 1952 delegates from sixty-two civic and housing organizations met at the McBurney YMCA to protest the entire Title I program, the loyalty oath for public housing tenants, and Metropolitan Life's racial quotas at Stuyvesant Town. Several Save Our Homes groups were featured, along with vivid testimony of hardships faced by black and Puerto Rican refugees from site demolition. The ALP was also behind the Chelsea Tenants Council's efforts to defy the New York Port Authority's clearance of five thousand residents from the approaches of the Lincoln Tunnel. In a well-organized campaign, the Chelsea Tenants leafleted buildings, advised tenants to band together against demolition, and vowed to delay evictions for years.[42]

Threats to urban redevelopment—the good Title I projects along with the bad—forced housing liberals to choose between the Moses program and the Save Our Homes intransigents. Many remained silent or vented an uneasiness, which to Moses was as useful as silence. While the State Committee Against Discrimination (SCAD), for instance, conveyed to the Board of Estimate its displeasure toward the CSC's Title I work, its criticism remained behind the scenes. Its intervention was limited to a quiet study of relocated families from Title I sites and to cooperation with the CHPC and the American Jewish Committee on a City-Wide Committee on Housing Relocation Problems. Supporters later conceded that the City-Wide Committee was "marked with confusion as to purpose and method" and never united on a program. SCAD, for its part, failed to fill the breach. While worried that the Save Our Homes zealots might dominate the debate against Title I and relocation and fearful that it was forfeiting involvement in "one of the city's most serious minority housing problems," SCAD nevertheless voted not to assume "any great responsibilities" in the relocation controversy.[43]

Moses's prodding finally forced committed redevelopment liberals off the fence. Skillfully exaggerating Housing and Home Finance Administration's doubts about the city's Title I progress, including Morningside-Manhattanville, Moses warned that he too might lose interest in the Morningside package. This was enough for MHI to assemble the ultimate sales pitch, which included dubious census data to make a "stronger case for physical deterioration" of the site, Father Ford's personal lament that his parishioners were fleeing "this festering sore," and CSC data on the influx of low-income groups that "definitely proves that it is deteriorating and it is blighted." MHI director Orton made the rounds at Housing and Home Finance, while his staff experts in cooperative housing reached influential Democrats on Capitol Hill. A few days later Truman administration officials gave their hearty endorsement, which also broke the logjam in the city. Further Board of Estimate hearings were rendered academic, although the Save Our Homes contingent had become so versed in Title I technical manuals that it raised embarrassing, largely unanswerable questions about the CSC's plans for relocation. The Board of Estimate braved three hundred diehard protesters and approved Morningside-Manhattanville on January 15, 1953.[44]

In defeat, Save Our Homes managed to hang on in a caretaker role. Still dominating Manhattanville Civic Association meetings, the group turned its expertise to strictly practical questions, such as Do you sign a loyalty oath before entering projects? Is a woman with children, but no husband, eligible for public housing? Will the city pay moving expenses? Elizabeth Barker's message mixed cold fury with sound advice for desperate site tenants—"Organize to save rent control. Every week we'll have a meeting somewhere, even in the apartments. Don't get hysterical. Keep people in the houses. Don't race around." Both Save Our Homes and the Manhattanville Civic Association continued to dispense rent and relocation advice and to hold weekly information nights that emphasized the peculiar rights of relocatees. "As long as you remain here and pay your rent, you are a project site tenant. The City and Morningside Heights are *required by Law* to help you." Save Our Homes remained active on the site as late as

1954, when it sponsored a bitter dispute contesting MHI's "diligence and sincerity" in carrying out its relocation responsibilities. But as demolition proceeded, it remained a champion of only a forlorn remnant, the large number of blacks and Hispanics struggling for "reasonable offers" for public housing or private rentals.[45]

During the Title I controversy, tenant opposition proved more substantial and liberal critics played far more ambiguous roles than observers have heretofore admitted. Much of the time, Moses was careful to direct his Committee on Slum Clearance onto marginal black and Hispanic neighborhoods, generally isolated, unorganized, and "invisible" in the early 1950s. Harlem's few tenant groups remained significantly still. Jesse Gray's Harlem Tenants Council, an ALP faction hanging on in the ghetto, was too weak to serve as an instrument of mass agitation. The venerable Consolidated Tenants League was a mere specter, clinging to its clientage with the Housing Authority. What remained were scattered lower-middle-class ALP clubs and Save Our Homes committees. But their rhetoric and motives were already discounted as Communist-tainted by liberal housing reformers. The liberals remained ad hoc committees of committees, with little grass roots support and too much faith in back-room consciousness-raising, hardly an even match with the best bureaucratic infighter of his time. Of course, liberals might "go public" with their doubts, but not with the impact of a Moses publicity barrage. Besides, in the early 1950s SCAD and the American Jewish Committee were preoccupied with providing open access to housing for the city's racial minorities, an effort that won passage of the Austin-Wicks and the Brown-Isaacs laws, which barred discrimination in state- and city-aided projects. These triumphs, accompanied by bitter SCAD attacks on the spurious aid given minorities by Communists and the ALP, ironically provided nondiscriminatory seals of approval on the Title I program, if not on its methods of relocation. But the distinction was lost on the public and, when it counted, on the liberals as well. They went along with the ends, if not the means, of Moses's redevelopment. They tried to hold out for adequate, humane relocation. But when that position meant jeopardizing glittering high rises or aligning closely with Save Our Homes radicals, the liberals began to weigh the costs of their quibbling intervention.[46]

During the winter of 1953–1954, lingering tenant anger had combined with the liberals' criticism of relocation to shape a new sensitivity in Washington and New York toward bulldozer removal. The Dwight D. Eisenhower administration, anxious to lower federal spending on Title I, approved the new concept of urban "renewal" in the Housing Act of 1954. Newly elected mayor Robert F. Wagner, Jr., an astute compromiser, tried to find some middle ground between Czar Moses and the housing liberals who worried about the social cost of redevelopment. The new sensitivity was skeptical about large-scale clearance for high-rise apartment slabs on superblocks, but enthusiastic about small-scale brownstones and townhouses and their networks of middle-class families. It was strong enough to force Moses to choose his targets with more care, and it gave opponents far more powerful weapons to resist his encroachments. Yet, while angry lower-middle-class tenants had helped shape this new appreciation for small-scale urbanism, its immediate beneficiaries were upper-middle-income preservationists, the first wave of the new era of urban "gentry."

Moses still scored his victories, but they came on carefully prepared ground, through indirection rather than frontal assault and from opponents already softened by the promise of relocation to public housing. In December 1953 the Board of Estimate gave the preliminary go-ahead to yet another Title I project, controversial "Washington Square Southeast." While Greenwich Villagers were up in arms, their real outrage may well have been the realization that many had unwittingly contributed to the plan's audacious cynicism. Moses had apparently remembered liberals' suggestions about the Village's undesirable "fringes," when they defeated his "South Village" proposal in 1951. This time, Moses refashioned his dream of an arterial highway through Washington Square with a redevelopment package between West Broadway and Mercer Street and the low-income Mary K. Simkhovitch Houses slated for the "South Village" site. Preservationists and New York University officials had been won over by the promised stability of real estate near the park, while liberals again conceded the inevitability of redevelopment for commercial buildings and "narrow truck-clogged streets" on the southeast. Villagers objected to public housing south of Houston Street and were adamant against the highway through their beloved park. But while liberals and ADA-ers sniped at the plan's expensive apartments and the bisected park, an unexpected dissident group, the Lower West Side Civic League, speaking for tenement residents and small manufacturers, lashed out against the proposed Simkhovitch Houses: "'Slum clearance' here would mean clearing *out* of crowded slums in Harlem and elsewhere *into* these Village projects." In the end, Moses rammed through the Board of Estimate most of his original plan for Washington Square Southeast, including the high rises and arterial roadway. But he could not have done so without NYU and the Washington Square Association. He also appreciated the "Italian interests" in whose behalf he killed the Simkhovitch Houses, his expendable bargaining chip all along.[47]

The next near-crisis in the Title I program was also occasioned by mounting tenant protest, but this time against a backdrop of civic dismay about scandalous contracts at Manhattantown. During 1955, sordid facts began to dribble out about lucrative deals made with CSC insiders, while the plight of site tenants became an ugly and undeniable issue for city policymakers. In February, after a tenant was killed at half-demolished Godfrey-Nurse, Jesse Gray's Harlem Tenants Council leafleted the surrounding neighborhood. Urban League officials and Congressman Adam Clayton Powell, Jr., then met Moses, who would not concede much. He merely assigned an aide to speed relocation, while pledging quick demolition of dangerous, abandoned tenements under his control. But the controversy would not subside, as Harlem agitation touched off intervention by outside liberals. During summer 1955, attorney Harris Present, Urban League secretary Edward Lewis, and Ira S. Robbins of the CHPC organized the City-Wide Committee on Housing Relocation Problems, which stirred newspaper inquiries about the fate of Title I site residents. The backlog of site residents awaiting new shelter had "seriously impeded" the program's progress, acknowledged realtor James Felt, one of Moses's most influential supporters. Facing another grave challenge, Moses threw down one of his support-me-or-I-quit ultimatums to Mayor Wagner. His threats to bring all construction to a halt forced the Board of Estimate's approval of clearance projects then pending, abruptly thrusting aside the relocation debate. The City-Wide Committee on Housing Relocation Problems had split down the middle about confronting the mayor and chose not to do so, while State Rent Commissioner Charles Abrams contented himself with Moses's reassurance that site residents would have the full protection of the Multiple Dwellings Law until their homes were razed. Again, housing liberals had backed down rather than force a confrontation.[48]

The resolved crisis, however, raised the curtain on widespread discontent, stirred by a loose coalition of civic and neighborhood groups, which enjoyed unprecedented attention from city agencies. With fears that two thousand low-income Yorkville families faced imminent eviction for speculative construction, State Rent Commissioner Abrams in November 1955 conducted hearings with witnesses from the Lenox Hill Neighborhood Association, Yorkville Save Our Homes, and other tenant groups. In Greenwich Village, Moses's plans for the four-lane artery through Washington Square faced a formidable new antagonist, the irrepressible *Village Voice*, and neighborhood groups ready to block traffic with their bodies. By January 1956 a coalition led by the Department of Church Planning and Research of the Protestant Council, SCAD, and Harris Present, chairman of the new City Council on Relocation Practices, met at the West Side ADA to condemn the Title I program and the havoc of relocation. Commanding new media attention, public agencies again nerved themselves to intervene. The city council, provoked by the Lenox Hill Neighborhood Association and Yorkville Save Our Homes, held week-long hearings during which East

Harlem and Yorkville tenants told how speculative landlords thrived on "human misery." The Urban League urged the city to repossess Manhattantown, Godfrey-Nurse, and North Harlem for public housing sites, while the Women's City Club and Charles Abrams recommended a moratorium on slum clearance. At this juncture, the regional housing and home finance administrator charged that the CSC's laxity had allowed private sponsors to run four Title I projects close to default.[49]

Shrewdly, Moses focused the Title I debate on his own terrain—the Lincoln Square site, where he could present a dazzling cultural center to the liberal cognoscenti and an elaborate relocation package for 6,018 site families. He appointed a special CSC group on relocation, then announced that 25 percent of the displaced would be guaranteed public housing. When Lincoln Square residents began continuous picketing at city hall and sent a telegram blitz to federal officials, Moses brought his enormous pressure to bear. While the CSC made glib promises of five hundred co-op units on the site and public housing nearby, Moses threatened to resign unless Title I got more "cooperation" from the Wagner administration. Finally, he tossed some conciliatory gestures at the housing liberals. He sent the new City Planning Commission chairman James Felt to an ADA luncheon to defend the city's relocation record and to argue that slum clearance could not await complete solutions to relocation. To the Citizens Housing and Planning Council, Felt made a more significant offer. His City Planning Commission would study the Upper West Side near Lincoln Square as a possible new "urban renewal area," presumably safe from large-scale demolition.[50]

Moses would carry on other projects after Lincoln Square, but he came up against steadfast, skilled opposition by neighborhood groups. When Moses pressed his arterial roadway through Washington Square in 1958, he encountered twenty-two ad hoc organizations that held meetings and collected thirty thousand names on petitions, and the *Village Voice*, which helped organize the insurgency. That spring, the park savers, led by Jane Jacobs and Eleanor Roosevelt, icon of the Village Reform Democrats, put tremendous pressure on the Wagner administration and Carmine DeSapio's Tammany organization finally to bar Moses's automobiles from Washington Square. When the CSC earmarked 8.3 acres between 24th and 27th streets east of Third Avenue for redevelopment, a new group, Gramercy Park Neighbors, spiritedly lobbied for the alternative of rehabilitation and selective demolition. On the East Side, Sloan-Kettering Hospital's expansion plans, thwarted by the Lenox Hill Neighborhood Association and Yorkville Save Our Homes, produced an agreement in which the medical center's real estate developers would absorb the costs of private relocation. And on the Lower East Side, CSC proposals for Title I co-ops at Cooper Square touched off local tenant opposition organized by East Side settlement worker Selma Burdick, who had close contacts with Planning Commissioner James Felt.[51]

By 1959 both the institutional and ideological support for Title I had completely eroded. Shaken by controversy over "unjust" evictions, growing youth-gang violence, and "the behavior of the problem families . . . [that] threatened the reputation of the whole housing movement," the New York City Housing Authority was undergoing a not-so-quiet crisis. Some observers argued that the New York system needed a two-year "breathing spell" on new tenant admissions "to concentrate on building a more favorable reputation of the projects." The Housing Authority could no longer be that convenient dumping ground where Title I developers "externalized" the costs of relocation. In mid-1959 the *New York Times* climaxed a half decade of growing doubt with a devastating review of urban redevelopment, which concluded that Title I had destroyed much of the housing of the poor and given them no alternative but the impersonal, crime-ridden public projects. Searching for a way out, many planning experts focused on James Felt's "spot" renewal, advocated with growing vehemence by community groups on the Upper West Side, at Cooper Square, in Greenwich Village, and in Chelsea. That year, when an outraged Citizens Union documented the insiders' deals between the CSC and Tammany realtors, Mayor Wagner scrapped the CSC for a new Housing and Redevelopment Board dominated by James Felt and realtor J. Clarence Davies. Both were liberals with a reputation for listening to neighborhood views on redevelopment and for sympathy to selective "renewal" rather than bulldozer clearance. Subsequent observers, such as Jeanne R. Lowe and Robert Caro, related these changes to the liberals' outcries, to good-government audits, and to newspaper scrutiny given Title I after 1957. But more important was the crisis in public housing, the growing neighborhood opposition, and the citywide coalition of tenants up in arms. In the climate largely shaped by tenants themselves, housing liberals could no longer turn a deaf ear to their protest.[52]

The new tenant voice emerged with the spring 1959 formation of the Metropolitan Council on Housing from tenant councils and neighborhood protest groups across the city. Its first meetings revealed visible links with the past, such as Helen Harris from the Bronx Council on Tenants and Housing (which was still holding daily rent advisement at the same storefront, 910 Southern Boulevard); Esther Rand and Frances Goldin, veteran ALP organizers from the Lower East Side now involved in the recent turmoil at Cooper Square; and Jane and Robert Wood, from the Chelsea Tenants Center. There were new faces, fresh from the war against Title I: Miriam Moody and Edward Schaffer of Gramercy Park Neighbors, a middle-class protest group; Staughton Lynd, from Cooper Square; and social work liberals from the University Settlement and the Community Council of Greater New York, who reflected the growing unrest among tenants on welfare and the "advocacy" movement in casework ranks. Their joining into the most influential radical housing voice since the old City-Wide Tenants Council was an auspicious event in the city's postwar history. For the first time since the chilled anti-Communist atmosphere of the early 1950s, a political thaw had allowed Save Our Homes radicals to project their viewpoints on citywide forums and expect to be heard.[53]

But if the political climate gave Met Council's radicals the opportunity, the new liberals' enthusiasm for "neighborhood renewal" made it imperative for them to act. Across the city, public interest was turning away from Moses and toward the neighborhood liberals' gearing up of the first pilot programs in community renewal. In the late 1950s, Chelsea's influential settlement house, the Hudson Guild, transforming a small rent clinic into a broad, paternalistic intervention in community housing, had provided the prototype for local tenement rehabilitation that the Wagner administration later formalized as the Neighborhood Conservation Program. In Yorkville, the luxury apartment boom along Third Avenue forced the Lenox Hill Neighborhood Association to similar efforts at ameliorative housing action. A Lenox Hill staff worker, Victor Remer, organized the Yorkville Housing Committee, which started with tenant counciling and wound up as the planning agency for middle-income cooperative housing to "maintain a balanced community." In both neighborhoods, Save Our Homes radicals dismissed these as clumsy attempts by liberals to fashion a more palatable kind of Title I clearance.[54]

By spring 1959, however, liberals' initiatives could no longer be shrugged off. Liberal Democrats and their trade union allies at the United Housing Foundation held a "slum prevention" conference at which they proposed housing rehabilitation for the Upper West Side. In a throwback to Octavia Hill paternalism, the headworkers of participating settlements would undertake rent collection and social counseling at the properties undergoing renewal. The conference was followed by the Wagner administration's proposals for a centralized relocation bureaucracy to identify available shelter and expedite relocation. By then, as well, Victor Remer's Yorkville success had brought him into the Wagner administration's Neighborhood Conservation Program. It was still in the start-up stage and working under federal demonstration grants in Harlem (coordinated by the Community Service Society), the Lower West Side (by the Hudson Guild), and Bedford-Stuyvesant (by another settlement, Colony House). But Remer was a tireless advocate of the idea that housing blight could be reversed by combining city assistance to landlords and consultative service to tenants. As so conceived, Neighborhood Conservation amounted to a strategy of community maintenance involving close cooperation between city agencies, civic groups, and landlords, with tenants and their spokesmen left out in the cold.[55]

Many Met Council charter members had had their brushes with the liberals' brand of community renewal. Jane and Robert Wood's perspectives had been shaped by a messy tenant fight against redevelopment in Chelsea. Their Chelsea Save Our Homes had originally joined hands with the local settlement, the Hudson Guild, on the Chelsea Community Council, but they could not go along when Guild headworker H. Daniel Carpenter insisted on cooperation with the relocation efforts on the "Penn South" Title I. Save Our Homes' withdrawal split the Community Council, but its vow to continue the fight against Penn South carried many neighbors along. The Woods were a tough, yet self-effacing, mix of Catholic Worker pietism and early 1930s confrontation. "We are not a rent clinic," Jane Wood told an interviewer in 1962. "We pick out the worst houses on a block—and we go in and organize the tenants." They earned the loyalties of the neighborhood's working-class Catholics and its old-line political club, Horatio Seymour Democrats, while somehow managing to stay on good terms with the predominantly Jewish reformers, the New Chelsea Democrats. At a meeting at the Horatio Seymour Club in late 1962, Jane Wood pilloried Carpenter for lending his support to the Wagner administration's Neighborhood Conservation Program and charged that it would rival Title I as a ravager of tenants.[56]

The most creative tenant efforts came out of the University Settlement's confrontation with Title I at Cooper Square on the Lower East Side. In the late 1950s, University Settlement had thrown off its recreation-room traditions in the struggle to defeat the "Delancey" Title I. During that stand, when the community learned to distrust city officials and big-shot landlords, the University Settlement formed the One Mile Neighborhood Council, a self-conscious grass roots organization that prided itself on "open" meetings and no formal hierarchies. Thus the area's dissident groups had already been blooded when the Committee on Slum Clearance announced plans for the "Cooper Square" Title I—twelve square blocks between the Bowery–Third Avenue and Second Avenue, north of Delancey Street. The CSC envisioned 1,800 middle-income cooperative units on land already occupied by 2,400 housing units, mainly old law tenements, and some 450 furnished rooms and 4,000 lodging-house beds that served homeless men on the Bowery. Moses's bulldozers would have also swept away 400 small businesses, two churches, and the Cooper Square Settlement.[57]

Based on past practice, site tenants would have responded with protests organized by a local Save Our Homes committee, with which, in fact, Frances Goldin had already begun on the One Mile Neighborhood Council. But several social workers, touched by a radicalism alloyed with a sense of

Christian witness, had other ideas. Staughton Lynd, caught between social work and American history at Columbia University, was working at the University Settlement in early 1959 when he broke with the headworker's apparent acceptance of the Title I project. He joined Thelma Burdick of the Cooper Square Settlement and Walter Thabit, a maverick city planner at the New School for Social Research, to discuss alternatives to what Moses was handing down. At the outset, Lynd and Thabit agreed that Cooper Union, the churches, and other indigenous institutions had to be preserved as anchors in any renewal plan. They went on to attack relocation provisions, which they suspected the CSC had woefully underestimated. Lynd and Thabit conducted their own site survey, with Sarah Lawrence students going house to house among five hundred residents, finding that many were tightly knit Italians who wanted to hold on to their modest apartments. In the meantime, Frances Goldin and Esther Rand organized a system of block and house captains that brought out local residents to noisy protests at Cooper Square and city hall during 1959 and 1960.[58]

Through the Met Council network—organizers from Jane Benedict's Yorkville Save Our Homes—and money from the J. M. Kaplan Fund, alternative planning went forward. Lynd coordinated a series of presentations to public meetings of site residents, while Thabit's professional staff shaped up the final renderings. On July 31, 1961, what was now the Cooper Square Community Development Committee and Businessmen's Association presented the Wagner administration with its version of the future of Cooper Square. Boldly challenging the CSC's plan to raze nine blocks between Delancey and Ninth streets, Thabit's alternative spared five blocks and depicted an imaginative mix of high rises and open space along Third Avenue. It contained ample provision for housing middle- and lower-income site residents, plus artists' lofts and single-room-occupancy space (although even Thabit's plan, while recognizing the Bowery's "function" as a haven for homeless men, suggested that the flophouses be relocated south of Delancey Street). Thabit's work at Cooper Square was an impressive debut for "advocacy planning," as young architects in the 1960s would soon proclaim.[59]

The heart of Met Council, however, lay within its largest, most reliable affiliate, the Yorkville Save Our Homes Committee, run by Jane Benedict. Involved with radical white-collar unions in the 1930s, Benedict had gravitated to ALP clubhouse politics in Yorkville, working in Congressman Marcantonio's last campaigns and running (unsuccessfully) for local office. As the last chairman of the Yorkville ALP club on East 70th Street, she provided a decent interment for the local party when the wave of luxury high-rise construction hit the area in 1955. Rent control laws had never prohibited evictions that landlords claimed necessary for new residential construction, a loophole that particularly affected the elderly who lived on fixed incomes and were the least able to secure new shelter. This hard fact gave Benedict's tenant work its modus operandi and salient issue—individualized tenant casework that appealed to the elderly and a "moratorium" or complete halt to evictions and to the destruction of existing housing for new luxury units. When the old ALP cadre called a community protest meeting, several hundred packed the Jan Hus House to form the Yorkville Save Our Homes Committee. But once the excitement against gentrification died down, Benedict and her ALP veterans settled Yorkville Save Our Homes into the daily community services reminiscent of the old ALP clubhouses. Their work depended upon a seven-person executive committee, which everyone admitted depended upon the dominating presence of Jane Benedict. She and her handful of loyalists did the typing, ran the mimeo, licked the stamps, and passed out leaflets. They had neither the troops nor the inclination to engage in rent strikes; nor did they ever mount door-to-door campaigns to sign up supporters. Benedict recalled "a great reliance on the rent control laws, on filing forms." Tenants were urged to visit the Jan Hus House for advice on approaching city departments to request improvements in services and the Temporary State Rent Commission to apply for reductions in rents, and not to panic upon receiving an eviction notice. By the late 1950s, Yorkville Save Our Homes had become a reliable, comforting fixture in the community.[60]

For a while, Met Council was more taken with the impetuous program of Staughton Lynd than with the routine tenant work of Jane Benedict. Lynd personified Met Council's first duels against the housing policies of Wagner administration liberals. Lynd, Burdick, and the other veterans from Cooper Square gave Met Council its early involvement in alternative planning, which they conceived as a powerful instrument to give people control of their neighborhoods. Their standing committees launched inquiries into Multiple Dwellings Law violations, the continued Title I program, and the City Master Plan and followed these with sophisticated press releases to housing reporters at the *New York Times* and *New York Post*. In 1959, Met Council contested the last attempts by the CSC to extend Title I and disputed relocation plans at Lincoln Square and Cooper Square. In the public opinion war for Chelsea Title I, it prepared a conference of academics and community groups in 1960 that amounted to ambitious intervention in the planning process. Like the City-Wide Tenants Council of the late 1930s, Met Council's agenda had ranged far beyond the boundaries of "tenant issues."[61]

Met Council's forays into the realm of housing and city planning were always held hostage by particular interests caught up with rent control. The council's center of gravity remained the Yorkville radicals, who had the tightest coalition of support among elderly tenants and small businessmen, who could stage the most impressive street rallies and who possessed their blunt solution for city planning issues, the "moratorium" on demolition.

Events during 1961, when both state rent control and the Wagner administration were up for extension, showed how Met Council's large visions could become subordinate to the trivial debates orchestrated by the politicians. Early that year, Met Council, at the zenith of its influence, had forged a united front with the Manhattan Reform Democratic movement, which had made rent counciling a mainstay of its clubhouse routine. Yorkville assemblyman Mark Lane, supported by Met Council and Yorkville Save Our Homes, led a diverse coalition into the Housing Emergency Legislative Program (HELP), to coordinate mass demonstrations in the city and Albany that would "save" rent control. Under HELP auspices, Met Council and Assemblyman Lane's East Side organization held rallies, distributed thousands of leaflets, and bussed fifteen hundred protesters to Albany, where they demanded an end to loopholes in the rent laws and an immediate moratorium on demolitions. They dominated the legislative rent hearings with descriptions of wanton landlords whose unconscionable "hardship" applications forced thousands onto the streets. Jane Benedict ridiculed suggestions of liberals on the CHPC and United Neighborhood Houses for a modest leeway on controls and called their proposed 15 percent rent increase "a stab in the back." Again and again she referred lawmakers to Yorkville and other neighborhoods, where landlords had leveled twenty thousand low-income units to build luxury apartments starting at sixty dollars per room. But for all the fury, the Nelson A. Rockefeller administration rammed rent control, only slightly revised, through the legislature, after which Mayor Wagner, blaming the law's shortcomings on the Republicans, handily won reelection.[62]

Having joined the Wagner Democrats against the enemies of rent control, Met Council radicals found themselves stuck with a mayoral administration quite smug about the 1961 extension package. At the third annual Met Council conference in November 1961, members adopted the idea of mass demonstrations for the "moratorium." Assemblyman Lane called for "mass action" to force a tenement repair bill out of legislative committee. Keynote speaker Harris Present, citing the methods "used by the sit-in and Freedom Riders," called on Met Council to "court mass evictions" to win the "moratorium." But the politicians again pulled the rug out from under this militance. In spring 1962 Governor Rockefeller had the legislature hand the headache of rent control administration to the city. Mayor Wagner then proceeded to make controls "a supple and powerful instrument" within his "new look" housing program. He ordered his new Rent and Rehabilitation Administration (RRA) to make controls "serve the positive purpose of encouraging rehabilitation and repair" within an expanded program of "neighborhood conservation." To critics, such as Met Council, who contended that rehabilitation would outweigh controls at RRA, Wagner countered that for the first time a single agency "had the tools required to assist owners in rehabilitating rent controlled property while retaining rents which present tenants will be able to afford."[63]

Throughout 1962 the mayor posed as the champion of tenant interests. His Rent and Rehabilitation Administration plugged GOP rent "loopholes" and cultivated the support of organized tenants on the RRA Citizens Advisory Committee. He publicized tough standards against rent-increase applications for major capital improvements and new procedures to permit a complaint on behalf of several tenants that could be filed by their representative from the community. Tenants still tried to insinuate themselves in the policy debate. When Rent Administrator Hortense Gabel reported a December 1962 vacancy rate of 1.8 percent as continued evidence of the "oppressive" rental market, but argued for phased decontrol of luxury housing, she was jumped on by Met Council, which called her suggestion an outright attack on controls. City takeover had given tenant groups greater access to rent administrators, especially when Met Council broke bread with Manhattan's Reform Democrats. But Mayor Wagner built his successful third-term reelection on the skilled absorption of Reform, and his Rent and Rehabilitation Administration stood an even chance of repeating that coup with the tenant radicals. Certainly, Hortense Gabel was in the position to initiate policy, set the parameters of the rent control debate, and reduce Met Council to little more than reflex action.[64]

At a time when New York liberalism—and the Wagner administration in particular—was shaping the most creative housing programs since the city's liberation from Title I, Met Council radicals were demonstrating a decided turn toward tenant traditionalism. Already put on the defensive by press releases from Rent and Rehabilitation, Met Council suspected any measures that would weaken controls and saw the prime threat in RRA's rehabilitation policy. Met Council never did accept the concept of rehabilitation or the popular variants of the mid-1960s—neighborhood conservation and historic preservation. "We who live in areas where we have seen such rehabilitation," claimed Jane Benedict, "know that its ultimate purpose . . . is to get rid of the low-income people living there." In June 1963 Met Council launched an assault on the Neighborhood Conservation Program. Tenant investigators looked beyond remodeled buildings to the relocation load. They found that Neighborhood Conservation's war on building code violations was really focused on alleged overoccupancy, which explained why 1,444 families had been displaced since the program's inception. Met Council concluded that "overoccupancy" was a racist euphemism, since 95 percent of those displaced were blacks and Puerto Ricans, forced from "integrated" communities such as Chelsea back to ghettoes such as Bedford-Stuyvesant and the South Bronx. The Chelsea Tenant Council added, "Neighborhood Conservation means the green light to real estate speculators who would like to turn Chelsea into another Yorkville or Greenwich Village."[65]

Met Council called instead for "true" conservation based on a sweeping moratorium against demolition of habitable structures, accelerated construction of public housing on vacant land, and strict enforcement of the Multiple Dwellings Law. Either landlords would bring their properties up to standards or they would lose their properties to a city receiver and go to jail. But this adamance estranged Met Council from liberals, as Jane Benedict recognized in her testimony at the September 1963 City Planning Commission hearings. She defensively explained that Met Council did not "oppose the *idea* of rehabilitation . . . but is opposed to loading the burden of payments on tenants." That burden equitably belonged to landlords, she argued, forwarding a Met Council plan for a city loan bank that would extend twenty-year, low-interest financing for rehabilitation, plus limited tax abatement, to enable owners to shoulder the costs without raising rents. To suggest otherwise, as did Rent Commissioner Gabel, who ventured that modest increases should cover some of the costs and that most tenants should expect to spend up to 25 percent of their income on rent, was to invite a cold disdain. "A new figure loomed ominously at the hearings," was the way Met Council's *Tenant News* reported Gabel's participation. Tenants throughout the city were invited to "figure out for yourself" what the 25 percent limit would mean.[66]

Despite the first New Left calls for "mass action" by tenants, Met Council remained dominated by older Leftists who looked with mixed envy and uneasiness on the ferment underway in the city. Not until summer 1962, in response to the civil rights agitation sweeping Harlem and Bedford-Stuyvesant, did Met Council move from the conference room and legislative lobby to the streets, and then only with great caution. In June it sponsored an Organize Your House campaign, with a series of street rallies on the edges of Manhattan's garment center. Lunch-hour crowds were handed leaflets, printed in English and Spanish, that advised "What the Law Says Your Landlord Must Do." Leaders were surprised by the "gratifying" response, but the effort at mass mobilization was never sustained. At Met Council's November 1962 annual conference, the focus was again on advocacy planning, including a "fresh look" from several prominent planners. The resulting publicity justified a series of miniconclaves, Met Council "roundtables," that brought community activists to talk about racial integration, community participation, public housing, and rent control. Met Council regarded these forums as highly effective instruments for citywide consciousness-raising.[67]

Met Council's attitude toward tenant mobilization remained stodgy and conservative, until it was swept along by the civil rights movement in 1963. Although the clique around Jane Benedict at Yorkville Save Our Homes realized the need to react to the vogue in mass action, it ended up making a feeble gesture in the streets. Throughout summer 1963 it announced "vigorous" petition drives and street-corner meetings. But the Yorkville mobilization, which anticipated the December 1963 rent control hearings, was aimed at the media and downtown liberals. An actual canvas of Yorkville tenements still remained a novel, untried idea. That summer, Met Council had reached an acknowledged "milestone," with a special committee to "organize tenants throughout the city and to coordinate the work of [Met] Council affiliates." It proved a very tentative step toward mass involvement. Its largest direct operation—among tenants at Seward Park Extension—was really the work of local radicals. Otherwise, the new committee devoted its energies to street rallies on behalf of its traditional program, strong rent controls. While Met Council's *Tenant News* was filled with talk about sending organizers to "trouble spots" around the city, few were exploited. The mobilization, such as it was, went into overdrive for the December 1963 city council hearings on rent control, when locals collected signatures on huge petitions. In September 1963, when Met Council was joined by the Brooklyn-based Organized Tenants, Inc., and the Tenant Association of New York to form the Action Committee of Tenants, the largest tenant consortium since the 1930s set a remarkably circumscribed goal, "a huge rally and demonstration outside rent control hearings scheduled for December at the City Council." On the eve of the great Harlem rent rebellion, Met Council served notice that it would take on no large cause.[68]

Rent Strikes and Community Power, 1962–1971

As the 1950s receded, tenant groups around the city had inched to the brink of mass action. Several forces had brought them to this point. American Labor party radicals found their organizational energies released by the political thaw. Title I, a profound mobilizing experience, had goaded entire neighborhoods into angry coherence. Churches and social settlements had contributed their sense of Christian witness and parish democracy. But most important was an impatience with the tenement environment and a weakening of those institutions that had siphoned off radicalism in the slums. Democratic Reform, which had consigned Tammany to oblivion, wrecked the clubhouse system that had given poor people considerable access to city rent offices and the Housing Authority. More fundamental still was the obstruction in the Housing Authority itself, as social breakdown in the projects undermined public housing's function as a safety valve for the pressures of Title I. Nevertheless, radicals hesitated to tread on the unfamiliar ground of direct action and mass mobilization until the civil rights movement swept them up in its intensity. This force finally brought tenants into the streets, on rent strike, and ultimately to the euphoria of community power. But the mass strike would prove a cumbersome weapon. It would intimidate landlords, but not necessarily to invest in new housing. It would stampede politicians to adopt cosmetic repairs, but not constrain them to approve bond issues or let building contracts. When the strike spasm ended, it would fail to improve the housing of the poor, but it would greatly stimulate the idea that poor people could take hold of their housing environment. As such, the strikes would be a formidable mobilizing force for the next stage of social action.

In the late 1950s, social work activists across the city, driven by a moral outrage against the slums and perhaps a growing sense of despair, had edged toward mass tenant mobilization. Most still operated, of course, within a liberal consensus, which in practice meant helping neighbors bear the stress of site clearance for Title I. As we have seen, Chelsea's Hudson Guild and the Upper East Side's Lenox Hill Neighborhood Association had pioneered tenant work effective enough to arouse the envy of nearby ALP clubs. In East Harlem, the Union Settlement worked through PTAs and tenant councils "to approach and then work with such authoritarian figures as school principles and housing managers." The Community Service Society's East Harlem Demonstration, which hoped to foster "neighborhood identification, self-esteem, and community action," even contained a harbinger of the 1960s, the search for "indigenous" leaders to rally neighbors into effective self-help groups. But like the others, the Community Service Society's efforts still centered on cooperative ventures with city planning agencies.[69]

The best known of these initiatives, Mobilization for Youth, Inc. (MFY), a self-proclaimed vehicle for radical change, found itself mired in conventional tenant casework. Launched in 1961 as an innovative attack on gang delinquency on the Lower East Side, MFY planned to reach "unaffiliated" lower-class teenagers by sending youth workers to stimulate PTAs, block associations, and tenant councils. At their storefront on Stanton Street, MFY community organizers longed to become wholesale advocates for a steady stream of welfare and tenant clients. But rhetoric aside, Stanton Street handled housing clients in classic casework style—forwarding individual tenant complaints to the Rent and Rehabilitation Administration

(RRA). MFY staffers saw themselves consumed by endless paper work, tedious often fruitless meetings with tenants, and the monumental inefficiency of city agencies.[70]

Even Harlem maverick Jesse Gray remained caught in these traditional channels. An ex-ALP radical, Gray had organized a series of local protest groups (at times called the Harlem Tenants Council or Harlem Tenant and Welfare Council) and delighted ghetto rallies with his tilts against landlords. But his activities, expediting applications for reduced rent at the Harlem rent office, stayed within the rent control system. No evidence shows that Gray resorted to rent strikes beyond the occasional withholdings sanctioned by section 755 of the New York State Real Property Actions and Proceedings Law (sec. 1446(a) recodified in 1962). His forte was the vivid publicity event, such as a 1954 protest against the eviction of a woman confined to a wheelchair. He often boasted of a network of block committees, run by two, three, or four hundred "house leaders." But these were the posturings of a political adventurer in a Harlem no-man's land—the Fourteenth Assembly District, whose crumbling tenements were overshadowed by the Housing Authority's Stephen Foster Houses (menaced by teenage gangs and "problem families"). The Fourteenth's political clubs, torn by factional revolt against Tammany, could no longer provide effective services for constituents at the rent office or the Housing Authority. In 1959, Gray, already with contacts in the Foster Houses, led his Harlem Tenants Council to organize housewives in the six-story walk-ups on nearby 116th Street. They picketed four tenements and handed out leaflets that announced they had gone "on strike" against rat infestation, while Gray told the *Amsterdam News* that six thousand more stood ready to join the rebellion. But as the city responded with squads of health inspectors, the flare-up receded to the back pages of Harlem's tabloids.[71]

What ended tenant work-as-usual for Gray, ALP clubs, social settlements, and MFY alike was the accelerating civil rights movement, unwittingly reinforced by the Wagner administration. Harlem's Congress of Racial Equality (CORE) chapter typified the drastic change. Caught in the crosscurrents of civil rights and Muslim nationalism, New York (Harlem) CORE was forced to supplement its liberal open-occupancy campaigns with sharp attacks on ghetto slums. In late 1962 the chapter opened a housing clinic on West 125th Street and announced that "CORE investigation teams will visit the buildings, call on residents, inform them of their rights." By mid-1963 the clinic was helping to organize tenant associations. Although it still continued to assist tenants at the rent office, it was now ready to challenge landlords with "direct action," including pickets and rent strikes. The chapter's aggressive minority talked excitedly about organizing "street people" into a network of building and block councils that would mobilize

Harlem. Drawn along, national CORE secretary James Farmer unveiled pilot projects for Newark and Bedford-Stuyvesant, where CORE organizers would confront landlords. When national CORE subsequently extended its "roving picket line" to Harlem, the City Buildings Department quickly responded with its first mass inspection of slums since the mid-1930s. While Mayor Wagner vowed to "press the attack" on slumlords, inspectors, accompanied by curious tenants, prowled through Bedford-Stuyvesant and Harlem.[72]

At MFY this direct action radicalized what remained of traditional social work. Cooperating aggressively with tenant groups, Stanton Street resorted to pickets, demanded meetings with city commissioners, and advised on withholding rent to get needed services. The summer crisis also hastened the creation of the MFY Legal Services Unit and the Tenement Housing Program, the brainchild of political scientist and MFY advisor Frances Fox Piven. Legal Services was envisioned as a network of clinics where volunteer attorneys would dispense advice on welfare and tenant problems such as unfair evictions from public housing. The Tenement Housing Program, on the other hand, revealed MFY's impatience with storefront casework and near despair about building code enforcement. The program's heart was to be a central file of housing violations, arranged by address and owner, to enable MFY to target the worst landlords. By October 1963 the Housing Program had taken on a professional coordinator, three Hispanic community workers, and seven student volunteers to work with the clinics and the central file. But MFY insiders still complained that direct action was used only "sporadically" and that the housing program had "no overall plan."[73]

By fall 1963, in the growing glare of the civil rights campaign, this impatience finally ignited. On one level it flared in impromptu rebellion against summary eviction proceedings in the magistrate's courts. Scores of tenants, most without legal counsel but inspired by black protest, claimed that they no longer owed rents for rat-infested rooms or that "Welfare" told them they did not have to pay. Judges indulged only a few of these defenses. On another level, however, organized groups soon vied to be the first to apply the new advocacy, with New York University CORE jumping the gun on the Lower East Side. In early 1963 the NYU student chapter had tried to act against code violations in old law tenements on Eldridge Street, but was frustrated by city agencies that sat idle for months. Concluding that the city was "incapable of fast, decisive action," chapter radicals called for an immediate rent strike. They got pledges from 94 Puerto Rican and black tenants for a November 1 withholding and reassured the one-third on welfare that they could refuse to pay rent for apartments with Multiple Dwellings Law violations. CORE volunteers from prestigious liberal Democratic law firms arranged with city officials for a tough prosecution, which dragged on and resulted in a mere $300 fine. But the owner had had enough, and he pleaded with CORE to take over his tenements. The exhausted chapter had stumbled on the remarkable prospect of unnerving a whole class of "slumlords" on the Lower East Side. The radicals urged CORE to send property owners a message that "we do not mean to pick on just one or two of their buildings, letting them do as they please with the rest." These were heady days, particularly with the news of strikes spreading through Harlem.[74]

During the early 1960s, Jesse Gray had restyled his Harlem Tenants Council into the Community Council on Housing (CCH), but only the name had changed. It was still Gray and a few unpaid, part-time organizers, working those same blocks in the Fourteenth Assembly District—an operation, Mark Naison found, "that teetered on the edge of bankruptcy." After a mid-October 1963 protest at city hall, Gray decided to lead sixteen of "his" buildings on strike. Tenants, reporters, and the curious soon converged on the CCH storefront; at a mass rally in early December, Gray claimed fifty-two buildings, with three thousand tenants, ready to join the movement. While city leaders rushed inspectors to the scene and arranged for drastic rent reductions, Gray was assembling a Rent Strike Coordinating Committee of Harlem religious and political VIPs. From time to time he held rallies, set up more paper coalitions, and got token support from New York CORE and local labor leaders. But his pickets, his eviction protests, and his confrontation with the police remained media events. On December 30, eviction proceedings against thirteen tenants on East 117th Street were heard in court, accompanied by Gray's raucous entourage and eager reporters. When the city magistrate, at the urging of Gray's attorney, accepted the applicability of section 755 and ordered rents paid in escrow, Gray jubilantly announced the support of three hundred more buildings, with one thousand joining by January 15.[75]

Gray spent early 1964 juggling these claims, while chiding the Wagner administration to come up with substantive reforms. Regarding the Harlem strikes as the most explosive episodes in a wave of civil rights demonstrations, Mayor Wagner virtually endorsed "legal" rent withholding. He rushed to the state legislature an agenda for more inspections, more housing courts, stiff Multiple Dwellings Law penalties, and a bill to transfer escrow rents from the courts to the Department of Real Estate to pay for repairs. Gray emerged the hero among tenant leaders and at city rent-control hearings (having staged the day before one of his vintage stunts to dramatize Albany's responsibility for ghetto housing—a Rats to Rockefeller campaign). But his claims about the "spreading" strike soon jaded his media contacts. At the same time, the Wagner administration was applying what Michael Lipsky has characterized as deft, symbolic gestures toward the slums.

When Gray demanded action, city hall obliged by jailing the landlord and invoking the Receivership Law to take over the tenements that had touched off Gray's strike. By then, Gray was also caught up in name-calling feuds with the police commissioner and in a controversy over alleged radicals in the city antipoverty program. By spring 1964 the Community Council on Housing was sorting through court papers that liquidated the last strikes.[76]

Nevertheless, Gray's example inspired direct action throughout Harlem. For the radicals who left New York (Harlem) CORE to start their own East River CORE chapter, this meant plans for disciplined community organization. They envisioned "group area teams" of ten workers per block to stir grass roots issues and contact "gangs, street people, numbers runners, and anyone else whose presence on the block is conspicuous." By late March 1964 the chapter claimed to have brought fourteen tenements to rent strike and to have organized tenant councils in another eleven. But its great success came at the twenty-one-hundred-unit Robert F. Wagner, Sr., Houses, where the chapter's pickets won stays against "unfair" evictions and attracted tenants already mobilized by local school boycotts. In the East Harlem barrio, Ted Velez, a young social worker, claimed that his contacts with Jesse Gray had helped set up the East Harlem Tenants Council in 1962. Boasting a network of building captains, in early 1964, Velez resorted to section 755 rent strikes on East 123d Street to force landlords to make repairs. Gray's influence also helped push Reverend Norman Eddy's East Harlem group, the Metro-North Citizens Committee (MNCC), from tenant counseling to street demonstrations and rent strikes. During 1963 MNCC had attracted a modest dues-paying membership, with its weekly rent clinic and volunteers to scout tenements for building violations. In early 1964 Eddy met with Jesse Gray and other tenant radicals to bone up on the section 755 defense.[77]

Gray's apparent triumph also ended Brooklyn CORE's ambivalence toward ghetto organization. Until 1962 the chapter's middle-class blacks, concentrating on open-occupancy pickets, had nagging doubts about their failure to "reach the Negro masses." But in late 1962 and early 1963, members staged noisy demonstrations about garbage pickup along Gates Avenue and job discrimination at the Downstate Medical Center. By September 1963 a CORE "task force" began canvasing Bedford-Stuyvesant and found tenants cynical about the Buildings Department's new inspections and ready to withhold rent. The chapter began to organize buildings and negotiate with landlords. "We had reached the point where we did it systematically," recalled Major R. Owens, head of Brooklyn CORE's Housing Committee. "We'd move into an area—a whole block, and canvas the block, distributing leaflets, explaining what the program was all about." To get quick referrals from the Buildings Department, Brooklyn CORE lived up to its "well-known reputation for taking direct action against city agencies." After the first spontaneous strikes on Rochester Avenue, CORE quickly got the Buildings Department to document "horrid" conditions, and in court, Brooklyn CORE's attorney successfully gained a section 755 rent diversion. With that, CORE dispatched volunteers equipped with interviewer sheets, city rent-reduction forms, and membership blanks for a community tenants council. When landlords served dispossess notices, organizers distributed applications for rent reduction, requested immediate "cellar-to-roof" inspections from the city, and even scheduled a photographer's visit to individual apartments. Yet, by late January 1964, CORE's tenant council had less than fifty members, although it claimed that fifty-one buildings (four hundred families) had gone on strike the following month.[78]

On the Lower East Side, MFY's Community Organization staff seized on the rent strike as the instrument to arouse the neighborhood—and to placate local radicals who had sniped at MFY "paternalism." Goaded by NYU and downtown CORE and by militants from Met Council and Progressive Labor, MFY's rent clinics on January 11, 1964, launched the Lower East Side Rent Strike. Organizers agreed to deploy a few Trotskyites, Progressive Laborites, and MFY staffers, perhaps thirty in all, to the tenements north of Houston Street, from Third to Fifth streets. NYU CORE, reinforced by the University Settlement and Esther Rand's East Side Tenants Council, would send twenty-six regular organizers and five more on weekends to Eldridge and Forsythe streets, from Delancey to Houston. The Puertorriquenos Unidos and the Stanton Street clinic would "work" Seward Park Extension. Some leaders expected the strike to force beefed-up inspections, fines, and jail sentences for landlords. Others spoke of foreclosing on private ownership altogether, with tenements taken over by city receivers and the Housing Authority. These divergent goals, however, were forgotten amid the euphoria, during which MFY pledged twelve volunteer lawyers coordinated by a young antipoverty attorney, Richard Levenson. A broad tenant uprising seemed imminent.[79]

Kicked off with an evening street rally and publicity releases claiming that seventy-five buildings would soon "go out," the movement was compromised from the start. It soon became clear that on their rounds, organizers had made far more contacts than actual commitments among tenants. For their part, Levenson's attorneys faced serious difficulties obtaining posted Multiple Dwellings Law violations on which the section 755 defense depended. Three weeks after the rally, strike leaders voted to take on no new buildings unless 50 percent of the tenants were already withholding rent. One organizer conceded that the strike had begun with "a splash" of claims, and his force was only "now going back to do the detailed work" among tenants. But that did not help Levenson's attorneys, already overwhelmed by the need to transport tenants, request inspections, subpoena Multiple Dwellings Law records, gather photographic evidence, and keep track of endless adjournments. The defense pleaded for a paid legal coordinator and a great increase in volunteer lawyers. "This panel is insufficient to handle the volume of rent strike cases," Levenson concluded. "One or two out of five cases are won by tenants (pay rent into court or dismissal). Three of five cases lost (rent paid to the landlord)." By the first week in April, the legal staff served notice that it could no longer continue without more volunteers, particularly from national CORE. During that week, only two evictions were dismissed and one settled, compared to nearly fifteen decided for the landlords. Levenson could report no successful section 755 defenses.[80]

The fervor also ended at downtown CORE, where the strikes first took root on the Lower East Side. By May 1964 the camaraderie was gone at the tenements on Eldridge Street; the "people got scared off." The chapter, in any case, was consumed by work for Mississippi Freedom Summer (an obsession after the murders of three Student Nonviolent Coordinating Committee (SNCC) workers, including Michael Schwerner, a downtown CORE founder) and by a Lower East Side voter registration drive. Later that summer, downtown CORE did launch another tenant campaign, Operation Eastside, with pep talks to an eager team of twenty. Like the decentralized SNCC effort in Mississippi, volunteers were told to fan out on designated blocks, "work" assigned buildings, and act "on his own initiative . . . towards solving the individual problems of the building." At this juncture, an organizer's question, "What was meant by 'organizing' a building?" elicited further confusion. "Was the purpose of CORE merely to get the landlord to make repairs, the city to inspect, and possibly to have the rent reduced or were the people being organized for something more?" An MFY observer was appalled. Another mid-August session at the CORE loft seemed equally aimless, as "people drifted in and out, new faces and familiar ones, chaos, disorganization, fine talk about the way CORE was going to organize itself, and the neighborhood, and nothing really happens." By late August, downtown CORE's tenement activities came to a halt.[81]

Despite the glib talk that radicals need only move in among the poor and ignite their solidarity, tenant unions proved monumentally difficult to organize. The Stanton Street Tenants Association, prominent in Frances Fox Piven and Richard A. Cloward's account of the welfare rights movement on the Lower East Side, failed to gain much hold on the neighborhood. It depended on the wits of MFY organizer Luisa Montes who tried, but never managed, to get the association going as a real participant group. With a few trusted subordinates, Montes ended up running a tough, no-nonsense operation in the MFY storefront. She would take on only major cases with landlords and never lost her illusions about the need to "goose" tenants to collective action. During a typical day, she might see nine walk-in clients, who asked for help on anything from union pensions to getting rid of junkies lounging on a tenement roof. In between, she was on the telephone bargaining with landlords, encouraging tenants, and prodding the RRA. Major victories never occurred, nor did tenants rush to join. Montes's own data indicate that from January through June 1964 (during the Lower East Side Rent Strike), the Stanton Street Association dealt with 170 tenants in 82 buildings, but could claim an active membership of only 20.[82]

Radicals thought they would have little trouble mobilizing the poor against greedy landlords and callous city agencies. But they managed precious little mobilization because the poor swamped them with routine requests—usually for access to those very agencies. The Stanton Street Association became less a union than a one-stop convenience center for community services. During summer 1966, 45 percent of the cases involved applications for public housing, compared with 26 percent for building violations and rent overcharges. The association also dispensed welfare advice, sponsored English and sewing classes, and filled an obvious social void. Militant East River CORE, which took up tenant councils as a tool to mobilize Harlem, concluded with dismay, "Tenant councils have not proved to be long-lasting because their only reason for existence has been redress of grievances. Consequently, when the immediate grievance is removed or compensated for, the councils collapse."[83]

Certainly, few tenant leaders anticipated the extent to which they became the local agents of the New York City Housing Authority. By the mid-1960s the Housing Authority was landlord to more than one-half million in over one hundred projects, and the waiting list for coveted apartments was one hundred thousand families, a vast undertow of the city's poor. While radicals carped at the Authority's "sterile," "institutional" facade, the sheer magnitude guaranteed a wide variety of apartments, locales, and neighborhoods, an alternative housing mobility within its domain. No wonder a large proportion of inquiries at MFY storefronts concerned help with Housing Authority application forms and with Welfare Department payments of project security deposits and rent. MFY's proudest achievement in indigenous organization, the block action group Puertorriquenos Unidos, was overwhelmed by such requests. Its best-known mobilization was not a rent strike, but a sit-in at Housing Authority offices to demand a speedup in the process of applications for apartments. Such dependence weakened tenant militance everywhere. Gray's early influence in the Fourteenth Assembly District rested on an organizational base in the Stephen Foster Houses. Compared with the drudgery of canvasing dreary, six-story walk-ups, East Harlem CORE preferred the easier gains that came from negotiating with the project manager at the Robert F. Wagner, Sr., Houses.[84]

Membership in a tenant council rarely signified a determination to withhold rent, even under the "legal" strikes made possible by section 755. On the Lower East Side, MFY confronted a pervasive timidity, particularly among the elderly and those who sublet. Major Owens commented that Brooklyn CORE's work was inhibited by the tenant belief in the "myth of the landlord's invincibility." The Stanton Street Tenants Association struggled through the summer against an ingrained wariness hardly affected by the rent strike fervor. The strike's most salient characteristic, in fact, was the disproportion between exhaustive effort and meager outcome. The brief united front among the adjoining tenements on Eldridge Street was the product of NYU CORE's ten months of intensive organization and the stubbornness of one landlord. For at least twenty months, Gray had picketed across the Fourteenth Assembly District, particularly 117th Street, and produced few solid buildings and fewer strikers. Brooklyn CORE had marched along Gates Avenue for half a year, but the major response came from tenants already excited by the chapter's demonstrations for jobs at Downstate Medical Center. Whether Gray's opportunists, NYU CORE's impulsive students, Brooklyn's older, methodical professionals, East River's militants, or MFY's social work radicals, organizers mobilized few strikers, probably no more than 2 percent of tenants in those blocks.[85]

Meager success at grass roots mobilization reflected pervasive confusion at the top. Tenant leaders could not decide, much less act, on the merits of what might be called the "structural" versus the "territorial" approach to organizing the tenement poor, and they never overcame the fallacies of both. Groups like Brooklyn CORE and the Lower East Side organizers were confident that all they had to do was dispatch young volunteers to "work" specific blocks into an angry consciousness, then call a strike. This territorial approach not only romanticized the rebellious potential of the poor, it overlooked the complexities behind the stereotypical "slum"—the differences in tenement dilapidation, between lease holders and subletters, between families and single occupants, between the working poor and welfare recipients, between those resigned to substandard walk-ups and those aspiring to enter city projects. The typical Lower East Side neighborhood contained no great monopoly landlord against whom tenants could be organized like an industrial local or against whom judges could order some kind of class-action relief. These complexities produced infinite mischief when tenant leaders sought the standard section 755 redress. Bewildering patterns of property ownership, compounded by decentralized municipal courts and idiosyncratic judges, produced the legal chaos—bureaucratic delays, endless adjournments, and uncertain decrees—that embittered those who expected decisive justice.[86]

From time to time, rent strike leaders professed the disciplined "structural" approach of organizing all the tenants in buildings controlled by a single landlord and crippling his entire rent income. While Jesse Gray flirted with the idea, radicals on the Lower East Side pursued the notion that a slumlord Gordian knot could be cut by bold measures. This myth grew with organizers' frustrations. In mid-December 1963 an NYU CORE attorney soberly assessed what his young colleagues had stumbled into on Eldridge Street. The chapter's experience showed the limits of "uncoordinated, unsupervised activities by a local group" and of street demonstrations that lacked legal follow-through with city administrators. Organizing more than a handful of tenants had proved a vast undertaking. Any realistic campaign against the slums would take "an immense, coordinate effort of National CORE chapters and every competent professional and semiprofessional we can lay our hands on." The alternative to that immense mobilization was an "attack on the basic 100 landlords," but even that struggle would require persistent legal and financial resources, the involvement of "mature, National CORE people," and take "several years."[87] But few organizers had such caution. Lured by the glamor of direct action, they plunged ahead. With little knowledge of slum residents and less understanding of their housing aspirations, they embarked on a crusade that seemed irrelevant to most poor people struggling to leave the tenements.

The strikes' profound limitations at mobilizing tenants reinforced the cautious approach of many longtime activists. ALP veterans in the East Side Tenants Council quickly reoriented their work around those few occupants disciplined to withhold rent and prepared to pay for their own litigation—a kind of "business unionism" on the housing front. A similar withdrawal occurred at Yorkville Save Our Homes, where Jane Benedict tightened organizational lines to prevent the "premature" strikes that Jesse Gray's enthusiasm seemed to touch off. But for more distant observers, the strikes were poor people's rebellions with immense potential for radical change. They clinched the Students for a Democratic Society's commitment to action projects in working-class neighborhoods. They intoxicated many young professionals, including Columbia University law students and Pratt Institute architects, to lend their expertise to direct action in the ghetto. The New York chapter of the American Institute of Architects was roused by James Farmer and Jesse Gray to form the Architects Renewal Committee in Harlem (ARCH) to "increase the capacity for action of ghetto residents in the planning situation" with its "sense of potency, responsibility and purpose." Going the extreme, many black power advocates saw the strikes as the first step in the ghetto's foreclosure on white colonialism.[88]

But already, Wagner administration liberals were recovering their composure with housing programs designed to accomplish all that upstart tenant power had intended. The mayor's office hastily improvised the Emergency Repair Program, after MFY and East Harlem activists presented the idea to city housing experts. Emergency Repair relied on municipal "police power" to contract for the elimination of hazardous Multiple Dwellings Law violations, with costs recovered from liens on the property. Tenant activists assumed that they would initiate most complaints. A companion measure, article 7-A of the Real Property Actions and Proceedings Law, authorized tenants in a seriously dilapidated multiple dwelling to petition the courts to appoint a public administrator to collect rent and order repairs. Although article 7-A required tenants to furnish detailed violations and estimated costs, it seemed to hand them an important instrument for self-determination. The city also revitalized the Receivership Program, which allowed the courts to appoint a receiver to take over a decrepit building and make repairs paid for with rents and a prior lien. Local tenant and community groups expected to play a prominent role in the recommendation of appropriate buildings and receivers.[89]

These programs gave an invaluable boost to the Wagner administration's tattered image, but had little impact on the tenements. Their operations also failed to allow for significant tenant involvement in the long run. Emergency Repair proved an administrative nightmare, soon taken up by the Model Cities bureaucracy, when it expired due to lagging reimbursement by landlords. From the beginning, article 7-A proved far too technical and cumbersome for most tenant groups to handle without outside professional help. Under the Receivership Program, the city took over 117 buildings by 1965, when arrears in rents and soaring repair costs convinced the new John V. Lindsay administration to halt acquisitions. By then the city had switched its emphasis from legal withholdings to landlord-tenant mediation, exemplified by the RRA's Housing Repair and Maintenance Program. Landlords, whose building violations normally meant punitive RRA rent reductions, were given the chance to agree to scheduled repairs supervised by the city and paid for with restored rents. By the decade's end, cases were coming from the district rent office, the mayor's office, and city councilmen. A landlord-tenant conference presided over by an RRA ombudsman worked toward an agreement on escrow rents and repairs to ward off abandonment. In 1968 the RRA supervised cases in 303 buildings, which led just 44 landlords to compliance.[90]

While the strike fervor cooled noticeably by 1965, it left a residue of tenant militance that continued rent strikes on an isolated, almost experimental, basis. On the Lower East Side, young radicals at the University Settlement started an MFY-type housing drive called Action for Progress. Director Paul DeBrul, plunging into tenant work, organized the city's first building to petition successfully for a 7-A administrator. DeBrul admitted his basic strategy was to "make it so tough for the landlords as to make them sell out cheap." Similarly inspired, David Borden, an East Harlem community worker, proposed that Massive Economic Neighborhood Development (MEND), the local antipoverty committee, sponsor a block development program to send workers from storefronts to organize food and housing co-ops. Nearby, Reverend Norman Eddy's Christian witness at the Metro-North Community Council was driven leftward by a faction pledged to continued direct action. Meanwhile, ARCH's young professionals envisioned Harlem as the place to conduct a massive tutorial in people's architecture that could turn out pamphlets on tenant action, code violations, and slumlord economics. An ARCH Housing Action Training Institute would graduate scores of young community organizers with a fluency ranging from rent control and urban renewal to strikes and 7-A sponsorship.[91]

As it turned out, grandiose strategies and militant rhetoric proved just another distraction from the frustrating reality of organizing ghetto tenants. University Settlement's Action for Progress always attracted a greater response from middle-class Jewish cooperators along Grand Street than from Puerto Rican welfare tenants on Rutgers. DeBrul conceded that his tenant organizing got nowhere compared to the media impact of lead poisoning, an issue he hit upon in 1969. At Metro-North, radicals briefly took over, but could not alter what had become their stewardship over a dwindling housing stock. Beset by a wave of building abandonment, Metro-North's activists found relocation aid their foremost function. Anticipating the needs of seven hundred families, Reverend Eddy drafted a 1966 grant proposal, "A Humane Relocation Program for the Poor," and used antipoverty funds to train a small cadre to work with city relocation officials. Despite the dreams, the ARCH Training Institute amounted to a one-time 1966 summer project where twenty-one students worked on a program for rehousing the elderly and prepared a tenant handbook. ARCH mustered far greater enthusiasm, if less success, by supporting the last hurrah of the Harlem strikes, particularly article 7-A proceedings, which seemed tailored to its technical expertise. An ARCH task force of twenty architects, lawyers, and VISTA workers submitted forty rent-withholding petitions based on section 755 and article 7-A (over half the 7-A petitions presented since the law's inception), but after endless litigation, only seven brought essential repairs. ARCH expected real breakthroughs with the city's new "rent-impairing violations law," which permitted tenants to withhold rent where specific, hazardous building violations went unrepaired for seven months. With typical enthusiasm, ARCH envisioned the prospect of one million organized slum residents: "The net effect of such a massive, simple, legal rent strike would probably be to drive many marginal slumlords to abandon their buildings—and we are back at the Neighborhood Housing Corporation which would be created to take over the properties."[92]

Across the city, radical initiatives were being systematically absorbed by another legacy of the civil rights upsurge—the War on Poverty's Community Action Program and, ultimately, the U.S. Model Cities Administration. Everywhere, radicals found their visions overwhelmed by tedious code enforcement, relocation services, and public housing applications, which transformed their indigenous groups into outreach service for the Housing Authority and the U.S. Office of Economic Opportunity. If the rent strikes had been ignited by sweating, shouting young black men in Harlem, they were soon defused by cool, sleeves-rolled-up technicians on the housing staffs of John V. Lindsay or Robert F. Kennedy.

Brooklyn's foremost antipoverty agency, the Bedford-Stuyvesant Restoration Corporation (BSRC), deployed its small staff to organize tenant and block associations. Its major work, however, came as a counselor and supplier of teenage job trainees to the spruce-up campaigns of local brownstoners' associations. BSRC also ran a small mortgage pool for limited rehabilitation projects and helped line up applications with participating downtown banks. But like the MFY storefronts, the greatest daily activity remained housing referral, chiefly of applicants for the public projects. By 1968 BSRC had spurred only a modest amount of new construction. With help from Pratt Institute and other outside consultants, BSRC advised on article 7-A conversions at two tenements and provided technical aid for the co-op conversion of two others. While vying for an ambitious, federally funded, scatter-site, housing rehabilitation program, BSRC had actually completed work on six buildings containing fifty-three apartment units. By far, its greatest impact occurred through code enforcement and civic pressure in support of middle-class block associations worried about the spread of the Central Brooklyn ghetto.[93]

In the Bronx, the techniques of tenant organizing also came to serve the needs of conservative block associations and antipoverty corporations. Like Bedford-Stuyvesant, Morrisania's black middle-class churches and small homeowners provided support for the New York CORE's and the Urban League's provision of local community services to expedite housing complaints to the Buildings Department and sponsor tenement spruce-up campaigns. Black homeowners on Union, Prospect, and Fulton avenues were appalled that the Department of Relocation had chosen Morrisania as a dumping ground for hapless relocatees. In 1966 the Union-Prospect Block

Association and several churches formed the League of Autonomous Bronx Organizations (LABOR) to demand city code enforcement and guide preservation policies of the Morrisania Community Planning Board. LABOR was apprehensive about the ferment in the Hispanic South Bronx, a center of the expansive Hunt's Point Community Progress Corporation (HPCPC). In 1966 HPCPC claimed a force of 50 block workers, who visited 3,000 buildings and started 350 tenant councils and 9 block associations. It had also lodged block workers and social service trainees at outposts, like the Concerned Parents of Fox Street, the Trinity, Kelly, Cauldwell, and Simpson Street block associations, and an HPCPC "satellite" storefront on Prospect Avenue. The leaders claimed fluency in section 755, article 7-A, and Penal Code 2040 proceedings, with twenty buildings on rent strike and another ten already paying rent to the courts. Nevertheless, HPCPC, operating as just another, although the busiest, Bronx ghetto service center, shunted complaints to the rent office, Department of Buildings, Department of Health, and Emergency Repair Service at the rate of some 510 cases per month.[94]

Ironically, such efforts made the least headway in Harlem. With little patience for the legal mechanisms of rent withholding, Jesse Gray had absolutely none for the tedious litigation of article 7-A or receivership. Furthermore, he left behind no institutional apparatus after he quit tenant organizing to pursue his political ambitions in the state assembly. Elsewhere in Harlem, ARCH faced increased difficulty scrounging up volunteer professionals to work on projects beside rent strikes. ARCH's most successful liaison was with the Community Association of the East Harlem Triangle and MEND, which drew up a plan for staged renewal, which the city agreed to add to its "housing opportunity studies." In the barrio, getting new housing on the official agenda proved a pyrrhic victory for other activists. In 1965, with substantial city aid, Ted Velez's East Harlem Tenants Council prepared elaborate plans for 448 low-income units in four high rises on 122d Street. The Tenants Council also proposed to ease relocation by dividing the block for phased demolition. Negotiating for city tax subsidies and FHA mortgage insurance, Velez had come a long way from section 755 withholdings. The proposals, however, neglected detailed analysis of the housing needs and income levels of site tenants and revealed an attention to physical and zoning specifications reminiscent of the CSC's glossy Title I reports. The plan faltered, later to be taken up by the state Urban Development Corporation, a more likely sponsor of such ambitious blueprints.[95]

Large-scale rehousing plans, which seemed to lead back to the sterile monoliths of the 1950s, drove many tenant groups to the vogue in small-scale rehabilitation and "vest pocket" housing. Rehabilitation of existing tenements promised lower development costs and minimum displacement of site residents as well as maximum involvement by local residents in neighborhood planning. In reality, sponsors tended to be nonprofit foundations or national corporations (usually manufacturers of builders' supplies), run by professional, centralized staffs, responsive to technical design criteria impenetrable to lay influence. Such outfits, with their established contacts with antipoverty funding, readily overshadowed storefront groups. One study of 1,283 units, rehabilitated with FHA below-market-interest-rate (BMIR) mortgages, found that two-thirds were sponsored by a handful of philanthropic foundations only tenuously connected to localities. Even with city tax abatements and BMIR mortgages, rents on completed units were twice the previous levels, well beyond the reach of site residents. Projects required a "gut" rehabilitation that meant a tenant removal "no different . . . than what occurs in any clearance project," while on-site coordination between architects and contractors precluded all but the most passive tenant involvement. The greatest disillusion came with the stiff costs of remodeling old law tenements and the difficulty in obtaining steady rents from low-income tenants. A rare success, the Upper Park Avenue Community Association's thirty-five units on East 117th Street, solved the problem by subjecting tenants to an orientation course and draconian management. "The energetic neighborhood ladies who ran UPACA inspected every apartment every month," noted journalist Martin Mayer, "and anyone who flunked the inspection had a chance of taking the course again or getting out."[96]

By 1968 such housing endeavors fell under the aegis of Model Cities, whose housing component was the Lindsay administration's eight-thousand-unit Vest Pocket Program. Model Cities' attack on ghetto dilapidation began with guarded rhetoric about community involvement, together with meticulous documentation of every community meeting held and every citizen who approached a microphone. But Vest Pocket was controlled by the Lindsay-appointed Model Cities Policy Committee, which deployed planning initiatives, prepackaged by the City Planning Commission and Housing and Development Administration, for use in the three Model Neighborhoods. Each neighborhood had an elected planning committee, which tended to defer to paid planning directors, who usually contracted detailed studies out to minority architects credentialed with the Urban League or the Urban Coalition. Observers noted that the Harlem and South Bronx Model Cities committees "had only a limited idea of what they were supposed to do." In Mott Haven, this citizen participation deteriorated so markedly that the planning committee finally staged a sit-in at city headquarters to force convenient relocation schedules.[97]

In South Bronx Model Cities, Vest Pocket Housing became the object of a power struggle between the mayor's Model Cities Policy Committee and the War on Poverty–funded Hunt's Point Multi-Service Corporation (HPMSC), which operated as Ramon Velez's political club. Sheer caudillismo and low voter turnout in Model Cities elections allowed Velez to control South Bronx Model Cities, although control meant deference to prepackaged blueprints from the Housing and Development Administration. Velez's dominance also extended to hastily contrived block organizations, which sponsored most of the South Bronx Vest Pocket housing, and to the planning contracts aggrandized by a few architectural firms. Managing to absorb the few indigenous tenant organizations extant in the Bronx barrio, Velez's HPMSC monopolized what passed for neighborhood involvement. Rare exceptions, such as the South Bronx NAACP and the South Bronx Housing Association, were local church groups, brokered by outsiders, who represented citywide Protestant charities and foundations. The South Bronx's largest Vest Pocket project, the Bronx-Chester Urban Renewal, was hammered out by HPMSC and the Third Avenue Merchants Association.[98]

In Brooklyn, Bedford-Stuyvesant's middle-class block associations controlled early community participation in the 1966 Vest Pocket Program via their seats on the Central Brooklyn Coordinating Council (CBCC). While a few tenant groups were accepted on the CBCC, planning sessions were dominated by the block associations, supported by the Brooklyn Democratic organization. Vest Pocket sites were chosen with a middle-class concern to "help eliminate eye-sores in the midst of many of Bedford-Stuyvesant's residential neighborhoods." Technical studies were then contracted out to the Housing Authority and the firm of Raymond & May Associates, although active contributions came from churches and block associations, who later vied as sponsors of middle-income housing. Generally, sites were first delineated by community advisory groups and Housing Authority consultants, then presented to a series of community meetings, and finally confirmed by the Housing Authority staff. In Bedford- Stuyvesant, intrenched homeowners' associations backed by local political clubs could at times hold their own in hard bargaining with city agencies.[99]

The clubhouse-homeowners' dominance grew stronger when the Vest Pocket Program was absorbed into the Central Brooklyn Model Neighborhood in 1968. Throughout Bedford-Stuyvesant and East New York, local civic and church groups came forward as housing sponsors, but usually in denominational consortiums or with neighborhood fraternal lodges or Youth in Action community boards. Tenant councils proved too weak to participate, except in one instance as part of a local church consortium. In any case, decisive control gravitated to the few indispensable professionals—a black, Harvard-educated architect and his favorite collaborator, a downtown, white attorney—and to a few favored contractors, including one reputed to be Brownsville's largest "slumlord." This pattern of community projects taken up by a handful of professionals, nominally "indigenous," and by local "povertycrats," was repeated throughout Bedford-Stuyvesant. In Brownsville, a disciplined clubhouse, controlled by the state senator, made a mockery of citizen participation that was "weak and pathetic" and an outright scandal of the rehabilitation program.[100]

If the antipoverty and Model Cities programs had shown the sharp limits of community-controlled housing, optimistic claims came from other nonprofit local sponsors, particularly church consortiums lured into the field by the federal BMIR subsidies. In sheer numbers, these denominational efforts were a spectacular success. By 1971 eighty-one church-related, nonprofit corporations had sponsored over 32,000 units of low- and moderate-income housing. But again, the crucial role belonged to professional developers, accompanied by the scantiest local involvement. In the Bronx, 63 percent of 4,724 units were taken up by just four sponsors, brokered by the law firm of emerging Bronx Democratic leader Patrick Cunningham and prominent builder Richard Ravitch. Of Manhattan's 14,889 units, four consortiums organized by such institutions as Roosevelt Hospital and Columbia University took up one-third. Only one Manhattan tenant group, the Tenants Association of 107th Street, participated in a 300-unit rehab, again as part of a local church consortium.[101]

Two projects, heralded as models of extensive community control, provided better examples of liberal agencies' dominance of vague community aspirations. When the mixed Italian, Jewish, and Puerto Rican West Tremont block associations and churches rejected a Housing Authority proposal for a low-income project, Bronx borough president Herman Badillo and the Catholic archdiocese twisted arms to incorporate the lower-middle-class Italians and Puerto Ricans into an amenable group, the Twin Parks Association. Later, advocacy planners with the City Planning Commission suggested their own design, revised again by experts from the state Urban Development Corporation. The result was the twenty-two-hundred-unit Twin Parks, which a sympathetic observer called "massive structures thrust" into the neighborhood. Behind East Harlem's Upper Park Avenue Community Association (UPACA) were two local black women, former luncheonette partners, whose ambitions were discovered by the New York Federation of Reform Synagogues and a succession of overpowering city agencies. Housing and Development Administration officials hit upon the duo as the instrument for their vision of large-scale rehabs with BMIR subsidies. Making these neighbors a community force, the agencies granted them management of city-owned tenements and made it clear to the community that the UPACA women controlled waiting lists for new units to be built by the city. Once established, UPACA became the recipient of mortgages from the Bowery Savings Bank, guarantees from the Urban Development Corporation, and grants from the Ford Foundation. Its massive, thirty-two-story apartment towers, coveted waiting lists, and conservative management combined to make UPACA indistinguishable from the huge Housing Authority projects further east.[102]

Amid ebbing tenant initiatives, the spring 1970 "squatters" movement echoed earlier failures. Inspired by the last gasp of 1960s' direct action, local radicals, seizing vacant apartments slated for demolition, proclaimed the community's moral right to possession. Ad hoc move-ins occurred on West 15th Street in Greenwich Village and on 111th and 122d streets in the Morningside Urban Renewal Area. But squatting became systematic on West 87th Street and along Columbus Avenue, where buildings awaited luxury conversion or demolition for middle-income high rises as part of the West Side Urban Renewal. At night, blacks and Puerto Ricans, prying open boarded-up entrances and rigging makeshift living arrangements, presented the city with a fait accompli—either recognize their "ownership" or evict whole families in front of press photographers. Eventually, the Columbus Avenue Operation Move-In claimed one hundred participating families and, like an alternative housing authority, a "waiting list" of three hundred. They were supported by elaborate networks, including several West Side antipoverty agencies, and, in Morningside Heights, a solicitous Episcopal bishop.[103]

Nevertheless, the squatters could not shake off a basic ambivalence about their purpose. Some radicals envisioned the break-ins as a sustainable housing policy and sought city mortgage and rehabilitation commitments. Others, bitter at the advancing edge of tax-supported luxury conversions (which housing critics dubbed gentrification), tried to use the squatters as bargaining leverage to increase low-income units earmarked for the West Side. Many squatters evidently hoped the Housing and Development Administration would redesignate their occupied homes for low-income rehabilitation (some even offered a "moral" rent of 25 percent of their incomes), but others apparently expected to gain priority on Housing Authority waiting lists. The few Columbus Avenue menages were soon cleared away for the detested Mitchell-Lama projects. Those on 111th and 122d streets, really middle-income protests against expansion by Columbia University, remained longer thanks to the sufferance of the Cathedral of St. John the Divine and the new militant Columbia Tenants Union. The squatters, however, did dramatize the notion of community sovereignty over abandoned units, an idea made plausible by the application of tenants' "sweat equity" to reclaim them. At a time when the Richard M. Nixon administration seemed bent on ending traditional and costly federal subsidies to low-income housing, this people's rehabilitation lived on in feisty organizations, such as the People's Development Corporation (founded in 1974) and the Banana Kelly Community Improvement Association (1977) in the South Bronx.[104]

For all their direct action, West Side squatters exemplified the central dilemma that had plagued tenant councils and community groups since the rent strike upsurge of the early 1960s. They could mobilize tenant anger, but for how long? To what ends? Undoubtedly on the block level they could play a powerful role in building-code enforcement. With their area teams they could become tenement vigilantes, meting out a popular justice against unscrupulous landlords. Certainly the thicket of tenant councils, block associations, and antipoverty groups on the housing front engendered a new level of code enforcement, or at least the posting of code violations. One planner may have exaggerated that code violations "were issued with a vengeance" by the mid-1960s, but she was right to point out that they reached an unprecedented volume. While the city's inspection force doubled during the mid-1960s, the number of building code complaints nearly quadrupled, as did the number of posted violations—to an incredible backlog of 781,000.[105]

But this was a housing policy that went only as far as the Buildings Department wished to take it, as the Emergency Repair Program and other enforcement efforts showed. Tenant leaders could rally support around alternative housing programs, but these usually required a technical command beyond the resources of most community groups. Those few that acquired them ended up bestriding their communities like the landlords they had detested. Otherwise, to raise the prospects of alternative housing was to stimulate powerful community aspirations that could only be fulfilled by established city agencies. Community groups soon discovered that they could maintain a standing among their neighbors only insofar as they could negotiate with these professional city staffs. Inevitably this meant deals at downtown city offices, over Housing Authority blueprints, and within mortgage-bank estimates.

By the end of the 1960s, the remnants of the tenant movement had become disembodied from its radical tradition. Its chief asset, rent control, had become an embarrassing, decayed relic, which few had the political courage to inter. Despite its inflammatory rhetoric and progressive self-image, Met Council was living off old crusades, in danger of becoming the tool of the city's new privileged upper middle class. Standing firm on vigilant rent enforcement through the usual city agencies, Met Council never made more than a peripheral connection with a decade of rent strikers and squatters. It remained stubbornly distant from the rehabilitation and tax-abatement programs, which it viewed as landlord grabs. In the meantime, its ranks swelled with new middle-class recruits living in Manhattan and Brooklyn Heights Title I and Mitchell-Lama projects, where tenants tried to gain some leverage over their middle-income rents. Understandably, Met Council worked hard and took credit for the 1969 Rent Stabilization Law, which for the first time imposed annual ceilings on rent increases in post-1947 housing. Adding a rent-stabilized to the already rent-controlled sector in this housing economy was no small accomplishment, although it stemmed from Met Council's ability to conjure up a fearsome tenant vote than from its ability to deploy organized tenant councils.[106]

Met Council's focus on the single issue of rent control, moreover, forfeited its influence on the most important housing debate of the new decade, touched off by the scare word *abandonment*. The number of landlords who simply walked away from their tenements probably reached epidemic proportions by 1966, but the phenomenon remained a technical consideration, even as late as the 1969 municipal elections. It surfaced, only briefly, when Mayor Lindsay and his opponents traded charges about the city's failure to expand the low-income housing supply. A week *after* Mayor Lindsay's reelection, his political ally, state senator Roy M. Goodman, convened Manhattan hearings of his Senate Committee on Housing and Urban Development and heard the problem described for the first time as a dire emergency. Frank S. Kristof, chief economist of the state Urban Development Corporation, startled the inquiry with an estimate that thirty-three thousand units had been lost annually in the last three years. Roger Starr, executive director of the Citizens Housing and Planning Council, and Jason R. Nathan, outgoing head of the Housing and Development Administration, depicted spreading devastation that could only be stemmed by a drastic reversal of postwar housing policy. Citing a yet-to-be-released study by the New York Rand Institute, which showed that rents in the controlled sector failed to provide for even normal maintenance costs, these witnesses called for an end to the city's punitive rent reductions and code enforcement and to that "destructive" anachronism, rent control.[107]

Miscalculating the issue's potency, Met Council responded with ritual exorcism of this "Frankenstein monster" created by landlords and their stooges at Rand and the CHPC. But this no longer sufficed in an atmosphere charged by ghetto riots, black power demands, and Harlem school wars. Met Council notwithstanding, the city, already switching sympathies from the slum tenant to the tenement landlord, regarded him less a rapacious owner than an endangered entrepreneur, hounded out of neighborhoods that could not afford to lose his housing managerial skills, such as they were. With the *New York Times* leading the media, abandonment tales peaked in spring 1970, with a new focus on the psychology of the beleaguered landlord. With Kristof's estimate now an obsession, public fears were heightened by stories about neighborhoods like Hunt's Point in the Bronx, where drug addicts foraged in empty, arson-torched tenements and civic order ceased to exist. At this juncture, the release of reports by the Rand Institute, the Citizens Budget Committee, and Rutgers University economist George Sternlieb crystallized public dissatisfaction with current housing policies. Marshaling new data on tenement operations, Sternlieb characterized the typical rent control landlord as a small owner, overwhelmed by rising costs, ignorant of his rights under the complicated city rent formula, and fearful of renting his property to blacks and Hispanics. While Sternlieb urged a ten-year phased system of rent increases, he cautioned that lifting controls might only save those post-1929 structures still not too far gone.[108]

Met Council could take only limited comfort in the outcome. Obviously, rent control still gripped the city. It could only be challenged by outsiders, like Kristof and Sternlieb. Moreover, the Lindsay administration had to muster all this prestigious opinion behind its May 1970 proposal for a 15 percent, across-the-board rent increase and its Maximum Base Rent Program (MBR), which would have scrapped controls for a complex, computerized cost-of-operations formula (that approached the Rand concept of an economic rent). Met Council and liberals in the city council nearly derailed the plan, had not a fissure opened up in their traditional coalition of support. Local 32B of the Building Services Employees, predominantly black and Hispanic, was bargaining for higher wages and threatened an apartment house strike that spring. Landlords on the Metropolitan Fair Rent Committee shrewdly understood that 32B would more likely join the breakthrough of ceilings on rents and wages than side with Manhattan liberals to preserve anachronistic rent levels. With some last minute city council bargaining that delayed the 15 percent increase to August 1 and added a fig leaf requirement that landlords certify they had repaired building violations, MBR was passed in July. What began as an attempt to impose rational order and profit incentives on the housing industry ended up with chaos, as MBR rent calculations got bogged down and the district rent offices had to divert their own scarce manpower. MBR enforcement and appeals were paralyzed. Reminiscent of 1947, tenants found themselves largely on their own and began organizing Met Council affiliates with a vengeance. But accelerating inflation and the continued gentrification of Manhattan and downtown Brooklyn rendered the old tenant coalition badly frayed. Beset by landlords, by organized labor, and by the new ownership vogue among middle-class cooperators, the tenant movement faced the 1970s with less certainty and less legitimacy than ever before.[109]

What did the tenant movement accomplish after a quarter century of mimeographed leaflets, marches, pickets, and legislative lobbies? Perhaps most remarkable, its survival in the liberal city may have been achievement enough. Along the way, it could also count some important triumphs, some maneuvers that bought time for thousands in their apartments, and a good deal of consciousness-raising that eventually changed the political landscape of the city. Tenant groups had maintained the cause of rent control, a political orphan as late as 1942, at the center of New York's political agenda for the next thirty years. By the late 1940s the tenants' politics of preemption had made it impossible for realtors to dismantle controls as they had done in the 1920s and suicidal for politicians to try. In many communities, they elaborated a neighborhood enforcement that amounted to vigilanteism. ALP clubs, which constituted the tenant vanguard, kept this shred of radicalism alive, and maintained a community-service tradition that would become the heart of Reform Democratic politics. It is not too much to say that these sometimes lonely activists, these beleaguered ALP clubs, shaped the awareness of the dignity and integrity of neighborhoods that would become the most significant ingredient of the community-power movement of the 1960s.

Tenant groups had far less success in contributing to the decisions on public housing and city planning, which were fundamental to where New Yorkers would live in the postwar city. Of course, their early involvement in public housing was important in establishing the program's foothold. In the late 1930s and through the 1940s, the project unions affiliated with the City-Wide Tenants Council and United Tenants League were the most vocal advocates for expanded public housing. Their demonstrations, indeed their very deliberations, were taken by liberals as the best evidence of the spirited new democracy being nurtured by decent housing. In the debates over the Truman administration measures that led to the Housing Act of 1949, no one provided more graphic or eloquent support for this crucial area of domestic liberalism. But to be effective, the tenants always had to operate within a larger liberal coalition, which had the decisive contacts in Albany and Washington. Furthermore, the single most influential hand behind the enormous expansion of public housing in New York may have been Robert Moses, who evidently regarded public projects as the most expedient means to "externalize" the costs of moving tenants off Title I sites and to keep the program on track. Tenants made less headway in the more important realm of postwar planning and urban redevelopment. While the war had fatally disrupted the promising relationship between the City-Wide Tenants Council and planning liberals, cold war discord kept them warily distant during the crucial start-up debates over Title I. Even so, it remains questionable whether any kind of liberal-radical coalition could have restrained Moses at the height of his power. Under the circumstances, the tenants did well to blunt some of his initiatives, force him into tactical withdrawals, and wheedle as much relocation housing as they managed. Again, they were not able to carry this off alone, but depended upon the intervention of liberals. But this was no small accomplishment, particularly in an era of declining neighborhood newspapers and before the advent of "eyewitness" television reports. The tenants' forlorn protests against Title I helped mold the sense of injustice that would eventually change the course of urban redevelopment in New York and across the nation.

Their limited accomplishments came on the most slender resources. What evidence we have indicates that for this quarter century, at least, mobilization never reached hundreds of thousands, unless we count those who signed petitions and sent letters to their representatives. In project after project, few mass organizations were ever realized or sustained for long. The most successful occurred in the middle-class limited-dividend projects, which provided the mainstay of the City-Wide Tenants Council in the late 1930s. Of course, mass defiance broke out in East Tremont in the early 1930s, but such numbers were never duplicated, not even during the Harlem and Lower East Side rent strikes of the 1960s. Moreover, the mobilization achieved had the disheartening tendency to melt away at the first prospect of relocation from Title I sponsors or the Housing Authority. And much of the time, tenant groups survived as self-styled mediators with these city agencies.

In light of these findings, it seems dubious to accord women any particular success at grass roots mobilization, nor misconstrue their function in the movement. No doubt, women were active on this domestic front. They could circulate petitions, knock on doors, and picket in front of supermarkets with an ease few men could match. On occasion, they served as movement shock troops, as in East Tremont in 1932 or Long Island City in 1943. In both instances, after housewives had badly shaken realtors and city rent officials, male tenant leaders negotiated the follow-up arrangements. The fact was that women operated within the prevailing sexual division of labor, with which radicals remained quite comfortable. The ambiguity of this gender politics was well symbolized by events at Queensbridge in 1943. The demands of two thousand project women to serve their country in war factories were telegrammed by the male Queensbridge Tenants League secretary to the female War Manpower Commissioner. Generally, few women rose beyond this rank-and-file activism to assume leadership roles in the limited dividends, Harlem's Consolidated Tenants League, or the City-Wide Tenants Council. Males dominated policy-making at the latter and shaped its transformation into the 1942 United Tenants League. Men dominated Jesse Gray's entourage, organized the seige against landlords on the Lower East Side, and guided the earliest development of Met Council; the list could go on. When the time came to lobby at city hall or Albany, the tenants sent males. Of course, the Esther Rands and Jane Benedicts were conspicuous in the movement, but not overly so when compared to settlement house and social welfare groups or the Democratic Reform movement itself.

We should also be careful not to attribute to these tenant groups a vitalism rarely foreseen, let alone achieved, by tenant leaders themselves. There is no doubt that from time to time local groups elaborated sophisticated organizational structures and larger coalitions of considerable citywide impact. At a distance this looks something like a purposeful adaptation to the changing housing and political environment, an evolution of radical forms. But a closer look suggests that little of this had occurred. There is no evidence of an organization steadily evolving, creatively adapting to the housing environment. For one thing, there was no long-lived involvement, no long continuity in the struggle, chiefly because residential and professional mobility removed many activists from the scenes of long-term engagement. There is no evidence that the rent pageants of 1904 provided a kind of collective memory that shaped behavior on the Lower East Side in 1919, or that these earlier outbreaks influenced the tenant rebellions of 1932. Jesse Gray often acted as if he invented rent defiance, and he apparently believed this in his innocence. The activists on the Lower East Side and in CORE had only the vaguest notion that tenants had struck against landlords thirty years before—and no knowledge that their chief weapon, section 755, had been first put on the statute books in 1930. The oral history of the 1960s strikes in Harlem and elsewhere, presumably a rich depository of a people's tradition of tenant protest, reveals genuine surprise that such tactics had been used before. In short, each tenant generation believed itself unique in confronting problems in the housing environment, generally elaborating approaches in ignorance of what had been tried before.

Above all, any conclusions about the tenant movement's successful adaptation to the housing environment must be severely questioned in light of the disastrous outcome of the housing struggle in the 1970s. It seems moot to analyze multilevels of influence when tenants could not influence the housing arbiters who really counted. In the end, they could not come to grips with landlords, could not force them to listen to their blandishments, could not constrain them to continue to operate tenements when it was no longer in their interests, could not prevent them from simply walking away from their properties. In this failure, of course, tenants were no more able to deter footloose landlords than labor unions were able to deter footloose industrial employers. The abandonment of some five hundred thousand apartment units after 1965 was only the most blatant example of general disinvestment by property owners in aging northern cities. Tenant groups could hardly stem this tide, although as the closest observers of the housing scene, they could be faulted for refusing to face that grim reality while offering the most disingenuous solutions. By the mid-1960s, tenant leaders, alternating inflammatory words with rent strikes of growing sophistication, were putting tremendous pressure on selected landlords. Perhaps they can be excused for not realizing the consequences of their war on landlords, although that would accord them a naïveté in their understanding of economic power that most would have indignantly rejected. But many tenant activists were not naïve. They were "realists." They talked seriously of wholesale foreclosure of slumlords. They expected slumlords to be replaced by tenant activists, by sympathetic liberals, or by the Housing Authority or similar agency. Considering how much they railed against those liberals, the Wagner and the Rockefeller administrations, this expectancy was inconsistent at best. That the Housing Authority might enlarge its landlordship was still plausible in the early 1960s; but by 1966, after the sharp decline in public housing commitments and the negligible impact of the War on Poverty and Model Cities programs were clear, such rhetoric bordered on the irresponsible. This is not to say that tenant leaders should not have lashed out against slumlords. But what the public and the tenants themselves could have expected was for movement leaders, who professed to act with toughness and realism, to understand the limits on their ability to fasten on landlords in a property-owning society, to talk with the realization that they could only be reached by a careful mixture of incentives and sanctions, and to act in the knowledge that landlords, tenants, and city agencies had to pull together in the complicated process of providing for New York's housing stock. To do otherwise was to impose a chilling effect on housing entrepreneurship. In the end, it was hundreds of thousands of low-income tenants who found themselves out in the cold.

ACKNOWLEDGMENTS

Space permits only a partial acknowledgment of the many people whose aid made this essay possible. They include: David Klaassen of the Social Welfare History Archives of the University of Minnesota; Jerry N. Hess and Lee Johnson of the National Archives, Washington, D.C.; Joel Buckwald of the Federal Records Center, Bayonne, New Jersey; Val Coleman and Alfredo Graham of the New York City Housing Authority; Marian Sameth of the Citizens Housing and Planning Council; Dorothy Swanson of the Tamiment Library, New York University; Jack Noordhoorn of the Butler Library, Columbia University; Bernard M. Weinberg of the Morningside Area Alliance; and Jane Benedict of the Metropolitan Council on Housing. Joseph Spencer shared his data on the 1930s, and John McLoughlin's oral history tapes proved indispensable. Mark Naison offered prudent editorial advice, while Ronald Lawson remained a patient and generous project director. Nathan R. Fox and Rose M. Schwartz typed numerous drafts. My wife, Bonnie Fox Schwartz, helped with the early stages of research and remained a constant, meticulous editor.

An earlier version of my discussion of tenant activism in the 1960s appeared as "The New York City Rent Strikes of 1963–1964," *Social Service Review* 57 (Dec. 1983). It is published here with the permission of the publisher, The University of Chicago.

NOTES

1. Joseph Starobin, *American Communism in Crisis, 1943–1957* (Cambridge, 1972), pp. 54–77; and Maurice Isserman, *Which Side Were You On?* (Middletown, Conn., 1982), chaps. 7–8.
2. Grace Aviles to Edith Elmer Wood, Jan. 6, 1942; *Vladeck News and Views*, Mar. 19, 1942, both in Box 62, Edith Elmer Wood Papers, Columbia University; Sydney Jacobs, "Tenant's Needs and Problems as Seen by Social Service Agencies," Dec. 8, 1942, in Citizens Housing Council, Management Committee, Minutes, Citizens Housing and Planning Council.
3. United Tenants League of Greater New York, Press Release, Sept. 11, 1942; UTL and National Public Housing Conference, "Continued Occupancy in Public Housing," both in Folder 102, United Neighborhood Houses Papers, Social Welfare History Archives, University of Minnesota (hereafter cited as UNH Papers); Edmund E. Klein to Director, War Manpower Commission, Sept. 23, 1943; and related correspondence in Section 269, War Manpower Commission Files, Federal Records Center, Bayonne; May Lumsden to Kelsey Volner, Williamsburg File 688; F. Didisheim to Edmund B. Butler, Oct. 15, 1942; Memo, June 11, 1943; Mr. Boyle to Mrs. Lumsden, June 22, 1943; Memo from LMC, June 11, 1943, all in Queensbridge File 687, New York City Housing Authority, Central Files (hereafter cited as NYCHA-CF).
4. Arthur Simon, *Stuyvesant Town* (New York, 1970), pp. 15–41; Charles Abrams to Thomas E. Dewey, Apr. 3, 1943; Algernon D. Black and Charles Abrams, City-Wide Citizens Committee on Harlem, May 27, 1943, Reel 11; Exhibit 5, Transcript of Minutes (Board of Estimate of the City of New York), pp. 138, 154–155, 159, 161, 162, Reel 50, Charles Abrams Papers, Cornell University (hereafter cited as Abrams Papers).
5. Frieda N. Heilberg, "A Study of the Rehousing Needs of Tenants Who Will Be Displaced by the Stuyvesant Town Project in New York City," Master's thesis, New York School of Social Work, 1944, pp. 7, 9–10, 30–31, 38–41, 48–49, 56–57; Community Service Society, *The Rehousing Needs of the Families on the Stuyvesant Town Site* (June 14, 1945), pp. 16–19, 28–30; *New York Herald Tribune*, Feb. 24, 1945; *New York Times*, Feb. 24, 1945; Fay Seabrook to Marcantonio, Apr. 24, 1945, Box 13, Vito Marcantonio Papers, New York Public Library (hereafter cited as Marcantonio Papers).
6. James Felt to Abrams, Feb. 16, 1942; Goode A. Harney to Abrams, Nov. 3, 1943, all in Abrams Papers, Reel 11; "Urban Housing Management Association, Inc.," (New York Urban League, 1943), Box 71, Arthur C. Holden Papers, Cornell University; "Informal Meeting on the Riverton Project," n. d., Box 8, Algernon D. Black Papers, Columbia University (hereafter cited as Black Papers); *New York Times*, July 2, Oct. 30, 1946, Aug. 31, 1947.
7. "Informal Meeting on the Riverton Project," Black Papers, Box 8; "Statement of Policy on Federal Aid to Urban Redevelopment and Post-War Planning in the U.S.A., September 30, 1944," Box 11, Stanley M. Isaacs Papers, New York Public

Library (hereafter cited as Isaacs Papers); *Daily Worker,* Dec. 2, 10, 1944. Compare these comments with the sharp dismissals of redevelopment in City-Wide Tenants Council, *Tenant Newsletter,* Mar. 4, Apr. 3, 1940.

8. Consolidated Tenants League of Harlem, Minutes, Sept. 30, Oct. 28, Dec. 2, 9, 1943, Mar. 2, Apr. 13, Sept. 7, 1944; Leigh Athearn to Thomas I. Emerson, Oct. 5, 1943, Box 1207; Tom Tippett to Walter Hart, Apr. 12, 1944, Box 1208; Ivan D. Carson, Memo, Sept. 22, 1942, Box 1207, Office of Price Administration, Enforcement Branch, Record Group 188, National Archives; City-Wide Citizens Committee on Harlem, Minutes, Feb. 2, 1944, Black Papers, Box 8.

9. Persia Campbell, *The Consumer Interest* (New York, 1949), pp. 158–159; *Daily Worker,* Sept. 29, 1943; Michael J. Quill Association flyer, Apr. 12, 1945; undated Memo on prices, both in Box 7, Peter Cacchione Papers, Tamiment Library, New York University (hereafter cited as Cacchione Papers); *Daily Worker,* Aug. 20, Oct. 14, 17, 1943, Jan. 5, 1944; *New York Guild Lawyer* 2 (Feb. 1944): 8; 3 (Jan. 1945): 8.

10. "Schedule of Events, Housing Week, May 21–27," Folder 103, UNH Papers; *UTL Bulletin,* May 20, 1945, copy in Holden Papers, Box 72.

11. Davis R. B. Ross, *Preparing for Ulysses* (New York, 1969), pp. 238–242, 249–251; Mark I. Gelfand, *A Nation of Cities* (New York, 1975), chap. 4; Stanley M. Isaacs to H. Daniel Carpenter, Apr. 11, 1945; Harold Buttenheim to Isaacs, Apr. 10, 1945, Isaacs Papers, Box 11; Robert A. Caro, *The Power Broker* (New York, 1974), pp. 704, 758, 764, 1221.

12. *Bronx Home News,* June 20, 27, July 2, 1946. For local buyers' strike pressures on neighborhood stores, see coverage in the *Daily Worker* on Apr. 23, July 22, 24, Nov. 24, and Dec. 11, 1946.

13. Frances Burden to William O'Dwyer, Apr. 8, 1947, Box 1214; Helen Harris to O'Dwyer, June 24, 1947; Alfred K. Stern to O'Dwyer, June 23, 1947, Box 1122; O'Dwyer to Keyes Winter, July 2, 1947, Box 1214; General Resolutions Promulgated by the Temporary City Housing Rent Commission, Articles II, III, July 15, 1947; Mayor O'Dwyer, Statement, July 15, 1947, all in Mayor's Papers, Box 1214, Municipal Archives and Records Center (hereafter cited as Mayor's Papers); *New York Times,* Aug. 30, Dec. 10, 1947, Jan. 26, 1948.

14. Circular, Apr. 15, 1947; untitled, undated typescript list of Brooklyn tenant organizations; Myron E. Lemberger to Cacchione, Oct. 9, 1947, all in Cacchione Papers, Box 8.

15. *Daily Worker,* Aug. 22, May 31, 1948; Tenants and Consumers Council of Boro Park Petition to City Councilmen, July 25, 1947; and to Mayor O'Dwyer, July 25, 1947, Cacchione Papers, Box 8. See also Alice Gardner and Lillian Mettling to O'Dwyer, Aug. 12, 1948, Mayor's Papers, Box 1213.

16. Yorkville Tenants League leaflets in Marcantonio Papers, Box 25; *New York Times,* Oct. 30, 1948, quoted in Marcantonio to O'Dwyer, Dec. 21, 1948, Box 13; Tenants of 233 East 100th Street to Marcantonio, Jan. 10, 1949, Marcantonio Papers, Box 54A. Data on Marcantonio's tenant work among individual buildings can be found in Marcantonio Papers, Boxes 54A and 55.

17. *Daily Worker,* Mar. 21, Nov. 28, 1948; Tremont Tenants Council, "Tenants' Bill of Rights" (1949), Box 278, Robert F. Wagner, Sr., Papers, Georgetown University; Morrisania Consumer Co-Ordinating Committee, Resolutions, Jan. 8, 1947, Mayor's Papers, Box 1123.

18. *Bronx Home News,* June 2, July 3, 8, 1947.

19. Ibid., Dec. 1, 2, 11, 1946, July 9, 11, 21, Oct. 29, 1947.

20. *New York World Telegram,* Oct. 14, 1948; *Daily Worker,* July 23, 1950; Ben Davidson to Charles Abrams, July 30, 1948, Abrams Papers, Reel 12.

21. *New York Times,* Dec. 10, 1947, Mar. 15, 1948; George Mallouk to Robert F. Wagner, Sr., Feb. 2, 1949, and similar

complaints in Wagner Papers, Box 278; *New York Times*, Jan. 19, 1948; *Daily Worker*, Mar. 21, 1948.

22. *Daily Worker*, July 24, 1946. These comments are based upon lists of tenant organizations that demonstrated and testified at various postwar rent hearings and are found in the Marcantonio Papers, the Wagner Papers, and the Mayor's Papers.

23. U.S. Congress, House of Representatives, Committee on Un-American Activities, Investigation of Communist Activities in the New York Area, *Hearings*, vol. 21 (May 5, 1955), pp. 923–924, 927, 976; *Daily Worker*, Nov. 25, 1946, Feb. 8, Mar. 11, 1947, Nov. 30, 1948, Apr. 13, 1949.

24. *PM*, Sept. 17, 1947; *New York World Telegram*, Sept. 17, 1947; Phillip Good to O'Dwyer, July 28, 1947, Box 1122; Telegram, KVTA to O'Dwyer, Feb. 11, 1947, Box 1123, Mayor's Papers; *PM*, Nov. 27, 1947; *New York Post*, Dec. 27, 1947; *New York Times*, Dec. 27, 1947, Feb. 20, 29, 1948; *PM*, Apr. 13, 1948; *New York Post*, Mar. 12, 1948; *PM*, Mar. 29, 1948; *New York Times*, Apr. 1, 1948; *PM*, Apr. 13, 1948.

25. HUAC *Hearings*, pp. 920, 972, 970–971, 916; *New York World Telegram*, Dec. 3, 1947; Paul L. Ross to O'Dwyer, Jan. 29, 1947, Box 1123, Mayor's Papers; Miriam Sayer to Edmund B. Butler, Dec. 21, 1946; Inter-Project Council, "Protest Evictions and Rent Increases at City Hall" (Mimeo, January 29, 1947), and other correspondence in Queensbridge File 687, NYCHA-CF; *New York Post*, Dec. 17, 1947.

26. Queensbridge Tenants League, Memo, Aug. 13, 1947, Queensbridge File 687; George R. Genung to Maxwell Tretter, June 16, 1947, Red Hook File 687; Alice Brophy to James W. Gaynor, Oct. 11, 1948, Queensbridge File 687, NYCHA-CF; *New York Post*, Dec. 17, 1947; Inter-Project Tenants Council, "Public Housing Tenants Fight for the Home You Live In!" (leaflet, n.d.) and "Statement by Norman Pike," Mar. 24, 1949, both in Box 1213, Mayor's Papers; New York Tenant Councils on Rent and Housing to Marcantonio, June 4, 1949, Marcantonio Papers, Box 13; Program of Inter-Project Tenants Council, Oct. 19, 1949; John D. Tierney to Phillip Cruise, Oct. 29, 1949, both in Box 1121, Mayor's Papers; Samuel Schooler to W. L. Paulson, Jan. 3, 1955, Queensbridge File 687, NYCHA-CF.

27. "A 3,800-Unit Project for Long Island," *Insured Mortgage Portfolio* 12 (1947): 5–7; "Fresh Meadows," *Architectural Record* 106 (Dec. 1949): 85–97; Lewis Mumford, *From the Ground Up* (New York, 1957), pp. 3–19; Women's City Club of New York, Minutes, July 7, 1948; Citizens Housing and Planning Council, Notes of Fresh Meadows Facilities, n.d., both in UNH Papers, Folder 105; and Heinz Norden to Helen Harris, Oct. 17, 1950, UNH Papers, Folder 195.

28. For tenant council strength see Beatrice Alewitz to Marcantonio, Mar. 17, 1949; and list of tenant groups at Jan. 19, 1948, hearings of the McGoldrick board, both in Marcantonio Papers, Box 13.

The ability of the Housing Authority to use radical groups as its agents can be seen in the Marcantonio Papers, *passim;* and in Consolidated Tenants League, Minutes, Sept. 4, 18, 1947.

The impact of fair-housing legislation on Harlem's middle class is touched upon in Robert C. Weaver, *Dilemmas of Urban America* (New York, 1969), pp. 92–94; Kenneth B. Clark, *Dark Ghetto* (New York, 1965), pp. 57–61, 193–194.

29. *New York Herald Tribune*, Aug. 26, Sept. 5, 1947; *PM*, Sept. 10, 1947; Nessa Feldman to O'Dwyer, Nov. 13, 1947, Box 1213, Mayor's Papers; *New York Times*, Dec. 9, 12, 1947, Jan. 10, 19, 20, 1948; Paul L. Ross, Oral History, Columbia University Oral History Collection; Statement by Mildred Wickson before Mayor O'Dwyer, Mar. 24, 1949, Box 1213, Mayor's Papers; *New York Times*, Aug. 9, Sept. 15, 1949; Paul L. Ross to Board of Estimate, Oct. 10, 1949, Box 1212; Frances Goldin to O'Dwyer, Oct. 31, 1949, Box 1213, Mayor's Papers.

30. Isidore Blumberg to O'Dwyer, Dec. 29,

1949, Box 1213, Mayor's Papers; Daniel Carpenter, Memo, Jan 10, 1950, UNH Papers, Folder 105; *New York Times*, Mar. 29, 1950; New York Tenant Councils on Rent and Housing, Release, Feb. 2, 1956, in series 1, 1950, I–Le, American Labor Party Papers, Rutgers University (hereafter cited as ALP Papers); State of New York, *Public Papers of Thomas E. Dewey*, vol. 8 (Albany, 1950), pp. 783–786; Temporary State Rent Commission, Release No. 23, July 12, 1950, in Herbert H. Lehman Papers, Lehman Library, Columbia University (hereafter cited as Lehman Papers).

31. *New York Post*, July 20, Aug. 24, 1950; Arthur Schutzer's comments, Oct. 14, 1950; Ross Statement to Marcy Houses Tenants League, Oct. 12, 1950; State ALP Office, Memo, Nov. 10, 1950, with enclosed tenant questionnaires, all in series 1, Pri–R, ALP Papers; *New York Times*, Oct. 23, 25, 1950; Temporary State Housing Rent Commission, Release No. 36, Nov. 20, 1950; No. 38, Nov. 21, 1950; McGoldrick Address, Nov. 30, 1950, all in Lehman Papers; Citizens Union, Statement, Feb. 9, 1951, Box 1212, Mayor's Papers; *New York Times*, Jan. 17, 22, Feb. 13, 1951.

32. *New York Times*, Jan. 6, 8, 12, 1953; Citizens Housing and Planning Council, Committee on Rent Control, Minutes, Oct. 9, 1952, in UNH Papers, Folder 105; *New York Times*, May 1, 2, 3, 1953; *Citizens' Housing News* 11 (Apr. 1953), copy in UNH Papers, Folder 221; *New York Times*, June 11, July 10, Aug. 14, 1953; Charles Cook to Abrams, Jan. 27, 1955; Frances Goldin to Abrams, Jan. 29, 1955, both in Abrams Papers; and the *New York Times* retrospective on rent control published Dec. 19–21, 1960.

33. Joel Schwartz interview with Jane Benedict, Aug. 27, 1981; Schwartz interview with Jane Wood, Aug. 30, 1981.

34. Press releases and correspondence of the Citizens Conference on City Planning, UNH Papers, Folder 220; Stanley M. Isaacs, Notes for Planning Conference, Apr. 8, 1948, Isaacs Papers, Box 15; Citizens Union, Press Release, Oct. 28–29, 1950; C. McKim Norton to Impelletteri, Dec. 11, 1950, both in UNH Papers, Folder 220.

35. Alfred Rheinstein, "Proposal and Report," Mar. 17, 1953; S. F. Boden to New York Life Insurance Company, Jan. 29, 1954; Nassau Management Company, "Morningside Gardens—Management Proposal," June 22, 1956, all in files of Morningside Area Alliance (hereafter cited as Morningside Files).

36. Jeanne R. Lowe, *Cities in a Race with Time* (New York, 1968), pp. 45–109; Gelfand, *Nation of Cities*, pp. 152–156, 205–215; Caro, *Power Broker*, pp. 961–983, 1014; New York City Planning Commission, *Tenant Relocation Report* (1954); Committee on Slum Clearance, *Title I Progress* (Jan. 29, 1950), p. 25; New York City Housing Authority, *Annual Report for 1951*, pp. 23, 33; *Annual Report for 1954*, n.p.

37. Committee on Slum Clearance, *Report of New York City Slum Clearance Program under Title I of the Federal Housing Act of 1949* (July 15, 1957); *Daily Worker*, Sept. 6, 1950; Abraham E. Kazan, Oral History, Columbia University Oral History Collection, pp. 313–316, 327; *New York Times*, Sept. 18, 1955; Emil Morosini, Jr., to Charles Abrams, Apr. 3, 1951; *The Villager*, June 12, 1958, clipping; unsigned Memo, Feb. 21, 1951, Abrams Papers, Reel 51.

38. *Daily Worker*, Sept. 28, 1951; "Call to an Emergency Conference Protesting the High Rent Project of 'Manhattantown,'" Dec. 8, 1951; Ira S. Robbins to Nathaniel S. Keith, Mar. 19, 1952, both in Mayor's Papers, Box 1120; New York State Committee against Discrimination, Executive Director's Action Report, Dec. 10, 1952, UNH Papers, Folder 432.

39. Lawrence W. Orton to David Rockefeller, Jan. 3, 1953; Elizabeth R. Hepner, *Morningside-Manhattanville Rebuilds . . . A Chronological Account of Redevelopment in the Morningside-Manhattanville Area* (New York, n.d.), pp. 3–4, 13–14; Ruth

Senior to Orton, Apr. 1950; Morningside Heights, Inc., Community Advisory Committee, Minutes, May 15, June 19, Dec. 14, 1950, Jan. 11, 1951, all in Morningside Files; Mayor's Committee on Slum Clearance, *Report to Mayor Impellitteri and the Board of Estimate by the Committee on Slum Clearance Plans* (Sept. 1951).

40. *Daily Worker,* Oct. 26, 1951; Aiko Hoshino to Abrams, Apr. 9, 1952, Abrams Papers, Reel 51; Martha Dalrymple to Margaret B. Bartlett, Oct. 18, 1951; Robert Dougherty to Rockefeller, Oct. 24, 1951; Margaret B. Bartlett, Confidential Memorandum, Oct. 22, 1951; Morningside Committee on Cooperative Housing, Minutes, Oct. 30, 1951, all in Morningside Files; Joel Schwartz interview with Bernard M. Weinberg, Dec. 12, 1979; Committee to Save Our Homes, "An Open Letter to the City Planning Commission," n.d., Abrams Papers, Reel 51; Rev. George B. Ford to Philip J. Cruise, Nov. 23, 1951, Morningside Files; *Daily Worker,* Nov. 16, 1951.

41. *Amsterdam News,* Feb. 2, 1952; and minutes, leaflets, and other material of the Morningside Committee on Cooperative Housing, the Manhattanville Civic Association, and the Save Our Homes Committee in Morningside Files.

42. Ira S. Robbins to Nathaniel S. Keith, Mar. 19, 1952; Keith to Robbins, Apr. 8, 1952; Robbins to Keith, Apr. 15, 1952, with enclosed Memo; Robbins to Charles Horowitz, Apr. 23, 1952; Citizens Housing and Planning Council, Press Release, May 5, 1952; Mel Bernard to Impellitteri, May 7, 1952, all in Mayor's Papers, Box 1120; *Daily Worker,* May 5, 1952, Jan. 19, 1953; *Amsterdam News,* Oct. 4, 11, 1952; Port Authority of New York, *Report: Lincoln Tunnel Third Tube Tenement Relocation* (Feb. 1955), p. 6.

43. John McLoughlin interview with Judge Hortense W. Gabel, Mar. 11, 1976; NYSCDH, Executive Director's Action Report, Dec. 10, 1952, UNH Papers, Folder 432; McLoughlin interview with Harris I. Present, Feb. 12, 1976.

44. Morningside Heights Housing Corporation, Report to the Executive Committee, Sept. 11, 1952; Moses to Rockefeller, July 30, 1952; Margaret Bartlett to Rockefeller, July 31, 1952; Morningside Heights, Inc., to Harry Taylor, Aug. 6, 1952; Father George B. Ford to Orton, n.d.; Taylor to Nathaniel S. Keith, Sept. 2, 1952; S. F. Boden to Orton, Oct. 30, 1952, all in Morningside Files; Committee to Save Our Homes, "An Open Letter to the City Planning Commission," Abrams Papers, Reel 51; Bernard Segal to Morningside Committee on Cooperative Housing, Nov. 18, 1952; Martha Dalrymple to Bartlett, Dec. 11, 1952; Bartlett to Dalrymple, Dec. 15, 1952; S. F. Boden, Memorandum, Dec. 22, 1952; *Daily Worker,* Jan. 16, 1953, clipping, all in Morningside Files.

45. Records and leaflets of the Manhattanville Civic Association and the Morningside Committee on Cooperative Housing's records of site protests in 1954, all in Morningside Files.

46. McLoughlin interview with Gabel, Mar. 11, 1976; American Jewish Committee, Committee on Law and Social Action, Minutes of Executive Committee, June 3, 1947, Abrams Papers, Reel 11; McLoughlin interview with Present, Feb. 12, 1976; NYSCDH, Executive Director's Action Report, Feb. 21, 1951, Abrams Papers, Reel 50.

47. Material on the struggle over Washington Square Southeast in Abrams Papers, Reel 51.

48. Caro, *Power Broker,* pp. 979–983; *New York Times,* Feb. 6, 1955; *Amsterdam News,* Apr. 16, 1955; McLoughlin interview with Present, Feb. 12, 1976; *Real Estate Record* 175 (Mar. 12, 1955); *New York Times,* Mar. 13, May 14, 1955; Hortense Gabel to Abrams, May 13, 1955; Temporary State Housing and Rent Commission, Release No. 210, June 9, 1955, both in Abrams Papers, Reel 17; *New York Times,* May 22, 1955; *Daily Worker,* May 23, 1955.

49. *Daily Worker,* Nov. 17, 1955, Jan. 6, 1956; *New York Times,* Oct. 11, 1955, May

21, 25, Dec. 23, 1956; *Village Voice*, Nov. 9, Dec. 14, 1955; McLoughlin interview with Present, Feb. 12, 1976; McLoughlin interview with Frances Levenson, Feb. 26, 1976; *New York Times*, Jan. 17, 18, 23, 1956; *Daily Worker*, Jan. 16, 19, 1956; *New York Times*, Mar. 23, April 7, 14, 1956; *Daily Worker*, Apr. 16, 1956; *New York Times*, Feb. 2, 3, Apr. 7, 24, May 5, 17, 24, 1956.

50. *New York Times*, Apr. 17, 26, May 28, 29, 1956; McLoughlin interview with Present, Feb. 12, 1976; *New York Times*, May 25, 29, 30, June 1, 2, 14, 15, Aug. 30, 31, Sept. 9, 23, 27, Nov. 10, 1956.

51. McLoughlin interview with Present, Feb. 12, 1976; *New York Times*, May 16, 18, July 15, Nov. 20, Dec. 20, 24, 1957; *Village Voice*, May 1, 1957, July 2, Sept. 17, 1958; Kevin Michael McAuliffe, *The Great American Newspaper* (New York, 1978), pp. 91–98; Abrams to George Baughman, Mar. 19, 1959; Raymond S. Rubinow, Edith Lyons, Norman Redlich, and George Popkin to Abrams, Mar. 22, 1959; Joint Emergency Committee to Close Washington Square Park to Traffic, Press Release, Apr. 12, 1959, all in Abrams Papers, Reel 12; *New York Times*, Feb. 4, Aug. 3, Oct. 5, Dec. 28, 1957, Aug. 31, 1958; Kazan, Oral History, pp. 534, 538–540; Committee on Slum Clearance, *Report of the New York City Slum Clearance Program under Title I of the Federal Housing Act of 1949* (July 15, 1957), p. 3.

52. New York City Housing Authority, Meeting of Sponsoring Agencies and Center Directors, Minutes, Mar. 13, 1957; William Reid to Helen Hall, May 21, 1958; Citizens Housing and Planning Council, "Request for a Grant of Funds for Experiments with Social Services in Two Housing Projects," n.d.; M. Stauffer to Helen Hall, Dec. 6, 1958, all in UNH Papers, Folder 484; the series on Title I by Wayne Philips, *New York Times*, June 29–July 7, 1959; Donald W. O'Connell, Memo, July 1, 1959; Robert C. Weaver, "Housing in New York City," enclosed in Weaver to Dr. Frank S. Horne, Sept. 30, 1959, both in Ford Foundation Archives, Log 59–931.

53. Metropolitan Council on Housing, Minutes, June 4, 1959, in Mayor's Papers, Box 2122; John McLoughlin interview with Staughton Lynd, May 8, 1975; Metropolitan Council on Housing, *Tenant News*, Jan. 1963.

54. Harrison E. Salisbury, *The Shook-Up Generation* (New York, 1958), pp. 86–88; *Neighborhood Centers Today* (New York, 1960), pp. 191–195; *New York Times*, Jan. 1, 1964, clipping, and other clippings in Chelsea Vertical File, Municipal Reference Library; Schwartz interview with Jane Benedict, Aug. 27, 1981; Yorkville Civic Council, Minutes, May 17, 1960, Yorkville Save Our Homes File, Met Council (hereafter cited as YSOH File).

55. *New York Times*, Feb. 11, 1959; Yorkville Civic Council, Minutes, May 17, 1960; Yorkville Housing Committee, Minutes, Nov. 27, 1956, UNH Papers, Folder 129.

56. *Tenant News*, Dec. 1962, Nov. 1962, Apr. 1963; *New York Times*, Jan. 24, 1960, Chelsea Vertical File; Joel Schwartz interview with Jane Wood, Aug. 30, 1981.

57. Mary Beauchamp et al., *Building Neighborliness in a Community on the Lower East Side of New York City: A Report of One Year's Work* (New York, 1957), pp. 38–42.

58. McLoughlin interview with Lynd, May 8, 1975; Betty Woody, "Cooper Square: Community Participation in Urban Renewal in New York City," Master's thesis in Urban Planning, Columbia University, 1972, pp. 45–46; *New York World Telegram*, Mar. 1, 1960, Aug. 31, 1961; *New York Times*, Aug. 31, 1961.

59. Walter Thabit, *An Alternative Plan for Cooper Square* (Cooper Square Community Development Committee and Businessmen's Association, July 31, 1961).

60. *New York Post*, Aug. 8, 1963; Schwartz interview with Benedict, Aug. 27, 1981; Yorkville Save Our Homes, Release an-

nouncing rally on June 17, 1961; handwritten Memo, distribution of leaflets, June 10–17, 1961; Yorkville Save Our Homes Committee leaflet announcing meeting on Aug. 13, 1962, all in YSOH File.

61. McLoughlin interview with Lynd, May 8, 1975; Met Council, Minutes, June 4, 1959, copy in Mayor's Papers, Box 2122; *New York Times*, Oct. 17, 1959.

62. *Daily Worker*, Feb. 7, June 12, Oct. 16, 1960, Jan. 15, 22, Feb. 26, Mar. 12, 1961; Temporary State Commission to Study Rents and Rental Conditions, *Hearings*, Mar. 2, 6, 1963, pp. 109, 128–129; *New York Times*, Dec. 19, 20, 21, 1960; Office of the Mayor, Press Release, Dec. 14, 1960, Mayor's Papers, Box 5578; *New York Times*, Jan. 30, Feb. 13, 28, Mar. 3, 23, 1961; Statements of Mayor Wagner, Oct. 22, 25, 1961, both in Mayor's Papers, Box 5578.

63. *Daily Worker*, Nov. 26, 1961, Mar. 6, 1962; Statements by Mayor Wagner, Feb. 26, 28, 1962; Testimony by Mayor Wagner before the General Welfare Committee of the City Council, Mar. 19, 1962; Statement of Mayor Wagner to state senator MacNeil Mitchell, Mar. 26, 1962, all in Mayor's Papers, Box 5578.

64. *New York Times*, Oct. 16, 1962; Office of the Mayor, News Release, Apr. 9, 1963; Wagner Statement, Apr. 1963, both in Mayor's Papers, Box 5578; *New York Times*, June 7, 1963; Hortense W. Gabel to Wagner, Dec. 13, 1963, with "Report to Mayor Wagner on the Control of Residential Rents in New York City," Mayor's Papers, Box 5578.

65. Temporary State Commission to Study Rents and Rental Conditions, *Hearings*, Mar. 6, 1963, pp. 128–129; Metropolitan Council on Housing, "Neighborhood Conservation" (June 1963).

66. *Tenant News*, Oct. 1963.

67. Yorkville Save Our Homes Committee leaflet announcing meeting on Aug. 13, 1962, in YSOH File; *Tenant News*, Oct., Nov. 1962, Feb., Mar. 1963.

68. Yorkville Save Our Homes leaflets announcing monthly meetings on May 6, Aug. 5, and Sept. 3, 1963, in YSOH File; *Tenant News*, June, Sept. 1963, Oct., Nov. 1963.

69. *Neighborhood Centers Today*, pp. 191–195; *New York Times* clipping, Jan. 24, 1960, in Chelsea File, Municipal Reference Library; Yorkville Civic Council, Minutes, May 17, 1960, in YSOH File; "The Case for the East Harlem Project," n.d., L61-1037; Community Service Society of New York, "A Project Proposal for the East Harlem Neighborhood Conservation Program," June 1962, L62-1074, Ford Foundation Archives (hereafter cited as FFA).

70. Frances Fox Piven and Richard A. Cloward, *Regulating the Poor* (New York, 1971), pp. 290–295; Harold H. Weissman, "The Housing Program, 1962 to 1967," in *Community Development in the Mobilization for Youth Experience*, ed. Harold H. Weissman (New York, 1969), pp. 46–50; "The Community Organization Housing Program," Jan. 7, 1964, in *Mobilization for Youth, The Crisis*, vol. 6, Columbia University School of Social Work.

71. "Rent Strike: Concerning the Community Council on Harlem," *New Yorker* 39 (Jan. 25, 1964): 19–20; *Amsterdam News*, May 15, July 17, Aug. 21, Sept. 11, 1954, Feb. 26, Nov. 5, 26, 1955, Apr. 4, July 4, 1959; Clark, *Dark Ghetto*, pp. 159–160.

72. *New York Times*, Apr. 25, May 14, June 3, 1963, Mar. 28, 1964; *NY CORE, Action II* (Jan. 1963), copy in vol. 76, Congress of Racial Equality Papers, Wisconsin State Historical Society (hereafter cited as CORE Papers); reports, manifestoes, and other materials of New York CORE, 1962–1963, in vol. 381, CORE Papers; *New York Times*, June 7, 1963; *Amsterdam News*, July 27, 1963; *New York Times*, Aug. 22, 1963; *Amsterdam News*, Sept. 21, 1963; *New York Times*, Oct. 21, 26, 29, 1963.

73. Weissman, "Housing Program"; MFY, Executive Committee, Minutes, Sept. 4, 1963; "Proposal for a Legal Service Unit," n.d.; "Proposed Tenement Housing Program," n.d., all in folder MFY, 1963, Box

36; MFY, "Overview of Community Organization Program," Dec. 16, 1963, folder MFY, 1964, Box 39, Whitney M. Young, Jr., Papers, Columbia University School of Social Work; "The Community Organization Housing Program," Jan. 7, 1964.

74. Lipsky, *Protest in City Politics*, p. 59; letters, memos, and other material on the New York University CORE housing project in vols. 76, 299, and 384, CORE Papers.

75. *Amsterdam News*, Mar. 24, Sept. 22, 29, Nov. 24, 1962; Naison, "Rent Strikes in New York," p. 19; Lipsky, *Protest in City Politics*, p. 62; *New York Times*, Nov. 5, Dec. 6, 16, 1963; *Daily Worker*, Jan. 7, 12, 14, Feb. 18, 1964; "Rent Strike: Community Council on Harlem," pp. 19–20; "Rent Strike in Harlem," *Ebony* 19 (Apr. 1964): 113–120.

76. Lipsky, *Protest in City Politics*, pp. 65–71; *New York Times*, Jan. 7, 16, 20, Feb. 20, 1964.

77. Papers and reports of East River CORE in vol. 72, CORE Papers; John McLoughlin interview with Ted Velez, Feb. 24 and Mar. 1, 1976; *Amsterdam News*, May 2, 1964; East Harlem Tenants Council, "The East Harlem Block Project," n.d., in General Correspondence, 65, FFA; John McLoughlin interview with Reverend Norman C. Eddy, Jan. 15, 1976; *New York Times*, Apr. 26, 1964.

78. "Brooklyn CORE's Report to the National Council on Projects," Feb. 10–11, 1962; Benjamin A. Brown, Memo, Mar. 19, 1962; Oliver Leeds to Mayor Wagner, n.d., all in vol. 70, CORE Papers; John McLoughlin interview with state senator Major R. Owens, Apr. 22, 1976; Joel Edelstein, "Rent Strikes: What, When, How" (Students for a Democratic Society, Dec. 1963); *Amsterdam News*, Nov. 9, Dec. 7, 1963; Brooklyn CORE Rent-Strike Committee, "Progress Report," n.d., vol. 70; Allan Hoffman to J. McCain, Dec. 15, 1963, vol. 374; Brooklyn Rent Strike, handwritten notes, Jan. 20, 1964, vol. 299, CORE Papers; *Amsterdam News*, Feb. 29, 1964.

79. "Report of the Special Counsel to Mobilization for Youth to the Chairman of the Board and the Directors of Mobilization for Youth, Inc.," Nov. 25, 1964, pp. 34–35, in *MFY: The Crisis*, vol. 4; *Village Voice*, Nov. 5, 1965; *Daily Worker*, Feb. 25, 1964; Weissman, "Housing Program"; North of Houston Street Rent Strike, Minutes, Jan. 15, 1964; Eldridge Street Rent Strike Committee, Jan. 15, 1964; Lower East Side Rent Strike (LERS), Minutes, Jan. 18, 1964; LERS, Minutes, Jan. 15, 1964; Mailing List, Jan. 15, 1964, in Tenants Movement Research Project Files (hereafter cited as TMRP Files).

80. LERS, Minutes, Jan. 24, 1964; LERS, Executive Committee, Minutes, Feb. 2, 12, 19, Mar. 11, 25, Apr. 8, 15, 1964, TMRP Files; Weissman, "Housing Program"; LERS, Minutes of subcommittee, May 1, 1964, TMRP Files.

81. MFY Observer Reports, Aug. 11, 13, 17, Sept. 16, 17, 1964, TMRP Files.

82. Piven and Cloward, *Regulating the Poor*, pp. 290–295; Orlando Rodriguez, "TA History," enclosed with MFY Observer Report, June 8, 1964; MFY Observer Reports, June 8, 10, 11, 16, July 29, Aug. 4, Sept. 4, TMRP Files.

83. Weissman, "Housing Program," pp. 58–59; Blyden Jackson, John Burke, and Don Petty to James Farmer, "Proposals to Give CORE an Effective Organization in the Urban Black Community," June 22, 1965, vol. 8, CORE Papers.

84. Nathan Glazer and Daniel Patrick Moynihan, *Beyond the Melting Pot*, 2d ed. (Cambridge, Mass., 1970), p. 61; Jewel Bellush and Stephen M. David, eds., *Race and Politics in New York City* (New York, 1971), p. 100; Weissman, "Housing Program"; Blyden Jackson and Tina Laurence, "East River CORE, Progress Report," n.d., vol. 72, CORE Papers; East Harlem Tenants Council, "The East Harlem Block Project," n.d., General Correspondence, 65, FFA.

85. Major R. Owens, "Brooklyn CORE Rent-Strike Committee Progress Report," n.d., vol. 70, CORE Papers; MFY Observer Reports, June 1964, July 13, Aug.

20, 27, 28, Sept. 3, 1964, TMRP Files; Lipsky, *Protest in City Politics*, pp. 73–75; lists of buildings canvased by Jesse Gray, in *Amsterdam News*, Mar. 24, Sept. 22, 29, Nov. 29, 1962, July 27, 1963; Brooklyn Rent Strike, handwritten notes, Jan. 20, 1964; George Schiffer to Allan Hoffman, Dec. 10, 1963, vol. 299, CORE Papers.

86. MFY, Attachment No. 4, "Proposal for Expanded Legal Services" (June 29?) 1965, in MFY Papers, Box 8; Nancy E. LeBlanc, "Why Tenants Need Lawyers," Nov. 12, 1964, in MFY Publications, vol. 4; Jane Meyer, "Economic Description of the Real Estate Market on the Lower East Side of New York" (MFY Housing Department, April 1967), MFY Publications, vol. 9.

87. "Background on New York University CORE Housing Projects," n.d., vol. 76; George Schiffer to Allan Hoffman, Dec. 10, 1963, vol. 299, CORE Papers.

88. LERS, Minutes, June 11, 1964; Rent Strike Subcommittee Meeting, June 24, 1964, TMRP files; Yorkville Save Our Homes Committee newsletter announcing Mar. 10, 1964, March on Albany; Newsletter announcing Apr. 6 meeting, both in YSOH File; Irwin Unger, *The Movement* (New York, 1974), pp. 58–59; Paul G. Chevigny to Christopher Edley, Jan. 14, 1965, L65-37, FFA; Robert Alper, *Pratt Guide to Planning and Renewal for New Yorkers* (New York, 1973), pp. xvi–xvii; *ARCH News*, November 1966; Architects Renewal Committee in Harlem, Inc., "Prospectus, 1965–1966," L66-162, FFA; Stokely Carmichael and Charles V. Hamilton, *Black Power* (New York, 1967), pp. 172–173.

89. John McLoughlin interview with Ted Velez, Mar. 1, 1976; interview with Valerie Jorrin, July 12, 1980; Lipsky, *Protest in City Politics*, pp. 87–89, 91–96; Carolyn Odell, *Code Enforcement* (New York, 1972), pp. 32–39; Temporary State Commission to Make a Study of the Governmental Operation of the City of New York, *A Superagency Evaluated: New York City's Housing and Development Administration* (March 1973), p. 107.

90. Lipsky, *Protest in City Politics*, pp. 145, 92; Odell, *Code Enforcement*, pp. 52–60; Linda Einhorn, "An Adequate Response: New York City's Incentive Programs to Halt Housing Deterioration," Master's thesis in Planning, Columbia University, 1968, pp. 76–77, 82; *A Superagency Evaluated*, pp. 71–72.

91. John McLoughlin interview with Paul DeBrul, Apr. 6, 1976; David Borden, "East Harlem Block Community Development Program, June, 1964"; Christopher F. Edley to Paul Ylvisaker, Sept. 8, 1964; Edley to Frank Bowles, Oct. 27, 1964; Borden to Edley, Mar. 15, 1965, all in L65-82, FFA; John McLoughlin interview with Reverend Norman C. Eddy, Jan. 15, 1976; Norman C. Eddy, "Metro-North Demonstration Neighborhood: Planning and Development by a Poor Urban Community, August, 1966," in General Correspondence, 66; Architects Renewal Committee in Harlem, Inc., "Prospectus, 1965–1966"; *ARCH News*, Nov. 1966, both in L66-162, FFA.

92. McLoughlin interview with DeBrul, Apr. 16, 1976; Eddy, "Metro-North Demonstration Neighborhood"; ARCH, *Tenant Action Handbook*, rev. ed. 1965; (New York, 1968); *ARCH News*, Nov. 1966; ARCH Memorandum, June 1967, all in L66-162, FFA; *New York Times*, Aug. 28, 1966.

93. Bedford-Stuyvesant Restoration Corporation, *Program Operations* (n.d.).

94. John McLoughlin interview with Claudius Drew, Mar. 1, 1976; McLoughlin interview with Diane Paul, Jan. 21, 1976; McLoughlin interview with June Salters, Feb. 18, 1976; McLoughlin interview with Edythe Jenkins, Feb. 16, 1976; *Report of the Hunt's Point Community Progress Center, Summary of Activities, 1966–1967: Program Components, 1967–1968* (June 1967); South Bronx Community Progress Center, *Second Progress Report, 1967*.

95. ARCH, "Prospectus, 1965–1966"; ARCH to Louis Winnick, May 17, 1965; *ARCH Review*, 1964/5–1966, all in

L66-162, FFA; *ARCH News*, Nov. 1966; John McLoughlin interview with Velez, Feb. 24, 1976; East Harlem Tenants Council, "Presentation to the Housing and Development Board of the City of New York for the East Harlem Pilot Block Project, 1965," in General Correspondence, 65, FFA.

96. Charles Abrams, *The City Is the Frontier* (New York, 1965), pp. 184–193; Frederieke Taylor, *A Catalogue of Low Rent Rehabilitation in New York City* (Citizens Housing and Planning Council, 1968); Harold K. Bell and Granville H. Sewell, *Turnkey in New York: Evaluation of an Experiment* (Columbia University School of Architecture, June 1969), pp. 9–10; McLoughlin interview with Eddy, Jan. 15, 1976; *Model Cities Housing Corporations* (Washington, D.C., Jan. 1971), pp. 1–2, 42–43; Harvard-MIT Joint Center for Urban Studies, *Rehabilitating New York's Multiple-Dwelling Tenements* (Sept. 1968), pp. vi–ix; 1:8; 2:44–47; 3:8–15, 32, 45–50; 4:62, 88–90; Martin Mayer, *The Builders* (New York, 1978), p. 166.

97. John V. Lindsay, *The City* (New York, 1970), pp. 125–127; Raymond & May Associates, *Vest Pocket Housing in Bedford-Stuyvesant* (New York, 1968), p. 40; *South Bronx Vest Pocket Program* (Feb. 1969), pp. 2, 6–7; Stephen Mittenthal and Hans B. C. Spiegel, *Urban Confrontation* (New York, 1970), pp. 256, 284, 356; Mott Haven Planning Committee, *Mott Haven Plan/67* (n.p., n.d.).

98. Mittenthal and Spiegel, *Urban Confrontation*, pp. 250–253; *New York Times*, Aug. 16, Nov. 6, 1969; *Christian Science Monitor*, Oct. 4, 1969; Jonas Vizbarras, *Bronx Plan: A Report on Physical Development Planning* (Aug. 15, 1969), pp. 14–18; New York City, *Model Cities: Vest Pocket Housing Progress Report* (1969), appendix, pp. 20–22; New York City, Model Cities Administration, *Eighteenth Quarterly Report* (Dec. 1973), p. 13.

99. Raymond & May Associates, *Vest Pocket Housing*, pp. 44–45, 51, 74, 76; and issues of the *Central Brooklyn Coordinator*, Jan., Mar. 1967, reprinted in *Vest Pocket Housing*.

100. Herman Rollins to Eugenia Flatow, May 1, 1968; Lionel Payne to Flatow, May 1, 1968; Horace L. Morancie to Flatow, May 1, 1968, all in New York City, Model Cities Committee, *Bi-Monthly Planning Progress Report, May 1, 1968;* Temporary State Commission to Make a Study of the Governmental Operation of the City of New York, *Urban Renewal in Brownsville* (1973); George J. Washnis, *Community Development Strategies* (New York, 1974), pp. 377–383.

101. Leland Gartrell and Nick Herman, "Participation of Religious Institutions in Non-Profit Housing Corporations, New York City, 1971" (mimeo, Council of Churches of the City of New York, Apr. 1971); "Interfaith Housing Strategy Committee" (mimeo, Mar. 3, June 11, 1971).

102. Myles Weintraub and Rev. Mario Zicarelli, "Tale of Twin Parks," *Architectural Forum* 138 (June 1973): 54–55; Kenneth Frampton, "Twin Parks as Typology," ibid., pp. 57–58; Suzanne Stephens, "Learning from Twin Parks," ibid., pp. 62–67; Mildred F. Schmertz, "'Vest Pocket' Housing Brings a New Scale to the Bronx," *Architectural Record* 153 (June 1973): 121–128; John M. Goering, Maynard Robison, and Knight Hoover, *The Best Eight Blocks in Harlem: The Last Decade of Urban Reform* (Washington, D.C., 1977), pp. 2, 29–38, 45–57, 69–70, 74.

103. Rob Hollister, "The Politics of Housing: Squatters," *Society* 9 (July/Aug. 1972): 46–52; Emily Jane Goodman, *The Tenant Survival Book* (Indianapolis, 1972), pp. 79, 206; John McLoughlin interview with William Price, Feb. 16, 1976.

104. John McLoughlin interview with Marie Runyon, Feb. 13, 1976; Robert Jensen and Cathy A. Alexander, "Resurrection: The People Are Doing It Themselves," in *Devastation/Resurrection: The South Bronx* (Bronx, 1979), pp. 83–85.

105. Einhorn, "An Inadequate Response," pp. 16–17; Judah Gribetz and Frank Grad, "Housing Code Enforcement," *Columbia*

Law Review, vol. 66, p. 1289; and Frederic Berman, "Letter to the Editor," *New York Times*, Sept. 23, 1966.

106. *Tenant News*, vol. 7, Jan.–Feb., Mar.–Apr. 1969, May–June 1969.

107. *New York Times*, June 5, Sept. 23, Nov. 7, 8, 11, 16, 1969.

108. Ibid., Feb. 8, 13, 15, 23, 27, 28, Apr. 1, May 1, 10, 1970; *Tenant News*, vol. 8, Oct.–Nov., Dec. 1969, Jan.–Mar. 1970.

109. *New York Times*, May 13, 17, 21, 26, 27, June 4, 5, 18, 25, 26, 27, 28, July 3, 10, 11, 1970; Monica R. Lett, *Rent Control* (New Brunswick, N.J., 1976), pp. 11–17; *A Superagency Evaluated*, pp. 111–113.

5. Tenant Responses to the Urban Housing Crisis, 1970–1984

Ronald Lawson
with the assistance of
Reuben B. Johnson III

A Watershed for the Tenant Movement, 1970–1975

THE early 1970s represented a watershed for the tenant movement in New York City. Dramatic changes in the housing market and legislative climate presented the movement with new challenges and opportunities. First, severe decay and abandonment of the housing stock increased sharply in the late 1960s and early 1970s. Second, the system of rent regulations, the central features of which had been in place since 1943, was suddenly challenged and undermined: a law enacted by the state legislature in 1971 provided that the bulk of apartments with regulated rents would be decontrolled within a few years, while a measure passed by the city council the previous year introduced annual rent increases for apartments while they remained rent controlled. Third, the threat of tenant displacement took on new forms. In the neighborhoods of the poor the culprit was the many faces of abandonment: fires, absent services, unsafe buildings, the stripping of pipes and appliances from vacant apartments. For tenants of stable working-class and lower-middle-class neighborhoods the threats were gentrification, manifested in evictions to make way for luxury redevelopment and "brownstoning," and hospital expansion. And for tenants of desirable buildings, the threats took the form of two landlord strategies: cooperative conversions with the eviction of non-purchasing tenants, and "encouraging" tenants with rent-regulated apartments to move so that rents could be decontrolled under the new legislation and then raised sharply.[1]

Tenants responded to the new conditions with a sustained upsurge of organizing. The sources of this were diverse and often far removed from the Old Left–dominated constellation surrounding the Metropolitan Council on Housing (Met Council*). Groups with church ties often initiated efforts to

*Names of organizations and agencies are always spelled out in full on first use; abbreviations are often employed on subsequent references. The reader may wish to consult the List of Abbreviations located at the end of this chapter.

combat abandonment or to stem white flight and reverse incipient decay. Middle-income tenants, frequently veterans of the civil rights and antiwar movements of the 1960s, formed tenant organizations on their own: some took leadership when their buildings faced problems; others, New Left activists seeking a long-term constituency, were attracted to a movement where the basic organizing unit was the building where members lived. Politically ambitious persons also organized tenants once the potential of the movement for building a constituency was revealed. By 1973 eighty-three neighborhood tenant organizations existed in New York City, sixty-seven of which had been founded since 1969. Over one hundred service centers funded by the federal Office of Economic Opportunity also purportedly engaged in tenant organizing. A broader spectrum of tenants became active in the movement: the abandonment issue attracted the poor and members of racial minorities, while the threat of displacement and rent increases drew both working- and middle-class tenants. A clear majority of the activists in all segments, especially at the grass roots, continued to be women. Together this constituency had considerable political potential, for 75 percent of the city's population were tenants.

New issues also bred new strategies. Low-income tenants began taking control of abandoned buildings, rehabilitating them, and owning them jointly as cooperatives. Other tenant organizations began to intervene directly in the political process, where they drafted and lobbied for legislation, held legislators to account for their actions, and supported candidates, including, occasionally, tenant leaders running for office themselves. Meanwhile, the traditional strategy of the movement, the rent strike, was also evolving new forms.

Rent Regulations and the Politicization of the Movement

Since New York City's rent control law was originally enacted to meet an "emergency," it included a "sunset clause," meaning that the law would lapse if a continuing emergency were not affirmed and the law extended—usually every three years. In the late 1960s, leaders of the real estate industry came to regard the next extension by the city council, which was due by March 1970, as an opportunity to seek the passage of amendments that would weaken the rent control system. Spurred by the rising costs associated with the inflation accompanying the Vietnam War and a sharp drop in the vacancy rate from 3.2 percent to 1.2 percent between 1965 and 1968, real estate leaders launched their campaign.

Jason Nathan, the administrator of Mayor Lindsay's new Housing and Development Administration, was sympathetic to the contention that the rent system was causing rents to lag behind cost increases. Consequently, he contracted for studies to assess the impact of controls on the rental housing industry and to derive a cost-driven formula to set and adjust rents within the framework of rent controls. A Rand Corporation study found that housing abandonment had increased sharply in New York City during the second half of the decade, with an average of 38,000 units per year being abandoned as compared with 15,000 between 1960 and 1964. Moreover, while the inventory of "sound" housing had grown by 2 percent between 1960 and 1967, "dilapidated" housing climbed by 44 percent, and "deteriorating" housing by 37 percent. The study blamed housing decay to a large extent upon a "rent gap" between the controlled rents landlords received and the "economic rents" necessary for them to maintain their buildings adequately. A second study, by George Sternlieb of Rutgers University, also argued that rent control indirectly discouraged maintenance and capital improvements by reducing property values.[2]

These studies convinced city officials that rent control led to abandonment. Consequently, the Lindsay administration extended the rent control legislation, but then introduced a series of modifications to it known as the Maximum Base Rent (MBR) system, which became law in July 1970. This system used a formula to establish an "economic rent" for each apartment, which, because it was usually much higher than prevailing rent levels, was to be phased in gradually, with an initial across-the-board increase of 15 percent followed by 7.5 percent annually as long as the landlord was maintaining his building and providing services. The addition of annual increases to the rent control system, where 15 percent increases on turnover had previously been the chief source of rent escalation, was a considerable change.

The new law affected a large constituency: 1.3 million apartments were covered by rent control. In its newsletter for October–November 1969, Met Council had begun to warn its affiliates of possible attacks on rent control. However, apart from statements against changes at the city council hearings on the extension of the rent control law, there was little activity by tenant organizations to protect rent control during the crucial months early in 1970. The position against modifications found little support, even among tenants who would be affected by them. In a poll instigated by the city administration, Louis Harris and Associates found that 37 percent of rent-controlled tenants living in transitional areas thought rent hikes to cover increases in landlords' maintenance costs were "fair," while 35 percent thought they were "unfair" and 28 percent had "no opinion."[3] Only a few Reform Democrat and Liberal council members opposed the changes, and even they did not work closely with organized tenants. In the end the MBR law passed 27 to 10, with the *New York Times* lauding the majority.[4]

The tenant response to these changes in rent regulations was shaped largely by the internal dynamics of Met Council. Many of the new neighborhood organizations were not affiliated, and their isolation and inexperience limited their ability to operate in the political arena. Met Council, on the other hand, politically active throughout most of the 1960s, sent large delegations and key leaders to lobby in Albany and published a regular column by Frances Goldin in its paper, *Tenant News,* that detailed its political plans. During this time, Met Council had built an image of representing a broad coalition, with key politicians, planners, and lawyers taking part in its annual conferences.[5] However, toward the end of the 1960s it had become pessimistic about the effectiveness of working through the political system and became more isolated and politically sectarian. In 1968 it announced that it would no longer endorse political candidates and signified disillusionment with political lobbying. Expressing support for civil disobedience, it reactivated its interest in the rent strike strategy and set out to develop a new form of strike to replace the section 755 form dominant since the Harlem strikes of 1963–1964. Early in 1970, Lester Evens and Richard Levenson, activist lawyers close to Met Council, devised the "rolling rent strike," under which strikers, refusing to place their rents in escrow, preferred, if necessary, to pay the landlord and then withhold their rents again the next month. The object was to force direct negotiations between tenants and landlords through lengthy court fights and fear of the tenants "skipping" with the rents in their possession. Several experiments with such strikes demonstrated that this form greatly boosted the independence and bargaining power of the strikers while attracting new activists to Met Council, especially veterans of the movements of the 1960s.[6]

Consequently, Met Council responded to the passage of the MBR law by calling for a citywide rent strike to protest the plan: "Do not count on legislators. Take matters into your own hands." On August 1, the day on which the 15 percent across-the-board rent increase took effect, Met Council renewed this call and began a Tenant Strike Campaign. With Met Council in the lead, tenant organizations in many sections of the city set out to organize strikes.[7] Tenant leaders thus reacted much more strongly once the increased rent bills were in hand than they had done in prospect. Nevertheless, while the campaign led to strikes in several dozen buildings, it never gained the momentum of a citywide strike and consequently had almost no impact on the legislative process. When, at the end of 1971, Met Council reviewed the strike and summarized the experiences of forty striking buildings, the focus of the story was on victories over individual landlords rather than clout with legislators.[8]

The only political opposition to the implementation of the MBR system came from the New Democratic Coalition, the reform wing of the New York Democratic party. In January 1971, under the leadership of Assemblyman

Richard Gottfried, Reform Democrat political clubs began a campaign to collect signatures so that an MBR repeal referendum could be added to the election ballot. Tenant organizations participated actively in circulating petitions. The drive, however, aroused strong opposition from other sectors of the Democratic party, civic groups, the news media, and the Lindsay administration. The *New York Times* denounced "demagogy on the rent front"; Commissioner of Rent and Housing Maintenance Benjamin Altman called the effort "irresponsible."[9] Ironically, this support from the Reform Democrats proved harmful to the tenant cause because it gave anti-rent-control forces "proof" that no New York City administration could ever administer rent control fairly or implement modifications in the law because "irresponsible" politicians and the huge bloc of tenant votes would eventually combine to repeal any changes.

This argument was used by Governor Rockefeller during the 1971 session of the New York State legislature to support a drastic reversal of the state's policy of allowing New York City home rule in rent matters. In proposing this change, Rockefeller cited the rapid deterioration of housing in New York City and said the laws were needed to provide incentives for private interests to begin the construction of new housing that would ease the housing shortage. One of the bills in the package removed rent regulations (both rent control and rent stabilization) entirely from apartments as they were vacated by their tenants ("vacancy decontrol"), while another prohibited New York City from imposing "stricter" rent regulations than those then in effect.[10]

Because of the speed with which these laws were introduced and passed, there was little time to organize opposition to them. Tenant organizations were caught off guard and put up even less opposition than they had against MBR. The only concrete action taken within the tenant movement was the calling of a citywide conference to organize a mass rent strike, which was endorsed by Met Council, the East Harlem Tenants Council, and Jesse Gray's Harlem Tenants Union. Met Council's *Tenant* had the following advice concerning efforts to apply political pressure: "While pressure should be kept on city legislators, there is not much influence a New York City voter can have on the State Senator from Canandaigua. Met Council has been on too many fruitless Albany trips in the past."[11] The calling of a mass rent strike was wishful thinking on the part of tenant leaders, for the tenant movement was without the necessary networks and had to organize buildings one by one.

The strongest opposition to vacancy decontrol in fact came from the city of New York. The Lindsay administration bitterly resented both the loss of power in the abrogation of home rule provisions and the fact that Rockefeller's legislation was introduced before its MBR system had been given time to have visible effect. The *New York Times* and several social welfare and "good government" groups backed the city in its opposition.[12] Nevertheless, these forces failed to prevail over Governor Rockefeller and his real estate supporters.

The political events of 1970–1971 showed that neither alone nor with the assistance of powerful allies were tenant groups able to stop the erosion of protective laws that had been in effect for twenty-eight years. Politically, these events represented the nadir of the tenant movement. Moreover, because Rockefeller's laws moved the decision-making arena for rent issues from the city council to the state legislature, they made it much more difficult for the tenant movement in New York City to influence such issues in the future.

At the time of the MBR and vacancy decontrol battles, many of the neighborhood tenant organizations were new. For the most part they had little knowledge of other organizations concerned with similar problems. However, between 1971 and 1973 contact between these organizations increased and played a key part in building the strength of the tenant movement in New York.

The Lindsay administration took the lead in helping to establish these communication networks. In so doing it responded both to its own chagrin at the passage of Rockefeller's laws and to fears concerning their consequences. The vacancy decontrol law eliminated tenant rights that had become traditional in New York City, such as the right to a lease and to renew it at the tenant's discretion, the right to periodic painting, the obligation of the landlord to maintain essential services, and almost absolute protection against eviction unless the landlord could prove, in court, that the tenant was unjustifiably withholding rent or destroying property. Tenant leaders were especially fearful that the law would provide landlords with an irresistible incentive to harass tenants into moving out of rent-controlled apartments.

Benjamin Altman, Lindsay's commissioner of rent and housing maintenance, the man responsible for pushing through the MBR law, responded to the new state laws by calling a meeting of tenant leaders to form an umbrella organization that would protect tenants against landlord harassment by organizing them "landlord by landlord" and promoting rent strikes if necessary. "The aim is simple," said Altman, "we'll establish tenant power."[13] Altman invited thirty representatives of neighborhood organizations and antipoverty groups that worked with tenants to the first meeting of his Tenant Advisory Committee (TAC). Several uninvited groups also demanded to be included and were admitted. Met Council, on the other hand, refusing to have anything to do with the body, dubbed Altman's initiative, in view of his MBR role, "cynical" and denounced the participants: "Company unionism never pays!"[14]

However, the members of TAC proved to be neither pliant nor patient. Within a month, thirteen of them had endorsed a letter to Altman pressing ten demands, one of which was that the city back the move to repeal the MBR law. Calling the demand "irresponsible," Altman refused. A week later seventeen of the forty members, declaring that the committee "served no effective function," resigned.[15] Significantly, the dissidents were a mixed group of activists from organizations representing both middle-class and poor minority neighborhoods.

Prior to the formation of TAC, tenant activists had not been aware of the variety and profusion of tenant organizations in New York City. With the exception of the clusters affiliated with Met Council and the City-Wide Anti-Poverty Committee on Housing, a group of antipoverty agencies that occasionally met but rarely did anything collectively, tenant organizations seldom interacted. No one had previously taken the initiative to organize a grand coalition that brought together all the housing and tenant groups of the city.

The dissident groups plus some others continued to meet together after the dissolution of TAC to plan a joint attack on housing problems. In August 1971, twenty-five groups from four of New York City's five boroughs formed the Federation of New York Tenant Organizations, which shortly afterward presented a list of demands to Mayor Lindsay.[16] Rent regulation issues remained prominent because the Lindsay administration was seeking to have the rent levels in the city excluded from President Richard Nixon's phase I price control program, and thus to have the scheduled MBR increases take effect on January 1, 1972. Although the tenant lobbying was ultimately unsuccessful, the publicity given their campaign to freeze rents led them into contact with tenant organizations in three suburban counties and with the National Tenant Organization (NTO), whose constituency was made up primarily of public housing tenants and whose executive director was Jesse Gray.

Realizing that tenants now needed statewide political strength in order to secure favorable housing legislation for New York City, a few of the tenant leaders from the city began to plan the formation of a statewide tenant federation. The organizations most involved in this effort included the West Side Tenants Union, Met Council, and the Harlem Tenants Union (HTU) from New York City and organizations in Rockland County and Albany. With the exception of the HTU representative, all the main figures on the steering committee were white and middle class. However, the connection between HTU and NTO provided by Jesse Gray also gave the organizers good contacts with organizations in upstate public housing projects.

The meeting to create the state organization was set for January 15, 1972, in Albany. However, because of Gray's prominence in NTO and his plans to run for the state assembly later that year, he did not want an independent state tenant leadership. Consequently, despite the participation of HTU in months of planning, Gray arranged to pack the Albany conference with upstate public housing tenants, to overturn the planned agenda, and to have his own candidates elected to run the new organization, which was then left to lie dormant. The conference thus resulted in great bitterness and division rather than the formation of a unified organization and a common agenda of issues to present to state legislators during the 1972 session.[17]

Many tenants received an unexpected respite from the first annual 7.5 percent MBR rent increase—due to take effect in New York City on January 1, 1972—because the city had great trouble setting up the information and computer systems that were to determine which buildings and apartments qualified for the increase. By the end of May the Housing and Development Administration (HDA) had issued only one-third of the expected one million MBR orders that were needed before landlords could increase rents. As a result, several landlord organizations petitioned the court to allow them to raise rents without the official orders, and Justice Paul Fino ruled in their favor. Consequently, six hundred thousand apartments were scheduled to receive 15 percent increases on July 1, and then the second annual 7.5 percent increase six months later. When the Lindsay administration chose not to appeal the decision but instead to issue "Interim MBR" orders that landlords could present to their tenants, tenant organizations from all over the city blasted the administration for allowing increases without requiring landlords to prove their buildings were without serious violations.[18]

Met Council reported that it was inundated with inquiries and requests for help from tenants. It did its best to counsel them, but did not take any action against the interim orders. However, two of the newer, more politically oriented neighborhood organizations, the West Side Tenants Union and Queens Presidents Council, each separately went to court to try to stop the orders. Although these cases ultimately failed, they illustrated the importance of the new organizations: unlike Met Council, which had little faith in the institutionalized channels of protest, the new organizations were more willing to work with politicians, to bargain and compromise when necessary, and to use political institutions, such as courts, to fight for tenant demands.[19] Meanwile, other organizations were pressing a campaign among politicians to protest the abuses of the MBR system. By the end of August the list of politicians endorsing this drive totaled thirty-five.

The MBR protest campaign was interrupted by the elections of November 1972. Tenant leaders ran in four state legislative assembly districts and were successful in two: Jesse Gray won in Harlem and Frank Barbaro, chair of the Bensonhurst Tenants Council, in Brooklyn. Tenant organizations also targeted other legislators whom they regarded as enemies.[20] Early in 1973

John Dearie, president of the Parkchester Tenants Association in the Bronx, was also elected to the assembly in a special election. The presence of tenant leaders in the legislature represented a significant development.

The rent control law faced renewal once again by the city council in the spring of 1973. At the first hearing concerning the legislation, in December 1972, tenant groups demanded the repeal of MBR. However, MBR had powerful supporters: the Lindsay administration, real estate organizations, civic groups such as the Community Service Society, and the *New York Times*. The latter, criticizing those councilmen who supported repeal, said that their actions were motivated by the upcoming elections; it warned, moreover, that any attempt at repeal would be overruled in court since the city was now prohibited from imposing stricter rent regulations.[21] Tenant organizations, however, continued their campaign, and in March 1973, 130 activists signed a statement calling for the repeal of MBR. Despite differences in strategy between Met Council and some of the newer organizations, their combined pressure, in an election year and perhaps with a cynical eye on the likely court outcome, produced the astonishing result of the passage of MBR repeal by a 34 to 1 vote.

As the *Times* had predicted, the MBR repeal began a series of court appeals that eventually found the action of the city council illegal. Nevertheless, the vote reflected the growing political strength of the tenant movement. Organized tenants were no longer concentrated in Manhattan, but could now be found in almost every neighborhood of New York City—middle income, blue collar, and poor; black, white, and Hispanic. No longer could the politicians from the outer boroughs look upon tenant activists as someone else's constituents.

Despite the growing strength of the movement, Met Council stood conspicuously apart from many of the newer organizations. In November 1972 it had purged its vice-chairman, Michael McKee, and eight other officers and board members, in an attempt to reassert centralized leadership by its Old Left faction.[22] Those resigning included most of the young, New Left–oriented members who had come to prominence as a result of the rent strike campaign and had occupied almost half the positions on the organization's executive board. In the face of the political defeats of 1970–1971 and the failure of the rent strike campaign to have a political impact, these young organizers had become restless and had attempted to move toward a stronger local focus with greater autonomy for their "organizing committees" in Brooklyn and Manhattan's Upper West Side. However, these moves were regarded with suspicion by the long-term leadership. They forced the new recruits out, only to watch them rise to leadership among the new, more legislatively oriented, tenant organizations.

The emergence of an effective tenant presence in the state legislature was triggered by the impact of vacancy decontrol on middle-income neighborhoods.[23] Testimony before a commission of inquiry headed by Assemblyman Andrew Stein confirmed that tenant fears, that the law would give landlords reason to "encourage" middle-income tenants to move in order to decontrol the rents of apartments in such neighborhoods, were being fulfilled.[24] Meanwhile, the construction of middle-income apartments, which had already declined sharply since the mid-1960s, was cut again by Nixon's freeze and changes in the policies of the federal Department of Housing and Urban Development (HUD). This in turn further strengthened the demand for housing and raised rents, especially in Manhattan.

As a result of these pressures on middle-income tenants, leaders of the new neighborhood organizations felt a need to establish a presence in Albany that would encourage legislators to strengthen rent regulations. Consequently, some of them made joint lobbying trips to Albany during the 1973 session of the state legislature, and toward the end of that year Michael Ehrmann, of the West Side Tenants Union, and Michael McKee, now of the new Brooklyn Tenants Union, established the New York State Tenants Legislative Coalition (NYSTLC). Although most of the original neighborhood organization members were from New York City, NYSTLC set out to act on its recognition that political strength in Albany depended on building suburban and upstate constituencies also. Strategically, it stressed "skilled" lobbying by a few informed leaders who would provide an ongoing presence in Albany and work with legislators there rather than Met Council's practice of taking a crowd of tenants to Albany on an annual protest.

The situation in Albany confronting NYSTLC during the legislative session of 1974 was changed dramatically by the resignation of Governor Rockefeller toward the end of 1973 and his replacement by Malcolm Wilson, who, though relatively unknown, had to face the voters a year later. Realizing that the vacancy decontrol law was a major source of disquiet among New York City tenants, Wilson took the unexpected step, for a Republican governor, of seeking the support of that constituency, and in so doing had his aides work closely with the leaders of the new federation.

Tenants gained considerably from the 1974 session. The Cooperative/Condominium Fair Practices Act required that 35 percent of tenants purchase their apartments in order for a conversion plan that would evict nonbuyers to go into effect. The "Langley Law" allowed upstate public housing tenants the right to elect up to two representatives to the governing boards of local housing authorities. The Preservation of Sound Housing Act made it more difficult for real estate developers to demolish economically profitable rent-controlled housing in order to erect new luxury buildings. Yet another successful bill limited the proportion of income paid by senior citizens in rents or, if they were homeowners, in property taxes. Ehrmann and the other NYSTLC stalwarts had drafted and lobbied actively for all these bills and had journeyed to the state capitol at least once a week to drum up support for them and to push them through the legislative process.

The NYSTLC constituency had a special interest in strengthening rent regulations. NYSTLC lobbyists were filled with secret jubilation toward the end of the session as they worked out an agreement with the governor's aides: indeed, Ehrmann was called by the head of the State Division of Housing and Community Renewal and asked to spend the whole of the last week of the session in Albany. However, when the agreement was revealed to the leaders of the state senate and assembly, they revolted and it unravelled. The result was a compromise law, the Emergency Tenant Protection Act (ETPA), which allowed the rents of decontrolled apartments to rise to market levels upon initial vacancy, but then limited further increases by placing them under the rent stabilization system. The law also extended rent stabilization to the suburban counties and gave all newly stabilized tenants the right to a lease and protection from arbitrary eviction.

During the 1975 session NYSTLC helped pass the Warranty of Habitability Law, a watershed in tenant protective legislation. Since the late 1960s, many politicians and "good government" groups had supported an "implied covenant" measure that would have required landlords to maintain their apartments in return for the rents they received; however, they were never able to get the bill passed. NYSTLC began to lobby for a similar, but more stringent, bill in 1974, and in 1975 it was enacted. This law transformed the lease, which had previously been one-sided in the obligations it created, to a contract with rent abatement penalties should landlords fail to provide necessary services or maintenance.

How can NYSTLC's extraordinary success in raising issues, defining the terms of legislative battles, and securing the passage of favorable legislation be explained, especially after the defeats suffered by tenants in 1970 and 1971? Until 1973, lobbying activity was restricted to Met Council, and its efforts in this respect had tended to be half-hearted. Its demands were also more radical than most elected officials would accept. Met Council would threaten and shout, but it rarely presented rational, informed arguments that legislators could understand or sustained pressure on them. The purpose of its lobbying pilgrimages seems to have been more to educate its members about the difficulty of making the system work than to secure legislative change: when nothing came of them, it used this to prove the futility of working within the political system. The emergence of NYSTLC and its more professional approach thus gave tenants a voice that was listened to in the state capitol for the first time in years. It was not content to protest and then hope that civic organizations or the city or state administration would devise a solution to tenant problems. It protested *and* presented its own solutions, often in the form of draft legislation, *and* participated in the formation of policy. Many legislators who had been alienated by the tactics of Met Council were receptive to NYSTLC, even though the demands of the two overlapped considerably. Moreover, NYSTLC gained credibility from the shrill presence of Met Council to its left, which made NYSTLC's demands seem reasonable, and from its statewide constituency. NYSTLC also had the advantage of operating in a more favorable political context—Governor Rockefeller's withdrawal had created greater flexibility—and of choosing legislation, such as the Warranty of Habitability and the Langley Law, that could be portrayed as so eminently reasonable that similar laws were being passed in other states.

Thus, by 1974 the tenant movement had developed the expertise to be its own advocate within the political process.

Coping with Abandonment: Tenant Control, Rehabilitation, and Ownership

When poor tenants were faced with the decay of their buildings and the disruption of services as the abandonment rate accelerated during the late 1960s, some, rather than suffering in silence until the situation became unbearable and then moving, turned to the central strategy of the tenant movement, the rent strike. However, many of those facing incipient abandonment did not achieve the results they hoped for from the withholding of their rents: rather than giving them the leverage to persuade their landlord to improve their living conditions, this strategy often hastened his exit, leaving the tenants still cold in winter but with a large collective bank account. By 1969–1970 some building organizations were responding pragmatically to this situation by spending the rents they had collected to buy oil and make urgent repairs. However, since the experienced leaders of tenant organizations—notably those associated with Met Council—initially regarded such tenant seizures of de facto control as too risky, this strategy was not fostered or publicized at that time.[25] Later, as experience in these isolated buildings taught movement leaders that tenants were not, through this strategy, inviting eviction, its use spread rapidly until, by the mid-1970s, it was the most common form of rent strike.

Meanwhile, several activist professionals—priests and lawyers—had suggested that one solution to the abandonment problem was to cede abandoned buildings to their tenants, thus creating low-income cooperatives. They raised the hope that owner occupancy could reverse decay and even curb the prevailing civil unrest by giving the poor and alienated a stake in the system. Some of these professionals, each originally acting in isolation, took the initiative in putting these ideas into action. The first low-income conversion to tenant ownership was initiated by a Harlem church in 1963; the second, sponsored by a lawyer, commenced in 1967; others followed rapidly.[26] At this point the concept attracted the attention of the city administration, and in mid-1969 Jason Nathan, HDA administrator, created an exploratory cooperative unit within the Office of Special Improvements (OSI) and staffed it with eight college interns—but gave them no resources, budget, or support staff.

In February 1970 Robert Schur, a West Side lawyer who had been prominent in promoting the plan, was appointed head of OSI and, having secured the promise of a budget for the purpose, pledged to get a co-op program off the ground. Schur utilized the Municipal Loan Program, which had been designed by the city to help landlords rehabilitate their buildings, and the federal Model Cities Program, to provide loans to tenants for the purchase and rehabilitation of deteriorated buildings. This cost was to be paid off, at low or no interest, by the new tenant cooperators. The extent of rehabilitation was usually curtailed—"moderate" rather than "gut"—in order to limit costs and typically was restricted to the "major systems"—plumbing, wiring, heating, the front door, and roof. All the co-ops were required by the city to incorporate as Housing Development Fund corporations,[27] which imposed income limitations. However, the majority did not take the second step of registering with the attorney general as formal cooperatives and thus avoided the costs of issuing a plan/prospectus and of allocating shares. Content to remain informal co-ops, they granted all tenant cooperators an equal vote at meetings. With Schur, able and committed, in command of an enthusiastic staff, the flow of would-be co-ops in the pipeline strengthened considerably.[28]

United Neighborhood Houses, a coalition of settlement houses, was so impressed by the potential of the low-income co-op movement that in 1971 it hired Robert Kolodny of Columbia University's Department of Urban Planning to map its development. Kolodny studied the movement at what turned out to be the time of its greatest expansion. By May 1973, when his report was finished, he listed 18 buildings that had completed the conversion process and 268 others that were at various stages in the pipeline. In many of the buildings entering the pipeline more recently, the tenants had already taken de facto control through the collective spending of their rents.[29]

The third strand of the evolving strategy of tenant ownership and control was the most dramatic of all: the rehabilitation of totally abandoned buildings by the would-be tenants themselves. The first examples of this strategy were initiated by a Catholic priest, Father Robert Fox of East Harlem, who, beginning in 1969, led a group of would-be tenants in the rehabilitation of two fire-damaged and derelict buildings on East 102d

Street. This procedure, dubbed "sweat equity" by Schur because it allowed financially poor people to gain equity in buildings through their labor, attracted considerable attention from the media because of some of the groups involved—a street gang, welfare mothers, teenagers. Initially most were Puerto Ricans; then blacks also "got a piece of the action." Those involved often formed local organizations that provided leadership for neighboring sweat equity projects. In other instances neighborhood organizations, such as Interfaith Adopt-a-Building, that were already organizing rent strikes began to sponsor sweat equity in vacant buildings. Once again Schur utilized the Municipal Loan Program to fund building materials and, often, low wages for the "sweators." Behind the strategy lay dreams not only of owning good housing (this was gut rehabilitation, and in most instances architects redesigned building interiors), but also of securing job skills. Later projects included an explicit job-training component, funded by the Comprehensive Employment Training Act (CETA) program.

With the city's enactment of a new statute, Schur was able to beef up the hitherto small Receivership Program, which dated from the mid-1960s, from 15 to 250 buildings in a year. Under this program buildings with serious code violations could be taken from landlords before the buildings deteriorated too badly. Schur went on to experiment with granting management controls for such buildings to community organizations (mostly neighborhood tenant organizations), thus increasing the coterie of organizations involved in programs aimed at preserving decaying buildings. He saw this program as a major resource for co-op conversions—it could preserve buildings while buying time to develop the unity and skills of the tenants.[30]

By transforming existing programs that had been created with housing developers and landlords in mind, Schur had built an eclectic co-op program upon the foundation laid in the first spontaneous, sporadic efforts.

However, it proved to be a difficult time to be launching low-income co-ops, for the process was fraught with delays, disruptions, and frustrations, which sapped the morale of the participants. The city itself was the source of most of these disruptions—for two reasons:

First, the programs, being experimental, required flexibility, faith, and consistency from a complex city bureaucracy that proved inflexible, unbelieving, and capricious. Loan packaging often bogged down, and once construction was under way it frequently encountered delays in securing approvals of change orders and payment of requisitions.

Second, financial scandals and crises resulted in programs being suspended and their rules altered. The first of these was the Municipal Loan scandal,[31] which surfaced in 1971 and led to the suspension of the program. Despite the fact that corruption had been restricted to the private owners involved in the program, and thus the co-ops were not tainted, the scandal resulted in the suspension of loans to co-ops and the application of more stringent regulations to them once the program was resumed. These events made things much more difficult for the co-ops in the pipeline.[32]

Following the election of Mayor Abraham Beame in 1973, his appointment of Roger Starr as HDA administrator, and eventually the firing of Schur, the official climate became even less conducive to creating low-income co-ops. Finally, most of the funding programs collapsed altogether in September 1975 with the New York City financial crisis. A few of the many properties in the pipeline eventually made it to tenant ownership with the aid of the Association of Neighborhood Housing Developers (ANHD), a federation created in 1974 under the direction of Schur, and the Urban Homesteading Assistance Board (UHAB), a technical assistance unit fostered by the Episcopal Cathedral of St John the Divine. Most, however, were stillborn: of the 286 formed or would-be low-income co-ops in 1973, only 48 were eventually completed.[33]

Factors internal to the co-ops also compounded the difficulties of these programs. Many of the sponsors were themselves inexperienced and consequently inefficient. All sweat equity projects had at least some degree of conflict among the would-be tenants, conflicts caused, for example, by differentials in the amount of work, or "sweat," put into the building. And in a few cases friction between the contractors responsible for moderate rehabilitation and the tenants became so acute that it disrupted progress because tenants denied the contractors access to their apartments.

Delays caused overruns, sapped fragile tenant morale, and, where they interfered with employment, resulted in rent arrears. They also caused arrears in debt service payments, for loan agreements set the dates for debt service to begin and these dates passed with sweators still working on incomplete buildings and moderate rehabilitation properties still partly empty because vacant apartments were not yet available for rent. For many of the young cooperatives, these problems marred what was otherwise an exciting, innovative approach.

One of the directions successfully pursued by ANHD was the expansion of Schur's experiment under which HDA contracted with neighborhood organizations to manage buildings that had previously been managed centrally by HDA. This approach was institutionalized as the Community Management Program. ANHD saw such a procedure as helping to stabilize its affiliates by giving them a steady income through management fees and staff lines, as producing better, more sensitive management, and as preparing the buildings, through moderate rehabilitation under the program and the development of leadership among the tenants, to become tenant owned.

Met Council criticized initiatives leading to tenant ownership because it regarded them as governmental endeavors to escape responsibility and as leading to the cooptation of the tenant movement through involvement in programs and dependence on external funding. However, Met Council found that organizing in the most decayed neighborhoods, where the withdrawal of landlords often left tenants in de facto control of their buildings but without either sufficient income to make them habitable or the authority to discipline tenants who failed to contribute their rents, was an overwhelming drain on its organizers. Symbolizing a strategic change, it moved the site of its Bronx branch from Morris Heights, where it had been in the midst of rampant abandonment, to a more stable neighborhood near Fordham Road. It thus largely conceded the tenants facing advanced decay to the affiliates of ANHD.

The Fear of Displacement

At the beginning of the 1970s, several different sources of displacement threatened tenants in various sections of New York City. Although the diversity of the sources made it difficult for those threatened to join together defensively, the expansion of the tenant movement as a whole enabled these groups of tenants to be more successful at finding allies and strategies than were the earlier victims of government-sponsored urban renewal, who had tended to organize late and in isolation.

The 1970s began with the last major echo of earlier disputes over urban renewal. Many buildings on Manhattan's Upper West Side had been cleared of their predominantly poor and working-class tenants during the 1960s to make way for redevelopment. However, the continued presence of a large amount of vacant, sound housing awaiting demolition, in a most desirable area, was an affront to poor tenants seeking housing in an extremely tight market. Consequently, some of them, entering at night, took possession of buildings, fixed them up as necessary, and fortified them. When their actions received media publicity, other groups of tenants emulated them and organizers from Met Council came to help spread the idea further.[34]

The city found the squatters more difficult to remove than it expected. Eviction required force, which created unfortunate media images, and squatters often returned to the same or neighboring buildings. The city's response was to damage the buildings considerably during the eviction process, so that they could not be reoccupied, and to speed up the demolition timetable.

One result of the short-lived squatter movement was that some of the most persistent squatters were offered a long-abandoned city-owned building near the urban renewal site. This eight-unit building became the first sweat equity project to be completed and a major inspiration to others because of the quality of its gut rehabilitation and the fact that the bulk of the work was done by two welfare mothers.

A new source of displacement grew out of a decision by the state administration during the second half of the 1960s to begin making long-term low-interest mortgage funds available for hospital expansion. New York City hospitals began, without publicity, to buy up surrounding buildings and to draw up plans for new wings, staff housing, parking lots, and buffer zones to separate them from poor communities. Typically, relocation companies were hired as building managers with the express purpose of emptying the buildings so that they could be torn down.

In some instances the tenants went passively, such as those in the way of the expansion of the New York Eye and Ear Infirmary in Manhattan's East Village. But other hospitals found their tenants organizing against them. As some of these organizations gained publicity, the various groups found out about one another, built networks, encouraged other groups of threatened tenants to organize, and eventually formed their own federation, Citywide Save-Our-Homes Committee. By 1972–1973 its members included tenants organized against the expansion of Columbia-Presbyterian, Mount Sinai, Beth Israel, Columbus, and St Claire's hospitals in Manhattan and Methodist Hospital in Brooklyn.

The driving force behind this federation was Harriet Putterman, who had been galvanized into action to oppose the plans of Columbus Hospital, which had already demolished other buildings to make way for a new wing, to take the forty-eight-unit double building in which she lived and replace it with a parking lot for twenty-seven cars. The relocation company persuaded over half of the tenants to move within months, but by that time the ties between the other tenants had cemented, and they survived a standoff that lasted from 1970 through 1976. During much of this time the tenants kept the hospital off balance, with strategies that inluded a suit that would have blocked the state loan for the new wing and, later, a counterdedication featuring the activist priests, Daniel and Phillip Berrigan, timed to coincide with Cardinal Terrence Cooke's dedication of that wing. These strategies won for the tenants the scuttling of the planned parking lot and an agreement guaranteeing them tenancy for life.[35]

Not all of the members of Citywide Save-Our-Homes Committee were so successful. For example, when some of the leaders of the tenant organization confronting Methodist Hospital accepted individual deals from the hospital, the organization collapsed and the housing it was defending was demolished. The threat of hospital expansion diminished with the state's financial crises of the mid-1970s, and the federation and most of its constituent groups faded away.

Tenants threatened with displacement for luxury redevelopment had an even more difficult time because developers and speculators were much less vulnerable to adverse publicity than either the city or religiously affiliated not-for-profit hospitals, and the proposed sites tended to be more scattered. Nevertheless, a major focus for redevelopment during this period was Manhattan's Upper East Side between First and Third avenues, where activists formed Tenants against Demolition (TAD). Their strategy was again to build networks, to prevent individual contacts with the landlord, to refuse to discuss monetary offers to move, and to seek to harass the landlord through negative publicity or picketing his home or office. The goal was to create delays that would cost the landlord so much that he would eventually cut his losses and give up his plans. The landlord of the building in which the fiery president of TAD, Connie Adamec, was a tenant so overextended himself financially through a long and bitter struggle that he eventually sold the building cheaply to the tenants. In spite of the encouragement and skills imparted by TAD to the tenants of many buildings, most confrontations did not end so well for the tenants because of the resources behind most developers. Because of this frustration, TAD became a founding member of NYSTLC and thus secured wider backing for a bill that would make it more difficult for landlords to demolish housing that was running profitably. Although their Preservation of Sound Housing Act became law in 1974, the recession and municipal financial crisis were probably more important in relieving the threat of eviction at that time.

Co-op conversion represented another threat to tenants. At the end of the 1960s landlords began to realize that by converting rental buildings to cooperatives they could circumvent the restrictions on profit imposed through rent regulations and make much more than they would by selling a building to another landlord. Almost all of the early conversion plans allowed for the eviction of nonbuyers once the plan was declared effective by the attorney general. Although there were usually substantial numbers of tenants who were unable or unwilling to buy, they could do little because of the absence of protective regulations. Politicians took little interest in the matter initially because the number of conversions was relatively small and these were restricted to a few electoral districts.

In 1972, however, New York City's largest landlord, Harry Helmsley, released a plan to convert the first quadrant of Parkchester, an extensive development in the Bronx. Since this was not highly prized Manhattan real estate, his was a noneviction plan, leaving in place those tenants who did not buy. This provision did not hush the protests, but the plan was nevertheless consummated the next year. Meanwhile, the remaining quadrants of Parkchester, expecting the other shoe to drop, formed a strong organization and then strengthened their influence when their leader, John Dearie, was elected to the state assembly in 1973. During that year rumors circulated that Helmsley was also planning to convert two other large developments: Tudor City in Manhattan and Fresh Meadows in Queens. Both developments formed strong tenant organizations that attracted the attention of their local legislators. All three of the Helmsley development tenant organizations became founding members of NYSTLC, where they made common cause with the West Side Tenants Union and tenant organizations from suburban Westchester County, which were also trying to cope with several local conversion packages. As a result of their concerns, NYSTLC gave high priority to lobbying for legislation that would help protect tenants in buildings where eviction plans were launched. The result was the passage in 1974 of legislation that prevented an eviction plan from being declared effective unless 35 percent of the tenants had bought their apartments.

By the mid-1970s the recession and financial crisis were causing the demand for cooperative apartments to fall sharply. Consequently, the number of conversion plans also declined significantly. Thus, economic forces aided tenants in shaping the initial wave of displacements during the 1970s. Only the threat of abandonment continued unabated at mid-decade.

The Evolving Rent Strike

As the tenant movement grew more diverse in the early 1970s, the rent strike became a far more flexible and effective tool. For the first time multiple forms of strike were used concurrently as organizations shaped the strategy to meet the particular housing problems and ideological and stylistic preferences of their local members.[36]

As we have seen, simply withholding rent, whether via a section 755 action or a rolling rent strike, was ineffectual with a landlord who was no longer committed to his building, so building organizations had begun to use withheld rents to buy what was most needed. One of Met Council's most prominent leaders, Frances Goldin, eagerly endorsing the new strategy in 1970, saw it as akin to the action of the West Side squatters, which Met Council was already supporting. However, Met Council, afraid that such tenants would be evicted because they could not produce the rent if so ordered by the court, repudiated Goldin. Nevertheless, the structure of the movement allowed those building organizations that wished to experiment with the strategy to do so without committing the whole movement to it; then, once the strategy was proved safe and effective, it could be endorsed and publicized by the federations and spread via the movement networks.

Many of the new middle-class constituents of the movement in the early 1970s still regarded the rent strike as too radical a strategy for themselves personally, in spite of real fears of blight and decay encroaching on their neighborhoods. Consequently, some organizers promoted what they called the "rent slowdown." This was not really a strike, but a strategy in which all tenants held back their rents until the middle of the month, when the tenant leader handed them all to the landlord at the same time. It was an eloquent demonstration of tenant solidarity and, therefore, also a warning to the landlord, who often responded to tenant grievances at this point. For the tenants it was in fact an organizational and emotional preparaton for a strike should the landlord ignore the warning.

Article 7-A of the Real Property Actions and Proceedings Law had been enacted in 1965, in the wake of the Harlem Rent Strike. The article allowed the tenants of a building where disrepair was imperiling "life, health or safety" to petition a court to appoint an administrator for the building who would collect rents and use them to fund repairs, fuel, utilities, and maintenance. Such an administrator also had the authority to rent vacant apartments and dispossess nonpaying tenants. This provision was used very little until 1974 because of legal complexities in bringing the action and the demand of the law that the administrator be a lawyer, accountant, architect, or real estate manager—few of whom were willing to take on a demanding assignment that paid very little. However, in 1974 this rule was relaxed, and tenants were added to the list of potential administrators. Several local affiliates of the Northwest Bronx Community and Clergy Coalition (NWBCCC) then adopted the strategy as a means of getting a landlord off the backs of striking tenants and of securing the greatest possible flow of income by giving them authority to rent vacant apartments and discipline nonpaying tenants. The use of this strategy gradually spread to other tenant organizations, while the city also began to bring cases against landlords. Met Council was adamantly opposed to the strategy for several years, most especially because it rejected on principle the concept of tenants evicting one another. Nevertheless, when it found that tenants it had organized were spending their rent monies on repairs and their efforts were faltering because some nonmembers were taking a free ride, it reversed its position and decided reluctantly to utilize the strategy.[37]

Meanwhile, Met Council's rolling rent strike, with its stress on direct negotiations between the building organization and the landlord, had been preempted as a result of changing court practices and decisions in the first half of the 1970s. During this period a firm legal basis for rent withholding under conditions of decay or absent services gradually emerged, and judges encouraged landlords and tenants to negotiate settlements in the corridors of the court and then register them officially. Judges fostered such practices because decaying housing was causing crowding of the court and the rolling rent strike had made tenants unwilling to place rent monies in escrow. Such practices became especially common after the establishment of separate, much less formal, housing courts in 1973. Since Met Council preferred to sponsor negotiations on the tenants' home turf, it initially advised strikers to refuse opportunities to negotiate in court corridors. However, it accepted these arrangements as the norm once it realized that tenants were usually eager to negotiate and settle.

The introduction of negotiations into court was a practical move toward the acceptance of the lease as a contract, with mutual obligations, which was presaged by the passage of Warranty of Habitability laws in several states in the early 1970s and by the emergence of this principle in New York case law during the same period. The enactment of this principle into law in New York State in 1975 completed the process. As a result of these changes, the rolling rent strike became unnecessary. Tenants without services had the right to withhold rent until their grievances were corrected as well as the right to receive rent abatements for their pains. Negotiation, arbitration, and settlement became the order of the day in the housing court.

Met Council's attempt to call a mass rent strike as a political weapon in 1970–1971 had failed. However, in June 1975 the tenant steering committee at Co-op City, a fifteen-thousand-unit subsidized middle-income development in the northeast Bronx with primarily Jewish and black tenants, announced a rent strike that confirmed the political relevance of the strategy. The strike, which protested yet another in a series of rent increases, lasted thirteen months, during which time the tenants' checks were hidden at undisclosed locations. With more than 90 percent of the tenants participating, huge amounts—eventually $25 million—involved, and a sense of drama attracting considerable publicity, the strike became the focus of political attention. Because the rents were needed to pay interest on state bonds issued to build the development, the state's credit rating and ability to borrow money in the public capital markets was undermined. Nevertheless, a series of government threats during the strike came to nothing. The resolution of the strike, arrived at with Secretary of State Mario Cuomo acting as mediator, turned control of the development over to the tenants' committee. Thus, Charles Rosen, the charismatic strike leader and a former printer, became head of the management team. However, because of the government condition that management collect sufficient rent "to cover, first and foremost, mortgage interest and amortization and, in addition, all operating and maintenance expenses," rent levels continued to rise steeply, beginning in July 1977 with an agreement that brought them almost to the level rejected by the steering committee at the beginning of the strike two years earlier, together with an increase of $50 per room in the equity payment.[38] The tenants became disillusioned with their managers when they continued the politics of confrontation, with disputes over payments, and in 1979 voted the original leadership out of office.

In summary, by the mid-1970s the rent strike had become part of the legal arsenal of weapons available to tenants. Rents that were once kept safely in court could now, with city support, be spent directly as needed by the building—the city concluded that it had to give higher priority to preserving housing in the city than to the niceties of property rights. Meanwhile, what was once perceived as a revolutionary threat had been transformed into a mechanism recognized in law and official programs for the redress of grievances. Its practice had been routinized through the adoption of standard formats (such as those detailed in organizing manuals),[39] and the development of its own jurisprudence (both laws and bureaucracies). By the late 1970s its use extended to representatives of the entire socioeconomic spectrum of tenants.

Multiple Federations and a Diverse Constituency

From 1936, when the first federation, the City-Wide Tenants Council, was formed, until the early 1970s, the structure of the tenant movement in New York was three tiered, topped by one main federation.[40] However, in 1973 and 1974 two other key federations, NYSTLC and ANHD, joined Met Council, the dominant federation since 1959. The emergence of multiple federations represented an important development in the history of the tenant movement in New York. This new situation reflected the diverse interests of the broader, larger tenant constituency that was mobilized in the early 1970s.

NYSTLC, which later changed its name to the New York State Tenant and Neighborhood Coalition (NYSTNC), initially represented the newer, politically sophisticated, and largely middle-class neighborhood organizations of the city and suburbs. Its goals were determined by the particular interests of its members, and it frequently recruited new members by agreeing to adopt their goals as part of its program. There was little attempt to ensure that the various positions it supported were consistent ideologically. Indeed, when members initiated ideological discussion it was usually postponed on the grounds that there were more urgent matters to consider and immediate decisions to be taken.

ANHD served tenants at the opposite end of the spectrum—primarily low-income blacks and Hispanics. However, the leaders of its affiliates included both a mixture of white, middle-class, college-educated community organizers and professionals and local "community people." The latter tended to be young and were better educated or more skilled than the average community resident. Most of the original affiliates were led by white males who had been inspired by the New Left ideals of the 1960s. However, when these moved on, the lieutenants who moved up to replace them were community people. Several of these were women. Indeed, the top positions in ANHD itself were eventually held by women. Thus even the rehabilitation segment of the movement, where the leadership had originally been strongly male dominated because of its stress on technical and financial expertise, came to reflect the predominance of women members at the grass roots.[41]

The chief emphasis of ANHD was on developing, imparting, and using technical skills that would reverse decay in poor neighborhoods by encouraging tenants to take greater control of their situations. Initially ANHD had two primary goals. One was to help member organizations raise money because they needed full-time staff to deal with the complex housing problems in their communities. The other was to pressure city government to expand and streamline programs that could improve the living conditions of tenants in these neighborhoods. It hired a paid staff to supply technical assistance to member organizations and to represent it in contacts with city agencies. In its first eighteen months, the period preceding the city's financial crisis, its membership grew from seven original neighborhood organizations to almost sixty.

Although, initially, the work of NYSTNC and ANHD was separate, they began to cooperate on certain projects as time passed. The leaders of the two federations were close ideologically and had developed skills that were useful to one another: for example, Schur was excellent at drafting legislation while the NYSTNC leaders had lobbying ability. As a result, some of the ANHD members also joined NYSTNC, not only swelling its membership but also increasing its black and Hispanic constituency.

The emergence of what it saw as two competing federations made Met Council uneasy. It responded by asserting frequently that it was *The* citywide tenants' union and by keeping a critical eye on the stands taken or actions performed by the others, especially NYSTNC. Met Council had itself been changing. Until 1970–1971 its only members had been organizations. However, during the rent strike campaign it had also begun to recruit strikers as individual members who paid dues and had a vote at its policy meetings. It had generated high hopes of attracting a large membership—a goal of two hundred thousand was mentioned—and, consequently, of gaining political influence. But while Met Council organized effective rent strikes that allowed the tenants to win improvements in their buildings, its efforts to educate the strikers were meeting with only minimal success: barely 10 percent of the early recruits renewed their membership for a second year. This disappointment had contributed to the split in Met Council at the end of 1972.

As time passed, Met Council returned to one of the ideas that had been pushed by the young organizers it had purged, and it began to establish a presence at the neighborhood level through creating a series of local branches. By 1976 eight branches were operating—four in Manhattan, three in Brooklyn, and one in the Bronx. Each was open one or two nights per week and served both as an organizing clinic where questions were answered and building strategies planned and as a gathering place where members were educated in Met Council's ideology and methods and were drawn into further involvement. This new approach was extremely successful, and the branches rapidly eclipsed in importance the scattered organized buildings and the independent affiliates within the organization. Met Council's membership climbed from 2,000 at the beginning of 1972 to almost 4,500 by September 1973, helped by a steep increase in membership renewal to almost 40 percent. Its individual membership continued to increase rapidly during the succeeding three years and passed 7,500 by September 1976.[42] The resulting influx of membership dues (ten dollars per year for employed members) allowed Met Council to add three full-time organizers, who in turn recruited more members, mostly by organizing rent strikes through the branches.

Met Council's identification with the rent strike strategy and its use as a lever to gain repairs and services from landlords meant that most of its effort and constituency lay along the edges of decay, among the white working-class and white-collar workers—that is, its membership was found primarily among tenants between the two sectors represented by NYSTNC and ANHD. While one of its staff, Bess Stevenson, was successful in building a strong branch in Harlem, even there it typically dealt with buildings that did not face the acute situations endured by neighboring ANHD affiliates.

Throughout much of the 1970s Met Council was developing its long-term goals. Although its ideal had long been public housing, it now discarded this because it allowed tenants insufficient control; at the same time, declaring that poor tenants should not be forced to shoulder responsibility for any housing problems that might develop, Met Council rejected co-ops. Instead, it developed the concept of "housing in the public domain," which would replace the private landlord, housing-for-profit system with a system that coupled public ownership and responsibility with tenant control. The major force in the development of the ideology was Peter Hawley, husband of long-time Met Council chairperson, Jane Benedict, and himself one-time president of the American Labor party. In 1978, after years of consensus building, he authored a book setting out the approach.[43] However, it was not Met Council's radical ideology that was primarily responsible for its growth—the goal was too distant to attract large numbers. Rather growth was a result of the fit of its strategies to the needs of constituents in the neighborhoods it served. Still influential, it remained fairly isolated, set apart by its ideology, its style, and its rejection of the pragmatic strategies of the other segments of the movement, which it regarded and portrayed as "selling out" to politicians and the real estate industry.

Recognition, Prosperity, Expansion, and Frustrations, 1976–1984

As New York City recovered from the 1975 financial crisis, the real estate industry reorganized its political forces to increase pressure on rent regulations, and the revival of the housing market resulted in renewed threats of tenant displacement. These dangers, however, initially paled beside a new prominence that was achieved by the tenant movement: private and public attempts to ameliorate the decay that continued to ravage the neighborhoods of the poor brought an unheralded prosperity to a segment of the movement, while concurrently activists won new measures of political recognition. Nevertheless, such progress also raised questions concerning the direction and ultimate impact of the movement.

He Who Pays the Piper: The Proliferation and Decline of External Funding

In the second half of the 1970s, large amounts of external funding became available to tenant organizations sponsoring the rehabilitation of abandoned buildings and their conversion to low-income co-ops. Then, toward the end of the decade, when the city of New York unexpectedly found itself the landlord of thousands of tenants in decayed housing, it utilized federal funds to become the most avid of all promoters of low-income conversions. However, when the cutbacks in federal funding began to be felt in the early 1980s, following the election of Ronald Reagan, the earlier euphoria over external funding was replaced by a period of reevaluation.

Organizations at all three levels of the tenant movement had, before the mid-1970s, typically existed in the slack in the lives of a handful of people, in borrowed space (often in the apartment of one of the founders), using an available phone, and relying on a member with access to a mimeograph machine at work to run off publicity fliers, membership forms, and so forth. Expenses were met from the pockets of the leaders and organizers themselves, by "passing the hat" at meetings, from the proceeds of fund-raising events patronized by members and their friends, and from membership dues. However, such resources proved inadequate to sustain organizations trying to help tenants cope with spreading abandonment and could not begin to support the costs of rehabilitating low-income housing.

Prior to New York City's 1975 fiscal crisis, most programs to rehabilitate abandoned housing and convert it into low-income cooperatives focused solely on the individual buildings. Only more sophisticated, extramovement sponsors, such as the Settlement Housing Fund, tried to have their overhead costs included in the rehabilitation budget, and then these amounts proved totally inadequate to cover the staff time expended.[44] However, in these early years neighborhood organizations began to draw small support from a variety of private sources, such as churches (priests of the Catholic church, in particular, became involved in neighborhoods where valuable institutions were in danger of destruction as parishioners fled decay), foundations, banks, and the manufacturers of materials used in sweat equity rehabilitation, which financed low staff salaries in some instances. The Community Management Program also provided salaries for managers and repair personnel.

The financial crisis wiped out funding for the rehabilitation of all would-be low-income co-ops except for a few sweat equity projects that included CETA job-training components. Those affiliates of ANHD that had gained Community Management contracts from the city continued to receive that income. The rest did what they could to combat decay through organizing tenants, sometimes choosing to do this full time while surviving on unemployment benefits, and making lists of buildings that could only be saved through rehabilitation. Meanwhile, Schur's eagle eye was open for possibilities to increase their effectiveness by securing funds for their endeavors.

One such opportunity arose when, toward the end of 1975, the city proposed accelerating its program under which abandoned buildings were demolished. ANHD affiliates were strongly opposed to demolitions when they saw the buildings as sound and rehabilitable. They argued that such buildings should be sealed, rather than demolished, in the hope that rehabilitation funds for them would become available. When the city planned to use federal Community Development funds for demolition, ANHD threatened to tie up the funds in extended litigation. Rather than risk this, the city met with ANHD representatives and agreed to fund demolition and sealing as a single program and to accept the recommendations of local organizations concerning which buildings should be sealed rather than demolished. ANHD members were subsequently awarded sealing contracts. Meanwhile, contracts were signed for the first three of fourteen projected sweat equity buildings under which unemployed persons received on-the-job training funded by grants through CETA and the Law Enforcement Assistance Act.

Yet other ANHD members began to receive weatherization contracts from the Department of Housing and Urban Development (HUD).[45]

Meanwhile, the ongoing sweat equity projects were attracting a great deal of media attention: there was drama, and eye-catching photographs, in both the personnel involved and in the transformation of the abandoned buildings. The Renigades, a "youth gang for the people" in East Harlem, made especially striking copy during 1974–1975. Then, in March and April 1976, the People's Development Corporation (PDC) in the Morrisania section of the Bronx and Adopt-a-Building on Manhattan's Lower East Side were covered in key television newscasts. The report featuring the latter's initial sweat equity co-op conversion project on the CBS Evening News with Walter Cronkite presented it as an alternative to abandonment and as an example to other cities across the country. Its experiments with solar and wind power, and then the sweators' victory in court which forced Consolidated Edison, the utility company, to buy the excess electricity generated by its windmill, were highlighted in succeeding months.[46] Such favorable publicity helped ease negotiations between HUD, HDA, and the Chemical Bank, which eventually, in 1977, led to the announcement of a National Urban Homesteading Demonstration Program, under which these two neighborhood organizations received contracts for twelve sweat equity projects utilizing CETA-funded labor. Opportunities for neighborhood organizations to sponsor the rehabilitation of abandoned buildings were thus clearly beginning to revive by 1977.

Meanwhile, however, a rift between Bob Schur, executive director of ANHD, and the federation's Operations Committee, or board, was widening, and in July 1977 Schur was forced to resign. The man who was unsurpassed at finding ways in which to use HDA and federal programs innovatively had been less successful in running an organization: he did not take directions well from his board and was inclined to go behind its back when it disagreed with him. His exit was a huge loss; since ANHD had been created as a vehicle for him, it was almost impossible for anyone to succeed him there. The federation floundered for several years thereafter, going through three executive directors in rapid succession at the outset.

In October 1977 the situation of organizations grappling with the problems of housing abandonment changed dramatically when President Jimmy Carter made an unexpected, two-stop visit to the South Bronx. One stop was on Charlotte Street, in the midst of utter devastation; the other was on heavily decayed Washington Avenue, where he inspected the almost completed initial PDC sweat equity site and responded appreciably to the contrast it offered to the abandonment he had seen. This incident triggered a rash of favorable publicity for the rehabilitation efforts of tenants in New

York City. The next morning the *New York Times* told the world that "A Loan and Some 'Sweat Equity' Create an Oasis Amid Desolation."[47] Heady times followed, as this segment of the movement received backing from churches, foundations, professionals, and all levels of government.

The rapid increase in external funding transformed many of the neighborhood organizations, especially those that had already begun to attract attention. PDC found that the delays that usually beset its proposals were suddenly truncated, with the result that its budget increased to $4 million and its number of members and employees to 250—both tenfold increases—in a year. The growth of Adopt-a-Building was equally dramatic. Its three leaders had survived on unemployment checks while organizing full time in 1975, and the following year they had put together minor church, city, and foundation support; now grants and contracts multiplied, and by 1978–1979 its budget stood at $2.7 million, while $1.5 million more flowed as mortgage funds to finance building rehabilitation. By 1980–1981 its budget had passed $4 million and its paid staff ninety.[48]

Many of the other ANHD members also showed substantial, though more modest, increases in funding. In 1976 ANHD surveyed twenty-seven of its affiliates and found that twenty-two of them were receiving $6.2 million in external funds—an average of $282,000 each. Of this amount, 75 percent flowed from Community Management and job-training funds, while another $1 million came from Model Cities and Community Development antipoverty grants.[49] When, in 1980–1981, attempts were made to reinterview the leaders of the 135 neighborhood organizations and federations studied in 1974–1976, it was found that 55 of the 89 still functioning had received $39.5 million—or a mean of $718,000 each—from a much wider variety of external sources in 1980. This figure omits the many organizations created since 1977 to compete for the newly available funds. The enthusiasm of funders was so great that, for example, HUD extended the homesteading demonstration to two other neighborhood organizations, and thirteen buildings, with a commitment of $2.2 million, despite the fact that the first phase of the demonstration was already far behind schedule.[50]

This expansion had a profound effect on ANHD. As early as March 1978 it had become the largest CETA umbrella group in New York City, funneling trainee personnel to its affiliates. It channeled almost all its attention into administering the program for the next four years. This represented a remarkable narrowing of its focus.

The impact of the sudden flood of external funding was even greater for most of the recipient neighborhood organizations. On the one hand it allowed them to implement new goals, such as rehabilitation, tenant ownership and management, imparting skills to tenants, and creating jobs for them, that had previously been outside the scope of the tenant movement. On the other hand, it led frequently to the displacement of previous goals. Some funders demanded specific changes in proposals before funding them: some foundations, for example, refused to fund the organizing of rent strikes. More often, neighborhood organizations tailored their proposals to meet the known preferences of funders or plugged into programs where the funders had already set the rules. The Community Management Program, for example, insisted that the neighborhood organizations with contracts manage the buildings directly rather than help tenants manage the buildings themselves, which led some neighborhood organizations to protest that they would become bureaucratic stand-ins for landlords. However, the majority of contractors accepted the roles assigned them and usually ceased trying to organize tenants altogether. The most usual reason for goal displacement, however, was that the sudden surge of funding for specific tasks squeezed out activities that were not covered by the grants. The leaders who, while their neighborhood organizations were small and largely internally funded, frequently spent much of their time organizing tenants to use their collective leverage against housing problems, now found themselves administering large projects, meeting stringent reporting requirements, and writing new funding proposals in order to keep income flowing. Since most grants were categorical, flexible funds were scarce—amounting, for example, to only 3.9 percent of Adopt-a-Building's total budget in 1980 and only 2.0 percent of Los Sures'.[51] Consequently, the typical neighborhood organization found itself working intensively on the few buildings it was funded to rehabilitate or manage and no longer trying to organize the tenants of the neighborhood.

When organizations previously staffed by volunteers first received external funding, the service of the staff was usually excellent: they could now work full time for a cause they cared about, but where their previous participation had been limited to their spare time. They therefore typically showed high commitment by working long hours and often continuing unpaid in their positions for months if breaks in funding occurred. However, this level of commitment tended to erode as personnel turned over, especially when funding triggered rapid growth, diluting the influence of committed members and hastening bureaucratization. The strain of large changes in scale was compounded when many of the new employees were CETA workers with no background in the movement, who were available primarily because they needed a job, not because of commitment to the cause. Moreover, under the rules of the program they usually had to be replaced by new recruits, often just as they were being socialized to the goals and ideology of the organization. External funding also had the effect of drying up the pool of volunteer participants.

Nowhere was the impact of dramatic, uncontrolled growth felt more acutely than at PDC, which had been made a symbol of the rehabilitation segment of the tenant movement by a fifteen-minute visit from President Carter:

> PDC . . . met none of the basic conditions for the survival of a small, complex business: its management had no experience working as a team; there was little trust between workers and management; the operation was badly under-capitalized especially in terms of covering administrative overhead and cash flow needs; it did not have good relations with its vendors, and vertical lines of authority had never been implemented. PDC's managers had control over neither their workforce nor their balance sheets.
>
> As for the homesteaders, pulling sweat "became just labor, a negative thing." Homesteaders were "working for the money, working as long as they could." Sweat time became the price workers had to pay to get a CETA job, instead of a commitment to an apartment, to themselves, to the community. Between late August, 1978, and January, 1979, over a third of the homesteaders were either fired or quit.[52]

Finally, the firing of a group of workers in February 1979 was followed by two months of arson, break-ins, theft, protest, and violence, which included the destruction of PDC's financial records. Within a few weeks most of the managers were fired or quit, and by the end of the year PDC's visionary leader, Ramon Rueda, had also resigned and most of the senior homesteaders had pulled out: only supervisors and no-show CETA employees were left.

Doug Moritz, the leader of Los Sures, one of the best-known and most successful neighborhood organizations, whose budget eventually topped $6 million, commented retrospectively in 1980 that the funded programs "diverted us from organizing, from an educational thrust. We sacrificed our local base, as we failed to educate the new tenants who moved in, and came to be seen—rightly—as part of the establishment." A board member of ANHD stated that "collectively we lost the involvement of local people, and instead adopted a contractor relationship with only a few buildings. As a result we can no longer say that we represent, or are even in touch with, the neighborhoods."[53] Many of the neighborhood organizations stopped organizing tenants just when the rent strike strategy of spending rents on services and repairs, and thus seizing de facto control of buildings, was being widely accepted and could have become a way of building considerable strength at the grass roots and forcing input to policy. Other organizations, whose formation was stimulated by the availability of external funding, never learned to organize tenants at all. The warning of Met Council concerning the danger of cooptation present in accepting external funding had been shown to contain considerable truth.

Some organizations managed to retain their combativeness after receiving external funding. This was possible when they retained flexibility because they continued to raise a substantial proportion of their income internally and their external funding was spread over multiple sources, with much of it coming from churches and other local institutions. Nevertheless, any degree of dependence could create a dilemma: for example, a group of neighborhood organizations working together in the Northwest Bronx Community and Clergy Coalition, which had earlier received financial support from local banks, found later that if they wished to protest against investment redlining in their neighborhoods, they would need to pressure these funders.[54] That they nevertheless chose to press ahead is a result, in part, of the protection afforded by their multiple sources of funding. Needless to say, the income from these banks dried up.

Some of these neighborhood organizations (notably members of NWBCCC) so succeeded in overcoming the problem of combining paid staff with volunteers that they achieved the highest participation levels of all. Participation was encouraged in several ways. Since their primary internal source of income was fund-raising (through dances, concerts, brunches, festivals, raffles, basketball games, and so forth), tenants whom they had helped were able to show their gratitude by selling (and buying) tickets. Not only did this approach create slots for those who otherwise would not have been active, but both the ticket selling and the events themselves strengthened social networks. Second, these organizations typically attempted to form block associations where they already had one or two well-organized buildings. These created opportunities for building activists to become involved outside their own building organizations but close to home, where they were concerned about the fate of the buildings and network ties could ease access. Block associations also created an intermediate but unfunded locus of activity, where tenants were less likely to feel the urge to leave the work to salaried organizers. Third, because these organizations typically addressed multiple issues, constituents were more likely to find a continuing relevance there once their initial issue was settled. Participation was therefore less ephemeral.

The City's In Rem Crisis

In 1978 a major new ingredient was added to the abandonment/rehabilitation/tenant ownership landscape. A new city law, Local Law 45 of 1977, allowing properties to be taken in rem—that is, foreclosed for tax arrears—once their owners were one year behind in payments rather than three years as previously, took effect. By this change the city council had hoped to accomplish two things: (1) to encourage owners to pay what was owed rather than lose their properties; and (2) to reduce the decay of those buildings taken by the city. However, the law's result was that the flow of buildings eligible for vesting by the city increased substantially, so it suddenly found itself the largest owner of deteriorated housing, a situation it was totally unprepared to manage. Between 1978 and 1981, vestings brought more than 16,500 residential properties to city ownership, and in 1981, demolitions and sales notwithstanding, more than 8,000 in rem buildings containing almost 112,000 units remained in city hands. Of these, 34,000 units were occupied. Eighteen percent of the occupied units were in buildings categorized as dilapidated, a rate four times that in the city as a whole. Their tenants were overwhelmingly drawn from racial minorities (only 19 percent white) and the poor (with a median income of $6,865, only 62 percent of that of all renters).[55]

In developing its response to the in rem crisis, the city administration had to take three factors into account: (1) housing activists were insisting that it was essential that much of this housing stock be preserved as a housing resource for low- and moderate-income people;[56] (2) it would not be possible to sell most of the property to private landlords without special incentives; and (3) the city did not want to own and manage the property permanently. Consequently, the city experimented with the concept of selling buildings to their tenants and installed Philip St. Georges, formerly head of UHAB, the chief source of technical assistance to sweat equity buildings, as head of a new Division of Alternative Management Programs (DAMP) within the city housing agency, which was itself symbolically renamed the Department of Housing Preservation and Development (HPD).

The main DAMP programs utilized two familiar tenant strategies. The first was the Community Management Program (CMP), whose goal was the sale of the properties after moderate rehabilitation to either the tenants as a co-op or the managing neighborhood organization, which could then continue to manage them. Since moderate rehabilitation of the buildings would continue under the supervision of the managers and at city expense (using federal Community Development funds), purchasers would escape the burden of debt service added to their rent.[57] The second program, the Tenant Interim Lease Program (TIL), was a variation on those early low-income co-ops where the tenants had taken the initiative without the help of a sponsoring neighborhood organization. In this case, organized tenants could gain experience through managing their building, while rehabilitation that was much more limited than under the CMP was carried out under city auspices; ultimately tenants could purchase the building and form a low-income co-op. The purchase price under both programs, as voted by the city Board of Estimate, was to be $250 per unit. Other alternative programs had the Housing Authority, private management companies, or previous 7-A administrators managing and potentially buying buildings. By the end of 1979, one-third of the occupied in rem units were enrolled in a DAMP program, and almost two-thirds of these were in TIL or CMP.[58] The city had unexpectedly donned the mantle of chief sponsor of low-income co-ops.

The TIL program grew by far the most rapidly. In part this was because, with its limited rehabilitation component, it cost the city least. In part it was because TIL was the natural route taken by tenants who were already in de facto control of their buildings as a result of spending their collectively held rent monies.

The commitment of the city administration to maintaining in rem buildings as a low-income housing resource began to waver as early as the second half of 1979. Mayor Edward Koch regarded the program as too costly: the total bill to the city between 1978 and 1981 was $342 million, while it raised less than $100 million in rents—rent collection during the first three years averaged less than 50 percent. The administration began to focus instead on selling buildings and minimizing interim management costs while maximizing the ultimate sales price. A moratorium on auctions, which had been imposed as a result of pressure from tenant activists, was lifted, and sales resumed in November 1979 with a fanfare of media publicity that attracted the lower middle class and boosted prices. Concurrently, there were reports that the city was delaying approval of sales of property to tenants at $250 per unit in Manhattan neighborhoods where the market was reviving: Mayor Koch told a heated town meeting in Clinton, the site of the proposed convention center, that he would not let tenants buy in rem units at $250 and then stand to make a profit by selling them.[59]

Tenants in DAMP buildings had already responded to rehabilitation efforts and their opportunities for input to management with rent collection rates exceeding 85 percent. Nevertheless, the administration pressured both TIL and CMP for sales because it feared that since two years had elapsed without them, the tenants were preferring to remain under city ownership as a hedge against unexpected costs and problems. Eventually, in mid-1980, the first five TIL buildings were sold to their tenants. The CMP, however, did not sell its first building until 1982. Consequently, four of the nineteen CMP contracts were cut out in 1980. Meanwhile, the city was delaying vesting so that it could slow the influx of in rem buildings, and thus left the tenants in many newly abandoned buildings to fend for themselves.[60]

Many of the TIL buildings had organized without the help of a neighborhood organization, and the structure of the TIL program reinforced their isolation. Nevertheless, their common problems—such as the impact of the seemingly inevitable rent increases on poor tenants, the need for more rehabilitation, protection from major problems that might emerge once the tenants had taken control, and a guarantee of the disputed $250 purchase price—created networks that eventually resulted in the formation of the

TIL Coalition. Its meeting with HPD commissioners early in 1980 elicited a promise of section 8 funds as a buffer against rent increases, but nothing firm on their other demands.[61]

By early 1984 a total of 115 TIL buildings had been bought by their tenants, while tenants were managing another 92 in the pipeline. TIL was regarded by the city as the most successful of the DAMP programs. However, the modest level of city-funded rehabilitation in these buildings meant that many tenant co-ops would have to borrow after purchase to complete the work.

The Reagan Presidency: Reevaluation, Convergence, and Divergence

The election of Ronald Reagan at the end of 1980 resulted in cuts in the budgets of the neighborhood organizations engaged in rehabilitation and in the elimination of programs they had come to rely on. Thus, the CETA programs were discontinued, section 8 was phased out, and Community Development funds were no longer restricted for use by the poor. In 1983 a HUD-sponsored study of the impact of budget cuts on eighty neighborhood groups, half of which were in New York State, found that the greatest impact was caused by the elimination of CETA funds, which had removed the bulk of the staff of the organizations. Other cuts had been felt first in "soft" services, since the construction pipeline was slower to come to a halt.[62]

Organizations faced major strategy revisions as a result of the cuts. Bonnie Brower, executive director of ANHD, announced at a retreat that the loss of ANHD's CETA contract had removed about half of its staff of thirty together with a good deal of what had become its direction. There was talk of lean times, self-reliance, and survival, and Brower announced a new emphasis on policy advocacy for neighborhood development. Robert Schur, in his last article before his sudden death in March 1982, argued that the rehabilitation segment had responded to the availability of external funds by moving from confrontation to cooptation, only to find that the government then canceled its part of the bargain. Rehabilitation neighborhood organizations were left with the choice of competing with one another for a piece of the shrinking pie or getting "back to basics" by becoming confrontational in order to force authorities to respond to them. Schur urged them to organize communities as they had once done but had now forgotten how to and, because to be alone was to be weak, to build networks by reactivating and radicalizing their federations. Steve Katz, one of People's Development Corporation's early activists, agreed: they had expected rents would be decontrolled within a few years, while a measure passed by the city council the previous year introduced annual rent increases for apartments while they remained rent controlled.[63] Also, the threat of tenant displacement took on new forms. In the neighborhoods of the poor the culprit was the many faces of abandonment: fires, absent services, unsafe buildings, the stripping of pipes and appliances from vacant apartments. For tenants of stable working-class and lower-middle-class neighborhoods, the threats were gentrification, manifested in evictions to make way for luxury redevelopment and "brownstoning," and hospital expansion. And for tenants of desirable buildings, the threats took the form of two landlord strategies: cooperative conversions with the eviction of nonpurchasing tenants, and "encouraging" tenants with rent-regulated apartments to move so that rents could be decontrolled to regulate how such amounts could be used. The gap between the needs of the older, larger, sophisticated members of ANHD and the younger, smaller organizations undermined Brower's attempts to build cooperating networks.[64]

The Reagan cuts gave further impetus to the determination of the city administration to rationalize programs dealing with the in rem crisis. Once again lack of unity hampered the tenant response. For example, the CMP, which had already undergone shrinkage from nineteen to fifteen contracts in 1980, was said to be facing much greater cuts again in 1981. However, in spite of the existence of a Community Management Coalition sponsored by ANHD, members acted to protect their own interests at the expense of others, rather than attempting to protect them all by utilizing their combined clout.

However, in 1982 the pressing need to resolve the dispute over the purchase price of units in TIL and CMP buildings demonstrated that bridges could be built. At issue was the refusal of the city to sell twelve TIL buildings in Clinton to their tenants for $250 per unit, as promised and originally voted. The tenants in many TIL buildings, recognizing that the decision reached concerning the Clinton properties would affect them all, organized into a cohesive, articulate force, which orchestrated a campaign that won coverage in the major media and then presented a focused, disciplined, powerful display of anger at meetings of the Board of Estimate. The board finally voted that the $250 sales price would be retained, but that on resale of apartments appraised at more than $2,000 the city would "recapture" 40 percent of the owner's profit. This compromise decision, which revealed a concern for the recapture of profits that the city usually did not have when it made subsidies to developers or corporations, failed to protect the buildings in sought-after neighborhoods from gentrification while also refusing the opportunity to help stabilize them as housing for the poor by channeling profits back into the co-ops.[65]

At the beginning of 1982, tenants belonging to the Union of City Tenants, an organization representing tenants in in rem buildings, challenged the right of the city to increase their rents without first improving services and claimed that their rights to due process and to equal protection were being denied. The Koch administration had, in 1979, obtained the passage of a bill through the city council giving HPD the right to raise rents in city-owned buildings, thus eliminating the protection of rent regulations for in rem tenants. Rent increases were seen as essential to returning buildings to profitability and thus to securing their sale back to the private sector. Increases were not in fact implemented until late in 1981, and it was these that were the subject of *Laureano v. Koch*. Behind this challenge lay the fact that the median gross rent: income ratio for in rem tenants already stood at 36 percent as compared with 28 percent for all renters in the city: to tenant leaders these were the last buildings where rent increases should have been imposed in order to make them profitable. In November 1982 Judge Sheldon Levy, in the state supreme court, ruled in favor of the tenants and ordered HPD to promulgate rules, regulations, and procedures governing rent increases before reinstating any rent hikes. In June 1983 this ruling was upheld by the state appellate division.[66]

Buildings organized by Met Council had initially refused to enter the TIL program. However, the *Laureano* decision temporarily removed one of Met Council's objections to the program—that it would clear the way for rent restructuring. Met Council had also become aware that in rem buildings in DAMP programs were obtaining better repairs and that other in rem buildings were now more likely to be auctioned to the highest bidder, which left tenants without opportunity for input and at the mercy of small speculators and hustlers who were prepared to buy buildings in decaying neighborhoods. Pragmatically, Met Council decided to reverse its position and support tenants who chose to enter the TIL program and ultimately buy their buildings.[67]

Meanwhile, the sweat equity program had remained separate from DAMP, but by 1980 its promise had faded considerably. The HUD demonstration project had faltered: of the twelve buildings planned for phase I, only seven went into production, and it seemed likely that four of these would not be completed. Difficulties integrating CETA with sweat equity and the internal problems of both PDC and Adopt-a-Building were seen as chiefly to blame. Moreover, the strategy was also having economic problems because costs had risen to such an extent that the income groups originally involved could no longer afford the projected rents. The resulting pessimism led HPD to make only two sweat equity loans in two years at the end of the 1970s and to effectively kill sweat equity in 1980 when the cost per unit passed $30,000. A total of only fifty buildings with 583 units had been completed or were in process using sweat equity.[68]

In 1981 a group of tenants that had been frustrated when Commissioner Anthony Gleidman killed sweat equity proposed that the city make a grant to cover the cost of highly skilled work in a row of buildings on Amsterdam Avenue; they would then do the rest. The buildings would be affordable because they would not carry a mortgage. The city eventually signed, and its cost turned out to be $5,000 per unit. The new program was dubbed "urban homesteading," and other buildings followed the first into the program. HPD has since issued two "requests for proposals," the second with so much hoopla and so little critical information that the crowd that appeared at the advertised time to collect application forms took on the dimensions of a riot. Moreover, since the total available for grants was only $1 million, it was announced that preference would be given to those needing the lowest grants. Ultimately, 519 applications were received for a maximum of perhaps a dozen or so grants. Those that called on UHAB, the traditional source of technical assistance for sweat equity projects, found they were refused: "We can't in good conscience give assistance," said Cheryl Edmonds, veteran of the first sweat equity project to be completed and guide to every form the strategy adopted since then, "This just isn't a low income program, we are already overloaded, and this is doomed to fail."[69]

The Reagan years brought reevaluation and greater agreement on the importance of tenant organizing, confrontation strategies, and the worth of the DAMP programs. However, the budget cuts also brought increased competition among tenant organizations for the funds available and greater efforts by the city to conserve its resources. The result was that within the rehabilitation segment of the tenant movement there were several instances of individualistic behavior by neighborhood organizations—a divergence that clashed with the calls for unity. Withdrawal from dependency on external funds was proving difficult. The problem of how best to mobilize resources for organizations representing the poor in their struggle with housing decay and abandonment remained unsolved.

New Displacement Targets: Redlining and Gentrification

Many of the trends that had led to the displacement of tenants in New York City during the first half of the 1970s eased sharply around the time of the city's financial crisis in 1975: the bottom fell out of the market for co-ops, thus removing much of the incentive for conversions for a couple of years; demolition for luxury housing was considerably curtailed by a building slump for most of the succeeding decade; and hospital expansion became unpopular amidst talk of excess beds and the need for cost cutting. However, the problem of displacement had not really gone away.

Redlining

The threat of encroaching abandonment to contiguous neighborhoods inhabited primarily by white ethnics and employed members of minority groups continued apace. In the second half of the 1970s the organizations trying to combat abandonment focused on a new target: the banks and their practice of "redlining," whereby certain geographic areas were singled out as bad risks for demographic reasons, such as racial change, so all applicants were denied loans regardless of their personal credit worthiness. The housing analysts associated with these organizations were well aware that the causes of housing abandonment were complex. However, they held that redlining played a key role by setting up a self-fulfilling prophecy concerning neighborhood decay: by making mortgage financing difficult to obtain, it reduced demand for properties, thus causing their values to fall and encouraging owners to "milk" their buildings by postponing repairs, cutting services, and even not paying taxes in order to earn a profit under the new conditions.[70]

The threat of redlining had already become a national issue, thanks to the efforts of National People's Action, a Chicago-based national federation whose members mostly represented modest homeowners but also included ANHD and NYSTNC. Its lobbying played a key part in the passage of two laws by Congress: the Home Mortgage Disclosure Act of 1975, which obliged banks to release data, by zip code or census tract, concerning the number and value of mortgages made annually, and the Community Reinvestment Act of 1977, which bade federal regulatory agencies weigh the extent to which a bank was reinvesting in areas surrounding its branches before approving the opening of new branches, acquisitions, or mergers.

Following the passage of the first federal law, concern about redlining in New York State increased in 1976. Both the Assembly Banking Committee and the New York City Commission on Human Rights held hearings; the New York Public Interest Research Group issued a study of Brooklyn, where it found little mortgage availability and none at all in the mostly black northern half of the borough; the Brooklyn Reinvestment Coalition, representing twenty-five organizations, became especially vocal; and an ad hoc New York Reinvestment Coalition was formed.[71]

By 1979, using the information available under the disclosure law and the threat of the reinvestment law, local pressure on savings banks was producing results. Most dramatic was the first major test of the reinvestment law, when a Park Slope organization, South Brooklyn against Investment Discrimination (AID), successfully challenged an application before the Federal Deposit Insurance Corporation by the Greater New York Savings Bank to open a branch on Manhattan's East Side. As a result of its research, AID was able to show that although nine of the bank's sixteen branches were in Brooklyn and 80 percent of its deposits were from that borough, only 6.5 percent of its real estate loans were made there. Although such challenges required "a vast amount of research," a total of seven more from within New York City were pending at the time. They were made easier by the networks built within the Coalition against Redlining in New York City (CAR), which was closely linked to NYSTNC.[72]

Meanwhile, the hopes of CAR that such challenges would encourage banks to increase mortgage availability voluntarily were being fulfilled. The first was an agreement signed by the Dime Savings Bank of Williamsburg with the Greenpoint/Williamsburg Committee against Redlining, which promised $1 million annually in real estate loans, low down payments, and the evaluation of applicants individually on their merits. It also agreed to enforce the "good repair clause" in mortgages, under which a bank could threaten foreclosure if a property were allowed to decay, to advertise the availability of mortgages, and to inform community organizations of properties in foreclosure. The following year NWBCCC achieved success in its long campaign with four banks, some of which were among its prominent early funders. These signed a "proclamation of cooperation," promising to finance the moderate rehabilitation of two hundred buildings, both multiple dwellings and one-to-four family houses, to advertise the availability of such loans aggressively, and to enforce the good repair clause. Two years later NWBCCC reported that the use of the latter clause had been successful: three buildings had been foreclosed, which made the threat real and an excellent organizing tool that gave tenants leverage with recalcitrant landlords via their banks.[73]

By the early 1980s, however, interest rates had skyrocketed, which made the availability of loans a moot issue since few could afford to borrow, and reduced many of the savings banks, with their large portfolios of long-term low-interest real estate loans, to the point of collapse. Consequently, CAR, turning its attention to the commercial banks, used the existence of federal regulations as a lever to arrange a meeting with representatives of twelve of them. These had traditionally made few real estate loans—indeed, half of them had made none the previous year—and certainly not to low-income borrowers. The result of the meetings was that two of the banks, Chemical and Manufacturers Hanover Trust, agreed to consider the financing of repairs in multiple dwellings on a case-by-case basis.[74]

Gentrification

The upgrading of older neighborhoods and the consequent displacement of the long-term residents had occurred in the early 1970s in such neighborhoods as Greenwich Village and Chelsea, parts of the Upper West Side and the Upper East Side, and the sections surrounding Brooklyn Heights. The chief concern of tenants organizing against displacement at that time was the replacement of existing housing with luxury high-rise buildings. However, when such construction slowed after the mid-1970s, tenant attention shifted to the threat of the transfer of the existing housing stock to a richer clientele who could outbid the older residents. Such gentrification had in fact been fought building by building in Chelsea from 1970 onward by the Chelsea Coalition on Housing (CCOH), which followed the traditional strategies of urging and helping tenants to "hang in there" and getting back at harassing landlords with negative publicity. Occasionally it was especially inventive and, therefore, effective. For example, in 1982 members discovered that a landlord who had been using notably grim harassing tactics to empty buildings needed to apply for an extension of his permit for a sidewalk café for his clam house, which he had been able to upgrade from local eatery to fashionable restaurant as a result of the gentrification of the neighborhood. CCOH successfully opposed his application on the grounds that occupying the sidewalk was a local privilege that should not be accorded to such an unneighborly person.[75] In spite of such efforts, however, much of the poor Hispanic population has been displaced from Chelsea over the past fifteen years.

Late in the 1970s considerable national attention began to be paid to gentrification. One result was that the Housing and Community Development Act of 1978 required that HUD report on displacement. It responded in February 1979 that there was no problem of "significant proportions." However, when displacement was listed as the most serious problem by both Legal Services attorneys and their clients, a second study was carried out by the Legal Services Anti-Displacement Project. This examined the same data but arrived at contrary conclusions.[76]

Meanwhile, organizations in New York City had become increasingly concerned and active around the issue, in spite of a 1980 declaration by Housing Commissioner Gleidman that displacement was not a problem.[77] Gentrification there had developed two forms. The first was the upgrading of older but sound and potentially attractive housing in neighborhoods that, like Chelsea, were "close to the action." The second was the invasion, by speculators, developers, and "urban pioneers," of well-located neighborhoods housing the poor that were, until the recent rehabilitation efforts of neighborhood organizations, unthinkable because of their level of decay. The prospect of losing the people of the neighborhoods they were resuscitating began to haunt ANHD and its member organizations.

The opposing responses to neighborhood upgrading were well illustrated by a clash in Park Slope, Brooklyn, where gentrification had been progressing for a decade. The Fifth Avenue Committee, a member of ANHD, was committed to retaining an integrated community. Focusing on the lower Slope, which was earlier ravaged by decay but had been slowly gentrifying, it sought to protect the poor tenants there, who usually had no defense against eviction because they lived in small buildings exempt from rent laws. One of the strategies it sought to implement was the development of rent-subsidized housing. The Park Slope Improvement Committee, claiming that it would result in an undue concentration of poor tenants and therefore attract crime to the neighborhood, opposed this strategy. It argued that there was no need for rent subsidies where the private market was strong enough to attract upgrading—they should be reserved for weaker markets. A similar controversy took place in Manhattan Valley, the one neighborhood on the Upper West Side still to be gentrified, where developers went to court to argue that subsidized housing being built there by ANHD affiliates would maintain such a proportion of poor tenants there that it would prevent the upgrading of the neighborhood.[78]

Harlem's decay had deterred gentrification in spite of its excellent transportation and a location adjacent to some of Manhattan's prime real estate. When Mayor Koch announced that the city would sell thirteen vacant brownstone buildings there through a pilot lottery, this aroused considerable local opposition because it was seen as likely to trigger gentrification. Opposition was expressed in spite of the mayor's decision, in an effort to blunt such criticism, to triple the chances of local residents taking part in the lottery. Such is the concern about gentrification that local activists fear their own successful rehabilitation efforts could well trigger the process. However, Margaret McNeil, past president of ANHD and director of West Harlem Community Organization, which helps form low-income co-ops, manages and buys CMP buildings, and develops and manages moderate-income housing, disagrees. She regards such development activities as protecting local tenants and therefore as insurance against gentrification when it takes off.[79]

Gentrification is a much more imminent threat on the Lower East Side, which has housed several generations of the city's poorest, most recent immigrants, but is now, since it abuts the newly chic East Village, attracting speculators and undergoing rising rents and real estate prices. In a recent article, "The Lower East Side: There Goes the Neighborhood" in *New York Magazine*, an out-of-town speculator was quoted as saying,

> Ethnic businesses and services will gradually be forced out. Anyone else can be paid to leave. If you can get rid of rent-controlled tenants, renovate the place, and charge $700 a month, it's worth paying them $10,000 just to get them out and raise the rents. They'll be pushed east to the river and given life preservers. It's so clear. I wouldn't have come here if it wasn't.[80]

In 1981 Mayor Koch's proposal to convert city-owned buildings in the neighborhood into artists' housing with the help of substantial subsidies aroused a storm of community opposition coordinated by the Joint Planning Council of the Lower East Side (JPC), a coalition of twenty-five neighborhood groups. They had already seen what had happened after artists pioneered the transformation of Soho to a residential community: it became prime real estate, and most of the artists were in due course forced out. A public hearing at which the JPC showed that speculation, profiteering, and displacement were already occurring on the Lower East Side brought bitter, but effective, confrontation. Ultimately most of the members of the Board of Estimate deserted the mayor and voted to quash the plan.[81]

Such victories are rare before the forces of gentrification, and this one did little to slow their progress on the Lower East Side. In 1981 Robert Schur, the architect of neighborhood revitalization, saw that the strong recovery of New York real estate was spilling over into several of the neighborhoods where ANHD members were operating, with the result that it was turning around decay and driving up prices and rents. Arguing that such forces could not be defeated,[82] he suggested instead that they could be regarded positively as long as they did not cause displacement—the communities needed the infusions of money and the job opportunities that construction and renovation would bring, abandonment had left room for growth, and if integrated communities were created they would revitalize stores and create more effective demand for services. Revitalization without displacement was possible so long as it was planned. Schur suggested leaving all current privately owned housing to the private sector, and thus open to gentrification, and using city-owned and new housing to protect the existing poor population, including the local relocation of tenants displaced by gentrification. Since all city-owned buildings would be needed as a land bank, vacant structures should be sealed and rehabilitation phased as needed.[83]

The section known as Loisaida, the heart of the Lower East Side, has lost 70 percent of its population to the ravages of abandonment and 30 percent of its buildings have gone in rem. The immediate threat of gentrification to this area led JPC to take Schur's vision seriously, with the result that it worked on a detailed plan for over two years. The outcome represented a dramatic leap beyond the local, often building-by-building, struggles of its members against abandonment over the previous fifteen years. At the center of the plan were two components: "Make the Lower East Side a special preservation district where the cost of making millions from luxury housing development is to provide low-cost units as well"; and "make the neighborhood a special enforcement area, where ackowledged landlord practices of harassment and rent gouging can be spotted and rooted out, and where immediate assistance can be provided for both low income development and for those market rate developers willing to provide affordable housing."[84]

Although the city administration, knowing that such a plan was in the works, had bowed to pressure from JPC to delay auctioning Lower East Side properties, officials refused to meet with JPC once the plan was announced. Two months later Mayor Koch and Borough President Stein held an unexpected press conference, from which JPC leaders were excluded, at which they announced the outline of their own plan for the neighborhood. The plan made little provision to increase the number of low-income units beyond those already in programs. Moreover, it included proceeding with auctions of city-owned buildings, which were essential to the Schur/JPC plan as a resource for low-income housing. The impact of the plan, local activists concluded, would be to accelerate gentrification and increase city income through sales and higher tax assessments.[85] The threat of losing the people in the neighborhood they had helped revitalize had increased.

The Political Thrust

NYSTLC (later NYSTNC) had led the tenant movement into direct participation in the political process in 1974 and met with considerable success in its first two years. The phasing out of rent regulations, begun in 1971, was reversed (although the original strictness of rent control was not restored); the freedom of landlords to convert or demolish their buildings without considering the interests of their tenants was restricted; public housing tenants gained input to decisions concerning their developments; and the weakness of tenants within the tenant-landlord relationship was mitigated when the lease took on the mutual obligations of a contract. Although these outcomes were political reverses for the real estate industry, they by no means represented its political rout; indeed, the industry remained extremely powerful. Tenant activists found during 1976–1984 that their efforts achieved mixed results legislatively. During these years the political rhythm was set to a great extent by the sunset provisions of the rent laws because these occasions gave both sides the opportunity to attempt to amend the laws or to allow them to expire.

Both of the rent laws as well as the Cooperative/Condominium Fair Practices Act were due to expire in June 1976. The Housing Committee of the Council of Property Owners, an ad hoc coalition of New York City real estate groups, launched a strong advertising campaign upstate with headlines such as "Warning: Blumenthal-Beame Pressure State Legislators to Extend N.Y.C. Rent Control. This Means Higher Taxes for Upstaters. Which way will your legislator vote???" Advertisements showed stark pictures of abandoned housing and blamed this upon rent regulations. The Emergency Financial Control Board, the State Moreland Commission, and several leading papers and business weeklies also blamed the city's financial crisis upon rent regulations, which they claimed had caused abandonment and therefore the erosion of the city's tax base, and demanded that the regulations, rather than the housing, be abandoned.[86] The climate was not favorable to extension.

To make matters worse, there was open division among tenant ranks. Met Council felt threatened by the new prominence of NYSTNC—the more so because Michael McKee had become its chairperson. It therefore became more active politically, lobbying for its own comprehensive statewide rent control bill while, at the same time, NYSTNC sought support for a different bill with similar intent. Although the two had agreed to keep their disagreements private and did cosponsor one or two demonstrations for the first time, Met Council, later attacking the NYSTNC rent bill in an editorial, accused it of "compromising tenant rights," and told several legislators both during their mass mobilization in Albany and in phone calls not to sponsor NYSTNC's "landlord" bill. This opened the way for a classic example of "divide and conquer," when Democratic senate minority leader Manfred Ohrenstein used the presence of branches of both federations in his district as an excuse for supporting neither bill—a considerable blow to their chance of passage.[87]

Both federations regarded the Emergency Tenant Protection Act as weak, but they also saw its extension as vital when the alternative was deregulating what was by now a large segment of the rental units. They were helped by the fact that 1976 was an election year. However, the extension granted all three laws by the legislature was for just one year—to a nonelection year. The implication was evident to all: it would be easier to let the laws lapse, or at least weaken them, at that point. Meanwhile, pressure to abandon the regulations entirely continued to mount—from the press, banks, Washington, the Republican (majority) leadership in the state senate, as well as from the ongoing real estate campaign.

NYSTNC therefore geared itself up for a crucial defensive struggle in 1977. The problem was to develop a strategy that would at the very least extend the three pieces of legislation. Its leaders, prodded initially by a letter from Assemblyman Frank Barbaro warning of the danger of public infighting to the defense of the existing protenant laws, agreed it was essential to close ranks with Met Council.[88] Upon meeting with their Met Council counterparts, NYSTNC found it was much easier to plan joint action to protect existing benefits than to press for new programs.

NYSTNC's initial strategy for the 1977 legislative session was to convince the leaders of the Democratic-controlled state assembly to take a strong stand on the rent laws early in the session as a means of applying pressure to the state senate. The senate Republican majority leadership had regularly used delaying tactics on controversial measures in the hope that by the end of the session the urgency would be so great that the Democrats would make concessions in order to get anything passed at all. Because the senate leadership had gone on record as favoring an end to all rent regulations, it was felt that a last-minute consideration of the issue could not be risked.

The assembly obliged by passing a three-year extender bill. However, this was, of course, meaningless without senate approval. The lobbyists well knew that power in the senate was centered in the Republican leadership and that they needed external strategies to build enough momentum to overcome the resistance of Senator Warren Anderson, the majority leader. Consequently, NYSTNC chose to pressure the seven New York City Republican senators to sponsor the extensions. It reasoned that each of these senators had a sufficiently large tenant constituency for him to be threatened by an effective leafleting campaign in his district. If these senators joined the twenty-four Democratic senators on the pro-extension side of the issue, there would be a majority for their passage.

The first mobilization took place in Senator Frank Padavan's district in eastern Queens in March. Evidence of its impact followed quickly. As NYSTNC was preparing to leaflet the district of the second targeted senator, Martin Knorr, in southwestern Queens, the Republican senators from the city met in caucus on the rent issue and then in turn pressured their leaders. Before any of the leaflets in the second wave could be distributed, Senator Anderson came out with a proposal to renew the expiring rent laws for an additional four years, thus outdoing the Democratic bill that had passed the assembly. His bill also set up a temporary commission, whose members would be appointed by but not include any politicians, to recommend general reforms in rent regulations.

A few days later NYSTNC distributed an ebullient letter from Chairperson McKee commenting on what had happened:

> This is an enormous tenant victory and we should all play it that way. Our strategy worked. We decided to concentrate on the renewal of existing laws rather than pushing for stronger controls; I am more than ever convinced of the soundness of this strategy. We decided to concentrate on putting pressure on legislators in their districts, rather than in Albany. . . . Another crucial factor was that all tenant groups maintained a posture of unity. . . . This victory has greatly increased the prestige of the N.Y.S.T.N.C. in Albany. . . . While we have successfully lobbied for the enactment of significant legislation in the past, for the first time we have taken on a political battle and won. We played our cards carefully and well. We have been able to reverse the anti–rent control tide of the past two years.[89]

NYSTNC's strategy had triumphed in a year when the real estate leaders had felt they were in a position to gain ground. The latter's end-of-the-session strategy was undercut by the early action of the assembly, and the defection of the Republican senators left them weaponless: "It blew up in our faces in the midst of negotiations. The New York City Republican senators went off the deep end, intimidated by the tenant demonstrations."[90]

In contrast, the effort to extend the Cooperative/Condominium Fair Practices Act failed. In part this was because the NYSTNC lobbyists, distracted by the threat to the rent laws, gave it less attention. Assemblyman Edward Lehner, chair of the Assembly Housing Committee, in an appearance before the NYSTNC board, cited three reasons for the outcome: limited constituent pressure; the restricted number of districts where the issue was pertinent; and the feeling among officials that the real estate industry was correct that the stability of existing housing in New York City relied strongly on the ability of landlords to convert their properties, thereby giving tenants an economic stake in the future of those buildings and communities. It had indeed proved difficult to arouse rank-and-file support, in sharp contrast to 1974, partly because two large developments that had been threatened with conversion at that time, Fresh Meadows and Tudor City, had withdrawn from NYSTNC—the threat to them seemed to have abated and there had been policy disagreements because their leadership was more conservative than that of the federation. Another reason for the outcome was perhaps equally significant: many legislators felt that by extending the rent laws, they had given tenants their due, and it was now the landlords' turn. Indeed, the landlords with the greatest political influence probably had more at stake in the conversion law than ETPA. Conversions open the way to large profits, and it seemed that the law had stopped them almost entirely; on the other hand, since ETPA applied only to apartments that were previously decontrolled or uncontrolled, their rents were already fairly high.

Conversions remained a live and frustrating issue for NYSTNC throughout the remainder of the period as their pace rapidly picked up momentum. In spite of their spread throughout many areas of the state by the early 1980s, NYSTNC was not again successful in securing passage of legislation that covered the whole state. However, it did have the 35 percent minimum tenant approval restored in the areas most immediately threatened—New York City and the three suburban counties. Protections—for example, of senior citizens—were gradually improved over time, and the long-sought goal of 51 percent tenant approval was finally realized in 1982. However, these changes were drafted in such a way that they also made tenant approval of conversion plans easier to achieve in some buildings. On the other hand, the state senate leadership remained adamant in its rejection of what had become NYSTNC's key objective—a similar process of approval by tenants in residence at properties offered noneviction plans. Such plans became more and more frequent, especially after the passage of the 51 percent approval for eviction plans. In 1983 the legislature passed a statewide local option bill under which municipalities could bar eviction of senior citizens and severely disabled tenants in conversions. Some fifty towns, villages, and cities have opted for the law.[91]

Legislatively, then, 1977 proved to be a year of both victory and defeat for tenant political activists seeking to prevent the protections won in 1974 from lapsing. While legislators responded sharply to tenant pressure, they ultimately tried to balance the total outcome when weighing tenant and real estate interests. However, one new NYSTNC initiative, the Neighborhood Preservation Bill, was successful in 1977. This bill, the brainchild of Robert Schur, who had been elected to NYSTNC's board, sought funding to cover the administrative staff and expenses of "neighborhood preservation companies" (NPCs)—that is, neighborhood organizations primarily involved in rehabilitation and management. It set out to meet a key need of such organizations, for the external funding available was usually targeted so specifically that it did not provide for such essential costs as rent and administrative staff. In lobbying for such legislation, NYSTNC was trying both to cement the already close ties between it and ANHD and to strengthen its own constituency among black and Hispanic tenants. The bill gained the support of the leadership within the legislature and made rapid progress—it was difficult to be opposed to neighborhood preservation, especially when potential recipients were scattered in many of the state's electoral districts. The main question was whether funding could be found in a year of financial stringency. Eventually, with the support of Governor Hugh Carey, the program received an initial budget of $500,000 for its first six months and $5 million the next year. Eleven of the first fifty neighborhood organizations to be funded were ANHD affiliates. By 1982 total funding of this law had reached $9.6 million, with 250 recipient neighborhood organizations statewide.[92]

Another bill introduced by NYSTNC in 1977 banned retaliatory eviction. The bill sought to protect tenants from reprisals for joining a tenant organization or for making a complaint in good faith to a code enforcement agency. While this right was guaranteed to tenants covered by rent regulation laws, tenants in many upstate areas and those in small buildings excluded from rent legislation had no such protection. NYSTNC introduced this bill because it believed the bill established a basic civil right; there was as yet no great demand for the bill from its tenant constituency. Consequently, it took time to build support for the legislation, and it was not until 1979 that the bill was finally successful.

The effective cooperation in 1977 of NYSTNC and Met Council to secure the extension of the rent laws cemented a relationship that, in 1978 and again in 1979, allowed the joint introduction of a statewide rent control bill. This bill was in fact a modification of that introduced by NYSTNC in each of the two preceding years. The federations also worked together somewhat uneasily, with other neighborhood organizations and within an ad hoc group, the Coalition against Rent Increase Pass-alongs (CARIP), which had come into being initially to oppose and challenge a series of city decisions to add special increases to rents when costs, such as labor or fuel, rose sharply.

Michael McKee was the only tenant activist appointed to membership of the Temporary State Commission on Rental Housing, which had been mandated by the state senate in its extension of the rent laws in 1977. The 1980 report of the commission, with 114 bitterly contested recommendations and two minority reports, made almost no political impact.[93] However, McKee's frustration with the commission did contribute to a decision by NYSTNC that a system of rent regulations based upon the existence of a housing "emergency" that had to be reaffirmed regularly should be replaced by a permanent system. Thus NYSTNC proposed a Statewide Rent and Eviction Regulation Bill that would regulate rental housing "as a public utility, for the public good and in the public interest," and consolidate the various rent regulation systems into one unitary system presided over by a state agency.[94]

The announcement of this bill at the end of 1980 precipitated a bitter, public break with Met Council and CARIP, which regarded NYSTNC's retreat from the statewide rent control bill they had been sponsoring jointly (now known as the Flynn/Dearie Bill) as a betrayal. Met Council declared, in an editorial in *Tenant*, that Flynn/Dearie was a "rent control–type bill," where the only increases were for hardship. In contrast, the NYSTNC bill was a "rent stabilization–type bill" with annual increases such as those that had led to rapid rent increases under rent stabilization. The NYSTNC proposal was therefore "doing the landlords' job for them." NYSTNC leaders responded that *both* bills were study bills, introduced to raise concepts and ideas: Met Council was insisting on treating Flynn/Dearie as viable legislation, but in fact it had not gotten out of committee in three years. However, when a few months later Flynn/Dearie unexpectedly passed in the assembly, NYSTNC sent out a "tenant alert" urging tenants to push their senators to act favorably on it. Nevertheless, the senate blocked passage; this was repeated also in 1982.

NYSTNC continued to find fault with many aspects of Flynn/Dearie; however, it also began to take part in joint talks aimed at making acceptable modifications, and in fact gained considerable input to reshaping it.[95] By 1983 NYSTNC reported with enthusiasm that the bill had been greatly improved by redrafting. NYSTNC especially liked the bill's formula for rent increases, which was tied to the equity investment of the landlord in his building: "This is a novel economic concept, the first serious new proposal for fair rate of return in more than 30 years of rent controls."[96]

NYSTNC had been searching for internal unity, growth, and financial stability throughout its first decade. Initially an ad hoc federation, compromising extensively to develop united stands on issues and to maintain the support of varied neighborhood organizations, it had lacked discipline: members would go off and "do their own thing," often supporting only part of NYSTNC's legislative agenda and seriously detracting from its credibility as a tenant voice. However, the negative political climate engendered by the financial crisis of the city of New York and the new financial austerity of the state that followed led to a demand for more disciplined support. Consequently, the membership of the Columbia Tenants Union, which had attacked NYSTNC in its newspaper, was suspended, and other more conservative groups that had engaged in independent political action, such as the Fresh Meadows Tenants Association and the Tudor City Tenants Association, were not pursued when they failed to renew their memberships.

At the center of NYSTNC's plans for expansion lay the need to broaden its constituency geographically in order to increase its legitimacy with legislators. Consequently, NYSTNC's leaders established an independent nonpolitical entity, the Peoples Housing Network, which obtained foundation funds to allow it to employ organizers in different sections of the state. Although it was almost always short of funds, it was successful in helping to broaden NYSTNC's membership base. One of its strategies was to use the election of tenant representatives in public housing authorities under the Langley Law, a law NYSTNC had drafted, lobbied for, and later defended from attack in the legislature, as an opportunity to mobilize tenants. Later, following the passage of the Neighborhood Preservation Act, it saw the Neighborhood Preservation Companies (NPCs), which were situated all over the state, as potential recruits. A membership drive focusing on these groups in particular helped increase NYSTNC's membership from twenty-seven to sixty-three between April 1980 and May 1981. Only thirty-five of these were situated in New York City. A bylaw change that admitted organized buildings that were not attached to neighborhood organizations also brought it an increasing flow of middle-income members.

Initially NYSTNC set low membership dues and then tried to finance its lobbying activities by urging member groups to contribute regularly to this cause. Consequently, it lived from one financial crisis to another, and its members got used to responding to crises. In 1980 it decided to finance the salary of a lobbyist in Albany in order to increase its efficiency and presence there, and set a scale of dues based on the total income of its members. Consequently, it raised $8,000 in 1980–81—twice its total for the previous year. As its membership expanded, it became more ambitious, and in 1982–1983 it budgeted to cover part-time salaries for a statewide coordinator, a lobbyist, and a "federal issues coordinator." Once again it urged its members to voluntarily increase their financial commitments and succeeded in raising $26,000. It also took a first step in following the financial path earlier trodden by Met Council when it established a membership category of individual member with dues of $15 per annum. Its budget was still modest when compared with that of Met Council, which was based largely on individual dues.[97]

Met Council's rate of membership growth declined after 1976, in spite of an increase from three to five in its paid organizing staff. Consequently, when its rent for office space trebled, it was left in a financial squeeze. Its falling growth rate was related to competition from tenant organizations whose rent strikes drained away other potential recruits, the need of organizers to spend time with tenants who were already members, a decline in its renewal rate, and demands placed on the time of organizers by the intractable problems of decay. Met Council's efficiency was also reduced by increasing turnover of its paid staff, who, in spite of great dedication, burned out as a result of long hours at low salaries. This pattern became a matter of increasing concern for Met Council stalwarts as the original core of volunteer leaders was thinned by advancing age and as the time for the retirement of Jane Benedict, chairperson for a quarter of a century, approached and was finally, after earlier postponements, set for the end of 1984.

By the early 1980s Met Council's decline in new members turned into a contraction of membership, from a maximum of over 10,000 in 1980 to under 8,000 in 1983.[98] Met Council was going through major changes at this time: frustrated with the long-term results of its years of organizing, it chose to divert some of its resources and to become overtly more political and radical. A key symbolic issue was its decision to endorse political candidates. This led it to take a strong stand for Assemblyman Barbaro in his 1981 mayoral race on the Unity party ticket against Mayor Koch, who had antagonized Met Council through his antitenant policies, appointments, and rhetoric, such as "the free lunch for tenants is over" and "move if you can't afford the rent."[99] The next year Jane Benedict herself ran on the Unity party ticket as candidate for governor, with the ostensible goal of gaining fifty thousand votes and thus giving the party a permanent line on the ballot. However, she fell far short. Meanwhile, in a series of obituaries occasioned by the deaths of early Met Council activists, *Tenant* revealed the ties of many of them to the Communist party, a fact that had previously been kept under wraps—less than a decade earlier Jane Benedict had ordered that an issue of *Tenant* be drastically altered and reprinted because she feared that a center spread celebrating May Day might alienate some members.[100] Concurrently, however, and rather incongruously, Met Council worked politically as part of CARIP, which was chaired by John McKean, a sometime Republican candidate for the state assembly, whose organization, the Tudor City Tenants Association, had earlier pulled out of NYSTNC upon finding it too radical. Met Council saw CARIP as able to compete with NYSTNC; however, without Met Council, CARIP would have had little credibility.

In 1979 a suit forced the Rent Guidelines Board (RGB), the body responsible for setting increases within the rent-stabilized sector in New York City, to hold its meetings in public. The tenant federations cooperated in organizing their constituencies to attend the hearings. When the RGB announced the smallest increases on record, the pattern for subsequent years was set: meetings were held in a circuslike atmosphere before a noisy, confrontational, and packed audience of tenants, landlords and, it is said, "landlords" recruited for the day at central casting. This new focus on the RGB hearing represented an acknowledgment that the majority of tenants were now, as a consequency of vacancy decontrol and the ETPA, rent stabilized rather than rent controlled.[101]

In 1980 NYSTNC launched a campaign to separate the Rent Stabilization Association (RSA), an organization of landlords, from the administration of the rent stabilization system. The RSA had been taken over, after a power struggle in 1978, by a group of activist landlords pledged to use its economic resources to further the political goals of the real estate industry.[102] Intended to be a neutral administrative body, it was transformed into a real estate advocacy organization:

> Instead of adequately funding the CAB [Conciliation and Appeals Board], RSA has spent its dues on hiring lobbyists and public relations consultants, and paying lawyers to sue RGB, CAB and even HPD. RSA set up a front group, the Neighborhood Preservation Political Action Fund, to raise money for campaign contributions. NPPAF also ran radio ads upstate during the 1981 legislative session when the Emergency Tenant Protection Act was up for renewal, urging voters to lobby their legislators against "New York City rent control"—and failing to mention that the ads were run by New York City landlords."[103]

In July 1980 Congressman Ted Weiss demanded an inquiry into the budget of RSA, which, he charged, was being misused for political purposes. He had been alerted to this by NYSTNC, which had already issued a flyer raising questions about RSA encouraging and covering up rent overcharging. NYSTNC continued to carry out its own investigations, and in November 1980 Chairperson Bill Rowen informed Attorney General Robert

Abrams of forty-two specific violations by RSA of its statute. The upshot was that Abrams brought suit to prevent the RSA from lobbying or litigating on behalf of landlords. The suit also sought restitution of nearly $1 million in misspent dues. Abrams followed up by petitioning HPD commissioner Gleidman to suspend RSA's registration; however, Gleidman took no immediate action. In 1981 NYSTNC had a bill introduced in Albany to separate the RSA from the rent stabilization system and, by registering rents, to make it more difficult for landlords to overcharge their tenants, but it was not successful. A similar city council bill the next year also failed.[104]

The Emergency Tenant Protection Act was due to expire once again at the end of the 1983 session. This time, however, it seemed unlikely that there would be a simple extension of the law because of the pressure of support for several other bills. These included the Flynn/Dearie Bill, now supported by NYSTNC as well as Met Council and CARIP; the new governor, Mario Cuomo, was also on record as supporting the "principles" of this bill. Met Council and CARIP were optimistic about its chances because of its success in the assembly during the previous two years and promises of support they had garnered from within the senate; NYSTNC was more cynical about the worth of such promises. The NYSTNC-backed bills separating the RSA from the rent stabilization system and requiring the registration of rents were also introduced once again. All tenant organizations expressed support for extending rent regulations to unprotected geographic areas and a variety of previously excluded building categories. They also agreed in their strong criticisms of the rent stabilization system (and therefore of the current ETPA) for giving overly generous rent increases and poor enforcement, including insufficient penalties to deter rent overcharging, and that an important ingredient in correcting such problems was removing the RSA from the system. So strong was the combined tenant assault on the prevailing system that senate Republicans felt under attack. Nevertheless, the extent of opposition from real estate forces led NYSTNC to predict that the most likely outcome was a negotiated bill.

The negotiations turned out to be extremely tortuous, in spite of a degree of agreement on several issues in advance, and the end result inevitably contained compromises that left all parties partly unsatisfied. This result, as laid down in the Omnibus Housing Act, which was in fact a greatly amended extension of ETPA, was that the state Division of Housing and Community Renewal (DHCR) took over the administration of both New York City rent regulation systems, rent control, and rent stabilization. Both systems kept their separate identities but were consolidated administratively with DHCR's administration of ETPA and state rent control in the suburban counties. Rents were to be registered and treble damages for overcharging imposed. Tenants in housing owned by institutions and with unrelated roommates, both of whom had been rendered defenseless by recent court cases, were protected. On the other hand, the formula for hardship rent increases was liberalized, with mortgage interest rates included for the first time; rent-stabilized tenants no longer had the option of a three-year lease; and the period during which overcharge claims could be brought was shortened considerably. These impediments, together with the bitterness of CARIP/Met Council at the failure of the Flynn/Dearie Bill, caused NYSTNC to pause before publicly claiming a major share of the credit for the changes; nevertheless, the results of its campaign against the RSA and for a consolidated, state-run system that provided for registration of rents had been enshrined into law. NYSTNC foresaw potential for the expansion of tenant protections and political power by unifying the system and bringing unregulated areas and classes of housing within it if the tenant movement was strong and focused its attention carefully.[105]

The Omnibus Housing Law set up two situations on which tenants had to act if their rights were to be protected. One was the question of refunds for past overcharges, where the sunset was March 31, 1984, and the onus of proof was placed on landlords once applications were filed. The second was the registration of rents by landlords, where tenants had only ninety days to file challenges after the deadline for landlord filing of June 30, 1984. Failure to file a challenge had the effect of sanctifying the landlord's figures as the legal rent, no matter how inaccurate. NYSTNC geared up to warn tenants and supply them with information by publishing and widely distributing special explanatory issues of its paper, *Tenants and Neighbors*, and opening a hot line.[106] As a result, it found itself in the spotlight and attracted a flow of new individual and building members. Met Council, however, failed to focus on the situation as a major recruitment opportunity.

The state senate, in passing the new rent law, had insisted on handing the RSA the task of preparing a new administrative code for DHCR, which brought it both a handsome fee and also the opportunity to shape the form of future rent regulation. However, the RSA overplayed it hand. Its proposed code would have so gutted tenant protections that Attorney General Abrams found fifty violations of current landlord-tenant law in the code. Consequently, the code created such an uproar that it allowed the tenant movement, once again united around a major threat, to place so much pressure on the city housing administration, which was required to ratify the code, that it rejected the code altogether. The administration of the new rent law thus began with an outdated but not malevolent code inherited for the time being from the city and a bureaucracy that had begun to gear up for its task very late.[107]

NYSTNC has been building a worthy track record in Albany for a decade. During this time it has scored some notable, though rarely unmixed, successes. Drafting legislation and pressuring legislators, it has become a presence in Albany. During most of this time its presence has been maintained by the intense activity of only a few people: it was only with great difficulty that it could even muster occasional shows of mass support. There are structural factors at work here: some issues, such as rents, have larger constituencies than others, especially when what is at stake has come to be accepted as a right. The constituencies affected by other issues are often small, fragmented, and insufficiently mobilized. Member groups are so involved locally that they must feel that a broader issue is vital to their interests before they attempt to respond significantly. That is, there is a great distance, within the pyramidal structure of the tenant movement, from the grass roots building organizations via neighborhood and citywide organizations to the statewide level: a decision to push for a new law in Albany does not have the same immediacy to most tenants as a rent strike protesting the absence of heat and hot water in their own building. On some of their bills, therefore, NYSTNC leaders were in effect speaking in the name of a constituency that was barely aware of the issues involved. That is, the leaders acted as consumer advocates who analyzed the system, looking for inequities in it, and then drafted bills to alleviate them. The surfacing of a bill would create an opportunity to educate a constituency around an issue, but only sometimes was this done effectively.

According to McKee, in its earlier years NYSTNC had impact because the legislators believed it was stronger than it was. As time passed, and NYSTNC built loyal support in many parts of the state, its clout strengthened. Much of the credit for this belongs with NYSTNC leaders, especially McKee, for their careful research and planning and imaginative deployment of resources. Some of the laws NYSTNC favored were enacted to buy off potential discontent before it erupted. Legislators remember occasions when tenant leaders had successfully stirred up hornets' nests and targeted them accurately. The RSA code fiasco is a recent reminder. The Republican senators from the city have been especially aware of the pressure that NYSTNC can bring to bear on them, even when it appears rather limited to outside observers. Annual NYSTNC legislative conferences, each lasting two days, have also demonstrated a growing, though still small, grass roots strength. Meanwhile, the increased political activity of CARIP and Met Council, and the more open radicalism of the latter, when focused on legislative targets rather than on NYSTNC, have helped strengthen the credibility of NYSTNC and the political clout of the movement as a whole. Politically, the tenant movement has matched the real estate lobby in sophistication if not in wealth.

An Emerging National Focus and Structure

Tenant organizations have typically been formed reactively with particular problems in mind. Thus, building organizations have focused on landlords, neighborhood organizations on agencies, banks, or clusters of landlords that have been blamed for local problems, and federations on the local or state governments responsible for establishing the legal framework of the tenant-landlord relationship.

Until recently, there was little interest in forming a national federation focusing on the federal government because Washington, D.C., was not seen as the immediate site of the tenant battle. The major exception was the public housing sector, which was closely dependent on HUD for both funding and other policy decisions. Consequently, the National Tenant Organization was formed in 1969, and funded for three years by the American Friends Service Committee, to organize the public housing constituency. However, it devoted itself to posturing and personal aggrandizement and proved incapable of maintaining a national presence once the funding of its headquarters expired. The tenant federations within New York State such as NYSTNC knew the enormous effort needed to maintain a presence, during the legislative session, in Albany, which is only three hours by car from New York City. They realized that national distances and the scale of organization needed to maintain and make decisions within a super federation made it extremely difficult for a largely voluntary, local crisis-oriented movement to maintain a presence in Washington.

Nevertheless, by the mid-1970s common issues were emerging in several different states. Awareness of this caused the tenant movement in New York, and its three major federations in particular, to pay greater attention to the national sphere. One of these issues was redlining, which drew ANHD and NYSTNC to become involved with National People's Action, whose constituency was predominantly homeowners.

A second issue, rent regulations, applied peculiarly to tenants. New York had been the only state to retain World War II rent controls into the 1960s. However, the inflation that accompanied the Vietnam War led to demands in several states for protection from rent increases and the implementation of "second generation" regulations. Thus, the New Jersey Tenant Organization (NJTO), formed in 1969, spearheaded a campaign that won controls in more than one hundred cities. Similar local initiatives spread across the nation during the 1970s. They ran into especially strong opposition from landlords of properties with FHA-insured mortgages (which were often large developments), who fought them politically, in court, and finally complained to HUD that its mortgages were threatened by the rent laws. In

February 1975 HUD responded with a regulation providing that properties with federally insured mortgages could bypass local rent regulations if they were in danger of defaulting.[108]

Tenant activists saw this regulation as a considerable threat. A Met Council delegation protested to the HUD regional director, and then followed up with a memorandum, copies of which were sent to all members of the New York congressional delegation. Aware that these actions were insufficient for a national issue, Met Council told its members that it hoped to contact NJTO and tenant groups in Boston (which it did not yet know by name) with the hope of coordinating protests. Knowledge of tenant organizations in other states, and links to them, were still limited.

Meanwhile, in April 1975 the first issue of *Shelterforce*, a national tenant quarterly newspaper, was published in New Jersey by the National Lawyers Guild and a group of tenant organizers and community workers from in and around the city of Newark. The headline of its first issue was dramatically relevant to its purpose: "HUD KO's Local Rent Laws."[109] By reporting the spread of tenant organizing and rent control initiatives across the country during the next several years, *Shelterforce* helped strengthen a sense of identity among tenants and, in turn, inspired further activism.[110]

The first multistate endeavors developed slowly. Finally, in 1976 NJTO took the initiative in calling together tenant organizations from New York (Met Council and NYSTNC), Massachusetts and the District of Columbia to form an ad hoc Coalition against Federal Preemption of Local Rent Control. In July they met with HUD officials in Washington and then followed up by pushing their congressional delegations to intervene. The following year the New York and New Jersey federations formed the National Committee for Rent Control and spent an exploratory day lobbying on Capitol Hill. Meanwhile, Met Council had begun to publish extensive reports of the burgeoning tenant activity in other states. Excitement rose with the upsurge in organizing and demands for rent regulations that followed the failure of California landlords to fulfill their promises to share the tax savings resulting from Proposition 13 with tenants in the form of rent reductions. In 1979 New York tenants celebrated by having actress Jane Fonda, an activist from Santa Monica, California, where tenant muscle was being flexed, as keynote speaker at a large outdoor rally marking Tenant Unity Day.[111]

By the spring of 1979 many "informed sources" were suggesting that the Carter administration would respond to the galloping rate of inflation by imposing wage and price controls. *Shelterforce* and the other members of the National Committee for Rent Control saw this as an opportunity to push their cause—they must be ready to demand strong national rent and eviction control as part of the federal package. A meeting of the committee decided to call a "national tenant movement conference on rent control" in the fall. The resulting meeting drew more than one hundred tenant organizers and activists from fifty cities and seventeen states to Newark. It greatly extended networks among tenant activists, elicited commitments to continue working together, and laid plans for a full National Tenant Organizing Conference in Cleveland the next summer.[112]

The Cleveland conference brought together two hundred representatives from one hundred tenant organizations in fifty cities and twenty-five states. The major result was the formation of the National Tenants Union (NTU). The top structural level of the tenant movement, a super federation, was thus put in place.

Once again networks were extended and strategies shared and their effectiveness discussed. Ambitious plans were laid concerning a clearinghouse for information, the development of model programs, and the creation of a presence on Capitol Hill. However, problems arose concerning how these would be carried out—the organizational members were not willing to set membership dues at more than a token level.[113] This meant there could be no national office in the immediate future, and certainly no lobbyist regularly at Congress. It was suggested that the shortfall in funds could be made up by pursuing individual memberships—but issues before Congress are too far away to attract the attention of the average tenant concerned about services at home. Consequently, shortage of money has been a continuing problem for the NTU. On the other hand, the national reporting of *Shelterforce* acts as a clearinghouse, while annual national conferences continue to strengthen ties among activists.

The first political test for NTU was an unexpected amendment introduced in the House of Representatives in the fall of 1980 by Representative Chalmers Wylie (Republican, Ohio). This amendment, which would have prohibited the use of certain federal funds in cities with rent control laws, was brought at the instigation of the National Multi-Housing Council, a real estate lobby, as a means of knocking the steam out of the tenant movement after a striking 2 to 1 defeat of an anti-rent-control initiative in California in June 1980. NTU responded to the amendment by encouraging local tenant and community groups to contact the members of their congressional delegations to urge them to oppose the measure. Their efforts met with little apparent success, for the amendment passed the House with a comfortable majority, and much of the opposition to it that was expressed in debate came from conservatives opposed to federal interference in local matters rather than from supporters of rent regulations. Tenants were saved when the amendment died with the bill it was attached to. Following the election of Ronald Reagan, his transition team recommended the adoption of a similar measure to encourage local governments to abandon rent regulations. Such a bill was introduced in both 1981 and 1982 by New York senator

Alphonse D'Amato. Tenant lobbying in 1981, in particular, was credited with playing an important part in its defeat. These were tense times for the fledgling National Tenants Union, when a real estate backlash encouraged by a conservative administration threatened the progress that had been made in the late 1970s.[114] Meanwhile, the Reagan administration proceeded with its plans to dismantle many of HUD's programs and to slash its budget.

The new networks that began to link tenant activists across the nation after 1975 gave tenants the ability to respond politically at the national level. Although their limited resources hampered lobbying efforts in Washington, they were in a position to coordinate local political efforts against national targets. The 1984 annual conference of NTU, held in Detroit, grimly debated what delegates regarded as the attacks of the Reagan administration on housing and eventually adopted a resolution, proposed by Met Council, that NTU should sponsor an "evict Reagan" campaign during the fall campaign period. As a result, NTU prepared a brochure for its members' use during the election season that urged tenants to register to vote and then to use their votes to "evict Reagan."[115]

Tenant Impact: Retrospect and Prospect

The fifteen years between 1970 and 1984 were a period of growth, diversification, and increasing influence for the tenant movement in New York. Within the city the movement was no longer concentrated in Manhattan, but was now well represented in three outer boroughs with large numbers of tenants: Brooklyn, where it had become a presence in the early 1970s; the Bronx, where NWBCCC's eight affiliates represented real strength in the north and ANHD members were hard at work managing and rehabilitating buildings in the south; and Queens, where the long unorganized tenant terrain had sprouted a spunky local federation appropriately known as QLOUT (Queens League of United Tenants) in 1981, which brought together fifteen affiliates in predominantly white middle-class neighborhoods. Meanwhile, NYSTNC had continued to expand upstate in its endeavor to build a statewide federation, its membership climbing to a total of seventy organizations by 1983.

The expanded movement represented a previously unmatched diversity of tenants, no matter what dimension is considered: middle class, working class, and poor; black, white and Hispanic; political radicals and neighborhood-oriented conservatives. The result was an unheralded breadth of protest. South Bronx tenants seized control of buildings undergoing abandonment while West End Avenue tenants organized because their elevator operators were replaced by automatic elevators or their doormen no longer wore white gloves; tenants from all over the city pressured the meetings of the Rent Guidelines Board with their unruliness, while their leaders lobbied with finesse in Albany.

The increased influence of the movement was seen at all levels. Among buildings, movement strategies were perceived by tenants as having a positive effect. When the leaders of 153 building organizations, first interviewed in 1975–1976 while using strategies against their landlords, were reinterviewed eight years later, 80 percent reported that the actions had brought short-term gains and 59 percent reported that gains were retained over time. (The record was least positive in the more deteriorated neighborhoods—the 34 cases in which the situation got worse after the tenant action include 13 buildings that were abandoned and derelict.) Met Council, with its very careful implementation of strategies, scored higher than the other neighborhood organizations collectively: 71 percent as compared with 58 percent long-term gains. The few (7) buildings in the sample that underwent rehabilitation and conversion to low-income ownership were unanimously reported as showing both immediate and long-term gains—their transformation had been most dramatic.

A separate study of the first forty-six low-income rehabilitation/conversions ten to fifteen years later allows us to examine the track records of such buildings more closely. Respondents stated overwhelmingly, 73 to 7, that they preferred living in a co-op to having a landlord; they said that co-ops gave them control over their housing, a better place to live and better services, and at a lower cost. When asked to evaluate their co-op as a success or failure, the vote was 70 to 17 in favor of successes. A leader of one of a cluster of four successful co-ops in the South Bronx that were surrounded by devastation declared with justification that they were "a piece of heaven in hell."[116]

Although the influence of the movement has increased, limitations on its impact remain. For example, many of the early low-income co-ops, lacking the financial resources, skills, or will to make ends meet, are in financial trouble. Eight of the forty-six are in rem (that is, have been seized by the city because of unpaid taxes), another six are filed for the next vesting, and five others were previously in rem but have been redeemed by their tenant owners. That is, 41 percent of the co-ops are or have been in severe tax problems—problems of the kind that can remove tenant ownership and thus destroy the co-op. Moreover, 63 percent were at least two years and five months behind with their debt service payments in 1983. Only fourteen made all payments in 1982–1983; another fourteen made no payments at all. While HPD could legally foreclose on many of these properties, it has in fact done so in only one case: it would be obliged to manage them, which would be even more costly than merely foregoing the payments.[117] Experience with these co-ops has demonstrated that properties frequently need more income to cover costs than poor tenants can pay, even where profit is not on the agenda. Ultimately, then, housing issues cannot stand alone, especially when poor tenants are concerned. A broader vision is needed, one that sets out to link the tenant issue to others such as the need to alleviate unemployment and poverty; for if these issues are dealt with, then housing for the poor will be able to pay its way.

The tenant movement's strength has also been limited by membership turnover. Met Council has rarely achieved a 50 percent renewal rate, while that of most neighborhood organizations, which give renewal less attention, has been considerably less. Most building organizations tend to be organized around a particular internal goal, and once this goal is realized their raison d'être evaporates. Only 53 percent of buildings that were still inhabited eight years after organizing retained any degree of organization. The proportion remaining in contact with the neighborhood organization that helped them organize was only 40 percent, and in the majority of these the contact was maintained by one or two individual memberships. However, the tenant movement, like the labor movement, has the advantage of having real locals where people are in regular contact with each other whether organized or not. This can allow a building organization to pass into latency, ready to be revived when needed—the more easily if some tenants retain contact with a trusted neighborhood organization.

A major exception to this pattern occurs when a building becomes tenant controlled. Thus, low-income co-ops are much more likely to stay organized—indeed, they have to, almost by definition. However, they seem to be even more prone to lose contact with the neighborhood organizations that assisted them initially. While 84 percent of the sample of early co-ops reported that they had close ties with a neighborhood organization initially, only 23 percent currently have such ties. This has left the co-ops isolated, without links to the tenant movement. Indeed, few of them are in contact with one another—even those that originally had the same sponsoring neighborhood organizations. Rather than becoming sources of inspiration and building blocks of the movement, they have put all their energies into mere survival.[118]

At the neighborhood level, the housing market in New York City was subdivided into three sectors, each with its own problems for tenants, throughout this period. At the bottom lay neighborhoods inhabited by poor minority populations, mostly in the South Bronx and central Brooklyn, where tenants faced severe decay and abandonment. This sector was encroaching on contiguous neighborhoods as their previous white tenants fled and landlords, real estate brokers, banks, and city agencies created a self-fulfilling prophecy of decay by their responses to the new minority tenants. The top sector, concentrated mostly in Manhattan, was characterized by spiraling rents, conversions, and gentrification. It too was spreading, driven by speculation and the changing fortunes of city and suburbs following the oil crisis. In between these two sectors lay another made up of previously stable working- and lower-middle-class areas that were feeling pressure both from below, primarily in the outer boroughs, as population shifts triggered white flight from the mid-Bronx, neighborhoods such as Brooklyn's East Flatbush, and the belt surrounding the Jamaica ghetto in Queens, and from above, mainly in Manhattan, as gentrification spread from the East Village into the Lower East Side, from Chelsea into Clinton, and from the Upper West Side into Manhattan Valley, and as the brownstone revival spread outward from Brooklyn Heights and Park Slope. Tenant strategies had saved large numbers of buildings and stabilized many blocks in these neighborhoods, but had not rescued the neighborhoods from the ravages of abandonment and gentrification. Nevertheless, while the wars against market forces seemed lopsided, they continued to be waged.

The improved political outlook for tenants is a dramatic indication of greater movement influence. Within the space of a few years, tenants have moved politically from being solely reactive to seeking to shape housing policy, and in the process have to a large extent set the legislative agenda while succeeding in placing large new sections of the housing market—conversions, retaliatory evictions, landlord obligations within a lease, and bank mortgage practices—under government regulation. New court practices have been accepted, tenants have successfully claimed management and ownership of their buildings, politicians have been transformed into tenant advocates, the daily lives of those involved in both sides of the tenant-landlord relationship have been altered. But although this represents a considerable change for the better for tenants since 1970–1971, it does not mean that all has become rosy for them. Tenants have matched, perhaps even exceeded, the sophistication of the real estate lobby, but not its wealth. The result has been a tendency of the legislature to try to balance political outcomes—to compromise on particular pieces of legislation or to allow the tenants a victory on one issue but to hold firm for real estate on another. Most significantly, the many battles concerning rent regulations have not prevented considerable increases in rent levels under both rent stabilization and rent control since 1970, so the proportion of households with a rent:income ratio of over 25 percent jumped by over 20 points, from 35.5 percent to 56.6 percent between 1970 and 1981, and those with a ratio exceeding 40 percent, an extremely high level, almost doubled between 1968 and 1981 from 16.7 percent to 30.5 percent.[119] Tenant "victories" over the Emergency Tenant Protection Act have been limited to preventing rent increases from being sharper still.

A second dramatic indication of greater movement influence has been the flow of external funding to many tenant organizations. This funding allowed tenants to take over the management of their buildings, to rehabilitate them, and to own them cooperatively; it also enormously increased the number of full-time tenant activists and opened up movement career paths. However, it so shaped the goals and strategies of organizations that it raised the specter of cooptation. Meanwhile, in spite of their genuinely warm words for their homes, which flow from the contrast with other housing in poor neighborhoods, the low-income cooperators are indeed owners of last resort. While, from one point of view, the strongest endorsement of strategies featuring tenant control has been their adoption and promotion by government agencies, the buildings passed to tenant groups have usually been unwanted lemons, and government generosity has proved likely to be withdrawn just as soon as a private landlord would offer more for them.

The evolution of strategies during this period has been transforming tenant activism from a movement toward an interest group. The routinization of the rent strike has rendered it less radical and more predictable, while miring it in the labyrinthine corridors of the housing court. Most of the new approaches to the legislature, banks, agencies, and funders require sophistication, skills, and, in many cases, professional staff.

The tenant movement is now, in several ways, at a turning point. Many of the members of ANHD are being squeezed by cuts in funding and have been warned solemnly that they must get "back to basics." Met Council has chosen to divert resources from organizing to try to build broad political coalitions; it is also about to test new leadership, for Jane Benedict, its charismatic chairperson for the past quarter of a century, has retired, marking a changing of the guard. She is the last remaining major figure from the founding generation. And NYSTNC, which has added a rapidly growing stratum of individual members to its organizational affiliate core, is focusing on how it can expand tenant power further by modifying the Omnibus Housing Law to unify the rent system and bring unregulated areas and classes of housing within it.

Strategic innovation continues: for example, a large group of tenant activists drawn from NYSTNC, QLOUT, Met Council, ANHD, and independent neighborhood organizations formed a statewide Tenants Political Action Committee (TenPAC) early in 1984, which endorsed two state senate candidates in closely fought races and supported them with volunteer electoral workers as a counterweight to the real estate funds being channeled to their opponents. Their hope was to provide a victory margin and win influence in Albany in 1985, when the Omnibus Housing Law may be amended because it is due to be extended. The candidate credited TenPAC with providing the margin of victory in one of these cases; the other candidate was engulfed by a Reagan landslide in his district. Meanwhile, all three main federations are exploring the potential of the National Tenants Union. The spread of the structural pattern of the movement in New York to other states, and its expansion to a new super federation at the national level, suggest that there will be a new stability, sophistication, and coherence in the expression of tenant interests.

The precise directions the tenant movement will take in the future may not yet be clear. Nevertheless, it is certain that during the period 1970–1984 it developed a diversity, sophistication, and power greater than it has ever previously possessed.

ABBREVIATIONS

AID	South Brooklyn against Investment Discrimination
ANHD	Association of Neighborhood Housing Developers
CAB	Conciliation and Appeals Board
CAR	Coalition against Redlining in New York City
CARIP	Coalition against Rent Increase Pass-alongs
CCOH	Chelsea Coalition on Housing
CETA	Comprehensive Employment Training Act
CMP	Community Management Program
DAMP	Division of Alternative Management Programs
DHCR	State Division of Housing and Community Renewal
ETPA	Emergency Tenant Protection Act
HDA	Housing and Development Administration
HPD	Department of Housing Preservation and Development
HTU	Harlem Tenants Union
HUD	Department of Housing and Urban Development
JPC	Joint Planning Council of the Lower East Side
MBR	Maximum Base Rent
Met Council	Metropolitan Council on Housing
NJTO	New Jersey Tenant Organization
NPC	Neighborhood Preservation Company
NTO	National Tenant Organization
NTU	National Tenants Union
NWBCCC	Northwest Bronx Community Clergy Coalition
NYSTLC	New York State Tenants Legislative Coalition
OSI	Office of Special Improvements
PDC	People's Development Corporation
RGB	Rent Guidelines Board
RSA	Rent Stabilization Association
TAC	Tenant Advisory Committee
TAD	Tenants against Demolition

TenPAC	Tenants Political Action Committee
TIL	Tenant Interim Lease Program
UHAB	Urban Homesteading Assistance Board

NOTES

1. In addition to the sources cited, this essay includes data gathered from extensive participant observation of the meetings and activities of the Metropolitan Council on Housing, the New York State Tenant and Neighborhood Coalition, the Association of Neighborhood Housing Developers, the Urban Homesteading Assistance Board, and twenty neighborhood organizations, and in-depth interviews with the leaders of these organizations. Data were also gathered from surveys of the leaders of 89 federations and neighborhood organizations and 37 Office of Economic Opportunity–funded service centers as well as surveys of the leaders and members of 153 building organizations and 46 low-income cooperatives.
2. Ira S. Lowry, ed., *Rental Housing in New York City*, vol. 1: *Confronting the Crisis* (Rand Institute, 1970), pp. 3–7; Ira S. Lowry, Joseph DeSalvo, and Barbara Woodfill, *Rental Housing in New York City*, vol. 2: *Rental Housing in New York* (Rand Institute, 1971); George Sternlieb, *The Urban Housing Dilemma*, preliminary draft (Housing and Development Administration, 1970); idem, *The Urban Housing Dilemma* (Housing and Development Administration, 1972). See also David Bartelt and Ronald Lawson, "Rent Control and Abandonment: A Second Look at the Evidence," *Journal of Urban Affairs* 4, no. 4 (1982): 49–64.
3. *Tenant News*, Oct.–Nov., Dec. 1969; *New York Times*, Mar. 19, 1970; Louis Harris and Associates, "Transition Neighborhoods in New York City: The People's View of Their Housing Environment," Vera Institute of Justice, New York, 1969.
4. *New York Times*, June 30, 1970.
5. *Tenant News*, Dec. 1962, Feb., Nov. 1963, Mar. 1964, Jan., June, Nov. 1965, Jan. 1968.
6. Ibid., May 1968, June 1970; Debbie Shliom, *Your Home Is Your Hassle* (Metropolitan Council on Housing, 1971); Interviews with Lester Evens and Richard Levenson, 1981.
7. *Tenant News*, Sept.–Nov. 1970; *Tenant*, June 1971; *New York Times*, Aug. 1, 1970.
8. *Tenant*, Dec. 1971, Jan. 1972.
9. *New York Times*, Jan. 23, 27, Mar. 7, 1971.
10. Ibid., Apr. 28, 1971; *New York State Laws*, 1971, chaps. 371, 372.
11. *Tenant*, May 11, 1971.
12. *New York Times*, Apr. 28, 29, 1971 (editorial); Community Service Society, Housing and Urban Development Legislation in New York State, 1971, p. 16.
13. *New York Times*, May 31, 1971.
14. Met Council policy statement, June 11, 1971.
15. *New York Times*, July 13, 20, 1971.
16. Ibid., Sept. 2, 1971.
17. Interview with Michael Ehrmann, 1974; *Tenant*, Jan., Feb. 1972.
18. *New York Times*, June 17, 1972; *Benson Realty Corp. v. Walsh*, *New York Law Journal* 2:2–4; *Tenant*, Aug. 1972.
19. *Tenant*, Aug. 1972; Interview with M. Ehrmann, 1974; *New York Times*, June 17, 1972.
20. *Tenant*, Jan. 1973.
21. *New York Times*, Mar. 2, April 4, 1973.
22. *Tenant*, Dec. 1972.
23. In spite of the fact that the vacancy decontrol law was justified as an attempt to reduce housing abandonment by giving landlords more money to invest in their buildings, its prime impact was not upon rents in decaying neighborhoods, where demand for housing was contracting, but in the most sought-after areas. Indeed, the rate of housing abandonment was not af-

fected by the legislation.
24. *Report on Housing and Rents of the Temporary State Commission on Living Costs and the Economy of the State of New York to the Governor and the Legislature, by Assemblyman Andrew Stein Chairman*, Jan. 1974.
25. *Tenant*, July, Aug., Nov. 1971.
26. Interviews with Leroy Washington and Abe Gerges, 1983.
27. Type D corporations under section 402 of the New York Not for Profit Corporation Law.
28. Interview with Robert Schur, 1980. Other projects secured federal financing (236 and 221(d)3), and one, state Mitchell-Lama funds. For further details concerning the evolution of this strategy and the buildings involved, see Ronald Lawson, *Owners of Last Resort* (N.Y.C. Department of Housing Preservation and Development, 1984).
29. Robert Kolodny, *Self Help in the Inner City* (United Neighborhood Houses, 1973).
30. Interview with Schur, 1980.
31. The Municipal Loan scandal was occasioned, inter alia, by landlords collecting rehabilitation loans but doing little or no construction, by the making of loans that exceeded the value of the properties securing them, by failures to certify actual costs, and by neglect of the duty to encourage minority contractors, which had been one of the central objectives of the program [Committee on Charter and Governmental Operations, 1972].
32. Father Robert Fox, "Entrepreneuring on Sweat Equity," *In Business*, 1979, pp. 44–47.
33. Lawson, *Owners of Last Resort*.
34. *Tenant News*, Apr., May 1970.
35. William Worthy, *The Rape of Our Neighborhoods* (William Morrow, 1976).
36. See Ronald Lawson, "The Rent Strike in New York City, 1904–1980," *Journal of Urban History*, May 1984, for greater detail.
37. Margaret Gillerman, "7-A Law Gives Tenants a Way to Seize a Building—Legally," *City Limits*, Aug. 1978; interviews with Roger Hayes (1976), Bill Frey (1978), Jim Mitchell (1980), Claudia Mansbach (1980).
38. J. Clarence Davies Realty Company, *Consultants' Report: Co-op City* (n.d.); Jack Newfield and Paul Du Brul, *The Abuse of Power* (Penguin, 1978), pp. 300–310.
39. *Organizing Handbook* (Metropolitan Council on Housing, 1966); Shliom, *Your Home Is Your Hassle*.
40. The one exception was the period 1952–1959. The existing federation collapsed in 1952 following both the success in winning state rent controls and the onset of McCarthyite repression.
41. See Ronald Lawson and Stephen E. Barton, "Sex Roles and Social Movements: A Case Study of the Tenant Movement in New York City," *Signs*, Winter 1980, for further discussion of women as the major tenant movement constituency and recent leaders.
42. *Tenant*, Nov. 1973, Nov. 1974, Nov. 1975, Nov. 1976.
43. Ibid., June 1971, July 1975, June 1978; Peter K. Hawley, *Housing in the Public Domain: The Only Solution* (Metropolitan Council on Housing, 1978).
44. Clara Fox, *Neighborhood Preservation: The Role of Moderate Housing Rehabilitation and Cooperative or Mutual Ownership* (Settlement Housing Fund, 1974).
45. "The Fight against Demolition: A Victory for Community Housing Groups," *City Limits*, Feb. 1976; "CETA/CJCC Job Training Program Launched at Last," *City Limits*, Mar. 1976.
46. *New York Post*, Jan. 24, 1974; *Daily News*, Jan. 25, 1974; *New York Times*, May 11, 1975, Nov. 13, 1976, May 6, 1977.
47. *New York Times*, Oct. 6, 1977; *Daily News*, Oct. 6, 1977.
48. Steve Katz, "The Faded Dream of Washington Avenue," *City Limits*, Apr. 1983, pp. 19–20; interview with Susan Treanor, 1981.
49. Robert Schur and Virginia Sherry, *The Neighborhood Housing Movement* (ANHD, 1977).
50. Bernard Cohen, "Rehabilitating Sweat Equity," *City Limits*, Feb., Mar. 1980.

51. Interviews with Susan Treanor and Doug Moritz, 1980.
52. Katz, "Faded Dream of Washington Avenue," pp. 19–20 (quoting Ruben Rivera, another of the participants).
53. From interviews with Doug Moritz and anonymous, 1980.
54. Interview with Bill Frey, 1978.
55. Michael A. Stegman, *The Dynamics of Rental Housing in New York City* (HPD, 1982), pp. 7–8, 207–209.
56. *Tenant*, May, Sept. 1978; *City Limits*, Sept., Nov. 1978; "New Believers Buy Bite of Big Apple," *City Limits*, Dec. 1979.
57. The Management in Partnership Program (MIPP) was a variation on CMP. Here neighborhood organizations without experience in management gained it under the watchful eye of a commercial management firm. Thus, in effect, they went through an apprenticeship with the aim of graduating to the CMP.
58. *City Limits*, Dec. 1979.
59. "New Believers Buy Bite of Big Apple," *City Limits*, Dec. 1979; "$250 Buys More Sweat Than Equity in City's Low-Cost Housing Sales," *City Limits*, Dec. 1982.
60. Stegman, *Dynamics of Rental Housing in New York City*, p. 208; "Eimicke Ultimatum," *City Limits*, Feb. 1980; "Community Management Standards," *City Limits*, Mar. 1980; "Rent and Tax Aid for TIL Buildings But No Pledge on Sales, Repairs," *City Limits*, Apr. 1980; Bernard Cohen, "Over Hurdles and Snags, First TIL Buildings Are Sold to Tenants," *City Limits*, June 1980; S. Baldwin, "Funds and Direction for Community Management Program in Dispute," *City Limits*, Oct. 1980; "Housing Officials Consider Merger of Some Community Building Management Programs," *City Limits*, Jan. 1981; *New York Times*, June 7, 1980.
61. *City Limits*, Apr. 1980.
62. "New York's Neighborhood Groups," *City Limits*, Aug. 1983.
63. "Neighborhood Housing Developers Chart Their Course," *City Limits*, Dec. 1981; Rick Cohen, "What Hath Reagan Wrought?" *City Limits*, Aug.–Sept. 1983; Robert Schur, "Back to Basics: Organizing in the Age of Austerity," *City Limits*, Jan. 1982; Katz, "Faded Dream of Washington Avenue."
64. "Community Group Profit-Sharing," *City Limits*, Jan. 1981; "Neighborhood Housing Developers Chart Their Course," *City Limits*, Dec. 1981.
65. Bonnie Brower, "Requiem for a Housing Policy: Selling Alternative Management," *City Limits*, Oct. 1982; Susan Baldwin, "Tenants Win $250 Sales Pledge: But There's a Catch," *City Limits*, Dec. 1982; Julia McDonnell Chang, "Rebuilding Home: Tenants Take a New Lease on City Life," *City Limits*, Apr. 1984.
66. *City Limits*, Feb. 1982; Tom Gogan and Dave Robinson, "Judge Voids City Rent Hikes," *City Limits*, Dec. 1982; *City Limits*, Aug. 1983; Stegman, *Dynamics of Rental Housing in New York City*, p. 8.
67. *Tenant*, Nov. 1983.
68. Cohen, "Rehabilitating Sweat Equity."
69. Andrew Reicher, "Homesteading Is More Than Just Housing," *City Limits*, Apr. 1984; Tom Robbins, "NYC's Homesteading Programs: A Land Rush to Nowhere?" *City Limits*, Apr. 1984.
70. Homefront, *Housing Abandonment in New York City* (Homefront, 1977).
71. Kathy Sanders, "Greenliners Blast Assembly Banking Committee on Redlining," *City Limits*, Nov. 1976.
72. "Savings Bank Denied Branch," *City Limits*, May 1979.
73. "Historic Bank Pact," *City Limits*, Mar. 1979; "Four Banks Commit to Northwest Bronx," *City Limits*, Feb. 1980; Jim Mitchell, letter to editor, *City Limits*, Jan. 1982.
74. Tim Ledwith, "Reinvestment: Enter the Commercial Banks," *City Limits*, June 1981.
75. "The Chelsea Clam House Defeat", *City Limits*, Mar. 1983.
76. Tom Robbins, "Displacement Examined: From Both Sides Now," *City Limits*, June 1981; Richard LeGates and Chester Hartman, *Displacement* (Legal Services Anti-Displacement Project, 1981).
77. Robbins, "Displacement Examined."

78. Tom Robbins, "A Roar in Park Slope," *City Limits*, Jan. 1981.
79. Susan Baldwin, "A Game of Numbers in Harlem," *City Limits*, June 1981; "Managing West Harlem," *City Limits*, May 1983.
80. Craig Unger, "The Lower East Side: There Goes the Neighborhood," *New York Magazine*, May 28, 1984.
81. "The Defeat of Artists' Housing," *City Limits*, Mar. 1983.
82. Indeed, the author's study of "the impact of tenant strategies upon the social process of housing abandonment" in six neighborhoods in four New York City boroughs shows that the revitalizing forces of the market, once in play in two neighborhoods—Manhattan Valley and the Lower East Side—overshadowed all tenant strategies.
83. Robert Schur, "Holding the Line in the Neighborhood," *City Limits*, June 1981.
84. Jim Sleeper, "This Neighborhood Is Not for Sale," *City Limits*, June 1984.
85. "Furor over City's Lower East Side Scheme," *City Limits*, Aug. 1984.
86. *New York State Tax Guardian*, Spring 1976; B. Bruce-Biggs, "Rent Control Must Go," *New York Times Magazine*, Apr. 18, 1976; *Amsterdam News*, May 1, 1976; *Business Week*, May 24, 1976; "Disaster Area: Rent Control Has Helped Turn Gotham into One," *Barron's*, Apr. 21, 1975; "The Case for Ending Rent Control," *New York Law Journal*, Apr. 14, 1976; "Moreland Panel: End Rent Curbs," *New York Post*, Mar. 31, 1976. Abraham Beame was mayor of New York City and Assemblyman Al Blumenthal, from Manhattan's West Side, was Democratic majority leader in the state assembly.
87. Minutes, Southern Region Membership Meeting, NYSTNC, Jan. 6, 1977; *Tenant*, Mar. 1976.
88. Minutes, Southern Region Membership Meeting, NYSTNC, Jan. 6, 1977.
89. Michael McKee to NYSTNC members, Apr. 30, 1977.
90. Interview with Lester Schulklapper, lobbyist for the Real Estate Board of New York (REB) and the Metropolitan Fair Rents Committee (MFRC). See further in Ronald Lawson, "The Political Face of the Real Estate Industry in New York City," *New York Affairs*, Apr. 1980.
91. *Tenant*, Apr., Sept. 1979; M. McKee, "State Legislators Pass Group Funding, Reject Co-op Protection Bill," *City Limits*, June 1980; S. Baldwin, "The War of the Queens Garden Apartments," *City Limits*, Oct. 1981; "Co-op Alert," NYSTNC flier, May 19, 1982; "New Co-op Conversion Legislation," NYSTNC newsletter, July 11, 1982; M. McKee, "How the City Got a New Co-op Law," *City Limits*, Aug. 1982.
92. *City Limits*, Mar. 1978, Apr. 1979; *Peoples Housing News*, Jan. 1981; *Tenant and Neighbors*, May, Sept. 1982.
93. *New York Times*, Apr. 25, 1980.
94. "New York State Tenant and Neighborhood Coalition Proposed Statewide Rent and Eviction Regulation Bill Outline," *City Limits*, Nov. 10, 1980.
95. NYSTNC letter to John Dearie, Mar. 1980; *Tenant*, Jan. 1981; Minutes, Southern Regional meeting, NYSTNC, Jan. 22, 1981; NYSTNC executive board minutes, Dec. 14, 1980, Mar. 18, 1981; "Tenant Alert," NYSTNC, Oct. 1, 1981; Minutes, NYSTNC membership meeting, Jan. 31, 1982; NYSTNC executive board meeting, Mar. 21, 1982; "Tenant Protection Update," NYSTNC, Mar. 15, 1983.
96. "Flynn-Dearie Bill Pending," *Tenants and Neighbors*, May 1983.
97. NYSTNC flier, Dec. 1979; NYSTNC secretary to members, Apr. 1980; Minutes, NYSTNC board meeting, Mar. 1981; NYSTNC membership list, May 1981; Minutes, NYSTNC membership meeting, Jan. 1982; NYSTNC Bylaws Subcommittee to members, Sept. 1982.
98. *Tenant*, Dec. 1972, Dec. 1980, Feb. 1976, July 1984, Dec. 1983.
99. Ibid., Feb. 1981.
100. Ibid., Feb., Apr., 1981, Sept. 1982, Feb. 1979 (Ruth Beinart), May 1980 (Jack Rand), July 1981 (Esther Rand).
101. Ibid., Mar. 1974, June 1975, July 1977, Mar. 1978, Apr. 1979; *City Limits*, Mar., Apr. 1979.
102. See further in Lawson, "Political Face

of the Real Estate Industry in New York City."

103. Bill Rowen, "Anti-RSA Campaign Picks Up Steam," *Tenants and Neighbors*, May 1982.

104. "Complaints under Rent Stabilization in New York City," Fact Sheet No. 13, NYSTNC, Feb. 1980; "Abrams Probes Landlord Group," *Peoples Housing News*, Jan. 1981; Rowen, "Anti-RSA Campaign Picks Up Steam"; NYSTNC flyer, June 1982.

105. "Rent Control Showdown," *Tenants and Neighbors*, Feb. 1983; P. J. Kamens, "Rent Laws Due for an Overhaul," *City Limits*, Feb. 1983; M. McKee, "The Senate's 'Secret' Rent Bill," *Tenants and Neighbors*, June 1983; idem, "The New Rent Laws," *City Limits*, Aug. 1983; M. McKee, "New Rent Law Passed: State Takeover Raises Enforcement Hopes, Other Changes Challenge Tenants to Organize," *Tenants and Neighbors*, Sept. 1983; "Rent Curbs for Church and College," *City Limits*, June 1983; Jane Benedict, "The Package Deal—What Happened to Flynn-Dearie?" *Tenant*, July 1983; John McKean, "How the Senate Took a Walk on Flynn-Dearie," *City Limits*, Oct. 1983.

106. *Tenants and Neighbors*, no. 8, n.d. (ca. Oct. 1983); no. 11, n.d. (July 1984).

107. M. McKee, "Landlords Overplay Their Hand," *Tenants and Neighbors*, May 1984; "The Landlords' End Run," *City Limits*, Feb. 1984; Bill Rowen, "State Takeover Off to a Rocky Start," *Tenants and Neighbors*, May 1984.

108. Richard E. Blumberg, Brian Quinn Robbins, and Kenneth K. Baar, "The Emergence of Second Generation Rent Controls," *Clearinghouse Review*, Aug. 1978; John Atlas and Peter Dreier, "Mobilize or Compromise? The Tenants' Movement and American Politics," in *America's Housing Crisis*, ed. Chester Hartman (Boston, 1983); "HUD KO's Local Rent Laws," *Shelterforce*, Apr. 1975.

109. "Who Is Shelterforce?" *Shelterforce*, Apr. 1975.

110. "Fed Programs Squeeze Tenants," *Tenant*, May 1975; "HUD KO's Local Rent Laws"; "Battling Over Rent Control," *Shelterforce*, Winter 1976; "From the Grassroots: Progress of the Housing Movement in 14 Cities," *Shelterforce*, Winter 1977; "Rent Control Roundup: Tenants Battle around the Country," *Shelterforce*, Spring 1979.

111. *Tenant*, Sept., Nov. 1977, May, Dec. 1978, Oct. 1979.

112. *Shelterforce*, Spring 1979; "National Movement Looks to the 80's," *Shelterforce*, Fall 1979; *Tenant*, Dec. 1979; *City Limits*, Dec. 1979.

113. *Shelterforce*, Oct. 1980.

114. "Congress Tries to Stop Rent Control," *Shelterforce*, Oct. 1980; *City Limits*, June, Aug. 1981; *Tenants and Neighbors*, May 1982; Atlas and Dreier, 177; *Shelterforce*, Spring 1982.

115. *Tenant*, July 1984; *Shelterforce*, Aug. 1984.

116. Lawson, "Owners of Last Resort."

117. Ibid.

118. Ibid.

119. Stegman, *Dynamics of Rental Housing in New York City*, p. 157. The latter datum is not available for 1970.

Index of Names

(Page numbers in italics indicate illustrations.)

Abrams, Charles, 153, 155, 162
Adamec, Connie, 226
Aviles, Grace, 140

Badillo, Herman, 189
Bambrick, James, 119
Barbaro, Frank, 216, 258
Barker, Elizabeth, 156, 159
Beame, Mayor Abraham, *31*, 223
Benedict, Jane, *36*, 167–168, 172, 182, 232, 258
Berrigan, Daniel, 225
Berrigan, Phillip, 225
Black, Loring, Jr., 69
Black, Sophie, 120
Bogues, Leon, *36*
Bohm, Ernest, 68
Borden, David, 184
Breitman, Anne, *13*
Broun, Heywood, 119
Brower, Bonny, *36*
Brown, Earl, 150
Burdick, Selma, 164
Burdick, Thelma, 167

Cacchione, Peter, 129, 139
Cahan, Abe, 41
Callahan, Joseph, 69
Carey, Governor Hugh, 255
Caro, Robert A., 153
Carpenter, H. Daniel, 166
Carter, President Jimmy, *31*, 235
Claessens, August, 58
Cloward, Richard A., 5
Cohen, Stanley, 69–70
Craig, Agnes, 79, 81, 86
Cunningham, Patrick, 189
Cuomo, Governor Mario, 260

D'Amato, Alphonse, 266
Davies, J. Clarence, 164
Davies, John R., 82
Davis, Benjamin H., 153
Davis, Benjamin, Jr., 129
Dearie, John, 217
DeBrul, Paul, 184
Dewey, Thomas E., 142, 151, 152
Donnelly, George, 67
Dryfoos, Robert, *36*

Eddy, Reverend Norman, 177, 184
Eddy, William, *28*
Ehrmann, Michael, 218
Ely, Harry Allen, 66, 78, 82
Engel, Eliot, *36*
Epstein, Sophie, 60–61
Evans, Lester, 212

Farmer, James, 175, 182
Felt, James, 139, 162, 163, 164
Fino, Paul, 216
Ford, Father George C., 157, 159
Fox, Father Robert, 221–222

Gabel, Hortense, 170
Gisnet, Morris, 56
Gitlin, Leo, 69, 72
Gleidman, Anthony, 244
Goldin, Frances, 164, 166, 167, 212, 227
Goldsmith, Charles, 62
Goodman, Roy M., 192
Gottfried, Richard, 213
Gray, Jesse, *23*, *24*, 160, 174, 175–176, 180, 182, 186, 215, 216
Grenthal, Abe, 82

Haas, Albert, 147
Hamilton, James, 47
Hannah, Edward, 68
Harriman, W. Averell, 153
Harris, Helen, 145, 164
Harris, Patricia Roberts, *31*

Hawley, Peter, 232
Helmsley, Harry, 226
Herman, William, 56
Hilly, Arthur, 71, 72
Hirsch, Nathan, 60, 62, 65
Howe, Irving, 40, 105
Hylan, Mayor John, 53, 58, 60, 65, 68

Jacobs, Jane, 163
Jesse, George, 65

Kahn, Alexander, 56
Kessler, Milton, *26*, *27*
Klapp, William, 110
Klein, Joseph, 56
Knorr, Martin, 253
Koch, Mayor Edward, 241, 249, 258
Kolodny, Robert, 221

LaGuardia, Mayor Fiorello, 69–70, 113, 125, 128, 137
Lane, Mark, 169
Law, Langley, 257
Leichter, Franz, *36*
Levenson, Richard, 212
Lewis, Edward, 162
Lindsay, Mayor John, 192
Lockwood, Charles, 60, 72
Lowe, Jeanne M., 164
Lynd, Staughton, 164, 167, 168

McGoldrick, John, 110
McGoldrick, Joseph B., 151, 152
McKee, Michael, *26*, 217, 218, 252–253, 254
McNeely, Father Joe, *28*
McNeil, Margaret, 249
Malakiel, Leon, 55
Malkiel, Theresa, 54
Mann, Frank, 53
Marcantonio, Congressman Vito, 119, 129, 144–145, 150, 167
Montes, Luisa, 179
Moody, Miriam, 164
Moon, Henry Lee, 150
Moore, Marcia, 120
Moore, Richard, 97
Morales, Louis, *28*
Moritz, Doug, 238

Moses, Robert, 7, 137, 152, 153–155, 156, 158–159, 162–164, 194
Murphy, Edward, 69
Musicus, Milton, *28*

Nathan, Jason, R., 192, 210
Nazario, Robert, *28*
Norden, Heinz, 119–120, 123, 125

O'Dwyer, Mayor William, 149, 152
Ohrenstein, Manfred, 252
O'Neal, James, 66
Orr, Samuel, 56
Orton, Lawrence W., 156, 157
Owens, Major R., 175, 181

Palmer, A. Mitchell, 64
Perkins, Lamar, 99
Phillips, Donnellan, 115, 139–140
Piven, Frances F., 5, 175
Post, Langdon, 94–95, 113, 125
Powell, Adam Clayton, Jr., 129, 147, 162
Present, Harry, 162, 169
Pressman, Lee, 143–144
Putterman, Harriet, 225

Quill, Michael, 129

Rand, Esther, 164, 167
Ravitch, Richard, 189
Reagan, President Ronald, 233, 243, 265
Rhenstein, Alfred, 125
Rich, Harry, 72
Rivers, Francis, 99
Robbins, Ira S., 162
Robitzek, Harry, 69
Rockefeller, David, 156, 157
Rockefeller, Governor Nelson, 213, 218
Roosevelt, Eleanor, *20*, 163
Ross, Paul L., 154
Rowen, Bill, *35*
Rueda, Ramon, *32*, 238
Runes, Richard, *35*

St. Georges, Philip, *28*, 240
Saunders, Wilma, 120
Scanlon, Michael, 54–55
Schaffer, Edward, 164

Schur, Robert, *30*, 221, 223, 235, 255
Schwerner, Michael, 179
Smith, Governor Alfred E., 60, 74, 80
Solomon, Charles, 58, 62
Starr, Roger, 192, 223
Stein, Clarence, 74, 80–81
Sternlieb, George, 193, 211
Stevenson, Bess, 232
Sweet, Thaddeus, 66

Thabit, Walter, *25*, 167
Truman, President Harry S., 142

Untermyer, Samuel, 80

Velez, Ted, 177, 186, 188

Wagner, Robert F., Jr., 152–153, 163–164, 169–170, 175
Wald, Lillian D., 46
Weinberg, Robert C., 155
Weiss, Ted, 259
White, Walter, 150
Whitman, Governor Charles, 58
Wilkins, Roy, 150
Williams, Vernal, 115–116, 139
Wilson, Malcolm, 218
Wilson, President Woodrow, 68
Wood, Jane, 164, 166
Wood, Robert, 164
Wylie, Chalmers, 265

Zeumer, Lucille, 77

Subject Index

(Page numbers in italics indicate illustrations.)

Abandoned units and buildings, 41; community sovereignty over, 190; low-income tenants' control of, 210, 220–221; 1960s and early 1970s, 209; program to deal with, 234; rehabilitation by tenants, 221–222
Abandonment, 192; in Bronx, *31;* coping with, 220–224; demonstration after, 113, 162–163, 164, 171; increase in (late 1960s), 211; rent control and, 211; tenant takeover of buildings after, *37*
Academy Tenants Association, 77
Activism, rebirth of, 114–118
Adopt-a-Building, *28*
American Labor Party (ALP), 4, 129, 146, 156; considerations for clubs of, 134; during liberal rent control period, 153; rent clinics of, 143. *See also* Radicals
American Property Rights Association, *29*
Americans for Democratic Action, 146
ANHD. *See* Association of Neighborhood Housing Developers
Antisemitism, 71
Apartments: abandonment of, 31, 37, 113; construction rate of (1917–1930), *83;* demolition of, 113, 120, 162; removed from low-rent market, 121; transfer to nonresidential use, 121
Arbitration and mediation, 51, 61, 183, 229; Communist rejection of, 106; lack of authority to enforce, 62; municipal courts and, 75. *See also* Negotiation(s)
Association of Neighborhood Housing Developers (ANHD), 230–231, 234–236
Attorneys. *See* Lawyers

Bank loans, 246–247
Bedford-Stuyvesant Restoration Corporation (BSRC), 185
Black churches as landlords, 97–98
Black collective protests, 47, 98–99
Black landowners, 185
Black landlords, 97, 98
Blacks, 156; attempted removal of, 157; decline in tenant protests by, 147; displacement of, 171; landlords' fear of renting to, 193; relocation and, 160; segregation of, 97–98; special housing problems of, 99; sweat equity and, 222
Black tenant organizations, *19*. *See also* Harlem Tenants League
Block associations. *See* Tenant organizations
Bowery, 166
Bronx, 31; Battle of the, 102–112; buyer's strike to save OPA, 142; lack of civic order in, 193; President Carter's visit to, 235; tenant organizations in, 77–78, 145
Bronx Council of Tenant Leagues, 78
Bronx landlord organizations, 104, 106, 110
Bronx Tenants League, 54–56, 61
Brooklyn Tenants Union (BTU), 62–63, 72
Brownsville Tenants League, 62, 69
BTU. *See* Brooklyn Tenants Union
Building violations. *See* Housing violations

CETA. *See* Comprehensive Employment Training Act
Charitable agencies, 79
CHPC. *See* Citizens Housing and Planning Council
Church ties with housing and tenant groups, 4, 79, 156, 157, 172, 188, 209, 221, 234
Citizens Housing and Planning Council (CHPC), 158
City Rent Commission, 143
City-Wide Citizens Committee on Harlem, 139
City-Wide Housing Conference (1935), 118–119

City-Wide Tenants Council, *18*, *19*, 95, 118–127; active role of tenants in housing and, 135; Communists in, 96; end of role as advocate for tenants, 137
City-Wide Tenants League, 119
Civil rights movement, 174
Committee to Save Our Homes, 156–158, 159, 166, 167
Committee on Slum Clearance (CSC), 155–156, 166
Communists, 4, *17;* avoidance of, 129; in City-Wide Tenants Council, 96; desire for confrontation, 106; eviction protests led by, 99–102; rent strike movement led by, 95, 99–102, 112
Community conservation, 153–168
Community Council on Housing, *23*, 176
Community leaders: apolitical, 4; training of, 184
Comprehensive Employment Training Act (CETA): discontinued, 242; problems with workers under, 237; sweat equity programs and, 234, 235
Conference on City Planning, 154
Confrontation, communists and, 106, 129
Congress of Racial Equality (CORE), 174–179, 181–182, 185
Consolidated Tenants League of Harlem, *19*, 95, 115, 119–120, 129, 140
Consumers leagues, 54, 55, 56, 144
Conversion to cooperatives, *38*, 254; of abandoned buildings, 210, 220–224; eviction of tenants and, 209, 226–227; federally-funded low-income, 233; tax-supported luxury, 190
Cooperatives: created from abandoned buildings, 210; income limitations in low-income, 221; informal, 221; in interracial, 150; low-income, *28*, 270; middle-income, 156, 165, 193
Cooper Square Community Development Committee, *25*
Cooper Square Title I, 166
CORE. *See* Congress of Racial Equality
Courts, 73; as arbiters, 75; crowding with lease termination cases, 76. *See also* Judges
CSC. *See* Committee on Slum Clearance
Demolition of abandoned buildings, 113, 162–163, 164, 171; sealing vs., 234
Depression. *See* Great Depression
Discrimination, 160
Displacement and relocation of tenants, 154–155, 159, 162–164, 187; by construction projects, 121; fear of, 224–227; gentrification and, 248; new forms of, 209; revitalization without, 250. *See also* Evictions
District of Columbia rent control, 75
Division of Housing (New York State), *36*
Doubling up, 80

Economic power, naïveté about, 197
Emergency Committee on Rent and Housing (ECRH), 151
Emergency Tenant Protection Act, *28*
Evictions, 3, *14*, *16*, *17*, 151; banning of retaliatory, 255; cooperative conversions and, 209; cost to landlords, 58; courts clogged with, 64; dispossesses resulting in actual, 100; of elderly and disabled, 167–168, 255; expiration of leases and, 73; fear of widespread (1947), 143, 146; following World War I, 51; movement against, 95, 99–102; in 1908 rent strike, 46; in 1919, 64; period of notice before, 60; proposed moratorium on, 121; rebellion against, 175; union movers and, 63. *See also* Displacement and relocation of tenants
Experiments, 2; by minority tenants, *28;* strategic, 5

Fair Play Rent Association, 66–67, 70, 74, 85
Family size, determining rent by, 40
Federal demonstration grants, 165
Federal funds for housing, 233
Federation(s), 6, *36*, 230–233; Bronx, 78; first New York City, *18;* of neighborhood tenant associations, 120; of tenant organizations, 263–266
Financial scandals, 222–223
Foreclosure for tax arrears, 34, 239–242
Foundations, 187, 190
French (Fred M.) Company, 117

Gentrification, *37*, *38*, 190, 193, 247–251; as threat in working-and lower-middle-class neighborhoods, 209
Ghettoes, 147, 150, 182. *See also* Slums and slum dwellers; Tenements
Great Depression, 94, 95–102, 103, 110, 112–130
Greenwich Village, resistance to redevelopment in, 155, 161, 162, 163

Harlem: Communists in, 115; decline in tenant protests in, 147; Federal demonstration grants in, 165; OPA rent regulation in, 140; political leadership in, 98–99; rents in, 97; rent strike (1908), 45; rent strike (1934), 114; rent strike (1963–1964), *23;* riot in (1943), 129; support for rent controls in, 98; as war emergency area, 129
Harlem Tenants League, 68, 86, 95, 97–99
Heat and hot water, 54, 55, 56, 63; leases and, 57
Hispanics, *24*, 144, 155; displacement and relocation of, 160, 171, 248; ghettos of, 150; landlords' fear of renting to, 193; sweat equity and, 222
Home relief system, 96
Hospitals, expansion of, 225
Housing: alternative, 191; as a public utility, 256; rent gap and decay of, 211
Housing conditions: unsanitary, 80; in tenaments, 40, 47, 55
Housing courts, 228–229. *See also* Judges
Housing market, 3, 81; booming, 83; early 1930s, 96; effects of change in, 84; Great Depression and crisis in, 94; Lower East Side (1904), 41; in 1919, 64; in 1920s, 52; rent control and, 88–89; threat of anarchy in, 6; World War I and, 53, 59
Housing policies, public dissatisfaction with, 193
Housing projects: discrimination prohibited in, 160; income ceilings for tenants in, 149; middle-income, 150, 188; sponsors of, 188–189. *See also* Public Housing; *names of individual projects*
Housing referral, 185. *See also* Displacement and relocation of tenants
Housing and Rent Act of 1947, 142, 151
Housing violations, 178, 183, 191; MFY's central file of, 175; scouting for, 177

Income ceilings (tenant), 138; in housing projects, 149; in low-income cooperatives, 221
Income maintenance organizations, 96, 112
Inflation, 193, 263
Interest rates, 247
Interproject Tenants Council, 149
Interracial development, 139–140
Investment, reasonable return on, 104
Irish-Americans, rent strikes and, 109

Jacob Riis project, 140
Jews: in rent strikes, 109; in tenant organizations, 143, 145; upward mobility of, 150
"Jim Crow City," 139
J. M. Kaplan Fund, 167
Judges: criticism of landlords by, 64; power over rent increases, 68, 71; pressure on legislature by, 74; sentiment against Communist-led rent strike movement, 106–107, 110; sentiment (1908) against tenants by municipal court, 46; support of tenants by, 57. *See also* Courts

Knickerbocker Village, 18, 116–118, 119; tenants association of, 148

La Guardia administration: low-income projects and, 126; middle-income Stuyvesant Town and, 138–139
Landlord(s): black, 97–98; constraints on, 147; cooperation with, 197; CORE pilot projects to confront, 175; disinvestment and abandonment by, 196–197; drive against rent strikers, 110; as endangered entrepreneur, 192; "equalization" adjustments for, 152; individual victories over, 86–87; leasing of properties by, 54; loss of properties due to rent strikes, 105; loss of rental income and, 99; New York City as, *36*, 240; organizations of, 57, 104; profits allowed, 76, 87, 152; revenge against strikers, 62; small, *29*,

Landlord(s) (continued)
147; stereotypes of, 70; typical rent control, 193; viewpoints of, 57
Landlord-tenant relationship. *See* Tenant-landlord relationship
Laws and legislation, 116; "April Laws" (1920), 52, 72, 73; Austin-Wicks law, 160; Brown-Isaacs law, 160; Community Reinvestment Act (1977), 246; Comprehensive Employment Training Act (CETA), 234, 235, 237, 242; Cooperative/Condominium Fair Practices Act, 218, 251; development of guidelines for administration of rent, 76; Emergency Price Control Act (1942), 128; Emergency Rent Laws (1920), 52, 53, 75, 77, 80, 82, 85, 86, 87; Emergency Tenant Protection Act, *28*, 219, 252, 260; eviction from cooperative conversions and, 227; exemption from, 80, 82; Federal Housing Act (1949), 153–172, 195; Federal rent control law, 128–129, 134, 137, 140, 142, 143; Flynn/Dearie Bill, 256; foreclosure for tax arrears, 239–242; Home Mortgage Disclosure Act (1975), 246; Housing Act of 1954, 160; Housing and Rent Act (1947), 142, 151; Langley Law, 218, 257; lease-as-contract law, 219; Limitations on protection by rent laws, 80, 82, 85–86; MBR, 193, 212–213, 215–217; Mitchell-Hampton Redevelopment Companies Law, 138, 140; New York City rent control, 86, 128, 213; New York State Real Property Actions and Proceedings Law, 174, 177–179; not covering new tenants, 80; Omnibus Housing law, 261; prior lien law, 121; Preservation of Sound Housing Act, 218; rent decontrol, 21, 142, 209, 213–214; rent stabilization (1969), 192; rent withholding law, 174; revised rent law (1928), 85; senior citizens' rents and property taxes and, 218; state urban redevelopment law, 134; Warranty of Habitability Law, 219, 229
Lawyers: provided by tenant associations, 79–80; volunteer, 60, 62, 146, 175, 178
Lead poisoning, 184
League of Women Shoppers, 141
League of Women Voters, 141
Leases, 43, 73; as contracts, 219, 229; court cases regarding termination of, 76; heat and, 57; influence on bargaining, 58; lack of, 55
Legal assistance to tenants, 56, 146; by MFY Legal Services Unit, 175
Legal Services Anti-Displacement Project, 248
Legislation. *See* Laws and Legislation
Lessee system, 54
Liberals, 146–147, 154, 158, 160; City-Wide Tenants Leagues ties with, 122; importance to tenants, 194
Lillian Wald project, 140
Lincoln Tunnel, clearing approach to, 158
Lindsey administration, 183, 210; opposition to decontrol by, 213–214; Vest Pocket Program of, 187, 192–193
Loans, bad risks and, 246
Lobbying, 2, 126, 142, 154, 218
Lower East Side: organization of tenants in (1919), 63; population of, 41; protest (1904), 39–47; as special preservation district, 250
Lower East Side Public Housing Conference, 113, 118
Low income housing. *See* Cooperatives; Public Housing

Maintenance and services, 23; rent control and costs of, 192
Manhattantown, 155–156, 161–162
Maximum Base Rent (MBR) Program, 193; political opposition to, 212–213, 215–217; support for, 217
Mayor's Committee on Rent Profiteering, 60–62, 68, 88, 89
MBR. *See* Maximum Base Rent Program (MBR)
Mediation. *See* Arbitration and Mediation
Met Council. *See* Metropolitan Council on Housing (Met Council)
Metropolitan Council on Housing (Met Council), 2, *33*, 136, 165–172, 258; annual mass mobilizations of, 6; focus on rent control, 191–192; founding of, 7, 164; ideology of, 232; internal dynamics of, 212; move of, 223–224; new middle class recruits to, 191–192;

NYSTNC and, 252, 255–256; radical demands of, 219; rehabilitation and tax abatement programs and, 191; rolling rent strike of, 228; turn toward traditionalism, 170
Metropolitan Life Insurance Company: Riverton development of, 139–140; Stuyvesant Town plans and, 138–139
MFY. *See* Mobilization for Youth
MHI. *See* Morningside Heights, Incorporated
Middle-class tenants, 18
Mid-Queens Consumer Council, 141
Minorities: barring of discrimination against, 160; mixing of, 189; proposed prohibition of, 122. *See also names of specific minorities*
Mobilization for Youth (MFY), 173–175; Legal Services Unit of, 175, 178; rent clinics of, 175–178; Tenement Housing Program of, 175
Model Cities Program, 187
Morningside Heights, Incorporated (MHI), 156–160
Mortgages, 246–247; below-market-interest rate, 187; from Bowery Savings Bank, 189–190; threatened by rent laws, 263–264
Moving: to escape tenement conditions, 40; payment for expense of, 121
Mutual benefit society, 43

National Public Housing Conference, 138
National Tenants Union, 6
Negotiation(s), 45, 58, 229; reasonable return on investment as basis for, 104. *See also* Arbitration and Mediation
Neighborhood conservation, 153–168, 170–171, 250. *See also names of specific neighborhoods*
New Deal work relief programs, 111
Newspapers, rent strike of 1908 and, 46
New York City Housing Authority, project councils of, 148
New York City in rem crisis, 239–242
New York Rent Protective Association, 43
New York State legislature, 69–73; as arena for rent issues, 214; pressure on, 69, 74, 81; special session to pass new rent laws (1920), 74; tenant leaders in, 216–218
New York State Tenant and Neighborhood Coalition (NYSTNC), 2, 5, *26, 30, 35, 36;* cooperation with ANHD, 231; influence and actions of, 218–220, 230, 252–262; Met Council and, 252, 255–256
New York Times, 71
NTU. *See* National Tenants Union
NYRPA. *See* New York Rent Protective Association
NYSTNC. *See* New York State Tenant and Neighborhood Coalition (NYSTNC)

Office of Economic Opportunity, 210
Office of Housing Expeditor (OHE), 142–143
Office of Price Administration (OPA), 130; Harlem rent control and, 140–141; phase out of, 141–143; rent controls and, 128–129, 137, 142–143; tenant councils and, 141
OHE. *See* Office of Housing Expeditor (OHE)
OPA. *See* Office of Price Administration (OPA)
Open housing lobby, anti–Communist, 154
Owners. *See* Landlord(s); Tenant-landlord relationships

Park West, 155
People's Development Corporation (PDC), *31, 32*
Picketing, 110, 123
Police: confrontation with, 176; as mediators, 123; reaction to perceived Socialist-led rent strike (1908), 45; strike suppression by, 106
Police power, 80
Political clubs, Irish-American, 109
Politicians, 4, 57; interest in housing, 59, 65, 82; pressure on, 69
Poor families: government responsibility toward, 96; right to a profit vs. needs of, 87
Private developers, blighted residential acreage sold to, 155
Professionals: underemployed, 127; as volunteers, 61, 62, 124, 182–183, 186
Profit: allowed landlord, 76, 87, 152; right to a, 87

Protests and demonstrations, 141; Communist-led, 109; consumer, 142; Great Depression and, 94, 109; as hallmark of Jewish tenants, 47; Lower East Side (1904), 39–47; techniques of, 41–43. *See also* Rent strikes
Public good, Emergency Rent Laws and, 87
Public Housing: bond issue proposed for, 68; campaign for (during Great Depression), 94, 112–114; first, *20;* government construction of, 125–126; pace of, 113–114; reformers and, 112
Puerto Ricans. *See* Hispanics

Queensbridge Tenants League, 149–150

Racial discrimination: laws against, 160; proposed prohibition of, 122
Radicals, 3–4, 125, 149, 156; absorption of initiatives of, 185; city antipoverty program and, 177; in CORE, 176, 177; Jewish, 145; Jim Crow issue and, 154; the poor and, 180
Rat infestation, 174
Reagan presidency, 242–245, 265–266
Real estate companies, 2
Real estate interest groups, 3–4
Real estate market. *See* Housing market
Receivership Program, 183, 222
Redevelopment. *See* Urban renewal and redevelopment
Redlining, 245–247
Red Scare, 52, 64, 66, 69–70, 77, 88
Rehabilitation: financing of, 171; rent control and, 169–170; slum prevention and, 165; small scale, 186–187; sweat equity, *31, 32,* 222, 223
Relocatees: fate of, 162; rights of, 159
Relocation of tenants. *See* Displacement and relocation of tenants
Rent: disputed, 75; economic, 193; family size and, 40; Federal experiment in setting levels of, 128; labor exchange for, 100; needy family aid for, 79; New York City home rule on, 213; rate of collection of, 241; reasonable, 76; return on assessed values and, 152
Rent control advisory boards, 151
Rent control movement, politicization of, 210–220
Rent controls and regulations: campaign for wartime, 94; challenges to, 209; city ownership of buildings and, *34;* dismantling of wartime, *21,* 142; District of Columbia, 75; Federal, 128–129, 134, 137, 140, 142–143; lifting of selected, 153; maintenance costs and, 192; New York City, 86, 128; New York City financial crisis and, 251–252; New York State, *22,* 152; in 1960s, 191; OPA and, 128–129, 137, 140–141; politics of, 150–153, 210–220; property values and, 211; rehabilitation and repairs and, 170; responsibility for enforcement of, *36;* tenant response to changes in, 211–212
Rent decontrol, 21, 142, 209, 213–214
Rent decrease(s), 43; to offset tenants' fuel costs, 55
Rent Guidelines Board, *33*
Rent increase(s), 244; "April laws" and, 52; chief mechanism for (under rent control), 22; the homeless and, *38;* inflation and, 263; judges' discretionary power over, 68; low percentage of "hardship" (Bronx), 147; postponement of, 116; reaction to impending (1907–1908), 44–45; resistance to exhorbitant, 87; tied to equity investment, 256–257
Rent law. *See* Laws and legislation
Rent profiteering, Socialist vote and, 59
Rent slowdown, 227–228
Rent stabilization Law (1969), Metropolitan Council on Housing and, 192
Rent strikes, 2–4, 227–230; in Bronx (1932), 102–112; Communist-led, 102–112; community power and, 172–197; demands and issues in, *9, 15, 17, 18, 19, 23;* Eastern European Jews and, 6; as effective tactic, 58, 178; emergency rent laws (1920) and, 75; first mass, *9;* Hispanics and, 24; as last resort, 123; leaders of, 182; limitations of, 182; new wave of, 107–110; 1904, *9, 10;* 1907, *10, 11, 12;* 1907–1908, *10, 11, 12,* 44–47; 1917–1920, *13–14;* 1930s, 6–7, *15;* 1960s, 4, *23;* origin of, 42; the poor and, 182; reactions against, 106–107; rolling, *26,* 228; threat of, 69; women and, *10,* 42
Rent wars (1943–1955), 137–153

Rent withholding, 56; legal basis for, 228; legal (New York State), 174; vs. mediation, 183
Repairs: by city and charged to landlords, 121; escrow rents to pay for, 176; rent control and, 170
Riverton (Metropolitan Life development), 139–140

Save Our Homes Committee, 156–158, 159, 166; challenge to Cooper Square Title I, 167
SCAD. *See* State Committee against Discrimination (SCAD)
Section 755 of New York State Real Property Actions and Proceedings Law, 174, 177–179
Services and facilities, rent withholding and, 229. *See also* Heat and hot water
Settlement houses, 94, 221
Slums and slum dwellers, 113, 155, 165, 166; CORE and, 174. *See also* Committee on Slum Clearance (CSC); Tenements
Socialists, *11*, 43, 54; creation of Mayor's Committee on Rent Profiteering and, 87; election promises of, 65; election victory of (1919), 66; fading of tenant leagues of, 52, 87–88, 1918 election and, 58; split of, 76–77; suspended and expelled from New York State legislature, 52, 66, 72; tenant organizations and, 57, 67; tenant uprising of 1908 and, 45
Socialist Women's Consumers League of the Bronx, 54, 55
Social work activists, 173
Speculation, *38*, 54
Squatters, 190–191, 224
Stanton Street Tenants Association, 179–181
State Committee against Discrimination (SCAD), 158, 160
Stuyvesant Town, 138–139; Tenants Committee against Discrimination in, 154
Subletting, 54
Sweat equity, *31*, *32*, 190, 222, 223, 235, 244; job training and, 234

Taxes: assessments for, 68; exemptions for new construction, 83; overdue, 239–242; seizure for nonpayment of, *34*, 239–242
Tenements: campaign to improve (during Great Depression), 94, 113; children in, *12;* conditions in (after 1908 strike), 47; construction of, 53; facilities in, 40; in Harlem, 174; taken over by city, 177; upgrading of, 113
Tenant action: limits and constraints on, 4–5; temporary nature of, 47
Tenant activism, 1, 130, 173
Tenant advocacy as a career, 115
Tenant appeals, ignoring of, 85
Tenant education, 79–80
Tenant-landlord relationship, 1, 45–46, 55, 57, 99–100. *See also* Arbitration and mediation; Negotiation(s)
Tenant leaders, 6, *11*, *36*, 42–44; actions against, 62, 63; as agents of New York City Housing Authority, 180; conservative, 88; middle class, 95; in New York State legislature, 216–217; Socialist, 67; social workers, 173; women, 6, *36*, 44, 128
Tenant leagues: Bronx, 77–78; campaign against, 64–65; make-up and leadership of, 67; Socialist, 62, 67, 73–74, 86
Tenant movement, 2–3, 86, 173, 233–266; accomplishments of, 193–197; Blacks and, 6, 150; changes in housing market and, 84–85; diversity of, 266; Great Depression and Communist leadership of, 101; influence of, 267–269; Italians and, 6; Jews and, 6, 9, 150; lack of awareness of historical continuity in, 196; leadership of, 6, *11*, *36*, 42–43, 67, 88; origins of post-World War I, 54; Puerto Ricans and, 6, 150; strategic innovation in, 270; threat to, 193; victories of, 7; weakness in, 59
Tenant organizations, 57, 147, 179, 271; achievements of, 51, 267–269; alternatives to Socialist-led, 61; black, *19*, 95; building and neighborhood, 5, 41, 68, 124, 153, 185, 188, 216, 239; conservative, 52, 67, 77, 88; decline of, 85, 148; demonstrations of strength of, 81–82; following World War II, 141–142; funding for, 233–245; fund raising by, 239; in the Great Depression, 95–99, 103, 110, 114–130; growth of New York City (1947), 143; with leadership tied to Democratic and Republican organizations, 52; middle class, 185;

Tenant organizations (*continued*)
model of, 116; number of members (1919), 63; political thrust of, 251–262; in slum neighborhoods, 120, 173, 174; Socialist, 52, 67; stable, 5. *See also* Tenant leagues; Tenant movement; *names of specific organizations*
Tenant rights, 52; housing shortage and, 89; of relocatees, 159
Tenants: categories of, 73; choice of legal responses to landlords, 147; cooperation with, 197; as developers, 135; difficulties in organizing, 124, 182, 184; improvement in legal climate facing, 124; income ceilings on, 138, 149; involvement in housing decisions, 135–136; lawyers for, 60, 78–79; as managers, 136; middle class, 114, 119; new, 80; organized, 217; rights of relocated, 159; selling buildings to, 240; stereotypes of, 70; survey of, 81. *See also* Displacement and relocation of tenants
Title I. *See* Laws and legislation, Federal Housing Act (1949)
Toilets, 55
Triborough Bridge, condemnation to make way for, 120–121

Unemployed Councils, 103, 112
Unions and union movement, 41, 67–68; evictions and, 63
United Tenants League (UTL), 115, 128, 138–141; endorsement of private-sector initiatives by, 154
Upward mobility, 148, 150
Urban homesteading, 235, 236, 238, 245
Urban Homesteading Assistance Board (UHAB), *28*
Urban League, 139, 187
Urban renewal and redevelopment, *25*, 138; change in course of, 195; corporate irresponsible, 139; federally-aided, 140; Housing Act of 1954 and, 160–161; indigenous institutions and, 167; relocation problems and, 154–155, 158, 159, 162–164; threats to, 154–159; Title I and, 153–172
UTL. *See* United Tenants League

Vacancies and vacancy rate, 53, 80, 83, *84*. *See also* Housing market
Vandalism, 70
Vest pocket Program, 187
Violence, 62
Volunteers: combining paid staff with, 237–239; commitment by, 237; lawyers as, 60, 61, 62, 146, 175, 178; professionals as, 61, 62, 124, 182–183, 186
Voting power of renters, 85

Wagner administration, 176, 183; creative housing programs of, 170
Washington Heights Tenants Association (WHTA), 66, 74
Washington Square, proposed highway through, 161–163
Washington Square Southeast project, 161
Whites-only plans of Metropolitan Life Insurance Company for Stuyvesant Town, 139
WHTA. *See* Washington Heights Tenants Association
Williamsburg Bridge, making room for, 41
Williamsburg Tenants League, 63
Women, 5, 6–7, 10, 54; as activists, 41–42, 141, 174, 195–196; in Battle of the Bronx, 104; as leaders, 6, *36*, 44, 189
Women's Consumers League, 54, 55–56
Work relief Programs, 96

Yiddish newspapers, 42
Yorkville Save Our Homes Committee, 168

Contributors

Ronald Lawson is professor in the Department of Urban Studies, Queens College–CUNY, and is the author of *Brisbane in the 1890s: An Australian Urban Society.*

Mark Naison is associate professor of Afro-American studies and director of urban studies, Fordham University. He is the author of *Communists in Harlem during the Depression.*

Jenna Weissman Joselit is a research associate in history at the YIVO Institute for Jewish Research in New York and the author of *Our Gang: Jewish Crime and the New York Jewish Community, 1900–1940.*

Joel Schwartz is associate professor in the Department of History, Montclair State College.

Joseph A. Spencer is executive director of the New York City Transit Authority's Transit Adjudication Bureau.